UNSETTLED STATES

AMERICA AND THE LONG 19TH CENTURY

GENERAL EDITORS: DAVID KAZANJIAN, ELIZABETH MCHENRY, AND PRISCILLA WALD

Unsettled States

Nineteenth-Century American Literary Studies

Edited by

Dana Luciano and Ivy G. Wilson

NEW YORK UNIVERSITY PRESS

New York and London

NEW YORK UNIVERSITY PRESS
New York and London
www.nyupress.org

References to Internet websites (URLs) were accurate at the time of writing.
Neither the author nor New York University Press is responsible for URLs that
may have expired or changed since the manuscript was prepared.

Library of Congress Cataloging-in-Publication Data
Unsettled states : nineteenth-century American literary studies /
edited by Dana Luciano and Ivy G. Wilson.
pages cm. — (America and the Long 19th Century)
Includes bibliographical references and index.
ISBN 978-1-4798-5772-2 (hardback : acid-free paper) — ISBN 978-1-4798-8932-7
(pb : acid-free paper)
1. American literature—19th century—History and criticism. I. Luciano, Dana,
editor of compilation. II. Wilson, Ivy G., editor of compilation.
PS201.U57   2014
810.9'003—dc23   2014009794

New York University Press books are printed on acid-free paper,
and their binding materials are chosen for strength and durability.
We strive to use environmentally responsible suppliers and materials
to the greatest extent possible in publishing our books.

Manufactured in the United States of America

10 9 8 7 6 5 4 3 2 1

Also available as an ebook

CONTENTS

Introduction

On Moving Ground

DANA LUCIANO

In the early morning of December 16, 1811, the first of a major series of earthquakes struck the Mississippi Valley. The earthquakes continued through the following spring, numbering over 1,800 in total. Centered in the Louisiana territory, in a region now shared between southeastern Missouri and northeastern Arkansas, their effects were felt for over a million square miles. They cracked sidewalks in Washington, D.C., damaged buildings in Savannah, Georgia, destroyed huge tracts of forest, and permanently altered the course of rivers; local legend held that during the worst quakes, the Mississippi flowed backward. The riverbank town of New Madrid, for which both the earthquakes and the fault line later designated as their cause would be named, was all but destroyed by months of shaking and flooding.[1]

Preoccupied by the War of 1812 and border conflicts with Indian nations, the state responded to the earthquakes rather slowly. When it did, it used them as another occasion to reassert already-familiar national narratives: those of American exceptionalism, found in the ability to persevere through hardship, and American compassion, seen in the nation's willingness to sympathize with and assist the earthquake's victims. The General Assembly of the Missouri Territory, in an 1814 appeal to the federal government for aid, vividly depicted the displacement of "our unfortunate fellow citizens, [who] are now wandering about without a home to go to, or a roof to shelter them from the pitiless storms," and affirmed its confidence that the "just light in which these calamities are viewed by the enlightened humane government of the United States" would result in the federal provision of material aid. This appeal to sympathy as a defining feature of the American character was shored up by a distinctly nationalist appeal: since the U.S. had, the previous year, sent economic aid to Venezuela after a devastating earthquake there, the Assembly went on to observe, it would surely be no less willing to help "a portion of its own citizens."[2] The nationalistic appeal of the General Assembly was taken up in Congress, and the following year, the New Madrid Federal Relief Act (1815) translated this account of the event into policy. The act not only ratified what was due to "fellow citizens," but, in effect, who counted as such—though the Native population in the affected zone was higher than the white population, no attempts were made on the part of the nation to compensate Native tribes, even "allied" ones, for the losses they suffered, nor even to track those losses.[3]

For both regional and national legislators, the New Madrid earthquakes counted as merely a "natural calamity," an unavoidable and causeless tragedy that could be resolved by the application of enlightened national sympathy and the passage of time.[4] Yet while the state response folded the earthquakes into a narrative of national continuity and coherence, others framed them differently.[5] Viewing American settlers' social or imperialist behavior as a cause of the quakes, Christian and Native American revivalists demanded a departure from national narrative, reinventing the space and time surrounding them. Christians of varying denominations read the earthquakes as an effect of divine will: some argued that the quakes were obvious retribution for the sinful life generally led in the western territories, while others located them in a grander timeframe, as the fulfillment of biblical prophecy. A writer in the *Connecticut Gazette*, cataloguing many of the extraordinary occurrences enumerated above, concluded: "May not the same enquiry be made of us that was made by the hypocrites of old—'Can ye not discern the signs of the times."[6] The multidenominational Christian revival movement that sprung up in the region after December saw a distinctive pattern of responsiveness from area residents: converts flocked to churches whenever the tremors intensified, and attendance fell off again when the land was relatively calm. These on-and-off disciples were aptly known as "earthquake Christians," their relationship to messianic time shifting in tandem with the ground beneath their feet.

The quakes were also read as "signs of the times" by Native tribes in the region. In this context, they served to amplify extant calls for resistance against the expansionist American state. The Shawnee leader Tecumseh was said to have foreseen, or even to have caused, the quakes as a means of promoting his pan-tribal federation and weakening white settlements.[7] Tecumseh interpreted the ongoing tremors as signs of encouragement, reportedly telling a band of Osage, at the end of 1811, "The Great Spirit is angry with our enemies; he speaks in thunder, and the earth swallows up villages and drinks up the Mississippi."[8] The quakes likewise intensified the religious and cultural practices associated with the pan-Nativist revival. The call for cultural renewal issued by Tecumseh's brother Tenskwatawa, the "Shawnee Prophet," resounded even more loudly against their devastation. Fasting and other responsive purification rituals coupled with a vehement embrace of his insistence on a return to traditional Native lifeways. Among the Creeks, some revivalists interpreted his call to abandon settler-style farming to incorporate the destruction of farm tools and killing of livestock. The religious revival fed into intratribal conflicts over the centralization of Creek national administration and privatization of Creek lands (part of the "civilizing" strategy of the U.S. Indian Bureau), giving rise to a series of confrontations that culminated in the Creek War of 1813–14.[9]

Though the extra- and counternational visions of the region and its possible futures that Christian revivalists and Native American resistance movements developed in relation to the quakes were omitted in the state's response, even that account could not entirely avoid acknowledging prior constructions of New Madrid that also deviated from the singularity of nationalist narrative. The fluctuating forms taken by the state in the period of settlement are indexed in the opening text of the 1814 appeal, which marked by a simple alternation of nouns the fact that the locality which had been, at the time of the earthquakes just two years earlier, the district of New Madrid in the Louisiana Territory was now the county of New Madrid in the Missouri Territory.[10] These ostensibly minor changes stand as the administrative trace of a longer history of geopolitical flux, of imperial conquest and escapist fantasy, utopianism, and disillusionment, beneath the ostensibly stable sign of "New Madrid." The settlement was founded in 1789 by Colonel George Morgan, an American Revolutionary War soldier turned disgruntled citizen and would-be expatriate, on land then under Spanish dominion; he had been encouraged in the venture by the Spanish minister Diego de Gardoqui, in line with that empire's policy of keeping U.S. expansion in check by lining the western bank of the Mississippi with ex-Americans whose loyalty to Spain would be secured by land grants. A former Indian agent, Morgan claimed that the land on which his colony stood was unclaimed by any Native tribe; he set aside hunting grounds for Natives whom he encouraged to move to the area, promising that its white settlers would be forbidden by law from fur hunting. Morgan imagined the colony as a transposition of the American revolutionary project, promising its white recruits U.S.-style democracy (which, significantly, included the right to own and import slaves) as well as freedom of religion. In this, however, he came into conflict with the Spanish governor of the Louisiana Territory, who, seeking to maintain control over the region, demanded that Catholicism become the colony's official faith and its residents be made to declare allegiance to Spain.[11] The vicissitudes of empire on the continent overtook this local conflict soon enough; after the turn of the century, New Madrid existed under three different imperial flags within a few years. Spain ceded the Louisiana territory to France in 1800 in a secret treaty, and France retained the territory for only three years before selling it to the United States in 1803, transferring New Madrid to the very jurisdiction Morgan had tried to escape in its founding.

The consolidation of American control over the ex-American Morgan's attempt at separation, the erasure of indigenous claims to the region, and the formal recognition of the state of Missouri in 1821, all, from an American nationalist perspective, were logical steps in the unfolding of the nation's destiny according to spatial and temporal coordinates envisioned as objective, singular, and inevitable: westward and forward, toward modernity and enlightenment. Yet the alternative accounts of place and time crowded onto the same ground are more than incidental from the perspective opened, in recent years, by critical rethinkings of the politics of time and space in the nineteenth-century United States. On this view, the cacophony of analytic, affective, national, and temporal claims circulating around the site of New Madrid before, during, and after the quakes no longer resolves into a singular, congressionally validated meaning; rather, it enables New Madrid to be viewed as a historiographic as well as geological "fault line," where competing readings, foreclosed historically, persist in and as critique. The earthquakes themselves, from this perspective, are not the main event: they are at once a pretext for, and a hyperbolic illustration of, the unsettled meanings of this place and time.

* * *

By opening this introduction with an account of an earthquake series, I am not suggesting that the present state of nineteenth-century American literary studies is akin to disaster. Far from it: the field is thriving, experiencing a renewed vitality, in no small degree because each of the terms in the phrase we use to describe it—"nineteenth-century American literary studies"—has become an axis of sustained interrogation and significant change. The portion of that phrase meant to distinguish it from other literary fields, to clearly demarcate its boundaries and contents, no longer does that work as self-evidently as it once did; a surge in critical attention to the historical and social production of space and place has instead begun to denaturalize what constitutes "America" itself, undoing its putative homogeneity as well as its self-evident configuration in (and as) space.[12] Critical attention to other flows and cultural currents—hemispheric, transnational, circum-Atlantic (and more recently, circum-Pacific), globalist, planetary—that expand or transcend national borders is generating a new map of "America," one which comprehends it, as Paul Giles points out, as both agent and object of globalization.[13] More recently, a new critical interest in questions of history, temporality, and periodicity has begun to trouble the "when" of the field, complicating the reflexive habits of periodization that organize fields according to distinct and self-evident centuries.[14] Temporally minded critics challenge the long-held assumption that, as Wai Chee Dimock puts it, "there can be a discrete, bounded unit of time coinciding with a discrete, bounded unit of space: a chronology coinciding with a territory," demanding closer thematic consideration and conceptual adaptation of alternate flows and rhythms of time.[15] These challenges to national and period demarcations emerged as consequences of—but also remain contemporaneous with—revolutions in content and method that addressed themselves to the coherence and self-evidence of the terms "literary" and "studies," respectively. These questions drove the ground-shaking critical and literary-historical movements associated with the 1970s, 1980s, and early 1990s, sparked by resistance to inherited canons and hierarchies of literary value, sustained by a vast and diffuse project of literary recovery, and extended by a new arsenal of critical approaches (Marxist, feminist, deconstructionist, postcolonial, antiracist, queer) that complicated the kinds of questions it was possible to ask about this dramatically enlarged collection of objects.[16]

It is by now a cliché to simply celebrate the productivity of ongoing uncertainty and dissension in cultural criticism. The project of *Unsettled States* is, rather, to consider how this uncertainty might unsettle and remap our critical relations to the field itself. The contributors to this collection were trained at a point when the earliest of the aforementioned interventions—the rejection of canons restricted to a handful of white, mostly male, authors and to a small number of genres and forms that counted as the "proper" objects for literary analysis—had already radically reshaped the terrain on which it was possible to think, as the range of objects, authors, and approaches engaged in these pages indicates. Yet the conversations generated across that range seek something other than an affirmative demonstration of inclusiveness or variety as the critical "common sense" we inherited from our forebears. Rather, they seek to develop ways of reading an "American literature" in motion, of improvising and identifying nodes of inquiry and invention attuned to the rhythms of a moving field.

Written by scholars working in the "minor" fields of critical race and ethnic studies, feminist and gender studies, labor studies, and queer/sexuality studies, the essays in *Unsettled States* share what we might describe as a diffusely minoritarian orientation. "Minoritarian," in the sense we are using it, does not name simply a coalition of those who have been minoritized, nor is it automatically continuous with "minority" subjects or marginal knowledges as such, though these have provided the most fertile ground for its development, in part because of the spatialization of minority existence: as Deleuze and Guattari point out, the "cramped spaces" to which minority subjects have historically been relegated, physically and/or structurally—spaces that are not outside the power of the majority, but are rather oversaturated with its contradictory impulses, overcrowded with multiple accounts of being—paradoxically enable the subjects confined there to develop new possibilities.[17] Minoritarian thought and action, in this sense, are distinguished from those of the majority by the form of their relation thereto. They do not seek representation within the majority, or the production of a coherent identity by virtue of which they might gain inclusion. Nor do they seek to overthrow the majority by means of direct confrontation. Their transformative work takes place through the multiplication of aesthetic, political, and ethical encounters; instead of seeking synthesis, they develop, through "myriad connections, disjunctions, and conjunctions," other ways of being.[18] As feminist critic Pelagia Goulimari explains, minoritarian movements distinguish themselves by virtue of their "processes of collective constitution"; they form themselves in and through movement, seeking not to settle into established forms, not to claim new ground, but to connect to it otherwise.[19] Pointing to the revolutionary changes accomplished by minoritarian movements in the academy, Goulimari wonders whether they will be able to "tolerate the seeming loss or chaos of intermixing, better able to produce a new kind of thinking that takes place across, between, and together."[20] Our answer is an emphatic yes. We seek in this collection to develop cross-connections between multiple "minor" fields, not to abolish their specificity but to engage and activate their disparities. *Unsettled States* is not trying to carve out a space for something like "minoritarian studies," nor to engage in a debate with "majoritarian" Americanist criticism—whatever the latter might look like. Minoritarian criticism, in the sense we intend, is always on the move. Improvisational and speculative, it roams the field, seeking opportunities, nodal points around which its thinking might gather and transform itself. We have no interest in opposing or overthrowing a "majority," nor in legitimating our work against its values: our investments are in discovering what else might take place in a world in flux.

To mark this collection as a minoritarian project also does not mean that its contributors are identified with Deleuzian thought as such; in fact, that critical idiom does not play a central part in any of the essays included here. The goal of this collection, rather, is to demonstrate how minoritarian critique may be actualized without automatic recourse to this (or to *any* singular) critical approach. The critical possibilities of becoming-minor, we might say, are actualized by contrapuntal rather than unified methodology. The essays presented here are drawn together, then, less by the establishment of topical or methodological "common ground" than by a shared sense that *moving* ground offers more compelling possibilities for collective projects drawn together by "myriad connections, disjunctions, and conjunctions"—projects that do not speak with a unified voice but vibrate against and across themselves, maintaining a commitment to criticism as a creative, ethical practice of persisting on other terrain.[21]

Our claim that a multiplicity of critical perspectives is best suited to this sort of project is not quite the same as an embrace of critical "diversity"; diversity exists only within a given boundary or frame, and elements of a "diverse" set have no necessary relation to one another other than their co-presence within that frame. An aspiration to multiplicity over diversity, rather, seeks the kind of proliferative transformation fostered by those "myriad connections, disjunctions, and conjunctions" necessary to the positive activity of minoritarian critique. The kinds of conceptual and critical networks guiding our work are indexed in the geopolitical, historical, affective, and ethical resonances of the term "unsettled" itself, a rough synonym for the flux that animates our work. This critical keyword operates in a number of contexts, including critical multiculturalism, postcolonial and indigenous studies, spectral historiography, narratology, and queer, trauma, and affect theory. We seek here to bring together these divergent and ostensibly unrelated senses of the term, to multiply their points of contact in the service of a minoritarian reimagination of its geopolitical, historical, and ethical possibilities.

The challenge of thinking "unsettlement" was posited from the early 1990s on as a means of shaking off the stasis that was beginning to inhabit and inhibit the project of multicultural education. This usage surfaces in Michael Geyer's 1993 critique of the politics of general education. Noting with approval the changes in curricular content accomplished in the preceding decades, Geyer nevertheless pointed out that most forms of multicultural education had not yet lost the conceptual habits of the Eurocentric models they sought to displace. They remained, that is, exercises in "civilizational education . . . focuse[d], if not on empire, at least on regionally bounded, territorially integrated settlements."[22] The civilizational infrastructure of the "cultures" considered in multicultural education myopically overlooked contemporary global conditions, which, marked by migration, diaspora, and cultural and religious syncretism, are moving, as Geyer points out, in an opposing direction. A truly *critical* multiculturalism, accordingly, would eschew the essentially additive configuration of pluralist and diversity-based understandings thereof; rather than simply expanding the number of civilizations it sought to include, he proposed, it would affiliate itself with "regions, times, and peoples of unsettlement," suspending the conception of culture as a set of achievements in favor of "the ceaseless struggle to think and create orders and to provide meanings" that consideration of unsettlement would necessarily underscore.[23]

Postcolonial and indigenous studies have been the most productive arenas for thinking "unsettlement," in this sense, against the historical dynamics of settler colonialism: the transformation of the colonial drive in locations where the quest to transfer resources back to the metropole extended toward, or was supplanted by, the intention to remain on the land. Critical considerations of settler colonialism highlight the fluctuating relations between the "bounded" and "integrated" models of European nation Geyer indexes, and their dispersion and reaggregation elsewhere. In addition to distributing populations across the globe, colonial settlement dynamically restructures occupied land by means of a dual movement linking the generation of new cartographies and geopolitical imaginaries to the displacement or extermination of indigenous populations.[24] Both time and space become "settled" by means of this movement, as new cultural histories and trajectories are developed to secure and perpetuate the settlement's geographical revisions.[25] In the U.S., this work has involved strategies both of continuation, the affirmation of a fundamental connection between English and Anglo-American narratives, and of regeneration, the assertion of the foundational break that sets the U.S. apart from the corruption and misdirection of the Old World. The performative dimension of national history, as Tavia Nyong'o's contribution to this collection demonstrates, enables these movements to be synthesized strategically, creating a sense of intimacy with overwritten histories that both upholds and disavows their alignment with whiteness.

The national future is likewise "settled" by the micro-political arrangements of sexuality and intimacy that organize themselves in relation to macro-political visions of progress; these at once encourage the population of the colony with more settler bodies, provide mechanisms for disciplining other populations, and link individuals to national and cultural norms through the operation of domestic nurture as well as romantic desire.[26] For instance, as Kyla Wazana Tompkins's reworking of food studies in these pages shows, the domestic arrangements organized in the name of love established dietary channels for the further settling of colonial bodies. Yet these also positioned the mouth as a site of unauthorized and potentially unsettling cross-racial encounters, the possible deviance she aligns with "queer alimentarity." Conversely, as Hester Blum's consideration of oceanic consciousness suggests, the fantasy of freedom from the confines of national space, in the polar voyage, remained susceptible to recoding by familiar social hierarchies. *Un*settlement is thus not a definitive space-clearing gesture, but the critical remapping of multiple formations onto the "same" space in order to activate it differently.[27]

In this sense, unsettling is as much about narrative as spatial organization. Leaving a story "unsettled," in narratological terms, indicates not simply a lack of closure but the amplification of that lack by devices designed to underscore the drive toward or desire for that missing end. In refusing the sense of an ending, that is, the unsettled narrative makes us conscious of the internalized structures that habituate us to particular kinds of "closure" and modes of progress toward it. Speculative postcolonial thought invokes unsettlement in precisely this way: not simply as a troubled interval, a period without direction or order, but as an opening to undoing the futures upon which colonial history insists, a means of generating unforeseen arrangements and expectations.[28] David Kazanjian's essay in these pages conducts a compelling exploration of early Liberian settlers' letters to the U.S. as one such opening; instead of forcing these letters into continuity with the later historical record, Kazanjian uncovers in them improvisational forms of life that return to challenge our contemporary understanding of agency. From this perspective, then, unsettlement *moves* rather than mourns the state of things, activating both utopian and pragmatic attempts to imagine other ways of being.

Unsettling also signifies historically, in the sense of "unsettling the past": undoing and contesting received narratives, a move common to a number of critical historiographic practices. "Unsettling," in this context, indicates the complicating effect of historical recovery, drawing upon the conviction that the very work of collecting overlooked accounts of the past can be as transformative in our time as the work done by those forgotten subjects was in theirs.[29] Rodrigo Lazo's contribution to this collection performs a dual unsettling along these lines; reconsidering the archive for Latino literary studies, a recovered archive intended to challenge white supremacist history, Lazo dwells on the effects of recovering objects that not only don't "fit" but that counter this intention.

In some deployments, historical unsettling also casts doubt on the sufficiency or terminability of the work of recovery. The "unsettled past" may be not simply recovered but *unburied*, the Gothic inflection working to undermine the belief that *any* account of the past, however expansive, can be complete, can permit it to be laid to rest. Inflected this way, "unsettling" connotes a haunted historiography, one actively undone by the historical erasures and omissions it can neither ignore nor exorcise.[30] In postcolonial, critical race and queer studies especially, this usage aligns with the invocation of specters.[31] This body of work adapts two traditional characteristics of haunting—a hypercathexis of place and a reactivation of time—to the process of confronting historical phenomena such as slavery and genocide that defy reckoning, and that therefore demand an "openness to what exceeds knowledge."[32] As unsettled and unsettling figures, specters diffuse themselves across a number of vital critical tasks: the transformative demand for just recognition; the refusal to countenance looking away even from the most horrifying events, and the concomitant search for some kind of reparative response; a reclamation of other ideas, other ways of thinking or being from the past that may make such a response more thinkable; and a nonlinear understanding of time. Ghosts not only mark unsettled pasts, but by doing so they unsettle time, undermining linear, singular models of history and causality as they underscore the hybridity of the present and the radical uncertainty of the future.[33] Lloyd Pratt and Elizabeth Freeman's essays here consider two related aspects of unsettled time. Pratt identifies historical fiction, specifically the African American historical romance, as a speculative tool to counter the spectral silences of the fragmentary archive, while Freeman considers Mark Twain's novel of time traveling as a point of entry into the queer effects of "doing history badly": collapsing time, hypercathecting the past.

The overinvestment that marks Freeman's queer historiographer parallels the critical impulse that marks Avery Gordon's influential study *Ghostly Matters*. Unsettling the past by "following the ghosts" becomes, for Gordon, an enlivening process, insofar as it "is about making a contact that changes you and refashions the social relations in which you are located."[34] Like Freeman's, Gordon's is an affective historiography, reflecting a desire and a willingness to be touched and moved by other histories, and to carry that movement into one's own world(s). This willingness is linked to the final deployment of "unsettlement" that I will consider here: the condition that trauma theorist Dominick La Capra names "empathic unsettlement."[35] For La Capra, empathic unsettlement is a kind of witnessing that affectively registers the collapse of spatiotemporal distinctions that characterizes trauma, though without a subsequent collapse of the witness's identity into that of the survivor. In this sense, its distinctive play of distance and intimacy attempts to avoid the difficulties that attend sympathetic identification. Glenn Hendler's essay in this volume reconsiders those difficulties as it considers a limit case for sympathy, identification with the state, as a means of exploring the operation of the impersonal in sympathy. Empathic unsettlement as La Capra understands it, though, seeks a different arrangement of distance and intimacy in the act of bearing witness, one that troubles the boundaries of the witnessing self without overtaking that of the survivor.

Noteworthy in La Capra's account is the connection he posits between empathic unsettlement and style or form, his assertion that the unsettling afterlife of empathic witnessing takes shape in and as writing. For historians and other "secondary witnesses," he insists, empathic unsettlement "should register in one's very mode of address," should "have stylistic effects in the way one discusses or addresses certain problems."[36] We can understand this contention in terms of an ethics of unsettlement bringing together affective and aesthetic experience. And whereas La Capra, a historian of the Holocaust, considers unsettlement solely in terms of traumatic experience, we ought also to consider pleasure as effecting a potentially ethical unsettlement. Gordon's work acknowledges the pleasure that attends even the recognition of sorrow; contact with the spectral or unsettled past, she contends, can "help you imagine what was lost that never even existed . . . [can] encourage a steely sorrow laced with delight for what we lost that we never had." Those responses, in turn, can lead the critic to the generative work of seeing anew: "that moment in which we recognize . . . that it could have been and can be otherwise."[37]

Thinking the *otherwise*, the task to which minoritarian criticism commits itself, is, therefore, dependent on qualities of attention attuned to affective and aesthetic experience. In this light, the recent renewal of interest within nineteenth-century American literary criticism in questions of aesthetics takes on ethical significance. What Shelley Streeby refers to in her response as the "gate-keeping function" of aesthetics, the ability to determine what counted as real literature and what did not, has begun to be transformed, in recent years, by a wave of criticism seeking to develop a more capacious understanding of what "aesthetics" might mean. Guided by the conviction that, as Cindy Weinstein and Christopher Looby insist, "social and political life always has a sensory and aesthetic dimension,"[38] this more flexible and politically aware conception of aesthetic experience lends itself to minoritarian uses. From this perspective, the "aesthetic question" may most usefully be rendered not as what aesthetics *is* but what it *can do*—what kinds of connection it can illuminate and intensify, and what other worlds it might make possible.

* * *

The configuration of this collection—divided into three sections, each of which closes with a short response tracing connections among the essays therein—deliberately evokes the format of a conference, though the "conference" that it maps never took place outside these pages.[39] We have adopted this form in an effort to replicate the sense of conversation that such live gatherings generate, to emphasize the connectedness of the work herein to the flows and crosscurrents of thought in the field. We do not intend this collection to offer "representative" selections of contemporary work on these topics: the accuracy and vitality of any such representative project would demand the inclusion of topics and perspectives (for instance, indigenous or Native studies, Pacific Rim studies) not presented in this volume. Nor should our provisional condensation of multiple crosscurrents of thought into the conversations presented here be taken to confirm the separateness of those conversations, since connections flow across the collection's sections as well: Freeman and Nyong'o, for instance, both consider nonlinear forms of time travel, while Kazanjian and Tompkins both grapple with the politics of settler colonialism. The arrangement of this collection, that is, seeks neither to isolate nor to conclude these conversations, but to underscore their status as such—as ongoing and lively circuits of exchange.

The collection's conversations are organized into three sections, "Archives Unbound," "States of Exception," and "Speculative Sexualities," reflecting three nodal points in contemporary Americanist thought—time, space, and embodiment—that have been particularly enlivening for minoritarian thought. The first, "Archives Unbound," unsettles time as it explores the construction of the archive for cultural analysis, considered not as a self-evident repository of history but as the effect of cathecting complex temporal crosscurrents. The second, "States of Exception," explores ways that unmapped spaces, both transnational and hyperlocal, can operate to interrupt and regenerate states of being. The third, "Speculative Sexualities," engages affect theory's preoccupation with bodily capacities as it builds upon Michel Foucault's crucial, yet often overlooked, reminder that "sex" is not a given but a speculative element in modernity, asking what "sex" might look like when set adrift from the oppositions that stabilize our contemporary understanding thereof. Yet these nodes cannot be isolated from one another. Hence "States of Exception" aligns its unmapped spaces with bodies in precarious situations; "Speculative Sexualities" highlights the pasts and futures that sex organizes and disorders; and "Archives Unbound" illuminates the role of attachment in creating the repositories we associate with history.

Archives Unbound

The essays in our first section draw on contemporary debates about the authority and operation of the archive and the function of historical memory. Even as poststructuralist thought has repositioned the archive as a problem rather than simply a resource, the "hunger for a recorded past," as Anjali Arondekar points out, sharpens in the face of conservative and fundamentalist appeals to tradition as foundation for their ways of knowing.[40] Critics in minoritized fields have begun to interrogate the persistence of our need for archives, examining the quasi-religious faith in their ability to produce answers about the past and hence to authorize or stabilize our continued existence. Official archives, as scholars of slavery and indigeneity in the U.S. have shown, are radically incomplete and skewed in ways that frustrate particular knowledge projects. What Jenny Sharpe refers to as the archival "tautology of facts" perpetuates the marginalization of historical subjects whose actions were not considered noteworthy in their own times.[41] The silences, omissions, and distortions of the archive have caused some scholars to turn away from it altogether, while others generate alternate historiographic practices, inventing ways to make those absences speak differently.[42] Even for those scholars who remain invested in traditional archival research and recovery practices, the archive is understood less as a discrete collection of documents than, as Ann Laura Stoler puts it, "a force field that animates political energies and expertise, that pulls on some 'social facts' and coverts them into qualified knowledge, that attends to some ways of knowing while repelling and refusing others."[43] The essays in this section correspond to the depiction of archive not as "fact" but as force field—a moving construction of the archive that unbinds its possibilities as it reorients how, where, and when we encounter it.

Rodrigo Lazo's essay, "Confederates in the Hispanic Attic: The Archive against Itself," opens on an encounter with what we might term the awkward historical object: the recent publication of data recording the contributions of Hispanic Confederate soldiers to the war effort, which contradicts the self-image of the Hispanic archive as it has sought, in line with the contemporary aims of U.S. Latina/o studies, to document a history of anti–white-supremacist resistance. By confronting material that is ostensibly undesirable, rather than simply absent,

Lazo's essay puts into relief the ideological mandates that shape how and why archives are perceived and apprehended. Such questions circulate around artifacts such as the Cuban Confederate Colonel Ambrosio José Gonzales's 1853 *Manifesto on Cuban Affairs Addressed to the People of the United States* and the ambiguous sympathies of the Reconstruction-era novelist María Amparo Ruiz de Burton—texts that trouble the desire to "locate a particular outcome," a reading of Latina/o studies as always oppositional, through archival labor.

In "Historical Totality and the African American Archive," Lloyd Pratt uses Edward P. Jones's *The Known World*, a twenty-first-century novel concerning slave ownership among African Americans, as a foray into larger questions about the possibilities of historical totality. Pratt questions whether the discernible absences inherent to archival practices around slaveholding in the Americas must constitute a permanent obstacle to the possibility of totality. He locates a resource in the African American historical romance, not only because it imagines a way across the gaps and fragmentation of the historical record, but precisely because its emphasis on human relationships resists the obfuscation of historical truth we know as reification. In this way, the historical romance finds the necessity of speculation about the past not only no obstacle but a positive gain.

Tavia Nyong'o, in "Race, Reenactment, and the 'Natural Born-Citizen,'" addresses the aggressively "historical" claims of the Tea Party movement as it reinvents and reorients the Revolutionary War archive. The temporal bend that loops the Tea Party to the revolutionary event it cites as carrying the weight of its anti-statism, Nyong'o argues, camouflages its stronger historical investment in the 14th Amendment's post–Civil War reversal of the foundational terms of citizenship. Tracking the "queasiness" of this time-shifting alliance with white racial innocence, Nyong'o sets a contemporary performance of archival reenactment—the collective reading aloud of the U.S. Constitution as the 112th Congress opened in January 2011—against the creative engagement with citizenship conducted in David Walker's 1829 *Appeal to the Coloured Citizens of the World* as it affectively undoes the amnesiac innocence of such performances.

Shelley Streeby's response, "Doing Justice to the Archive: Beyond Literature," engages these essays alongside the case of anarchist activist

Lucy Parsons, whose 1913 arrest for "selling literature without a license" (in the form of a printed collection of anarchist speeches) allies the perennial question of what constitutes literature with the section's interrogation of what constitutes the archive and the history to which it ostensibly refers. Streeby charges the conversation with the force of critical interdisciplinarity, affirming that the questions opened here demand an active openness to the evocations of a lively past in contexts beyond the traditional terrain of literary studies.

States of Exception

The essays in the second section dwell in and upon particular (dis)locations in space and time. The exceptional cases they consider—situated in extranational or hyperlocal contexts—set the social and affective relations familiar to the U.S. nation-state askew. The "outside" status that marks these situations—polar voyages, the earliest years of black American settlement in Liberia, the New York City draft riots of 1863—not only expose the tenuousness of nationalized modes of belonging; they also force us to confront the precarity of life, in the removal of structures of order and/or comfort. As Jonathan Elmer notes in his response, the exceptional conditions into which the essays inquire differ from the removal of citizenship by the power of law, the reduction from directed and qualified to "bare" life that marks the "state of exception" as Giorgio Agamben has defined it. Rather, they mark the distancing, at once willed and compelled, of norms for the regulation of behavior, expression, attachment, and futurity. Their attention to bodies *in extremis*—frozen into polar ice, living "close to death" in the new Liberia, or exploding into riotousness—carries out the work that Judith Butler identifies as central to a generatively critical humanities: to "return us to the human where we do not expect to find it, in its frailty and at the limits of its capacity to make sense."[44] These explorations of precarity align with a minoritarian humanism, a humanism that does not want to restore an unreconstructed "full humanity" but to activate other ways of apprehending its potential.

David Kazanjian's essay, "Unsettled Life: Early Liberia's Epistolary Equivocations," exposes the fault lines of black diaspora theory by examining how black settlers from the U.S. were suspended in a social subjectivity that resisted being congealed as specifically American or Liberian. Reading Phyllis Wheatley and Ouladah Equiano alongside and against the nineteenth-century archive of letters authored by Liberia's earliest black American settlers, Kazanjian identifies resonances of two conventional positions on settlement: the allure of diaspora's racial romanticism and the imperialistic impulses of an American nationalism. His nuanced consideration of the letters' language, however, settles for neither of them, instead exposing the conditionality and "equivocal agency" of Liberian settler-subjects as they speculated on the meanings and improvised on the practices of freedom.

Hester Blum's "The News at the Ends of the Earth: Polar Periodicals" also dwells on the kinds of writing and forms of imagination that emerge when familiar modes of self-location remain at a distance. Reading newspapers produced by nineteenth-century sailors aboard polar exploration vessels, written to fill some of the endless night hours during winters spent frozen within the polar ice, Blum finds an exhilarated sense of liberation from national constraints and the advocacy of a new perspective on the globe. Yet even as this new perspective was claimed, Blum notes, literary labor also became a means of reinstalling social hierarchies, though the traces of this reinstallation were edited out of reprints of the papers circulated onshore, revealing an attempt to portray shipboard life as more harmonious than it actually was.

Glenn Hendler's essay, "Feeling Like a State: Writing the 1863 New York City Draft Riots," also addresses the reemergence of forms of social ordering from within the exceptional moment. Collating an archive of materials around the 1863 draft riots in New York City (novels by Edward Ruffin and Anna Elizabeth Dickinson, and Herman Melville's poem "The House-Top: A Night Piece"), Hendler outlines these works' attempts to find an adequate form for depicting the riots, which, for Dickinson and Melville, involves an identification with the state itself as the force that must be hailed to contain the violence. Attending to the part played by the impersonal in the process of sympathetic identification, Hendler's essay demands and enacts an expansion of the types of objects generally considered by affect theorists.

Jonathan Elmer's response, "Impersonating the State of Exception," opens by addressing the limitations of a strictly juridico-political understanding of the state of exception in relation to the activation of alternative political knowledges linked to what we might call "unauthorized" states of exception. Considering three essays in this section against one another and against Melville's "Bartelby, the Scrivener," Elmer draws their elaboration of writerly politics toward an interrogation of the extent to which aesthetics can do justice to the question of a humanity that "requires acknowledgment on grounds that can never be provided."

Speculative Sexualities

The final section, "Speculative Sexualities," insists that the history of sexuality is not concerned only with what looks to us like "sex"— that is, with recognizable sex acts, homo- or heterosexual. Sex, in these essays, charges unexpected social sites and bodily processes, and the plasticity of the body renders it both a capacious tool of disciplinary power and a field of creative possibilities for remaking relations to history, sociality, and the self. A speculative history of sexuality—one that does not take the location of "sex" as given, but rather, follows attentively to see where it might lead—demands distinctively speculative and literary modes of reading, a willingness to engage in the kind of close reading that Elizabeth Freeman elsewhere describes as "too close for comfort."[45] This sustained textual intimacy produces surprising results, identifying the imaginative construction of worlds in which sexual difference, and the (re)productivity that orders that difference, is set aside, enabling sex to center on taste, or acoustic receptiveness, or timeplay. At the same time, the focus on Anglo-American writers in these essays might also remind us of the role of nineteenth-century biopower in aligning whiteness with sexual normativity, calling into consideration the extent to which these alternative sexualities might or might not unsettle the perpetuation of whiteness's propriety as the nation's destiny.[46]

Kyla Wazana Tompkins's and Elizabeth Freeman's essays both center on the anxieties surrounding the practice of masturbation in the nineteenth century, though they address the topic of alternative sexualities from very different angles.

In "Eat, Sex, Race," Tompkins, focusing on the role antebellum reformist campaigns played in a bodily (rather than genitally) centered history of sexuality, considers the emergence of dietary correctives to the practice of masturbation in the work of Sylvester Graham, tracing out the way his endorsement of whole-grained breads as a corrective to sexual excitement remaps both nation and globe by means of the "political life of the mouth," an orifice that was as much concerned in the sustenance and reproduction of a purified whiteness as were the genitals that could be overexcited by improper eating. What Tompkins terms "dietetic biopower" is, however, always haunted by the specter of improper consumption, a possibility that connects the mouth not only to the genitals—the site, presumably, of the masturbatory habits that improper diet helped to cause—but, queerly, to the anus, that unspeakably breachable boundary whose erotic potential serves as a reminder of "the liberal individual's ethical responsibility to the other."

Freeman's "Connecticut Yankings: Mark Twain and the Masturbating Dude" foregrounds Twain's humorous take on the anxieties surrounding masturbation, both explicitly, in his 1879 speech to a men's club concerning the "science of onanism," and implicitly in his 1889 time-travel novel *A Connecticut Yankee in King Arthur's Court*. Freeman reads the latter through the lens of a long-standing alignment of "bad" historiography with effeminacy and sexual deviance. If part of the work of being a good American is "getting at history in the right manner," then the bad historical practices that surface in Twain's novel not only critique the contemporary American vogue for things past but also, unexpectedly, work to make a future for sexual deviance in the inaccessible materials of that distant and discarded history.

Peter Coviello's response, "What Came Before," synchs Tompkins's and Freeman's divergent considerations of the autoerotic with a developing critical decentering of binary frameworks for sexual orientation. Their willingness to speculate on how autoeroticism might orient the body otherwise moves away from modern sexuality identity altogether, insofar as it necessarily conceives sex as a property of the self. What the antimasturbation movement used to call "self-abuse" paradoxically *unselves* sex, rendering it unsuitable for modern sexual identity's understanding of sex as a property of the self. Coviello examines the resonances between their accounts—in which the unselving of sex renders the body a tool for making other kinds of contact—and the elaboration, in Henry David Thoreau's journals, of an erotics of sound that offers intimations of a more expansive corporeality.

* * *

Thoreau's enraptured experience of sound—the aftermath of a dream in which he and Bronson Alcott "fell to quoting & referring to grand & pleasing couplets & single lines which we had read in times past"—may serve to point us, by way of conclusion, to a consideration of the recent turn toward enchantment as literary-critical method. Affirmations of pleasure, intimacy, and faithfulness to literary and cultural objects are articulated forcefully against the habits of distance, suspicion, and demystification attributed to a previous generation of critics. Enchantment, as Nancy Bentley observes, posits itself as an ethical rethinking of the goals as well as the methods of critique, enabled, in part, by the aforementioned reconsiderations of time and space that permit us to come closer to the past, overcoming the distance and disenchantment advocated by the earlier methods.[47] The speculative, as well as affective and ethical aspects, of postdisenchanted critique resonate suggestively against our understanding of minoritarian criticism as a means of encountering the world otherwise. We are, however, wary of overemphasizing the divide between "distanced" and "intimate" critique, as well as over-Oedipalizing the generational divide often used to explicate the emergence of enchantment. Though we agree with Stephen Best and Sharon Marcus when they resist the compulsion to "[have] a political agenda that determines in advance how we interpret texts," we would not align this resistance, as they do, with the emergence of a new "political realism" about the limited effect of cultural criticism on the contemporary world-historical situation.[48] Such appeals to "realism" imply that the political possibilities of critique are given in advance— indeed, that politics itself is already a known form, a position minoritarian criticism resists. That is not to say that we cherish the fantasy that our interventions will leap off the page directly into the midst of ongoing geopolitical struggles. The flows that animate minoritarian thought move very much in the reverse direction. The problems with which the essays in *Unsettled States* grapple—the possibility of freedom, definitions of history and identity, the rise of new conservatisms and forms of white supremacy, the ongoing policing of bodies, the reenergizing of the social imaginary—are urgent ones, permissive of no easy resolution. Yet in affirming a continued commitment to what Bentley calls the "the kind of political desire that is a signature of cultural critique,"[49] we are committed, as well, to its ongoing transformation, reinvention, and self-interruption—to leaving the very ground of "politics" uncertain, unsettled, the animating principle of a criticism that remains on the move.

NOTES

1. Published accounts of the earthquakes and surrounding events include James Lal Penick, Jr., *The New Madrid Earthquakes* (Columbia: University of Missouri Press, 1981), and Jay Feldman, *When The Mississippi Ran Backwards: Empire, Intrigue, Murder, and the New Madrid Earthquakes* (New York: Free Press, 2005); also Robert Sidney Douglass, *History of Southeast Missouri, a Narrative Account of its Historical Progress, its People and its Principle Interests, volume one,* chapter XIV, "New Madrid Earthquake" (Chicago: Lewis Publishing, 1912), pp. 212–33.

2. See *Resolution by the General Assembly of the Missouri Territory, for the Relief of the Inhabitants of New Madrid County, who have Suffered by Earthquakes.* Washington, D.C.: A & G. Way, Printers, 1814.

3. See Penick, *The New Madrid Earthquakes,* pp. 120–21. As it turned out, the slow diffusion of the provisions of this act and waves of corruption and fraud prevented many of the affected from receiving due compensation for their losses. Land fraud became so common, in fact, that the term "New Madrid claim" was synonymous with fakery and fraud. See Penick and Feldman.

4. The quoted phrase belongs to a congressional representative from Missouri, Joseph James Russell, who, a century later, read into the congressional record a report of the events, including a dramatic description of the quakes by an eyewitness. Russell's commemorative recitation of the event, focusing solely upon the perspective of white settlers, upheld the ameliorative federal response it received, in the form of the New Madrid Relief Act, as a logical move toward the binding of the local to the national. Although, as he acknowledged, most of the federal aid sent failed to serve its intended purpose, ending up in the hands of speculators and swindlers, the ability of Congress to act in response to this "great natural calamity" implicitly marks the episode as a confirmation of national progress. Joseph James Russell, "Remarks on the Centennial of the New Madrid Earthquakes." December 16, 1911. Washington. D.C. Mss. of congressional speech of Congressional representative from New Madrid's district, held in Huntington Library. 4 pp. typed.

5. I am grateful to Jonathan Hancock for introducing me to the range of responses to the New Madrid quakes in a presentation at the Huntington Library, July 2012, based on his doctoral dissertation in history, "A World Convulsed: Earthquakes, Authority, and the Making of Nations in the War of 1812 Era" (University of North Carolina, 2013). See also his article "Shaken Spirits: Cherokees,

Moravian Missionaries, and the New Madrid Earthquakes," *Journal of the Early Republic*, 33.4 (Winter 2013): 643–73.

6. Quoted in Penick, *The New Madrid Earthquakes*, p. 1.

7. One account of his visit to the Creeks in early December 1811, just before the first earthquake struck, holds that when tribal leaders were unmoved by his recruitment speech, he declared, "You do not believe the Great Spirit has sent me. You will know. I leave Tuckhabatchee directly, and shall go straight to Detroit. When I arrive there, I will stamp on the ground with my foot, and will shake down every house in Tuckhabatchee." Quoted in Penick, *The New Madrid Earthquakes*, p. 124. See also John F. Gall, *Tecumseh's Earthquake: A Bit of Ohio and Mississippi Valley Folklore* (Chillicothe: Dave Webb, 1954).

8. Quoted in Penick, *The New Madrid Earthquakes*, p. 125.

9. For an account of the intertwining of religious, economic and geopolitical struggle in pan-tribal resistance, see Gregory Evans Dowd, *A Spirited Resistance: The North American Indian Struggle for Unity, 1745–1815* (Baltimore: Johns Hopkins University Press, 1993). On the Creek War, see especially Joel W. Martin, *Sacred Revolt: The Muskogee's Struggle for a New World* (Boston: Beacon Press, 1993).

10. See *Resolution by the General Assembly of the Missouri Territory*. What remained of the Louisiana Territory after Louisiana was admitted to statehood was renamed the Missouri Territory in June 1812 in order to avoid confusion. The southeastern portion of that territory became the state of Missouri in 1821.

11. Max Savelle, "The Founding of New Madrid, Missouri," *Mississippi Valley Historical Review*, 19.1 (June 1932): 30–56.

12. On the spatial turn in American literary studies, see Wai Chee Dimock, *Through Other Continents: American Literature Across Deep Time* (Princeton: Princeton University Press, 2006) and "Planet and America, Set and Subset" in *Shades of the Planet: American Literature as World Literature*, ed. Wai Chee Dimock and Lawrence Buell (Princeton: Princeton University Press, 2007), 1–16; Paul Giles, *The Global Remapping of American Literature* (Princeton: Princeton University Press, 2011); and Hsuan Hsu, *Geography and the Production of Space in Nineteenth-Century American Literature* (Cambridge: Cambridge University Press, 2010). On the transnational turn in American literary studies, see Anna Brickhouse, *Transamerican Literary Relations and the Nineteenth-Century Public Sphere* (Cambridge: Cambridge University Press, 2004); Shelley Fisher Fishkin, "Crossroads of Cultures: The Transnational Turn in American Studies," *American Quarterly* 57.1 (2005): 17–57; Kirsten Gruez Silva, *Ambassadors of Culture: The Transamerican Origins of Latino Writing* (Princeton: Princeton University Press, 2002); Rachel Lee, *The Americas of Asian American Literature: Gendered Fictions of Nation and Transnation* (Princeton: Princeton University Press, 1999); Paula Moya and Ramón Saldívar, eds. *Fictions of the Trans-American Imaginary*, special issue of *Modern Fiction Studies* 49.1 (2003): 1–180; Carolyn Porter, "What We Know That We Don't Know: Remapping

American Literary Studies," *American Literary* History 6.3 (1994): 467–526; Claudia Sadowski-Smith and Claire F. Fox, "Theorizing the Hemisphere: Inter-Americas at the Intersection of American, Canadian, and Latin American Studies," *Comparative American Studies* 4.1 (2004): 5–38; José David Saldívar, *Border Matters: Remapping American Cultural Studies* (Berkeley: University of California Press, 1994) and *Trans-Americanity: Subaltern Modernities, Global Coloniality, and the Cultures of Greater Mexico* (Durham: Duke University Press, 2011); and Sandhya Shukla and Heidi Tinsman, *Our Americas: Political and Cultural Imaginings*, special issue of *Radical History Review* 89 (2004): 1–250. Other important scholarship on transnationalism incorporating discussions of the Americas includes Pheng Cheah, *Cosmopolitics: Thinking and Feeling Beyond the Nation* (Minneapolis: University of Minnesota Press, 1998); Inderpal Grewal, *Transnational America: Feminisms, Diasporas, Neoliberalism* (Durham: Duke University Press, 2005); Paul Jay, *Global Matters: The Transnational Turn in Literary Studies* (Ithaca: Cornell University Press, 2010); Winifred Fluck, Donald E. Pease, and John Carlos Rowe, eds., *Re-Framing the Transnational Turn in American Studies* (Hanover: Dartmouth College Press, 2011). Important recent titles on hemispheric literary studies include Susan Castillo, *Performing America: Colonial Encounters in New World Writing, 1500–1786* (London: Routledge, 2005); J. Michael Dash, *The Other America: Caribbean Literature in a New World Context* (Charlottesville: University Press of Virginia, 1998); Earl Fitz, *Rediscovering the New World: Inter-American Literature in a Comparative Context* (Iowa City: University of Iowa Press, 1991); Claire F. Fox, ed., *Critical Perspectives and Emerging Models of Inter-American Studies*. Special issue of *Comparative American Studies* 3.4 (2005): 387–515; Sean Goudie, *Creole America: The West Indies and the Formation of Literature and Culture in the New Republic* (Philadelphia: University of Pennsylvania Press, 2006); Caroline F. Levander and Robert S. Levine, eds., *Hemispheric American Studies* (New Brunswick: Rutgers University Press, 2007); Gretchen Murphy, *Hemispheric Imaginings: The Monroe Doctrine and Narratives of U.S. Empire* (Durham: Duke University Press, 2005); Susan Scott Parrish, "The 'Hemispheric Turn' in Colonial American Studies," *Early American Literature* 40.3 (2005): 545–53; and José David Saldívar, *The Dialectics of Our America: Genealogy, Cultural Critique, and Literary History* (Durham: Duke University Press, 1991).

13. Paul Giles, "The Deterritorialization of American Literature," in *Shades of the Planet*, p. 39 [39–61].

14. Recent work on the temporal turn in American literary studies includes Thomas Allen, *A Republic in Time: Temporality and Social Imagination in Nineteenth-Century America* (Chapel Hill: University of North Carolina Press, 2008); Elizabeth Freeman, *Time Binds: Queer Temporalities, Queer Histories* (Durham: Duke University Press, 2010); Dana Luciano, *Arranging Grief: Sacred Time and the Body in Nineteenth-Century America* (New York: NYU Press, 2007); Jeffrey Insko, *The Ever-Present Now: Romantic Presentism and Antebellum American Literature* (forthcoming);

and Lloyd Pratt, *Archives of American Time: Literature and Modernity in the Nineteenth Century* (Philadelphia: University of Pennsylvania Press, 2010).

15. Dimock, *Through Other Continents*, p. 28.

16. No footnote can hope to do justice to this body of work. Useful guides to key issues and critical texts include Paul Lauter, *Reconstructing American Literature* (New York: Feminist Press, 1984) and *Canons and Contexts* (New York: Oxford University Press, 1991), and John Carlos Rowe, *The New American Studies* (Minneapolis: University of Minnesota Press, 2002).

17. See Gilles Deleuze and Felix Guattari, *Kafka: Toward a Minor Literature*, trans. Dana Polan (Minneapolis: University of Minnesota Press, 1986). For an influential account of the relations between minority existence and the creativity of minoritarian worldmaking, see José Esteban Muñoz, *Disidentifications: Queers of Color and the Performance of Politics* (Minneapolis: University of Minnesota Press, 1999).

18. Gilles Deleuze and Felix Guattari, *Anti-Oedipus: Capitalism and Schizophrenia* (Minneapolis: University of Minnesota Press, 1983), p. 315.

19. Pelagia Goulimari, "A Minoritarian Feminism? Things to Do with Deleuze and Guattari," *Hypatia* 14.2 (Spring 1999).

20. Pelagia Goulimari, "'Myriad Little Connections': Minoritarian Movements in the Postmodernism Debate," *Postmodern Culture* 14.3 (May 2004).

21. Deleuze and Guattari, *Anti-Oedipus*, p. 315.

22. Michael Geyer, "Multiculturalism and the Politics of General Education," *Critical Inquiry* 19.3 (Spring 1993): 528 [499–533].

23. Geyer, "Multiculturalism," p. 533.

24. See especially *Unsettling Settler Societies: Articulations of Gender, Race, Ethnicity and Class* (London: Sage, 1995); Patrick Wolfe, *Settler Colonialism and the Transformation of Anthropology: The Politics and Poetics of an Ethnographic Event* (London: Cassell, 1999) and "Settler Colonialism and the Elimination of the Native," *Journal of Genocide Research* 8.4 (2006): 387–409; Alyosha Goldstein and Alex Lubin, eds., "Settler Colonialism," special issue of *South Atlantic Quarterly* 107.4 (2008); Lorenzo Veracini, *Settler Colonialism: A Theoretical Overview* (Basingstoke and New York: Palgrave, 2010) and "Introducing Settler Colonial Studies," *Settler Colonial Studies* 1.1 (2011): 1–12; and Michele Grossman and Ceriwiden Spark, "Unsettled States," special issue of *Postcolonial Studies* 8.3 (2005).

25. Wolfe, "Settler Colonialism and the Elimination of the Native," p. 388.

26. The coimbrication of settlement and sexual normativity highlights the resonance of "queering," another critical term that activates the disturbance of sedimented forms, against "unsettlement"—though it is less useful, I think, to treat the two as synonyms, lest this activation of "queer" become an affirmation of its transcendently resistant capacities, to the detriment of identifying those spaces, times and forms where queerness's "unsettling" effect is notably, and sometimes violently, partial. Scholars working in queer indigenous studies, for instance, note the lack of attention in most queer U.S.-based criticism and political

practice to the specific power relations that characterize settler colonialism. (Two important recent studies of the politics of sexuality in relation to Native American history and politics are Mark Rifkin, *When Did Indians Become Straight? Kinship, The History of Sexuality, and Native Sovereignty* [Oxford: Oxford University Press, 2011], and Scott Lauria Morgensen, *Spaces between Us: Queer Settler Colonialism and Indigenous Decolonization* [Minneapolis: University of Minnesota Press, 2011]). For this reason, the queer scholarship contained in this collection is less invested in "queering" as a solely a mode of resistant undoing—the kind of queering indexed in Lee Edelman's assertion that "queer can never describe an identity, it can only ever disturb one"—than in queering as a practice of generating speculative connections, the sense evoked, for instance, in Eve Kosofsky Sedgwick's reminder that one of the meanings of the term "queer" is "across or athwart." See Lee Edelman, *No Future: Queer Theory and the Death Drive* (Durham: Duke University Press, 2004), p. 17; Eve Kosofsky Sedgwick, "Queer and Now," *Tendencies* (Durham: Duke University Press, 1993), p. xii.

27. See, e.g., Mishuana Goeman, "The Tools of a Cartographic Poet: Unmapping Settler Colonialism in Joy Harjo's Poetry," *Settler Colonial Studies* 2.2 (2012): 89–112.

28. Two publications in postcolonial studies that share the main title of this volume might serve to illustrate these inflections. Ian Lustig's important study *Unsettled States, Disputed Lands: Britain and Ireland, France and Algeria, Israel and the West Bank-Gaza* (Ithaca: Cornell University Press, 1993) examines the sustained and violent border disputes that constitute the wreckage of colonial occupation in these three regions. A more recent special issue of the journal *Postcolonial Studies* evokes unsettlement as at once a sustained articulation and critique of settler colonialism and, crucially, as the energizing of a demand for another future, an as-yet-unknown post-settler one. See Michele Grossman and Ceriwiden Spark, Introduction to "Unsettled States," *Postcolonial Studies* 8.3 (2005): 235–41.

29. See, e.g., Jo Ann Levy, *Unsettling the West: Eliza Farnham and Georgiana Bruce Kirby in Frontier California* (Berkeley: Heyday Books, 2004).

30. See, e.g., Macarena Gómez-Barris, "Documenting Absence: Ghostly Screens Unsettle the Past," in *Where Memory Dwells: Culture and State Violence in Chilé* (Berkeley: University of California Press, 2009), chapter 4.

31. Some key works include: Renée Bergland, *The National Uncanny: Indian Ghosts and American Subjects* (Hanover: University Press of New England, 2000); Avery Gordon, *Ghostly Matters: Haunting and the Sociological Imagination*, new edition (Minneapolis: University of Minnesota Press, 2008); Pheng Cheah, *Spectral Nationality: Passages of Freedom from Kant to Postcolonial Literatures of Liberation* (New York: Columbia University Press, 2003); Ivy G. Wilson, *Specters of Democracy: Blackness and the Aesthetics of Politics in the Antebellum U.S.* (New York: Oxford University Press, 2011); Ian Baucom, *Specters of the Atlantic: Finance Capital, Slavery, and the Philosophy of History* (Durham: Duke University

Press, 2005); Terry Castle, *The Apparitional Lesbian: Female Homosexuality and Modern Culture* (New York: Columbia University Press, 1995); Carla Freccero, *Queer/Early/Modern* (Durham: Duke University Press, 2006); Christopher Peterson, *Kindred Specters: Death, Mourning and American Affinity* (Minneapolis: University of Minnesota Press, 2007).

32. Colin Davis, "État Presént: Hauntology, Spectres and Phantoms," *French Studies* 59.3 (2005): 379.

33. See especially Jacques Derrida, *Specters of Marx: The State of the Debt, the Work of Mourning, and the New International* (New York: Routledge, 1994), p. 11.

34. Gordon, *Ghostly Matters*.

35. Dominick La Capra, "Trauma, Absence, Loss," *Critical Inquiry* 25.4 (Summer 1999): 696–727. See also Amy Shuman, "On the Verge: Phenomenology and Empathic Unsettlement," *Journal of American Folklore* 124.493 (Summer 2011): 147–74.

36. La Capra, "Trauma, Absence, Loss," pp. 699, 723. La Capra goes on to argue that "empathic unsettlement also raises in pointed form the problem of how to address traumatic events involving victimization, including the problem of composing narratives that neither confuse one's own voice or position with the victim's nor seek facile uplift, harmonization, or closure but allow the unsettlement that they address to affect the narrative's own movement both in terms of acting-out and working-through" (p. 723).

37. Gordon, *Ghostly Matters*, p. 57.

38. Cindy Weinstein and Christopher Looby, "Introduction," *American Literature's Aesthetic Dimensions* (New York: Columbia University Press, 2012), p. 8. See also Christopher Castiglia and Russ Castronovo, "A 'Hive of Subtlety': Aesthetics and the End(s) of Cultural Studies," *American Literature* 76.3 (September 2004): 423–35.

39. Several of the contributors to this volume (Rodrigo Lazo, David Kazanjian, Hester Blum, Glenn Hendler, Kyla Wazana Tompkins, and myself) first gathered at an invitational symposium organized by Ivy Wilson at the University of Notre Dame in April of 2008, entitled *Unauthorized States: Antinomies of the Nation and Other Subversive Genealogies;* however, with the exception of one portion of Hendler's essay, none of the work in this volume was presented at that conference, nor did its sessions employ the format or critical framework we have adapted here.

40. Anjali Arondekar, *For the Record: Sexuality and the Colonial Archive in India* (Durham: Duke University Press, 2009), p. 2.

41. Jenny Sharpe, *Ghosts of Slavery: A Literary Archaeology of Black Women's Lives* (Minneapolis: University of Minnesota Press, 2003), p. xiii.

42. See, e.g., Sharpe's expansion, in *Ghosts of Slavery*, of the space and time of the U.S. slavery archive, weaving together oral narrative, song, mythology, and contemporary neoslave narratives.

43. Ann Laura Stoler, *Along the Archival Grain: Epistemic Anxieties and Colonial Common Sense* (Princeton: Princeton University Press, 2009), p. 22.

44. Judith Butler, *Precarious Life: The Powers of Mourning and Violence* (New York: Verso, 2004), p. 151.

45. Elizabeth Freeman, *Time Binds: Queer Temporalities, Queer Histories* (Durham: Duke University Press, 2010), p. xxi.

46. Roderick Ferguson's *Aberrations in Black: Toward a Queer of Color Critique* (Minneapolis: University of Minnesota Press, 2003) outlines some of the ways in which a racialized heteronormativity operated as a precondition of U.S. citizenship, visible, for instance in the Freedmen's Bureau's postbellum administration of marital norms as a corrective to the "nonmonogamous and fluid intimate arrangements elaborated by slaves" (86).

47. Nancy Bentley, Introduction to "Forum: In The Spirit of the Thing: Critique as Enchantment," *J19: The Journal of Nineteenth-Century Americanists* 1.1 (Spring 2013): 148.

48. Stephen Best and Sharon Marcus, "Surface Reading: An Introduction," *The Way We Read Now,* special issue of *Representations* 108 (Fall 2009): 16.

49. Bentley, "Introduction," p. 150.

PART I

Archives Unbound

1

Confederates in the Hispanic Attic

The Archive against Itself

RODRIGO LAZO

John O'Donnell-Rosales's compendium *Hispanic Confederates* is an impressive and disturbing contribution to the archive of Hispanic history. "The War for Southern Independence saw thousands of these men flock to the Confederate cause," O'Donell-Rosales writes in an introduction. "Whole companies were raised, composed fully or partially of Spanish/Hispanic men."[1] And these included not only white Creoles but also "Mestizos of Spanish/Native American ancestry," Minorcans of Florida, Sephardic Jews, and even a handful of "Asian men from the Philippines" who used Spanish in their correspondence and had Hispanic surnames.[2] O'Donnell-Rosales's project is archival in the sense that it is recuperative and amasses information, but it does not offer either extensive analysis of Hispanic affiliations with the Confederacy or a narrative of events; rather, it provides a list of more than 6,175 men who fought in the war, and thus the book's 149 pages are made up of just that—names with accompanying information on rank, brigade, and militia. The author speculates that even more offspring of Hispanic women may have joined the ranks but are difficult to identify because they did not have Hispanic surnames. The archival impetus here is to collect and preserve, so that scholars and/or descendants of soldiers can look up who fought in the war. The book organizes the information under a banner that is both ethnic (Hispanic) and political (Confederates) and determines who is included through the use of surnames.

Calling attention to thousands of these Confederates adds interesting twists to the history of people of Latin American descent in the United States, and it raises questions about the transhistorical endurance of identity. As a field, Latino studies has gained momentum in the last thirty years from the work of scholars who sought to challenge exclusion and white supremacy in U.S. society.[3] As Juan Poblete has noted, "The emergence of ethnic studies in the 1960s can be seen as the victorious result of the pressure of social movements or as the price that the radical movements of the 1960s had to pay in order to be heard and legitimized at the institutional level."[4] Poblete presents an important tension between the impetus of the projects, born out of Chicano/a and Puerto Rican social movements, and the institutionalizing effects of establishing a field of study. Historical research has led to a capacious and messy Hispanic archive. In 1993, for example, Genaro Padilla expressed surprise at finding texts by men in gray: "That a *Mexicano* would ever be part of the Confederacy had simply never crossed my mind."[5] At the same time, Padilla's own contributions in *My History, Not Yours: The Formation of Mexican-American Autobiography* opened research avenues that confronted how economic elites in the nineteenth century led lives that at times clashed with the working-class dimensions of the Chicano movement. Since the early 1990s, numerous studies, including Jesse Alemán's edition of the Civil War narrative of Loreta Velazquez, "Cuban Woman and Confederate Soldier," have called attention to the temporal contradictions of Latino/a identity formation across historical periods.

Temporally speaking, I would distinguish between a Hispanic archive that stems from a capacious notion of ethnic descent and cuts across centuries and Latino studies as a field with commitments that emerge from the late twentieth century. The construction of an ethnic archive clashes with the premise of an academic project committed to progressive political perspectives (keeping in mind that the premise was never monolithic). Theoretical discussions have pointed to the complicated relationship between an "archive" as a repository of documents and the word "archive" as an analogy for the collection of information that sustains an academic field.[6] In this case, the search for and construction of a Hispanic archive dovetails but is not commensurate with Latino studies. Fields of study seek physical archives for artifacts, books, and materials or their digital counterparts in order to produce research. In turn, a second archival formation emerges (books, figures, authors, events, key terms) that represent the field's concerns. But the two are not symmetrical, and thus a Hispanic archive will not necessarily run parallel to the progressive political positions of a Latino present. Rather, a Hispanic archive may call attention to the way Latino studies' attempts to situate identity in history creates contradictions and brings forward a multiplicity of political commitments. O'Donnell-Rosales's book exemplifies the dispersal inherent in a Hispanic archive. On the one hand, it offers a scholarly contribution that calls attention to the often-overlooked participation of Hispanics in U.S. historical events and it shows how Latino history can open new vistas in historical study. On the other hand, the very notion of a Hispanic Confederate is a reminder that a scholarly enterprise is likely to turn up skeletons. The archival work undertaken by O'Donnell-Rosales shows how the organization of information from the past may lead to a cultural and political disjunction that is the result of identifying a historical group by contemporary terms and investments.

That disjunction is the result of identifications that cut across time. Hispanics with sympathies for the Lost Cause may find solace in knowing that some ancestor fought in Confederate garb, which explains my title's invocation of Tony Horwitz's popular *Confederates in the Attic: Dispatches from the Unfinished Civil War* (1999), a hilarious and frightening account of battle reenactments and the ongoing purchase of the war in historical imagination. Horwitz's descriptions of contemporary invocations of the Civil War raise questions about the relationship of historical conception to a present embodiment of the past. At the end of the battle, the reenactors are still alive, having performed an identification that was only partially successful. Comparable to how battle reenactments motivate bodily experiences that connect to events from the nineteenth century, the historical aspirations of Latino studies posit continuity from people in the past to the present. Identity seeks to reach across time. But such identifications speak more to the imperatives of a field's archival claims and the organization of information in the present than the actual items inside the attic's—or the archive's—dustier ends. Attics can lead to unexpected discoveries and even uncomfortable histories, and in that sense they are similar to archives. If the journals, monographs, canonical writers, and departmental web pages of Latino studies are to be displayed on the coffee table, then it's in the attic where we find the letters, documents, and objects that appear out of place, such as a Confederate flag.

This article is about the persistence of archival structures as well as the endurance of elements within the archive that challenge the archival sign organizing the content. The ongoing investment in archival formation and the circulation of a sign naming the archive are part of a process that Jacques Derrida recognized as "consignation," meaning not only to deposit or entrust but also a gathering together. "*Consignation,*" he writes, "aims to coordinate a single corpus, in a system or a synchrony in which all the elements articulate the unity of an ideal configuration."[7] An attempt to articulate an ideal configuration in a shared time is the aim of a national archive, but it can also describe the formation of a field of study based on an ethnic subject. Like a nation-based archive that reaches to the past to sustain its present ideological commitments, Latino studies seeks ancestors and antecedents that can convey continuity. This idealistic proposition is likely to clash against some of the material that is ultimately gathered within the archive.

I begin this essay by considering archival persistence. Although the project of Latino studies emerged from a challenge to monolithic and exclusionary forms of knowledge organization, the attempt to establish a legitimate academic field led back to an investment in an archive. I consider the persistence of the archive in the work of two theorist/writers whose work was motivated by anti-archival longings that ultimately led to the formation of archival ouvres. By returning to meditations on the archive produced by Derrida and Hélène Cixous, I show how texts, particularly Cixous's *Manhattan,* that offer forceful arguments against the archive, can lead to archival formations. That theoretical premise will move to a discussion of the Hispanic archive, which I argue is being constructed not only through academic but also broader social and media conceptions of a Hispanic past. Looking at a peculiar interpretation of Annie Proulx's story "Brokeback Mountain," I show how the naming of archives and a reversion to personal names leads to the dispersal of an archival formation. My final section looks at the way contradictions in archival holdings, the elements that challenge consignation, can also foment renewed interest in an archive and support its ongoing development. To show how that process works, I turn to what I call the María Amparo Ruiz de Burton Archive.

Messy Attic/Persistent Archive

Recent discussions of the power wielded by archivists have invoked several potent metaphors: the archive as temple, prison, and restaurant. As Randall Jimerson has noted, the temple invokes the archivist's authority to shape memory and valorize certain objects that are treated as treasures; the prison emphasizes the controlling aspect of archival work and the protective role of archival institutions; and the restaurant brings forward the archivist's importance as an interpreter of the menu (finding aids or catalogues) and conveyor of the goods within a repository.[8] At stake in these metaphors is the role of the archivist in instituting a site for veneration, protection, and intellectual nourishment. Without denying the importance and influence of archivists, who can wield significant influence because of their knowledge of contents, I introduce the attic as a site that emphasizes the multiplicity of objects within an archive. Unlike the metaphors discussed by Jimerson, the attic emphasizes the passing of time and forgotten objects. Attics are filled in a haphazard way and they contain (or hide) items that might otherwise be thrown away. The attic emphasizes the unpredictable force of archival holdings. How do items in the attic break away from the organizing principle of the archive? The attic is packed with unexpected objects and their stories, and thus the desire to locate a particular outcome might run into an inversion or a shift. At least since *The Madwoman in the Attic,* the attic has been associated in academic work with revisionary approaches that emphasize stories previously excluded from dominant narratives of literary and cultural history. But what if the new stories move in directions that differ from the revisionary vision?

Let's take an example from the attic. At the Library of Congress (the first archive of the United States) is a dedicated copy of *Manifesto on Cuban Affairs Addressed to the People of the United States* (1853) by

Ambrosio José Gonzales, the so-called "Cuban Confederate colonel" who served as chief of artillery for General P. G. T. Beauregard. Gonzales did not receive significant attention until researchers became more sensitive to the presence of Latinos and particularly Cubans in U.S. history. Recent work includes a book-length history of Gonzales and several other studies.[9] Gonzales offers another example of the contradictions that emerge when an archival text speaks for itself. The *Manifesto* is remarkable for its defense of representative government and its call for Cuban independence from Spain at the same time that it displays a profound ambivalence on the question of slavery. Writing in the wake of failed filibustering expeditions to Cuba and a few years before the U.S. Civil War, Gonzales rails against the Spanish crown's support of the slave trade in Cuba "for the special benefit of the Queen Mother, the [island's] Captain-General, and a powerful Spanish clique in Havana."[10] He argues that as a result of slavery Cuba has become "not only a mart for African captives, but the point d'apuui for European despotism in America." The illegal continuation of the slave trade is among a litany of Spanish abuses that include excessive taxation, the prohibition of arms, and the use of military courts for criminal offenses.

But Gonzales's opposition to the slave trade does not seem to extend to slavery itself. He sees "blacks" as well as Chinese indentured servants as perpetuating a system of fear in his native island: "While slaves and Asiatics are thus introduced, white colonization is discountenanced, that the threat of a colored population may be held to the Cubans."[11] This invocation of a black "menace" is a nod to a policy of *blanqueamiento* (whitening, whitewashing) that had been advocated by other Cubans. As such, the critique of the slave trade becomes a rhetorical opportunity to attack Spain. In keeping with this ambivalence, Gonzales throws his military lot in with a cause that would have retained slavery in the southern United States.

But if Gonzales offers a masculine example of Confederate alliances, the curious case of Loreta Janeta Velazquez, Confederate soldier in drag, shows just how creative Hispanic Confederates can become. As Jesse Alemán has shown, the proposition that Velazquez fought in drag, an example of "the instabilities of gender and national identities," disturbed supporters of the Confederacy, including General Jubal Early. "Early found it downright offensive that a narrative about a woman masquerading as a Confederate soldier would be in circulation," Alemán writes.[12] Early's response is an example of an archival conflict; his expectation is challenged by a text in the archive.

What Gonzales and Velazquez have in common is a multiplicity of subject positions: they are connected to multiple nations, multiple wars, and for Velazquez even more than one gender. Gonzales is both Cuban and Confederate, and by the terms of O'Donnell-Rosales, Hispanic. According to his pamphlet, he is also a naturalized U.S. citizen. In addition, he is on the losing side of more than one military conflict: the filibustering expeditions of Narciso López and the Civil War. At the same time, Gonzales is well connected and moves in elite circles. His pamphlet is dedicated to Caleb Cushing, the attorney general under President Franklin Pierce. It is written in Warrenton Springs, Virginia, and published in New Orleans. Gonzales is the type of historical actor whose experiences would defy the singularity of an archival concept. If anything he calls attention to how an archival starting point will inevitably lead to partial knowledge of historical figures. In her study of colonial archives, Ann Stoler has emphasized the fragmented nature of colonial archives, the way they "mark the distance between recognized and disqualified knowledge, between intelligible accounts and those deemed inappropriate for exchange."[13] The "inappropriate," she continues, is not necessarily something that can be described in other than piecemeal fashion.

The archive is always inadequate. But while the contents of the archive are likely to be partial and to upset the starting point of someone conducting research, such challenges do not necessarily destroy the archival terms of consignation and certainly not the archive itself. The edifice and the attic remain. And this persistence is apparent in the critical apparatus surrounding Cixous's *Manhattan: Letters from Prehistory*. In some ways, this is a book about a woman who crosses the Atlantic to do research on literary masters even as she is grappling with a variety of personal challenges, including the death of her father and the loss of a child. She goes to the archive to ward off death. Or we could say that she seeks to escape her present. During an archival trip to Yale's Beinecke Rare Book and Manuscript Collection she meets and falls in love with an impressionable wanna-be writer, Gregor, a man with Kafkaesque name and an aspiration to be another Poe. That experience remains in her memory (a personal archive full of notes and images) for decades. But the bare plot aside, *Manhattan* is a book about attics, both personal and archival: "Later on, in the eighties, I was disagreeably surprised to rediscover, in one of those far too numerous boxes brooding on their volcanoes in the back of my life, into which at variously dated moments of panic I have tossed a hodgepodge of treasures and trash that render later excavations forever unbearable, a small yellowed envelope without anything written on it, containing a lock of extremely fine sandy hair."[14] That is the language of the attic: "treasures and trash," "excavations," unmarked "envelopes," unexpected mementoes. At first she is not even able to place the content in a recognizable set of associations. Whose hair is it? Her dead child's? The lost lover's?

Lest there be any question of the relationship between archive and memory, the running narrative switches from the personal attic to the Beinecke and to other archives across decades. Cixous's choice of the Beinecke is instructive for it is a repository that complicates the distinction between archive and museum. A testament to the power of Yale University and the opulence of its collections, the Beinecke holds not only ancient manuscripts and Greek and Roman papyri, but also papers for writers whose names could make up an anthology of English and American literature (Byron, Franklin, Conrad, Wright). The researcher and her love interest both seek some kind of regenerative power among dead authors. At the Beinecke, the narrator says, "Literature changed the corpse of my father that was all I asked: the sublimation of the corpse I tell my brother is what I was looking for" (*M* 62). In some ways, the Beinecke (and the lover) offer a reprieve, but more to my point is that archival work is always about unearthing corpses, whether sublimated or not.

Despite the narrator's search for sublimation, the Beinecke has other ideas. The researcher comes to recognize that "a Library is in so many ways like a Necropolis, this Beinecke where untold volumes testify to illness and deathbeds" (*M* 72). Suddenly, the dimensions of the universe from which she tries to escape emerge in the texts before her. She contemplates "the still warm manuscripts of those always prematurely dead authors who've vanished and taken with them the eternal nothingness of the hundreds of books they didn't write." Death becomes an archival absence that influences her interpretation.

In the face of loss and the impossibility of escaping the presence of death, she continues moving: "In the USA I didn't go from city to city but from one Library to the next, and even from one manuscript collection to the next. In my mind I took the boat that was moored between the columns of the British Museum for the monumental Beinecke Library, even if in reality I had to cross cities roads ports oceans ports cities airports roads that went from Paris to London to New York to New Haven to Buffalo" (*M* 61). As the years pass and she returns to her personal archive repeatedly, the movement continues. And the circularity persists: "I had such love for Literature, therefore for him I thought, thirty-five years after Gregor's exit, the idea comes to me of the suffering he had sown for himself, I loved literature and believe he was it, whereas he knew he had borrowed it" (*M* 177). At the end, the narrator is no closer to sifting archival remnants from the events, and it would be tempting to read *Manhattan* as a deconstruction of the archive, except that Literature persists. The author is not dead and neither is the archive. They come back with a vengeance both as the memory that will not go away but also in the apparatus of the author, Hélène Cixous. The friend who helps create the Cixous archive is Jacques Derrida.

Perhaps the most important opponent of the archive, always seeking to deny its presence, Derrida participates in the establishment of the Cixous archive. In a slim volume titled *Geneses, Genealogies, Genres, and Genius: The Secrets of the Archive*, Derrida considers Cixous and *Manhattan*. On the one hand, Derrida echoes the point I made in the first part of this article: "The archive's trustees may find themselves, because of the archive's devious structure, dispossessed of all power and all authority over it. The archive won't let itself be pushed around, it seems to resist, make matters difficult, foment a revolution against the very power to which it feigns to hand itself over, to lend and even to give itself."[15] The word "feign" implies that the archive is an invention or even a forgery. From the beginning, before the archive can even revolt against itself, the terms are feigned.

But why is Derrida, delivering the opening talk at a symposium in 2003, returning to an argument against the archive a few years after *Mal d'Archive* (1995)? The occasion is the donation of Cixous's letters, notebooks and dream journals to the French national library: the foundation of an archive of materials by and about Cixous at the

Bibliothéque Nationale de France. Once again, Derrida emphasizes all that the archive cannot know and cannot hold. Cixous's secrets, her dream-work, her genius all create a space outside of knowledge as circumscribed by the archive. The sleight of hand is the following return to Literature (with a capital L). Derrida on the Beinecke: "I know well this renowned edifice whose walls of stone let in an inoffensive natural light, from the sun, to illuminate the archives of so many of the greatest writers of the 'Omnipotence-other' of world Literature. In the mammalian chamber of this Beinecke library, the author tells us she read, in all the languages, three *Ulysses,* Homer's, Shakespeare's and Joyce's. Each of the *Ulysses,* every one of their brilliant [*géniaux*] inventors, is potentially incommensurable with any library supposed to house them, classify them, shelve them."[16] That is a valiant defense of Literature, and a suggestive introduction into rarefied company for Cixous, whose "great oeuvre" also cannot be contained by the archive. Literature, in this case *Manhattan,* holds secrets that it will not reveal.

The archive cannot contain all that Literature, per Derrida. Something does escape. Something or someone always migrates, and perhaps the best archival work in the future will move into those unforeseen directions. But my point here is that the archive is persistent, even in the face of its own limitations. Somehow the archive always comes back, as it does with Cixous. And when the story of Derrida is retold, someone will have to consider how this lively critic of the archive became archivized in the Derrida Papers and in an entire apparatus of Derrida studies.[17] The key to the archival persistence as presented by Derrida and Cixous is in their use of Literature because this term is always deployed in conjunction with a name: the Author who proliferates. Derrida's gambit is to position Cixous among the great authors, just as he might be positioned as well.

The invocation of Literature and its author brings us back to the challenge we face in the Hispanic archive. While entries such as the pamphlet by Ambrosio Gonzales would not be classified as Literature by aesthetic archivists, the process of research retains the authorial subject. The Hispanic archive always presumes a speaker (or actor) behind the textual historical record. While Cixous and Derrida cannot escape the author, the Hispanic archive cannot do without the Hispanic subject—or the author, as we will see in the last section's discussion of Ruiz de Burton. In the next section, I want to consider how the Hispanic archive is intricately connected with popular conceptions of history and with the deployment of surnames that speak to a presumed descent.

A Latino (Heath) Ledger: What's in a Name?

I use the term "Hispanic archive" in two ways, one more general than the other. The mega-Hispanic archive is where popular representation and media circulation meet academic research: an accumulation of information, discourses, and texts that motivate a problem of subjectivity. Some of the functions of the archive are to name (make visible) and store (defend) that which might pass away. The Hispanic archive exists in many places and creates a subjectivity that is apparent and real. This archive simultaneously facilitates the commodification of ethnic subjects, the exploitation of laboring subjects, and the identification of academic subjects. It promotes the selling of products and bodies termed "Hispanic" and supports the development of labor power that is associated with an ethnic group. My second use of "Hispanic archive" refers to the accumulation of knowledge as a result of fields of study that emerge from the ethnic labels Hispanic/Latino, in other words the scholarly collection of texts that make up the historical record; a prime example of the latter is the Recovering the U.S. Hispanic Literary Heritage Project, but we could point to various scholarly and critical projects that contribute to the Hispanic archive. One of the challenges of historical work is accounting for people who were not defined socially by the ethnic labels we use today.

In the early nineteenth century, for example, the U.S. Census did not account for a multiethnic population, and certainly not for people of Latin American descent. The category "Mexican," for example, did not appear until the 1930 Census and then as part of "other races" not considered black or white.[18] The widespread accounting of a Hispanic/Latino population did not begin until 1970, and then as a question referring to "origin or descent" (Mexican, Puerto Rican, Central and South American, etc.). For scholars seeking to trace population figures in the nineteenth century or even to determine the background of a defined set of historical participants, often the only recourse is to find surnames. For example, since Confederates did not necessarily define themselves as Hispanic, O'Donnell-Rosales turned to surnames to identify the group of people in his archival record, a ledger of names.

In this recourse to surnames, academic work dovetails with popular usage of Hispanophone surnames to identify people as part of a transhistorical Hispanic panorama. A surname motivates one of the more curious inclusions in the Hispanic archive, one that emerged from an interpretation of Annie Proulx's story "Brokeback Mountain." In February 2006, on the eve of the Academy Awards for motion picture excellence, *The Los Angeles Times* asked several pundit types to opine on the nominations for best picture, which that year included a film about racial conflict in Los Angeles, *Crash,* and an adaptation of Proulx's story. The *Times* asked: What points did these particular movies overlook in the treatment of their respective topics? What was left on the cutting room floor? *Brokeback Mountain* drew an unexpected commentator, Alisa Valdes-Rodriguez, author of several novels, including *The Dirty Girls Social Club, Playing With Boys,* and *The Husband Habit.* According to her web site, Valdes-Rodriguez was named one of the twenty-five most influential Hispanics by *Time* magazine some years ago. And perhaps because of this representative honor, Valdes-Rodrigues decided to call out the makers of *Brokeback Mountain* for casting in the role of Ennis the late Heath Ledger, whom she describes as "an Anglo from Australia." Valdes-Rodriguez wrote, "The film is adapted from a short story by Pulitzer Prize–winning author Annie Proulx. In her story, one of the young 'cowboy lovers' is Latino, and in their adaptation, screenwriters Larry McMurtry and Diana Ossana kept the character, Ennis Del Mar, Latino."[19] Valdes-Rodriguez invoked the historical record, and implicitly set up a Hispanic archive, to support her claim for a Latino Ennis. She proposed that the first American cowboys were "caballeros from Spain" and continued by noting that the "states and cities of the American West still bear Spanish names given to them by Latino conquistadores." And she emphasized that unlike careless Hollywood, Proulx is aware of this "Latino history." And so ultimately, she said, *Brokeback Mountain* should have been film about Latinos and Hollywood had once again cut *us* out of the movies.

Valdes-Rodriguez must be joking, and yet there is a historical vision that sustains her caricature of a critique of exclusion. (And the point about Hollywood is not without merit.) The associations proceed as follows: Latino conquistadors, Hispanophone cities, Western American cowboys, Ennis Del Mar (in Anglo disguise), and Alisa Valdes-Rodriguez, the latter being one of *us,* a group identity based on affiliation throughout history. The claim is supported by Ennis's last name: Del Mar. The surname's supposed continuity facilitates an interpretation of the archive based on a fundamental assumption: genealogical and biological descent. Nothing in Ennis's actions or statements would lead us to conclude that Ennis is Latino, which effectively cuts social construction and self-identification out of the picture. If anything, Ennis shuns a social identification of any type. At one point he says, "I'm not no queer." To which we might conjecture that he would also say, "I'm not no Latino." Jack's response to the disavowal of queerness is, "Nobody's business but ours." In some ways, "Brokeback Mountain" is about a man who is unable and unwilling to define his own social identity.[20] By contrast, Valdes deploys identitarian affiliations by turning to an archival sign, a name that lassoes Ennis to a genetic Hispanophone past. Del Mar can take us back to the conquistadors only through a family lineage, a reversion to blood. Under this logic, Ennis is Latino by descent, not association. Under Valdes-Rodriguez's reading, the difference between the Latino Ennis and the "Anglo Australian" Heath Ledger is not cultural; it stems from a racial difference encapsulated in the term "Anglo," which she uses to mark Ledger as racially white. Because some Hispanics are light-skinned (and demographically have the option of identifying as "white"), the term Anglo is deployed with the full implication of whiteness beyond skin color. In the process, Valdes takes us back to the racial dimensions of the Hispanic archive, which sustains a discursive distinction between Anglo- and Spanish America as well as between white and brown.

If the Hispanic surname Del Mar sustains Valdes-Rodriguez's reading, that move is not at odds with the nonironic historical methodology employed by O'Donnell-Rosales. As we have seen, he turns to Hispanic surnames to develop his list of Hispanic confederates. They might be more accurately called "Confederate soldiers with Hispanic surnames." This is a particular serious matter when one considers, as I have noted, that names are a resource for historical work. As scholars look back at decades before the U.S. Census allowed people to self-identify as Hispanic/Latino/Chicano and to specify a country of origin, Hispanic surnames may be the most accurate, if not expedient, way to determine population numbers and thus establish a claim to a kind of ontology, albeit an onomastic one, within an Anglocentric country.

But while names can imply a continuity of descent, they also point to ruptures in historical progression. "Brokeback Mountain" does note historical antecedents through the use of names, but the point is the opposite of continuity. That past has become disentangled from a Latino present. Another Hispanic surname that appears in "Brokeback Mountain" is that of Joe Aguirre, the rancher who hires Ennis and Jack and spies on them. "Aguirre" goes back to the Basque region, from agir (open space, pasture) and in Proulx's story it is a "bandy-legged Basque" who sees them off to the mountain. Aguirre also take us into conquistador realms, at least in terms of film history, which gives us Werner Herzog's *Aguirre, the Wrath of God*, about a Spanish expedition in the Amazon. "Aguirre" with its double *rr* resists Anglicization, but we cannot say the same for "Del Mar," which can easily sound like Delmer. Nevertheless, Proulx does want to bring forth that the mountain holds a history buried under the myth of the Marlboro-type cowboy. In his spying ways, Aguirre emphasizes the need to see something that might otherwise not be apparent. Proulx writes that Ennis and Jack "believed themselves to be invisible, not knowing Joe Aguirre had watched them through his 10x42 binoculars for ten minutes one day" (262). So with Aguirre in the picture as a gawker it's possible to consider whether in this story there is some correlation between the Hispanic archive and the cowboy closet.

On the one hand, the story/movie calls attention to seemingly heterosexual people who negotiated social restrictions to develop same-sex relationships (or attempt to do so) in the mid-twentieth century. That story of closeted love is easily recognizable today. As critics of Ang Lee's *Brokeback Mountain* have noted, one possible reading of the movie is that it encapsulates a moment in time when a tragedy of impossible love seemed to be the dominant mode of homosexual experience. Heather Love, for example, writes, "While the unrelenting stigmatisation of homosexuality characteristic of earlier moments is hardly to be yearned for, the current appearance of homosexuality in the mass media as a happy and healthy lifestyle poses a new set of problems."[21] How dominant modes of representation, past and present, come to define populations is one of the conflicts of historical study.

The connection between the cowboy closet and the Hispanic archive is that they both call for an interpretation that fixes Ennis in a social position that responds to contemporary notions of identity. But in Proulx's story, sexuality and the Hispanic past are not commensurate. "Brokeback Mountain" emphasizes the love story, but the Hispanic remnant remains peripheral. Mexico is still an othered place of unfettered desire and even exploitation, and the Hispanic past emerges in names that offer a historical trace but not a context for the signification. The beauty of Valdes's silly reading is that it encapsulates how the investment in a present condition, a Latino identity, is the most expedient way to make sense of a past that may not be easily apprehensible. What was it like to be someone of Spanish or Portuguese descent in the northern American mountain West in some previous century? It would be impossible to answer that in a definitive way, and yet scholars have attempted to provide answers to that type of question, although often in the more particular experiences of national or local identities.

One of the challenges for Latino studies is how to recuperate a recognizable past that brings together disparate experiences (e.g., Cuban and Mexican). Kirsten Silva Gruesz has argued that in addition to the specific traditions of national groups, "if 'Latino' is to have any long-term conceptual staying power, it must grapple with the construction of a usable past that would be, if not *common* to all Latinos (what historical stories are?), intelligible and meaningful to that constituency."[22] Rather than focus on the different remnants, such a Latino history might seek the still invisible linkages among different populations. For Gruesz, this would make certain parts of history meaningful, which is important considering the ongoing elisions of a Hispanic past in the United States. That type of hopeful recuperation is a hallmark of Latino studies and drives research agendas, and yet it is also what grates against the dusty objects in the attic. What happens when one of the linkages involves the Confederacy? In a socio-political context, one response might be to define "Latino" in a way that sutures the rupture. But in the realm of academic study, such an antagonism leads to research results. In other words, it can begin to remake the Latino studies archive and its research agenda, helping it grow. The Hispanic literary figure who exemplifies this process is María Amparo Ruiz de Burton. Along with José Martí, she may be the only other Hispanic writer who has approached canonical status in nineteenth-century U.S. literary studies, and the tensions in her biography and in her writings have helped the formation of an archive.

The Ruiz de Burton Archive

Hispanic literary history offered an interesting contribution to the revisionist spirit in American literature of the 1980s and 1990s, namely a variety of newspaper articles, pamphlets, unsigned poems, and *corridos,* many of them in Spanish. The bulk of materials published in the nineteenth century would not be easily organized under a "great writers" approach. And yet scholars of the nineteenth century turned to a figure of authorial importance. Like an apparition of the Virgen María, Ruiz de Burton drew tremendous attention when her two novels, *Who Would Have Thought It?* (1872) and *The Squatter and the Don* (1885), were republished in the 1990s. These books engaged with a litany of themes and topics of interest to historicists (cult of domesticity, race, and gender), but perhaps most important for American literature, a field dominated by Anglophone writing, was that Ruiz de Burton published those novels in English. In some ways, Ruiz de Burton appeared to be a nineteenth-century antecedent to Chicana and Latina writers of the late twentieth century. Scholars in the field of Latino studies as well as those more generally interested in American literature published a variety of articles, and she became a keystone in the Recovering the U.S. Hispanic Literary Heritage Project.

But more than any other writer in Hispanic literary history, Ruiz de Burton has come to exemplify the tension between archival formation of Latino studies as a field and the antagonism of political affiliations from the past. Rosaura Sánchez and Beatrice Pita's editions of her novel came with important introductory material that claimed Ruiz as part of a Hispanic past and also characterized her as "subaltern" and emphasized her dispossession as a "Latina," "a Catholic," and a "Spanish speaker." She was an "outsider in Yankee territory."[23] The contours of Ruiz de Burton's life soon raised complications, including evidence that she could move as an insider in the highest levels of the U.S. government. For one, Ruiz de Burton displayed sensitivity toward the Confederacy at certain moments. José Aranda called our attention to the problems of heritage by questioning the critical investment in framing an upper-class light-skinned woman as a writer of resistance to white hegemony. In the most enduring image of Aranda's article, we see a letter from Varina Davis, Jefferson Davis's wife, saying that Ruiz de Burton is very angry with the Yanquis about "Mexican affairs, and we get together quietly and abuse them."[24] Ruiz de Burton's husband had been assigned to guard Jefferson Davis after the war, which brought her in touch with the highest echelons of the Lost Cause. It would be hasty and unfair to categorize Ruiz de Burton among Hispanic Confederates, but the friendship with the Davises explains how she has come to embody a conflicted authorial ontology in the Hispanic archive.

My point in returning to this particular debate is to show how the multiplicity of contradictory positions inhabited by Ruiz de Burton led to additional critical scholarship that helped to build the archive about her.[25] The "author" here persists not under the great-writers model or even as representative of a unitary ethnic community but rather as an example of conflicts between past and present and the complications of a life over various decades. Her novels speak to a variety of critical paradigms and could be positioned as part of California literature or the literature of Manifest Destiny. What if we were to consider the Civil War vision of *Who Would Have Thought It?* in relation to Reconstruction novels that fail to account for the racial tensions in the postwar period? *Who Would Have Thought It?* is published in the midst of Reconstruction and attempts to make sense of the U.S. military-political system through an elaborate setting that includes appearances by President Lincoln and nameless soldiers at Libby. Although not necessarily celebratory of the Confederacy, the novel reserves its harshest criticism for the North. Reconstruction politics provides one important context for this novel and shows the intricate twists in Ruiz de Burton's life and work. These twists, the multiple discourses of the past, grate against the synchronic idealism of a Hispanic present.

Rather than disqualify her as part of Hispanic or Latino history, all of the dusty articles in the Ruiz de Burton attic serve the formation of the archive. In other words, her archives are sustained by their inherent contradictions and antagonisms. The most extensive archival recuperation of Ruiz de Burton's personal writing is Sánchez and Pita's edition of *Conflicts of Interest: The Letters of María Amparo Ruiz de Burton* (2001).

This impressive volume, itself a kind of archive, contains letters spanning four decades.[26] In these letters we see Ruiz de Burton's developments from a young Mexican woman who moves to Monterey, California, in the wake of the U.S.-Mexico War and marries a U.S. Army
officer, to her final years, during which she is involved in a series of law-
suits and legal maneuvers related to her family's land claims in the San
Diego area and Ensenada, Mexico. The dates on the letters provide a
portrait of a woman on the move over her lifetime: Sonoma, San Fran-
cisco, Staten Island, Pittsburgh, Richmond, Norwich, San Diego, and
Mexico City, among other places. She died in Chicago.

While moves during the first part of her life are connected to her
husband's military assignments, later she creates her own trajectory,
which in some cases is in accordance with various economic projects.
It is important to consider her troubled experience as a woman trying
to make a profit in a capitalist economy. For twenty-five years, Ruiz de
Burton lived as a widow who sought ways to support her family while
retaining an upper-class lifestyle. Many of her letters are concerned
with the intricacies of legal battles over land titles for her properties.
Like Mariano Alamar in *The Squatter and the Don,* Ruiz de Burton had
to contend with squatters and to fight for title to the Jamul ranch near
San Diego, a property purchased by her husband. She returns to California from the East Coast in 1870 to fight for her claims to the Jamul
ranch. She goes to Mexico late in life in defense of her land holdings in
Baja. The movement prompts her negotiation of various social contexts,
including the Hispanophone world of Californios and the Anglophone
world of the U.S. legal system. In other words, she lives as both Ruiz and
Burton. She signs most letters "M.A. de Burton," a name that both connects her to Anglophone society but demands a recognition of her Hispanophone background through the use of "de." The tension between
Ruiz and Burton emerges repeatedly in the letters of the Sánchez and
Pita volume.

The letters, like items from an attic that gives us yet another picture,
depict a woman whose primary concern is economic well-being. Many
of the letters are directives about various legal disputes, investments,
and debts. "You probably know that my beloved and best of husbands
is no more and now upon me devolves the necessity of attending to
the matter you mention in your letter" (*Letters* 285), she writes about

a pending debt. Her use of "devolves" implies a kind of degeneration; she will have to get her hands dirty with money matters. Not long after taking over the finances, she becomes aware that her property in San Diego is under dispute. Ruiz de Burton sets off on her own archival search for proof that the Jamul ranch was purchased by her husband from the last Mexican governor of California, Pío Pico. She writes to Ephraim W. Morse, a merchant and lawyer in San Diego, "I want you to have the kindness to get Mr. Pendleton [the county clerk] and ask him to let you see, or he search with you, in the archives for the record of the title of Jamul which was given to Don Pío Pico by General (or Governor) Don Manuel Victoria in 1830. . . . Look well in the archives, please, and let me know what you find" (*Letters* 297–98). Like her modern-day heirs, Ruiz de Burton looks to the past to verify a claim to her present state, and thus seeks some type of veracity in the archives. The fight over Jamul will pursue her for many years because of questions as to whether Pico had title and also questions as to whether Mr. Burton completed the purchase. For Ruiz de Burton, the uncertainty about Jamul—the lack of an archival confirmation—creates significant economic anxiety.

In some cases the economic necessities prompted her to give way on her political beliefs. For example, this opponent of Manifest Destiny supports a colonization scheme in Baja California and even looks kindly on annexation because of the possibility that it would bring profits from her land holdings there. She wrote, "Nothing less than the purchase of the peninsula by the United States would restore to that unhappy country some of its lost credit. Or a well organized emigration backed by capital and begun in a less barren portion of the peninsula" (*Letters* 432). We could berate Ruiz de Burton for her support of annexation, but her letters also provide an opportunity to consider how financial struggles can come into conflict with political beliefs. In the same letter, she writes of her "very tender and perhaps foolish sentiment of patriotic love" (*Letters* 432) for Mexico.

The letters also shed light on her economic attitude about book publishing. Whatever literary aspirations and imaginative leaps motivated the writing of her novels, it also becomes clear that she writes for money. When *Who Would Have Thought It?* is published in 1872, Ruiz de Burton is motivated in part by the book market. In two letters to

Samuel Lathan Mitchell Barlow, legal counsel for the Lower California Company, a consortium of wealthy investors seeking to establish a colony in Mexico, Ruiz de Burton discusses her novel: "Did you get my book? And did you send the copies to the newspapers requesting them to give me 'a puff'?" (*Letters* 433). Concerned that Barlow is offended by something she has said, Ruiz de Burton writes, "I thought you to have too much gallantry to treasure up against a lady a feeling of anger; and in second place, because, I thought that after you had promised and pledged your word to have the book favorably noticed, that you would certainly not fail only because you felt some little irritation at something I said on a very hot day when I was very insupportable mentally and physically" (*Letters* 434). The last phrase is a Hispanic construction building on the word *insoportable,* closer to "intolerable" or, more colloquially, "cranky." Two months later, she writes to Barlow again: "I will write today to Mr. Lippincott [the publisher in Philadelphia] telling him to send *you* a copy, and then you must really do all you can for me. . . . I hope you will give me all the benefit of your influence with the New York Press, for I would like to make the venture a little bit profitable. I did not write for glory" (*Letters* 437–38). Someone hoping to make a profit from book publication in 1872 is not unusual. But it appears that that Ruiz de Burton would have preferred a best seller over critical acclaim.

Her literary vision emerged in conjunction with a sense that modernization and the changes brought on after the U.S.-Mexico War and the Civil War ruptured the purity of creative imagination. That is the point of a letter to her good friend Mariano Guadalupe Vallejo, written from Norwich, Vermont. Describing her daily visits to the shore of the Connecticut River, Ruiz de Burton explains the impossibility of a golden age of myth:

> Yo creo que estoy enamorada del río y si fuera en tiempos mitológicos no hay duda que el Dios del Connecticut respondería mis suspiros. Pero ya pasaron esos tiempos felices en donde uno podía agarrar a los Dioses de los cabellos. En estos tiempos de "railroads" y "magnetic telegraphs" no hay esperanza de volverse uno ninfa más que uno se enamore de los ríos, más fácil sería volverse rana, yo creo, y tal vez desaparecer en las muelas de algún francés. (*Letters* 242)

[I believe myself to be in love with the river and if these were mytho-
logical times I have no doubt that the God of the Connecticut would
respond to my longings. But those joyful times have passed when one
could reach for the Gods by the hair. In these times of "railroads" and
"magnetic telegraphs" there is no hope that one could turn into a nymph
nor fall in love with the river; it would be easier to turn into a frog, I
think, and probably end up in the teeth of some Frenchman.][27]

The sensuality of the nymph-like writer is ruptured by the intrusion of
code switching into the modern technology of the "railroad" and "telegraph." But more than positing a historical shift, the passage shows that
her inability to reach the heights of full sensuous experience is the result
of having to deal with her economic burdens. In the next paragraph,
she launches into a discussion of a mining project at the property near
Ensenada. She tells Vallejo that the Mexican government has authorized
them to import mining equipment through the port of Ensenada duty
free, and they have a contract with a mining company from Baltimore.
But due to conflicts in Mexico, she is unable to carry out the operation.
She follows up with a different type of imaginative reverie:

¡Ah! Que no haya un solo hombre *capaz* de mirar más allá de donde está
parado y con 30 hombres hacerse dueño de ese país que sólo necesita
brazos fuertes, guiados por una cabeza clara y previsora, para convertir
esa aridez en jardines, esos pedregales en oro! (*Letters* 243)

[Oh! That there is not a single man *capable* of seeing beyond where he
is standing and along with 30 men take over that country, which needs
only strong arms, guided by a visionary and clear-headed leader, to turn
the arid land into gardens and those stones into gold!]

The passage is reminiscent of Richard Henry Dana's line "In the hands
of an enterprising people, what a country this might be," which he
writes about California in *Two Years Before the Mast* (1840).[28] Unlike
Dana, who portrays depravity and laziness in racial terms, Ruiz de Burton takes issue with the political and social climate of Mexico, which
she sees as preventing the mining operation from proceeding. She
writes that all who have property in northern Baja would benefit from

the introduction of capital and industry, thus bringing modernity to a place suffering under "miserable conditions."

Documents from the Ruiz de Burton attic clarify that she sought profits from various investment projects. Her attacks on monopoly capitalism should be considered in light of her sense that small landholders such as herself were being edged out by Gilded Age capital accumulation. But that is only one part of a very rich and varied life, available through the archival recovery of Sánchez and Pita. The letters provide bumps and surprises in the attic of her Hispanic past. Rather than negating a Hispanic archive, Ruiz de Burton provides opportunities for more reading and additional recuperation.

The questions presented by Ruiz de Burton and Hispanic Confederates are connected to present-day debates over what it means to be *a* Hispanic or Latino. A researcher invested in a particular type of identity may encounter a different type of figure in the past. If "Hispanic" modifies archive—or identity, for that matter—then it is best to go in and look at the materials contained within that particular repository. Just as the archive can always be challenged by its holdings, Hispanic literary history's claim to a counter-narrative can stumble across its own troublesome past. That is one of the salutary if disturbing effects of items in the archive: finding someone or something we did not expect. The archive against itself is a condition under which an academic archive can flourish.

NOTES

I thank my friends at Penn State University, particularly Chris Castiglia, Hester Blum, and Sean Goudie, for inspiring this article and for their lively conversation. I also thank the editors of this volume for their helpful feedback.

1. John O'Donnell-Rosales, *Hispanic Confederates*, 3d edition (Baltimore: Clearfield, 2006), iv.
2. Ibid., viii–ix.
3. Throughout this article I distinguish between "Latino" as a contemporary term linked to university-based programs and post–Civil Rights social movements versus "Hispanic" as an ethnic label for people of Spanish and Latin American descent. These two terms are often used interchangeably, and that slippage motivates the types of contradictions that emerge from Hispanic Confederates.
4. Juan Poblete, Introduction to *Critical Latin American and Latino Studies* (Minneapolis: University of Minnesota Press, 2003), x.

5. Genaro Padilla, *My History, Not Yours* (Madison: University of Wisconsin Press, 1993), 35.

6. See Jacques Derrida, *Archive Fever: A Freudian Impression,* trans. Eric Prenowitz (Chicago: University of Chicago Press, 1995).

7. Ibid., 3.

8. Randall C. Jimerson, *Archives Power: Memory, Accountability, and Social Justice* (Chicago: Society of American Archivists, 2009), 3–10.

9. Antonio Rafael de la Cova, *Cuban Confederate Colonel* (Columbia: University of South Carolina Press, 2003); Philip Thomas Tucker, ed., *Cubans in the Confederacy* (Jefferson, N.C.: McFarland, 2002).

10. Ambrosio José Gonzales, *Manifesto on Cuban Affairs Address to the People of the United States* (New Orleans: Daily Delta, 1853), 4.

11. Ibid., 5.

12. Jesse Alemán, Introduction to *The Woman In Battle: The Civil War Narrative of Loreta Janeta Velazquez, Cuban Woman and Confederate Soldier* (Madison: University of Wisconsin Press, 2003), xi.

13. Ann Stoler, *Along the Archival Grain: Epistemic Anxieties and Colonial Common Sense* (Princeton, N.J.: Princeton University Press, 2009), 20.

14. Hélène Cixous, *Manhattan: Letters From Prehistory,* trans. Beverley Bie Brahic (New York: Fordham University Press, 2007), 48; hereafter cited parenthetically as *M.*

15. Jacques Derrida, *Geneses, Genealogies, Genres, and Genius: The Secrets of the Archive,* trans. Beverley Bie Brahic (New York: Columbia University Press, 2006), 11–12.

16. Ibid., 14–15.

17. Currently the Derrida Seminar Translation Project meets regularly to edit and translate the unpublished materials, mostly lectures, in the Derrida Archive. The goal is to publish dozens of volumes.

18. Clara E. Rodriguez, *Changing Race: Latinos, the Census, and the History of Ethnicity in the United States* (New York: New York University Press, 2000), 82–83.

19. Alisa Valdes-Rodriguez, *Los Angeles Times,* February 26, 2006, M3.

20. Del Mar can be translated as "of the sea," and we can imagine Ennis floating in the wilds of the ocean, unable to land on firm ground. He is out of place in the landlocked mountains of cowboy country.

21. Heather Love, "Compulsory Happiness and Queer Existence," *New Formations* 63 (Winter 2007–8), 55. At stake for Love is the conflict between two opposing dominant representations: the closet of an earlier period or the contemporary emphasis on a cheerful integration into the mainstream. Love would resist the extremes in favor of a conception of experience that allows for all of the above and more, but that also moves toward a general humanist view that raises questions as to the difference purported in a terminology of identification.

22. Kirsten Silva Gruesz, "The Once and Future Latino: Notes Toward a Literary History *Todavía Para Llegar,*" in *Contemporary US Latino/a Literary Criticism,* ed. Lyn Di Iorio Sandín and Richard Perez (New York: Palgrave, 2007), 117.

23. Rosaura Sánchez and Beatrice Pita, Introduction to *Who Would Have Thought I?* (Houston: Arte Público Press, 1995), viii.

24. José F. Aranda Jr., "Contradictory Impulses: María Amparo Ruiz de Burton, Resistance Theory, and the Politics of Chicano/a Studies," *American Literature* 70 (September 1998), 562.

25. If anything, scholars took her works to task for investment in whiteness and aristocratic positions. Both articles inspired a variety of critical work by Lisbeth Haas, Gretchen Murphy, Marcial Gonzales, Vincent Pérez, and many others. See, for example, Amelia María de la Luz Montes and Anne Elizabeth Goldman, eds., *María Amparo Ruiz de Burton* (Lincoln: University of Nebraska Press, 2004).

26. The letters are supported by numerous introductory articles and footnotes and supplemented with selections by and about Ruiz de Burton from newspapers. See Sánchez and Pita, *Conflicts of Interest: The Letters of María Ampario Ruiz de Burton* (Houston: Arte Público Press, 2001); hereafter cited parenthetically as *Letters*.

27. My translation.

28. Richard Henry Dana, *Two Years Before the Mast* (New York: Penguin, 1986), 237.

2

Historical Totality and the African American Archive

LLOYD PRATT

Edward P. Jones's 2003 novel *The Known World* recounts the fortunes of an antebellum Virginia plantation owner named Henry Townsend who is a former slave. In his freedom, Townsend elects to purchase slaves of his own. For many readers this novel's topical interest lies in its generally unfamiliar account of slaveholding among free people of color, while its stylistic appeal derives from the way that Jones combines acute realism with the expansive imagination of what Madhu Dubey terms "speculative fiction meets neoslave narrative."[1] For these readers Jones's novel unveils a troubling nineteenth-century world in which intraracial slavery marks a key feature of African American life.[2] By this account Jones's novel offers a critique of the humanist, additive, and heroicizing procedures that arguably dominate African American progressive history writing.[3] Such histories would represent people of African descent as strictly the targets of enslavement rather than as also participants in the peculiar institution, all the while adopting the questionable and under-theorized recommendations of mainline liberal U.S. historiography.

However, this novel's critique goes even deeper, taking issue with one recent account of African American thinking about the past.

According to this recent account, Jones's novel joins many other African American texts in casting doubt upon the liberal project of additive history writing associated with the recovery movements that have sometimes dominated African American writing about the past by highlighting the impartiality and incompleteness of the historical archive. I will be suggesting, however, that this novel actually differs from these seemingly like-minded (recent and nineteenth-century, literary and critical) efforts to reject liberal historiography. In particular, I will be proposing that Jones's novel does not engage in the "turn away from history" that Dubey has suggested characterizes many recent African American fictional encounters with the past. Nor does it embrace the "micronarrative" as a desideratum of African American history writing, an embrace that, like the turn away from history, has been characterized as following from black dissatisfaction with mainstream historiography and the compromised archive. In fact, Jones's novel implicitly repudiates this emerging emphasis within certain corners of African American intellectual and expressive culture on the importance of acknowledging the broken archive and on embracing the partial narrative, as well as the related sense that History is a sorry bargain for the disenfranchised. *The Known World* lobbies instead for the rewards of totalizing history. If this novel suggests that we must still seek to tell the history of totality, however, it also argues that the only way to tell that history is through a reconsidered encounter with the black past. It imagines this encounter to be modeled on but also a revision of the nineteenth-century intellectual and political projects of total history traceable to Marx, Hegel, and, as it turns out, early African American history writing. According to *The Known World*, I am suggesting, engagement with African America is a necessary (and perhaps even sufficient) condition of the total world history first identified in the nineteenth century as a resource for the struggle against injustice.

Through a series of interpolated tales about flawed surveyors, cowardly census-takers, careerist historians, and drunken mapmakers, Jones's novel cues us to consider what is at first glance a series of familiar questions about African American history: we are asked to ponder first whether the absences and obfuscations inherent to slavery's institutional and economic archives constitute a permanent obstacle to telling the history of black life.[4] If these absences and obfuscations in fact confound conventional research protocols and narratological methods, the novel next asks, then what would an efficacious black history look like? What formal practices would it necessitate? What would be its defining features? Nineteenth- and twentieth-century African American historiography and historical fiction have long sought to answer precisely these questions. John Ernest, Stephen G. Hall, and Marnie Hughes-Warrington have shown, for example, how a specifically black historiography extends at least as far back as the nineteenth century. Tracing the rise of African American history writing in a pre-professional mode, their accounts mirror Dubey's recent claims about African American speculative fiction's relationship to the past, as well as Susan Donaldson's framing of contemporary African American historical fictions of the American South as a species of historical theorizing. As I explain in more detail below, Dubey identifies metacritical impulses in black historical fiction that echo what Ernest argues was an early African American understanding of history writing as a critical intervention rather than a merely documentary realism, while Donaldson argues that African American historical fiction of the American South similarly generates alternative approaches to writing the African American past.

These studies together mark an intellectual communion connecting the speculative histories and historiographic essays written by nineteenth-century African Americans to the metafictional strategies of late-twentieth- and twenty-first-century African American historical fiction. They further indicate that this metacritical and historiographical black tradition highlights absences, elisions, and breaks in the archive. Recalling Phillip Brian Harper's influential work on the origins of the decentered postmodern subject, Ernest's and Donaldson's focus encourages us to understand the longstanding African American interest in the incomplete archive as in some sense postmodernist before and after the fact.[5] These critics and historians propose that the structured contradictions and elisions that dominate the African American experience of slavery and structural racism, as well as their archives, anticipate the world that would come to be known as postmodern. They suggest moreover that this world registers in both the form and content of African American history writing. The legacies of racial slavery and antiblack racism precipitate "nothing so much," Donaldson argues, "as those micronarratives that Jean-François Lyotard sees as emerging from the debris of master narratives shattered under the pressures of postmodernity."[6]

The Known World asks us to reintroduce the issue of historical totality into this conversation, reminding us that "universal history" and "master narratives" have persistently appealed to African American writers and thinkers.[7] A commitment to totalizing history is generally absent from emergent critiques of African American progressive historiography, including those I have just described; the postmodern as a period and postmodernism as a critical stance, which African American history writing and historical fiction are said to mirror, preclude the turn to "master narratives" that any theory of historical totality requires. Nineteenth-century African American writing's perceived emphasis on rejecting totalizing historical accounts would further suggest that African American postmodern historical metafiction represents not a break with but an extension of nineteenth-century African American historical thinking. The *longue durée* of racial slavery ends up registering as a composite of piecemeal "micronarratives" that precludes any dialectical account of historical totality.[8]

I nevertheless want to suggest that at least some of these histories and historical fictions may actually be taking up the challenge of producing an anti-reifying and totalizing historicization such as Lukács describes in *History and Class Consciousness*, while at the same time they seek to revise our sense of what a totalizing history looks like.[9] Lukács's key contribution in "Reification and the Consciousness of the Proletariat" is to show how contradictions, absences, and elisions come into view only at the moment that a totalizing impulse is already at play. This insight reveals that the micronarrative always exists in the context of the pursuit of a larger master narrative; by this logic the persistent African American questioning of history's contradictions follows from a totalizing impulse rather than being a sign of its rejection. According to Lukács, moreover, capitalist logic seeks to preclude the sort of synoptic vision that draws into focus the disjuncture among what on the ground look like highly rational laws, but which from a different perspective resolve into a congeries of productively incoherent contingent practices. Reification names the process of conceptual and experiential segmentation that commodity fetishism permits, that eventually impresses itself on all features of daily life under capitalism, and that obscures the overall logic of capital. A totalizing account of history such as Marxism offers both identifies and dissolves that segmentation, Lukács argues, allowing the whole of history to come into view. A totalizing view abstracts from particular local details, but it does not ignore them. A properly totalizing view instead transcends details to reveal those modes of human interrelationship that commodity fetishism obscures. If Marx famously suggests that commodity fetishism turns a relationship among people into a relationship among things, then Lukács demonstrates how accounts of totality can revisualize relationships among people who have misunderstood themselves as things.[10]

In what follows, I make the case that an ongoing African American attempt to revise our sense of how to produce the totalizing history that Lukács describes has been misrecognized as a wholesale rejection of the totalizing project. In order to make this claim, I will first offer a more developed characterization of the emerging consensus regarding the status of nineteenth-century African American historiography and history writing, focusing in particular on the influential work of John Ernest and Stephen G. Hall. I will then address in more detail Madhu Dubey's analysis of the recent turn away from realism in African American literature, as well as her sense of what this turn tells us about African American historical thinking. I do so in order to identify certain continuities and discontinuities connecting African American history writing to African American historical fiction. I next return to Jones's novel to propose that it offers a compelling account of how we might simultaneously acknowledge the problems of the injured archive and embrace totalizing historical impulses without dishonoring those injuries. I also consider Frederick Douglass's "The Heroic Slave" in the light of Lukács's account of properly anti-reifying historical fiction contained in *The Historical Novel,* pursuing the question of what Douglass's obvious debts to Scott might mean for his account of history. My conclusion draws a few axioms from Jones's novel and Douglass's novella, the most important of which concerns the relationship between the broken archive and accounts of historical totality. Jones's novel and Douglass's novella would suggest that the challenges of the former do not preclude the creation of the latter. Indeed they remind us that totalizing accounts of history typically assume a broken or occluded archive in advance, and that the hybrid modes of intellectual inquiry common to these accounts are a considered response to that brokenness. In this sense they permit us to remember that the empirical project of engaging with a documentary archive is quite different from the Hegelian, Marxist, and early black approaches to history. One might go so far as to argue that total history is the only kind of history possible in an unjust world that attempts to evacuate the many from the archive in service of the avarice of a few. In the end, these texts illuminate not only why it might be important to continue to pursue a "master narrative," but also how to revise its form and content such that it does justice to the history of African America and in turn the history of the world.

History, Historiography, and Literary Realism

In *Liberation Historiography: African American Writers and the Challenge of History, 1794–1861,* John Ernest offers a comprehensive account of how early African American history writing reconceived the office of the historian in relationship to emerging white ideologies of history. As he demonstrates in his introduction, Ernest is particularly concerned to show how African American historical writing early on detected a fundamental limitation of the sorts of historical practice introduced as the mainstream during this period. Mainstream U.S. and European historical writing came at this moment to favor comprehensive and "totalizing historical narrative[s]" that subordinated the spread of detail inherent to the archive to a coherent linear narrative of cause, effect, and transformation.[11] African American historical writing took a very different approach, Ernest argues, because early black historians understood that white supremacist ideology not only dictated that a Bancroft or a Parkman would never adequately address the contributions of African Americans to the emergence of the United States. White supremacist ideology also constituted the main "cultural dynami[c] that shaped and limited the preservation of the records of African American experience."[12] In other words, white supremacist ideology determined in advance that African American historical experience would be rendered inaccessible by excluding from the archives those documents suited to forming the backbone of a synthetic empiricist account of the African American past.

In addition to this clear and present exclusion of African Americans from the documentary trail of evidence, except as entries in chattel bookkeeping or the emerging scriptive technologies of the American judicial system, African American writers of history faced an additional burden. According to Ernest, these writers were forced to contend with the fact that there was something unspeakably sublime about the African American experience under slavery. Adopting a critical vocabulary drawn from discussions of the challenge of representation in a post-Holocaust moment, Ernest argues that these writers were developing a mode of depicting an "unrecoverable past," and that this past was "unrecoverable" not only because of archival exclusions.[13] It was also unrecoverable because it "resisted representation": "Beyond [their] necessary responses to racist historiography," Ernest proposes, "African Americans faced the troubling problem of representing a history that—in its fragmentation and especially in the depth of its moral complexity—resisted representation. How does one tell the story of the Middle Passage, or of slavery?"[14] Here the emphasis shifts from the nature of the archive to the nature of the story secreted in the archive. Even if a full documentary record of the Middle Passage had been at their fingertips, African American historians would have been faced with a task of narration made impossible by the very nature of the black experience rather than by any particular problem of the archive.

Faced with the compounded issue of the broken archive and the sublime terror of slavery, African Americans adopted, Ernest continues, a very particular historiographic stance. During the pre-professional period of African American historical writing, which both Ernest and Stephen Hall open to new scrutiny, these African American historians developed a metacritical account of history. Their method met the "specifically textual challenge of creating an approach to historical representation that could promote the development of a unified African American community."[15] This alternative approach to historical writing shifted the focus away from the details of history, many of which had been made unavailable by white archival procedures, and toward the very problem of writing history in a white supremacist world. In other words, African American historical writing emerged as a substantively metacritical and historiographical practice in the earliest stages of its formation: As Hall argues, "black writers constructed black history largely as a metahistorical narrative that simultaneously transcended and reinterpreted mainstream historical narratives."[16] As when Frederick Douglass opens his one piece of fictional writing, "The Heroic Slave," with a meditation on the elusive "marks" and "traces" of Madison Washington found in the chattel records of the State of Virginia, African American history writing during this period repeatedly turned to the question of its own enforced impossibility. This early emphasis on the inadequacies of the documentary archive has shaped the practice of writing about the African American past into the present moment. As Hall explains, "Scholars today often privilege nontextual manifestations of black culture as the dominant modes of early African American historical expression. Studying oral, vernacular, and commemorative culture and historical memory has become a prominent means of examining the ways African Americans re-create their past."[17]

We will return to Hall and Ernest in just a moment, but for now it seems important to acknowledge that Hall's list of "oral, vernacular, and commemorative culture" might also include "literature." The long and growing list of African American literary texts that seek to provide a way into the African American experience of the past suggests that African American literature (past and present) understands itself and has been understood as an archive of past experience rearticulated in the present moment. As Madhu Dubey explains, this literature in many respects "confidently claim[s] to reveal the truth of the past."[18] In a curious way, however, and notwithstanding Douglass's early comments, the African American literary tradition has had, Dubey argues, a longer road to travel to the metacritical impulse that Ernest and Hall suggest dates to nineteenth-century African American historical writing. Dubey documents how African American fiction writing, in particular, long labored under the demands of a social uplift model of realist fictionalizing that constrained the ability of these writers to open a space of imaginative possibility for African American futures. In other words, with certain notable exceptions, such as Charles Chesnutt's conjure tales, African American fictionalizing was tasked with the same charge of certifying the truth of African American life for white readers that had defined the fugitive slave narrative. As Dubey explains, "Notwithstanding certain errant flashes of fantasy and fabulism, the burden of realist representation began to ease off only by the 1970s, or the beginning of what is commonly termed the post–Civil Rights period, which . . . witnessed an outpouring of fiction that flouts the dictates of realism."[19] Given the willingness of nineteenth-century historians to point out the inadequacies of the archive and, therefore, the limitations of any mode of realistic writing about the past, the general unwillingness of fiction writers to pursue similarly metacritical stances until the 1970s may be understood as a legacy of what William Andrews has described as the "novelization of voice" in African American literature, a process whose origins tie later novelistic accounts of African American experience to the protocols of the fugitive slave narrative, including its demand for authenticity and authentication, its emphasis on certifiable detail, and its reluctance to abstract from the specific and the empirically verifiable.

As Dubey documents, however, when realism's longstanding dominance in African American fiction finally waned, it did so in significant and impactful ways. Dubey suggests that

> recent novelists of slavery undo historical authority by exploiting an exorbitantly fictive imagination, the faculty that had to be devalued in order to shore up the disciplinary standing of history as "the custodian of realism." Refusing to regard the past of slavery as history, speculative novels suggest that the truth of this past is more fully addressed by way of an antirealist literary imagination that can fluidly cross temporal boundaries and affectively immerse readers into the world of slavery. The turn away from history, then, becomes an immensely generative occasion for antirealist novels of slavery in the late twentieth century.[20]

Dubey's main point in the article from which this quotation is drawn is to contest one emerging consensus about historical novels of slavery that dispense with the protocols of realism in favor of a more capacious account of just what might be real. As she explains, one dominant view understands these novels as reclaiming the historical past. According to this consensus view, these novels of slavery, despite their dalliances with the speculative and fantastic, nevertheless "confidently claim to reveal the truth of the past."[21] Dubey contests this reading, suggesting that these novels should be understood as altogether turning away from historical knowledge as a useful resource. She sees these speculative historical fictions of slavery as proposing that the inequities of the past have rendered the past a useless resource. From a methodological perspective, then, we might say that Dubey's main interest lies in defining more precisely the form that the African American "turn away from history" has taken and now takes.

In addition to illuminating certain continuities and discontinuities linking fictional and nonfictional African American accounts of the past, Dubey's analysis usefully recalls us to the fact that there are many different ways to turn away from history, and it encourages us to take her procedural question about these differences and run it back through the arc I began with—the one connecting Hall's and Ernest's nineteenth-century African American historical writing to Dubey's and Donaldson's late-twentieth- and twenty-first-century African American speculative and historical fictions. If we do so we can agree that across the broad expanse of theorizing and expression that constitutes this tradition, the compromised archive is a primary concern. We can also agree that across this broad expanse of writing, African American historians and African American writers have grappled with the "partiality" and "incompleteness" of the archive. What I want to ask now is whether it necessarily follows from these facts that the African American intellectual tradition around historical knowledge has given up on the idea of a totalizing historical vision. In other words, have African American writers and historians conceded the idea of a total history to Hegel and Marx? Or have they simply been pointing to the added burdens and particular obstacles involved when universal and total history has to grapple with the history of African America? If the latter is the case, then how do we square the broken archive with the writing of a total history?

Distributed History

On the face of it, it seems clear that African American historical fictions and nineteenth-century histories produce totalizing accounts much more routinely than is imagined, to the extent that the partiality of clear concern to these writers comes into view as such in the context of their reaching toward totalization. Jones's novel in particular reminds us that one of the primary metacritical problems taken up by African American historical writing is in fact how best to write a history of totality in a world of partial vision. Among other things, *The Known World* asks: What mode or modes of artistic practice best replace reification with desirable forms of abstraction? What kind of thought understands how to transform the archive's details and its inadequacies into politically efficacious History? Those questions gather greatest force in *The Known World* in the *mappa mundi* section near the end of the novel. This section's emblematic account of an African American reaching toward a totalizing vision of history suggests both an obligation to the Lukácsian model and the necessity of certain signal revisions to it if black life is to figure in and figure as historical totality.

In this section, Louis, the brother-in-law of the now-deceased slave-holding former slave, Henry Townsend, writes a letter from Washington, D.C., to his widowed sister, Caldonia, describing his encounter with a slave named Alice who escaped from the Townsend plantation. It is important to know that before her escape from the Townsend plantation, Alice is perceived as a madwoman and roams the plantation late at night. Recalling Faulkner's Benjy, she freely accesses the far corners of the county. One day she disappears. Louis's letter details an encounter with Alice in a D.C. boarding house and her unusual form of expressive culture. He explains that in a dining room off the main parlor of the boarding house hang two objects.

> [P]eople were viewing [first] an enormous wall hanging, a grand piece of art that is part tapestry, part painting, and part clay structure—all in one exquisite Creation, hanging silent and yet songful on the Eastern wall. It is, my Dear Caldonia, a kind of map of life of the County of Manchester, Virginia. But a "map" is such a poor word for such a wondrous thing. It is a map of life with every kind of life made with every kind of art man has ever thought to represent himself. Yes, clay, Yes, paint. Yes, cloth. There are no people on this "map," just all the houses and barns and roads and cemeteries and wells in our [home town of] Manchester. It is what God sees when He looks down on Manchester.[22]

On the facing wall, Louis continues, hangs a second "Creation."

> This Creation may well be even more miraculous than the one of the County. This one is about your home, Caldonia. It is your plantation,

and again, it is what God sees when He looks down. There is nothing missing, not a cabin, not a barn, not a chicken, not a horse. Not a single person is missing. I suspect that if I were to count the blades of grass, the number would be correct as it was once when the creator of this work knew that world . . . In this massive miracle on the Western wall, you, Caldonia, are standing before your house with Loretta, Zeddie, and Bennett. As I said, all the cabins are there, and standing before them are the people who lived in them, ere Alice, Priscilla, and Jamie disappeared. Except for those three, every single person is there, standing and waiting as if for a painter and his easel to come along and capture them in the glory of their day. Each person's face, including yours, is raised up as though to look in the very eyes of God[. . .][23]

Alice's two *mappa mundi* constitute an anti-reifying vision of totality that permits the historical nature of slavery to come fully into view as a "relationship among persons," but they also urge us to consider which media and how many specific formal practices might be required for the particular work of an anti-reifying African American encounter with the past to take place. This normative question recalls Lukács's desire in his study *The Historical Novel* to determine what form of novelistic writing would be adequate to telling the history of class struggle; it also demands a careful rethinking of Lukács's normative project.

In order to understand what sort of practice of total history Jones's novel envisions, one must first mark the fact that the novel describes not one but two "creations." The first "creation," which resembles a county map, functions in the context of the novel as a critique of the mapmaking and surveying that go on elsewhere in the text. White surveyors are described as having limited skills that result in poorly constructed maps, but the novel suggests that Alice has walked each of the roads and byways rendered in her first creation. This critique cuts both ways, however, for the limitations of Alice's first creation are illuminated in the moment we learn of its supplementation by the second one. We come to recognize from the presence of Alice's second creation that the first one's scale prohibits representation of that which gives meaning to its roads and byways—which is to say human beings and the relationships among them. The second creation points to the evacuation of human forms from the first more familiar map-like project. As

Louis's letter indicates, the world of slavery is depicted in the second creation as a relationship among persons: "Every single person is there," he writes.

If these two creations go some way toward making clear that a totalizing vision of history must speak to the relationships among persons, the novel also identifies one additional formal element necessary to such a vision. It does so by virtue of including Jones's descriptions of these creations. Although the *mappi mundi* scene just described would seem to involve the unveiling of a key to the structure of the world that this novel describes, much in the way that certain editions of *Absalom! Absalom!* include Faulkner's genealogical and chronological key to the story, it is important to remember that in this moment Jones engages in ekphrasis, or the verbal description of visual art forms. Since Achilles's shield ekphrasis has been associated with a desire to represent the totality of a historical moment and the inability to do so in the medium of language.[24] Figures of ekphrasis in this sense connote that unaided writing is incapable of capturing the totality of a historical moment. Alice's creations might therefore be described as pointing to the novel's necessary failure fully to represent history—its reaching toward but never grasping a vision of totality. This could only be taken as a failure on the part of the novel, however, if we forget that the frustrated desire to represent the experience of slavery in language is a central feature of life inside the peculiar institution. Ekphrastic desire—if I could only see Alice's creations then I would fully comprehend this novel and the history it describes—regenerates one of the key features of African America: a longing for a bird's-eye view—a view of totality—in what is at first encounter (and often second and third encounter) a seemingly unmappable land not of one's choosing. In other words, Jones's novel has internalized the persistent sense within the black intellectual and expressive traditions that African diasporic culture has an obligation to document and reproduce the longing for perspective that characterizes the experience of enforced diaspora. With its ekphrastic description of Alice's creations, Jones's novel prompts an experience of perspectival desire that contributes to rather than confounding its totalizing project. Jones's novel proceeds as though the history writer's procedures and her formal practices must archive this desire for perspective as much as they capture the demographic patterns of the slaveholding south. Jones's novel also assumes that it is possible to do so. Rather than merely fetishize what is missing from the archive, a historian can and must determine how to document what it felt like not to know the known world. The history writer might in the end find herself required to work in a variety of different representational modes if she is to achieve the goal of a total history.

Although Frederick Douglass's "The Heroic Slave" (1853) does not involve the same attention to ekphrastic desire, it does indicate how in the mid-nineteenth century, the historical romance as it descended from Sir Walter Scott and was refigured in the United States went some way toward achieving the totalizing vision of history pursued in *The Known World*. As Paul Christian Jones has argued, there is very good reason to read Douglass's novella as working in the tradition of Scott's historical romances. Christian Jones specifically suggests that Douglass's novella in fact reflects an engagement with and revision of the southern (U.S.) historical romance, often known as the plantation romance. Where Scott's historical novels focused on the fortunes of what Lukács identifies as an "average man, clearly not an ideologue," in order to see the fullness of history playing out around him, the southern historical romancers imported the Romantic heroic figure of history into the historical novel.[25] Christian Jones suggests that that this importation of a Romantic heroic figure happens in "The Heroic Slave" as well, as the title might suggest. For Christian Jones this indicates Douglass's revision of the southern historical romance tradition, to the extent that Douglass's refigures the Romantic hero as a black man. From Christian Jones's perspective, then, the Lukácsian model would seem inapt. Where is the middle-of the-road figure that permits us to see the shape and impact of warring historical forces? Lukács argues that "Scott's greatness lies in his capacity to give living human embodiment to historical-social types. The typically human terms in which great historical trends become tangible had never before been so superbly, straightforwardly and pregnantly portrayed. And above all, never before had this kind of portrayal been consciously set at the centre of the representation of reality."[26] He continues on to suggest the "compositional importance of the mediocre hero": "Scott always chooses as his principal figures such as may, through character and fortune, enter into human contact with both camps."[27] Douglass's hero, Madison Washington, could hardly be described as mediocre.

That description might well be applied, though, to two central figures in the novella: the friendly Quaker, Mr. Listwell, and Tom Grant,
the white sailor who recounts the story of the revolt aboard the ship
Creole. Mr. Listwell in particular has been read as a stand-in for the
reader of the novella, the sympathetic white man or woman who might
imagine her- or himself in the role of aiding the fugitive slave by virtue of a proper mode of identification with the slave's flight. Marianne
Noble argues, for example, that we may understand Mr. Listwell as a
sign of Douglass's desire to make tangibly felt the possibility of alternative forms of sympathy in which the sympathetic white becomes as
much listener as witness. Noble argues that Mr. Listwell suggests how,
for Douglass, "When the two members of a dialogue are generously
willing to enter into the other's point of view, a deep communion is
available, even though fully meanings and true selves are never present nor graspable."[28] However, it is also possible to see Mr. Listwell and
Tom Grant less as sympathetic listeners and more as figures for the
mediocre historical hero that Lukács describes. In this sense Douglass's
"The Heroic Slave" reaches toward a full picture of the various warring historical forces at play in the Atlantic world, and particularly the
U.S., around the issue of slavery: Mr. Listwell and Tom Grant permit
the novella to stage a scenario in which a central and somewhat sympathetic figure "enter[s] into human contact with both camps." This is
not quite the bird's-eye view pursued in *The Known World,* but it does
restage the history of slavery as a story of human relationships translated into great historical forces. "The Heroic Slave" rewrites the history
of slavery as a relationship among people rather than a story of things,
while also doing justice to the broad historical significance and centrality to world history of those relationships.

Total Visions

If Jones's novel and Douglass's novella in this sense suggest that a total
history of African America is achievable, then what about a total history that is written at the scale of totality? A different way of putting this
is to ask: Whose world do we come to know in the process of reading
The Known World? In *A Faithful Account of the Race: African American Historical Writing in Nineteenth-Century America,* Stephen G. Hall,

like Ernest, suggests that early African American historians developed a historiographical stance alternative to mainline (white) U.S. and European historical writing. Hall focuses especially on the way that, while white historians of the U.S. and Europe turned increasingly to theories and practices based on a sense of national belonging, African American writers expressed much greater interest in the parameters of a "faithful account of the race," a practice which from the perspective of our present is counterintuitively a more expansive and global historiography. According to Hall, "By the 1830s, when white historians began to construct American history in increasingly nationalistic ways, drawing on Romanticism to construct ideal historical personalities and deriving crucial lessons from the immediate rather than the distant past, black writers, led by abolitionists trained in various clerical traditions, challenged this approach by trumpeting the authority of sacred, ancient, and modern history. In this way they preserved a more complex black subject who emerged from a review of *world* history rather than national history."[29] Hall's descriptive point here is to draw a line of demarcation separating the practices of African American historians writing black history from those of the white European and U.S. historians much more familiar to most readers. The conceptual intervention is equally important. Hall allows us to see that it was white European and U.S. historians who embraced what we might call "national micronarratives." Although Bancroft and Parkman would not have admitted as much, they were writing partial narratives organized around a parochial view that mistook the U.S. and Europe for the world. By contrast, according to Hall, "people of color throughout the nineteenth and early twentieth centuries viewed themselves in terms articulated by David Walker, as 'citizens of the world.'"[30] These same people of color, in their roles as intellectuals and historians, "used the intellectual culture of the nineteenth century, namely biblical, classical, and modern history . . . to frame a complex humanistic portrait of African American history that transcended the rise of the West with its attendant horrors of the Middle Passage and slavery and extended back to the 'first ages of man.'"[31] According to Hall, then, early national and antebellum African American historians proposed that the history of black people was the history of the world and vice versa. In this sense, they anticipated some of W. E. B. Du Bois's most memorable claims about the centrality of the color line to the modern world. Du Bois's great work *The Souls of Black Folk* opens: "This meaning is not without interest to you, Gentle Reader, for the problem of the Twentieth Century is the problem of the color line." A micronarrative this is not.

Hall, Jones, Douglass, and Du Bois remind us that African American history writing and historical fiction have not always dismissed the idea of a coherent totalizing vision of history. They have at least as often argued for a *better* totalizing vision capable of tracing what is from the perspective of a certain present seemingly impossible. If the traditions of African American historiography and African American speculative fiction described here are reconsidered in this light, we start to understand them as making a deeply demanding claim on the present. These texts are not retreating into the domain of the micronarrative to write a restricted history of the (black) nation. These texts pursue instead an account of totality that puts the experience and arrangements of blackness at the center of what it means to live this world. These texts also make the case that African American literature and African American history are and always have been world literature and world history—and not in a multiculturalist or additive sense. Precisely the reduction to topography, human relationships, and moral accounting that we see at force in *The Known World* and "The Heroic Slave" come into focus as a comprehensive mapping of human life under the conditions of modernity. In this totalizing vision of history, African American experience allows us to know this world—all of it.

What conclusions can we draw from these observations? First, the longstanding African American interest in damage done to the archive should not be mistaken for a full-scale retreat from totalizing visions of history. To do so would be to conflate the identification of a problem with one particular approach to solving it. Second, Jones's novel understands the conceptualization and representation of historical totality as a project necessarily distributed across media, genres, and formal practices. This is a lesson taught and a practice engaged in by African American writers, thinkers, and artists since at least Du Bois. It is worth remembering in this context that African American studies is an interdiscipline for reasons other than chronic underfunding. These observations also draw into focus a potential limitation of the Lukácsian model, as well as an obstacle to thinking through totality as a concept. As my recourse to Lukács on the historical novel would indicate, it is easy to confuse, as Lukács arguably does, the production of a totalizing vision of history with a linear narrative about the past. Although Lukács is useful and necessary here, he does not give us adequate tools for envisioning an account of totality that does not unfold as a linear narrative organized in fairly conventional terms. In this sense, he does not allow for a reality that is neither linear nor particularly susceptible to being subsumed by linear narrative. This is troubling not only because the great works of totalizing vision are neither particularly linear nor particularly narrative. (*Capital* is one of our most compelling accounts of totality, but its procedures are not those of linear narration. Anecdotes, algebraic equations, and reductions to principle all make an appearance, but it would be hard to describe them as adding up to something so straightforward as a narrative.) It is troubling also because assuming the linearity of time in the past underestimates the force of both slavery and capitalism to reorganize the order of time.

Ultimately, these texts prompt us to consider whether now might be an appropriate moment to revisit the project of historical totalization as it relates to the history of slavery and African American life. The intimidating expansion of the historical archives of slavery consequent upon the recovery work undertaken over the last one hundred fifty years, as well as the increase of data following from important digitizing efforts of more recent vintage, will tempt us to embrace the seemingly manageable micronarrative. *The Known World* suggests though that the world of slavery is a world we need to know in its totality if we are to know any world at all.

WORKS CITED

Bassard, Katherine Clay. "Imagining Other Worlds: Race, Gender, and the 'Power Line' in Edward P. Jones's *the Known World*." *African American Review* 42, no. 3/4 (2008): 407–19.

Baucom, Ian. *Specters of the Atlantic: Finance Capital, Slavery and the Philosophy of History*. Durham, NC: Duke University Press, 2005.

Donaldson, Susan V. "Telling Forgotten Stories of Slavery in the Postmodern South." *Southern Literary Journal* 40, no. 2 (2008): 267–83.

Dubey, Madhu. "Speculative Fictions of Slavery." *American Literature* 82, no. 4 (2010): 779–805.

Ernest, John. *Liberation Historiography: African American Writers and the Challenge of History, 1794–1861.* Chapel Hill, NC: University of North Carolina Press, 2004.

Hall, Stephen G. A. *Faithful Account of the Race: African American Historical Writing in Nineteenth-Century America,* John Hope Franklin Series in African American History and Culture. Chapel Hill, NC: University of North Carolina Press, 2009.

Harper, Phillip Brian. *Framing the Margins: The Social Logic of Postmodern Culture.* New York: Oxford University Press, 1994.

Jones, Edward P. *The Known World.* 1st ed. New York: Amistad, 2003.

Jones, Paul Christian. "Copying What the Master Had Written: Frederick Douglass's 'The Heroic Slave' and the Southern Historical Romance." *Southern Quarterly* 38, no. 4 (2000): 78–92.

Krieger, Murray, and Joan Krieger. *Ekphrasis: The Illusion of the Natural Sign.* Baltimore: Johns Hopkins University Press, 1992.

Lukács, György. *The Historical Novel.* Boston: Beacon Press, 1963.

Lukács, György. *History and Class Consciousness: Studies in Marxist Dialectics.* London: Merlin Press, 1971.

Mutter, Sarah Mahurin. "'Such a Poor Word for a Wondrous Thing': Thingness and the Recovery of the Human in the Known World." *Southern Literary Journal* 43, no. 2 (2011): 125–46.

Noble, Marianne. "Sympathetic Listening in Frederick Douglass's 'The Heroic Slave" and *My Bondage and My Freedom." Studies in American Fiction* 34, no. 1 (2006): 53–68.

Schoonover, Karl. *Brutal Vision: The Neorealist Body in Postwar Italian Cinema.* Minneapolis: University of Minnesota Press, 2012.

NOTES

1. Madhu Dubey, "Speculative Fictions of Slavery," *American Literature* 82, no. 4 (2010), 779.

2. Katherine Clay Bassard, "Imagining Other Worlds: Race, Gender, and the 'Power Line' in Edward P. Jones's *The Known World," African American Review* 42, no. 3/4 (2008), 407–9.

3. Bassard argues that "Jones shifts the ground of literary representation from the question of historical 'accuracy' and 'authenticity' and onto the terrain of language. This re-mapping away from the sociohistorical and onto the linguistic through the mistrust of historical documents, data, and the like demonstrates the powerlessness of written texts to yield what it is we really want most to know about the past: the complexities of relationships, emotions and motivations that make up the human experience" ("Imagining Other Worlds," 408).

4. For an influential account of how to engage the archive's absences so as to tell black and modern world history, see Ian Baucom, *Specters of the Atlantic: Finance Capital, Slavery and the Philosophy of History* (Durham, NC: Duke University Press, 2005).

5. Harper revises standard accounts of postmodernity by suggesting that one of the key features associated with the experience of postmodernity—decentered subjectivity—defined life for minority subjects well before the technological advances often associated with the advent of the decentered subject. Harper proposes in essence that postmodernity represents the extension of minority experiences of modernity to a greater number of majority peoples. In this reading the experience of minoritized subjects constitutes the chronological precursor to the experience of postmodernity, and attending to the conditions of minority illuminates the condition of postmodernity. Phillip Brian Harper, *Framing the Margins: The Social Logic of Postmodern Culture* (New York: Oxford University Press, 1994).

6. Susan V. Donaldson, "Telling Forgotten Stories of Slavery in the Postmodern South," *Southern Literary Journal* 40, no. 2 (2008), 273.

7. Ibid. Hughes-Warrington writes convincingly of the longstanding African American interest in universal history.

8. For a more detailed account of the sort of historical writing being done in the nineteenth century, see Stephen G. Hall, *A Faithful Account of the Race: African American Historical Writing in Nineteenth-Century America* (Chapel Hill, NC: University of North Carolina Press, 2009), 5–6.

9. György Lukács, *History and Class Consciousness: Studies in Marxist Dialectics* (London: Merlin Press, 1971).

10. For a different account of thingness in *The Known World*, see Sarah Mahurin Mutter, "'Such a Poor Word for a Wondrous Thing': Thingness and the Recovery of the Human in the Known World," *Southern Literary Journal* 43, no. 2 (2011).

11. John Ernest, *Liberation Historiography: African American Writers and the Challenge of History, 1794–1861* (Chapel Hill, NC: University of North Carolina Press, 2004), 25.

12. Ibid., 5.

13. Ibid., 7. For a cogent summary of recent accounts of unrepresentability in the context of the Holocaust, see Karl Schoonover, *Brutal Vision: The Neorealist Body in Postwar Italian Cinema* (Minneapolis: University of Minnesota Press, 2012), 1–3.

14. Ernest, *Liberation Historiography*, 22.

15. Ibid., 2.

16. Hall, *A Faithful Account of the Race*, 10. As Dubey points out, Ernest's and Hall's claims can be seen to rewrite for African American criticism much more familiar writings on history such as those of Hayden White. According to Dubey, "White contends that, for 'subordinate, emergent, or resisting social groups,' the realist imperative that has characterized history since its inception as a discipline can only appear as the crowning element of the very ideology they wish to oppose. Effective opposition must therefore be based on a refusal of realism, on 'a conception of the historical record as being not a window through which

the past 'as it really was' can be apprehended,' but rather as an impediment to proper understanding of the past" ("Speculative Fictions of Slavery," 784).

17. Hall, *A Faithful Account of the Race*, 3. Hall convincingly argues that this emphasis on the nontextual has its limitations. As he shows, "Central to the articulation of black historical voice was textual production, especially extended, book-length works, and its influence on and connection to the subsequent scholarly development of the field" (*Faithful Account*, 4).

18. Dubey, "Speculative Fictions of Slavery," 784.

19. Ibid., 780.

20. Ibid., 785–86.

21. Ibid., 784.

22. Edward P. Jones, *The Known World*, 1st ed. (New York: Amistad, 2003), 384.

23. Ibid., 386.

24. Murray Krieger and Joan Krieger, *Ekphrasis: The Illusion of the Natural Sign* (Baltimore: Johns Hopkins University Press, 1992).

25. Paul Christian Jones, "Copying What the Master Had Written: Frederick Douglass's 'The Heroic Slave' and the Southern Historical Romance," *Southern Quarterly* 38, no. 4 (2000).

26. György Lukács, *The Historical Novel* (Boston: Beacon Press, 1963), 35.

27. Ibid., 36.

28. Marianne Noble, "Sympathetic Listening in Frederick Douglass's 'The Heroic Slave' and *My Bondage and My Freedom*," *Studies in American Fiction* 34, no. 1 (2006).

29. Hall, *A Faithful Account of the Race*, 6–7.

30. Ibid., 11.

31. Ibid., 14.

3

Race, Reenactment, and the "Natural-Born Citizen"

TAVIA NYONG'O

When the Republicans rode a Tea Party–fueled backlash into a new majority in the U.S. House of Representatives in 2010, they organized a fittingly symbolic entrance act. On the second day of the 112th Congress in January 2011, the public witnessed an unprecedented spectacle, as the nation's business was held up for ninety minutes while lawmakers from both sides of the aisle took turns reading aloud the U.S. Constitution in its entirety on the floor of the House of Representatives. Congress members jockeyed to read particularly symbolic passages. A bipartisan standing ovation was reserved for former Student Nonviolent Coordinating Committee chairman and current Democratic Congressman John Lewis, who received the honor of declaiming the Thirteenth Amendment, enacted in 1865, abolishing slavery throughout the land.[1]

The U.S. Constitution is a document that is nigh universally available worldwide in print and electronically. It is a document that, besides being the basic law authorizing and organizing the political body that met to read it, had already been entered in full into the congressional record, twice before in the nation's past. Why bother, then, to proclaim it aloud? The exercise, by turns pedagogic and devotional, was widely understood in the media as a partisan rebuke of the passage of a health care law the prior year, a law which many in the new Republican majority held to be an unconstitutional extension of federal law over individual liberty. Some viewers of the broadcast proceedings detected partisanship in selective applause, with Republicans cheering the Tenth Amendment (1791) which limits the powers of the federal government, and Democrats cheering the Fourteenth (1868) which expands citizenship rights. One hardly needed this performance, however, to learn these partisan dispositions in the 112th Congress. Was this particular political performative, then, "*in a peculiar way* hollow or void," to quote a famous analyst of the speech-act, J. L. Austin's *How to Do Things with Words*?[2]

To answer this question is to explore the immense terrain Austin uncovered between the constative and the performative, between saying and doing. In particular, it is to make use of a distinction his analysis proposed between the illocutionary force of an utterance, that which is accomplished *in* saying something, and its perlocutionary force, of that which is accomplished *through* saying something.[3] While the illocutionary force of a performative speech act, such as calling a session of Congress to order, is exhausted in its enactment, its perlocutionary effects are durational and open-ended. We might even say that where the illocutionary directs our attention to performance effects, the perlocutionary focuses us on performance *affects*. It is these durational and open-ended performance affects that the otherwise hollow and void reading of the Constitution directs us to, to a set of concerns that are at once in excess of the political, and its remainder, that which is not fully accountable within a procedural analysis of law's workings.

As political theater, then, the reading was literally a waste of taxpayers' money, a wholly symbolic expenditure of time and resources in an exercise filled with redundant and repetitious *ressentiment*. And yet, in that very ressentiment—in that very "re-tonguing" or "re-sniffing" of the Constitution, as Eve Sedgwick's brilliant gloss on the word would have it—something political was indeed attempted.[4] Among Austin's commentators, Sedgwick has been perhaps most responsible for amplifying the discussion of performative affects, and her concept of the "periperformative"—all that can happen in and around (and in this case especially, after) a performative speech-act—is key to thinking through the resonances the Constitution has held in various political quarters down the centuries.[5] Key here is her comment that the peri-performative field of perlocutionary affects does not attenuate along a center-periphery axis, but "rarefies or concentrates in unpredictable clusters, outcrops, geological amalgams."[6] Avowing one's proximity to the Constitution—once heightened sensitivity to its rhetorical and moral force—allows a politician to set a contrast with one's partisan opponents who become, by implication, errant readers of the founding text. By yoking public feeling to an invidious distinction between direct and vicarious contact with national origins, a somewhat hokey civics exercise could thereby yield political dividends. It is from such a pernicious direct/vicarious binarism that the politically symbolic action of the Tea Party movement that emerged in the immediate wake of the financial crisis of 2008 and election of Barack Obama drew such force.[7] And it is with a distinctive rhetoric evoking a quasi-geological scale of time—excavating through the trash of recent subsoil to reach patriotic bedrock—that the movement staged its perlocutionary affects. Indeed, the concept of the perlocutionary force of the performative utterance enables us to parse the otherwise paradoxical language of direct access and temporal return at work in the most heated of Tea Party rhetoric. Although we cannot literally return to the past, the Tea Party's call to rededicate ourselves to the nation's founding promoted the conviction that we nevertheless can or somehow should stage such a return, that even as we forever fall short of an origins we must nevertheless continuously strive to live up to it. There is a kind of fetishistic pleasure in disavowal at work here, a pleasure activated in conscious knowledge that it is attempting the impossible, even the perverse. This pleasure ought to give pause to any theorist who might hope to assign the politics of enjoyment to the left. For those of working in the cross currents of performance studies and queer temporality, there is an occasion to revisit some of our own verities regarding the uses of pleasure, the subversiveness of nonchronological time, and the politics of surrogation.[8]

My analysis of the Tea Party–inspired reading of the Constitution as political theater is shaped by two books, on overlapping themes, and of shared political leaning, but of juxtaposed implication. Rebecca Schneider's *Performing Remains* (2011) and Jill Lepore's *The Whites of Their Eyes*

(2010) both engage aspects of historical reenactment culture in America.[9] From their respective disciplinary vantage points of theater and performance studies on the one hand, and social and cultural history on the other, these two feminist scholars take on historical reenactment, a performance genre that is often considered a bastion of white male identity politics. Both works stage a debate between history and memory in which the body is strongly implicated. While Schneider considers Civil War reenactment, and Lepore focuses on reenactments of the U.S. Revolution (in her home state of Massachusetts in particular), they share an interest in race, slavery, and its legacy, as any consideration of U.S. reenactment culture must. They both bear upon a nineteenth-century studies interested, as Ian Baucom has put it, less in the question of how time passes, and more in the question of how time *accumulates* in and as forms of (racial and national) property.[10] This concept of time as accumulation, while not the standard model of chronological time, is not yet either a model of time as a resource for pleasure. Or at the very least, our sense of what pleasures time gives us might be dramatically reconfigured so as to allow for a kind of pleasure-in-pain among the varieties of perlocutionary affects that follow in the wake of the foundational act. In his famous 1852 speech "What to the slave is the Fourth of July," Frederick Douglass summoned up one potent acoustic image of black perlocutionary affect in and around patriotic commemoration when he spoke of hearing "above your national, tumultous joy [. . .] the wail of millions, whose chains, heavy and grievous yesterday, are to-day rendered more intolerable by the jubilant shouts that reach them."[11] The sound of black bodies audibly surrogating the national Thing—whether in Douglass' rhetorical figure or in John Lewis's reenacting the abolition of slavery from the floor of Congress in 2010—serves as a reminder of the accumulation of time and the dispossessive force blackness asserts against it.[12] I will return to that dispossessive force—and its possible links to the perlocutionary—in my conclusion. Along the way I hope to show how both books open up, obliquely at some points, directly at others, the fraught question of how reenactment can as easily foreclose as enable a reckoning with the black radical strivings that are immanent to but never fully contained by the nation's story.

Tea Party politicized reenactments of an eighteenth-century war are, in some key ways, displaced reckonings with a nineteenth-century one. At their broadest, Tea Party activists engage matters of federal powers—the authority to abolish slavery principle among them—that were consolidated only in the wake of Union victory. On the issues of race, migration, and citizenship, the movement's judicial philosophy might even be thought of as a *relitigation* of nineteenth-century victories over states rights and what Alexander Saxton has termed white "herrenvolk democracy" (although it has not sought to contest women's suffrage which, logically, an appeal to the inerrancy of the founding framer's intentions would require).[13] An important tradition of Marxist historiography has long argued that the Civil War was the real American revolution (in terms of the revolutionary transformation of the mode of production by a national bourgeoisie)—in this light the Tea Party fetishization of the "founding fathers" can be thought of as a kind of Marxism-in-reverse. Not only was the Civil War not the real revolution, it shouldn't have happened at all.[14] All the festive tri-corner hats and Paul Revere rides occlude the very issues of slavery and federalism that the Founding Fathers themselves ultimately compromised upon as they drew up the Constitution.[15] Such occlusion is precisely the phenomenon that Schneider and Lepore seek to throw analytic light upon. They seek to articulate what is forgotten as well as what is remembered when history is commemorated for present political purpose.

As Lepore in particular makes clear, taking up the framing of the Constitution as a high point from which the country's politics has only devolved over time isn't simply ahistorical. It enshrines a peculiar political theology in response to secular historical change. This sacralizing mode gives form to collective memory as an apparatus that divides as much as unites, that consists in "the unsaid" as much as in "the said," as Foucault puts things.[16] And yet Lepore is too confident of the historian's craft to repel the past's ghosts, which is why I pair her methodological dressing down of the Tea Party with Schneider's much more ambivalent deconstruction of Civil War reenactors. My impulse here is to unwork the direct/vicarious binarism a little, whether it is used, as the Tea Party does, to set up the Constitution as sacred text or, as Lepore by contrast does, to detect their places of convenient historical amnesia and propose her own "direct" past. While her politically progressive vision of the past is personally preferable to me than the Tea Party, her polemical distinction between history and antihistory reinstates the direct/

vicarious binarism (historians directly engage the archive, whereas reenactors vicariously participate through cultures of political performance). Rather than sustain this binary, I propose instead to read the tendency to *sacralize* history against an abolitionist legacy of its *profanation*.[17] Profanation, like the perlocutionary, is a passionate unworking of the codes of the legal and historical performative, one that, as Stanley Cavell puts it, takes place within "the field of human interaction which is not governed by the conventions or conditions or rituals [of the performative] but represents the complementary field occupied by or calling for improvisation and passion and aggression."[18] In a sense this sounds like a field already occupied by Tea Party theatrics, but if it is so, it is all the more important to engage it.

History and Antihistory

History making is a cultural activity of the present, determined in the never-quite-final instance by the record and our methods for organizing, accessing, interpreting, and transmitting it. The elusive *real* of the past is withdrawn from the present both ontologically, in its being, and epistemologically, in the modes of our knowing it. Performance is the joker in the deck scholarship plays in this ontoepistemic game. Performance studies' attunement to the present and subjective encounter with the past foregrounds what history takes pride in delegating to other disciplines, and calls attention to bodies that history might rather leave dead and buried. In *Performing Remains*—whose theoretical position I have attempted to summarize above—Rebecca Schneider tracks the consequence of the indifference of history to its performative occasion, arguing that such indifference hobbles our grasp of exactly how history holds us, and why. She scrutinizes the live/mediated and actual/theatrical binarisms routinely invoked in criticisms of historical reenactment (alongside the direct/vicarious abovementioned). She shows how repeatedly a primary experience is held up over and against a second-hand one that is then castigated as easy, corrupting, and effeminate. Her ironic feminist identification with antifeminist Civil War reenactors (whose gender realism results in banning women from their faux battlefields) comes via commiserating in a shared stigma regarding a theatrical experience that those in the know, but only they, know to be real.[19]

Schneider take on historical reenactment is several steps away from the now familiar (if heavily criticized) postmodern critique of history associated with theorists like Keith Jenkins.[20] Her focus is less on the social or textual construction of the past, or even on the collective memory of the past, as it is on the past as something that can be taken on again like a second skin. Embodiment is key to her polemic, and she uses it to unlock an ontology of time typically seen as homogenous and unidirectional. As Schneider notes in her foreword: "To trouble linear temporality—to suggest that time may be touched, crossed, visited or revisited, that time is transitive and flexible, that time might recur in time, that time is not one—never only one—is to court the ancient (and tired) Western anxiety over ideality and originality. The threat of theatricality is still the threat of the imposter status of the copy, the double, the mimetic, the second, the surrogate, the feminine, or the queer."[21] Schneider's riposte against covert Platonic idealism in the historicist disciplines resonates both with Sedgwick's now classic formulation of the epistemology of the closet—in which a whole series of modern binarisms are structured, made knowable, and at the same time couched in a privileged unknowing—as well as with Elizabeth Freeman's more recent positing of "chrononormativity," or "the use of time to organize individual human bodies toward maximum productivity."[22] Both Freeman and Schneider emphasize a critique of linear, chronological time, asserting the possibility of time being experienced affectively, in "unpredictable clusters, outcrops, geological amalgams," which allows both history and our understanding of it to progress smoothly toward a complacent future, paradoxically positioning history against the backward looking, thinking, and feeling. Against these liberal historiographic niceties, Freeman and Schneider recall the subversive historical materialism of Walter Benjamin, whose theses against the concept of "homogenous, empty time" they evoke as they advocate a lingering, even a malingering, in the past.[23]

Such a view of temporality, while perhaps foreign to some academic historians, is not unknown to critical theory. While it raises the crucial point that time and temporality are embodied, it also begs the question of the politics of that embodiment. Here another heterodox historicist, Foucault, is relevant. Much like Schneider, Foucault enjoyed deconstructing the pernicious contrast between original historical knowledge and its theatricalized travesty.[24] But he also acknowledged the ambivalence of his parodies. He spoke mockingly of the historian who sought to offer the "confused and anonymous European" an "alternative identity" drawn from a past that, the more thoroughly it was scoured for verifiable origins, the more comprehensively it transformed historians into "street vendors of empty identities." Within the public sphere, according to Foucault, the historian and the reenactor are on equally shaky ground. The "new historian," the one who observes Foucault's ironic fidelity to the dissimulation of the archive, "will know what to make of this masquerade. He will not be too serious to enjoy it; on the contrary, he will push the masquerade to its limit and prepare the great carnival of time where masks are constantly reappearing."[25] This rhetorical inflation of the doublings of theater and the market into a cosmic carnivalesque is typical of Foucault's style, but it leaves only partially answered the question of enjoyment, which is here clearly directed less at the enjoyment of alternative identities drawn from the past, than from a distanced appreciation of the foibles of others, historians and their public alike, who are taken in by the reality effects of the archive. The dramatic reading of the Constitution in January 2011 is the kind of spectacle Foucault encourages us not too be too serious to enjoy. But as that example suggests, pushing the masquerade to its limit entails something different from assimilating oneself wholly to its terms. There is space within Foucault's rhetoric for a position that is neither idealistic nor theatrical, but devoted to a perpetual and restless questioning of the terms that sustain that difference.

A genealogical mode of critique might therefore highlight the ways in which performance and history do not neatly align with the direct/vicarious binarism. Instead, that binarism splits them, and is split by them, in complex and unexpected ways. True, the "Western anxiety over ideality and originality" Schneider associates with the linearity imposed by conventional historiography reemerges at the center of the right-wing historical reenactments she and Lepore examine. But the appearance of such concerns within the rhetoric and repertoire of those who self-consciously aspire to legal and political anachronism points out a twist in the otherwise smooth progression of straight time. Here I refer to the right-wing anxiety over returning to the original intentions of those idealized figures, the Founding Fathers. In the form of the legal doctrine and political performance of "originalism," such a deployment of the direct/vicarious binarism crosses both archive and repertoire, binding them tightly in a single, reactionary script. It is as if the adherents to originalism agreed with the Benjaminian account linking the linear concept of time and the liberal ideology of progress, and so much so that they, like he, sought to attack the latter by undermining the former.

The critique of linear time, that is to say, possesses limits of its own, and we cannot always valorize those who veer from the temporally straight and narrow, confidently equating linearity with chrononormativity. Deeply normative projects like originalism and Tea Party conservatism, as Lepore details, possess their own deviations from straight time. Their historical malingering, what is more, can be accompanied with a hierarchical, conservative, and zealous fidelity to "facts" that are resolutely antifeminist and antiqueer. And the pleasure they find in direct contact with the past is often won at the cost of another's trauma (as Douglass pointed out in claiming that the sounds of white patriotic feeling cut all the deeper into the wounds of the enslaved blacks).[26] Such a recognition pushes against any straightforward preference for embodied forms of knowing over knowledge generated by the archive. Robin Bernstein has recently argued that the distinction between archive and repertoire, even a distinction that insists upon their mutual interaction, misses the way racial meanings are scripted across a range of objects, affects, texts, discourses, and behaviors.[27] Although she doesn't herself call attention to this link, her method dovetails nicely with the new materialisms emerging across many different disciplinary locations (performance studies among them). In this new materialist or object-oriented approach, performativity is best understood not as a property specific to a range of human behaviors known as performances (however narrowly or broadly "performance" is construed) but as a capacity inherent in all social and even natural phenomena.[28] Embracing the performative and perlocutionary force of the past on the present does not entail a subsuming history to a wholly embodied or humanist method; it is more nearly "to expose a body totally imprinted by history and the process of history's destruction of the body."[29] When the body in question is the white national body, this process of historical destruction takes on a double-edged nature. Bernstein is able to show, through her genealogy of archival and material performatives, how white supremacy is transmitted in American culture through tacit knowledge as much as through official ideology, a point I will return to. The point to stress at this stage here is simply how reenactment's claim to have sidestepped textual history, with its plodding forward momentum, can align as easily with the conservative historicism Benjamin opposed as with the radical historical materialism he championed.

In her time spent with reenactors, many of whom *sotto voce* support the lost cause of Southern independence, Schneider repeatedly shows how performance of direct contact with a historical sublime depends upon various vicarious foils. Because the past forever withdraws from our approach, our direct reenactment of it is entirely composed of disavowed vicarious experience. This elusive character of the past is rendered tangible in object matter that "remains" on the scene, its phenomenological allure coming to stand in, metonymically, for the past as such. And this allure must somehow be verified: the reenactor must somehow be seen to be experiencing the past in order to experience it—another order of vicariousness. Thus, Civil War reenactors seeking contact highs with the thrill of the nineteenth-century trenches require the presence of contemporary spectators and observers whom they nonetheless ignore or keep out of sight, in a game of *fort-da* that would make Freud proud.[30] They strive to period authenticity in clothing, weaponry, gender, and diet, disattending such incongruities as the disparity between their average age and that of a Civil War soldier, and the massive, banalized fact of battlefield death on a scale still unmatched on American soil. This last misfire is memorably described in a repeated incongruity Schneider observes at the end of reenactments: when "the various cadavers strewn about the field would get up, dust off, and quite simply, *return to camp* . . . they rose up with a surprisingly exultant joy. Spectators often cheered as the tired corpses, clearly pleased with themselves, ambled off."[31] Life itself, filled to the brim with white racial innocence, would appear to be among performance's remains. Schneider identifies this exultation as a paradox, as if the reenactors ought to feel the weight of their own failure to go to the end of their fidelity of event and actually die. But the paradox is lessened when the pursuit of direct contact with the past is apprehended in the entirety of its fetishistic structure, where what is wanted is actually the substitute, no matter how avidly this wanting is disavowed. It is not simply that the reenactor, excepting certain extreme circumstances, cannot actually want to die for the cause. It is also that, as Bernstein shows through her study of the material and performative culture of American childhood, white racial innocence is transmitted through "scriptive things" that "contain massive historical evidence" that "habituate and thus deeply inscribe the body."[32] *Performing Remains* shows, with great brio, how reenactment works as an embodied performance of this fetishistic attachment to a lost object (in this case, the Lost Cause). As Schneider notes, "For many history reenactors, reenactments are more than 'mere' remembering but are in fact the ongoing event itself, negotiated through sometimes radically shifting affiliation with the past as the present."[33]

Schneider calls the affect produced in this radical shift in affiliation between past and present by the appropriately inexact name of "queasiness." I would supplement this name with Bernstein's "racial innocence," to clarify what is at stake when national origins are conveniently reimagined as the thrilling pursuit of white men.[34]

Queasy indeed was the affect produced by Republican attempt to pull the U.S. Constitution out of vicarious habit, and, through sheer audible force of repetition, re-cognize its binding force on the present. And filled was it also with the plausible deniability that accompanies racial innocence, even though the women and men of many races participated. Watching the televised proceeding, it was hard not to be struck by how inept the overall performance was; a well-rehearsed class of junior high students could have done better. Representatives flubbed lines, flipped to the wrong page, tried for a stirring effect or rhetorical high dudgeon, both of which fell flat on the Constitution's tinder-dry eighteenth-century legalese. A fundamental flaw took hold, as the eagerness to seize pride of place at the podium gave way to an eagerness to get it over with. What the televised reading disclosed was how exactly the Constitution is not a *rhetorical* document, despite its ringing opening flourish. Far better to have read the Declaration of Independence, a document that does have at least an honored place in American oratory.[35] The effort to read the Constitution as an ongoing event in the present only foregrounded the discrepancy between its illocutionary and perlocutionary force. If the intent was to restore the former by means of the latter, then the reading was an utter failure on its own terms.

But while such a discrepancy might be a source of easy pleasure for skeptics, beneath it lay deeper worries. The reading was staged in fidelity to a doctrine of constitutional interpretation of originalism, which holds, in brief, that the present nation is bound by the original intents of its founders.[36] For originalists, reenactment is more than mere memory but in fact and in law the ongoing event itself, insofar as that present is also always potentially the past, imagined as something that can be both preserved in perpetuity and be repeated without variation. Here we see the Constitution operating as a "scriptive thing," scripting social action not only in terms of textual or legal interpretation (which it of course also does), but also as akin to a play script or musical score from which a variety of political actions and scenarios can be derived.[37] And here we also see the constitutional performative opened up to its perlocutionary uses, to the "field occupied by or calling for improvisation and passion and aggression." Even as originalist jurisprudence looks backward, drawing on precedent and authority to establish "good law," originalist performance looks forward, rehearsing and reenacting the future as a potentially better and more faithful iteration of a now sacralized past.[38] The illocutions of originalist jurisprudence and the perlocutions of originalist political theater are thus dangerously conjoined.

Originalist historical reenactment and revisionism is the target of Jill Lepore's caustic polemic, *The Whites of Their Eyes*. Lepore follows, with a journalist's wry eye and a historian's factual handwringing, the doings of her local Tea Party activists, whose version of revolutionary history she juxtaposes with her own narratives from the same period. A social and narrative historian, Lepore's accounts highlight the perspective of the ordinary people—women, the enslaved, the impoverished, the unwell—who ghost the edges of the Tea Party's celebratory portraits of our "Founding Fathers." Because she finds herself in direct opposition to a suddenly emergent political movement whose appeals to history she finds more or less fraudulent, Lepore takes a harder line than Schneider against the attempt to live the past as present. "Chronology," she declares with flat tautology, is "the logic of time." "Chronology is like gravity. Nothing falls up."[39] Any alternative to this view is neither history nor memory (no one remembers the revolution any more, Lepore reminds us), but what she calls *antihistory*:

In antihistory, time is an illusion. Either we're there, two hundred years ago, or they're here, among us. When Congress began debating an overhaul of the health care system, this, apparently, was very distressing to the Founding Fathers. "The founders are here today," said John Ridpath of the Ayn Rand Institute, at a Boston Tea Party rally on the Common on the Fourth of July. "They're all around us."

To the far right, everything about Barack Obama and his administration seemed somehow alarming, as if his election had ripped a tear in the fabric of time.[40]

Lepore, unlike Schneider, is unwilling to tarry in this queasiness, perhaps because her reenactors, unlike Schneider's, are directly engaged in a reactionary white identity politics. Where the right-wing sentiments of Civil War reenactors are more or less ambient, the "period rush" of Tea Party activists is furiously partisan and politically instrumentalized. Tea Party activists even briefly pondered fusing their actions with those of their historical namesakes by throwing the text of the health care bill into the Boston Harbor.[41] While Lepore is not too serious to enjoy such mad literalism, she also opposes its fundamentalist historical ontology with an avowedly progressivist one. Much as a left-liberal tradition opposes originalism by holding the Constitution to be a "living" document, one that evolves over time, Lepore practices a narrative history that adapts to current needs (for instance she foregrounds stories of illness, a move calibrated to address contemporary health care debates).[42] Originalism, in her critique, is quasi-religious fundamentalist in its reverence to political scripture, which it urges us to read and reread with hermeneutic devotion, and then act out our lives in accordance with its mandates. Hers is a reform wing of the church of history, ever sensitive to possible omissions and exclusions.

Originalism is a doctrine, as the title of Lepore's book implies, that can make common cause with racial innocence and white supremacy, insofar as it idealizes a historical period prior to black citizenship (prior to women's suffrage and universal white male suffrage even). Here Lepore proceeds carefully from the empirically overwhelming whiteness of the activists she encounters to more substantive claims regarding their racial ideology and habitus. Of course, originalism is a doctrine represented in places as respectable as the U.S. Supreme Court (by Justices Scalia and Thomas). And, for their part, Tea Party activists have virulently repudiated the charge that their movement was racist. Indeed, the Icarus-like 2011 presidential campaign of Herman Cain seemed to have been lifted skyward by the determination on the part of the Tea Party he assiduously cultivated to demonstrate their willingness to rally behind a sufficiently conservative black politician. The whiteness that Lepore espies in Tea Party opponents of big government takes the shape less of a consistent, conscious antiblack racism than it does of the racial innocence that Bernstein and, in a related context, Scott Malcolmson point to as a basis for white privilege.[43] Bernstein points to the way scriptive things "contained historical memory while performing innocence, performing obliviousness to history and to race."[44] Originalism, especially viewed from the perspective of a social historian like Lepore, attuned to the multiple perspectives from which any given event must be considered, must seek to disavow all that it must be oblivious to, it must forget that it forgets as it remembers what it remembers. While ostensibly deeply concerned with history, originalism performs a strategic occlusion of the historicity of the Constitution, its conditions of emergence and transformation.

And yet, collective memory of the racial past cannot be easily assimilated to the "living" image of the Constitution as an evolving, progressive document. Lepore's progressive critique of right-wing antihistory doesn't so much push the masquerade to its limit as it backs off from the precipice, compares chronology to gravity, and asserts its natural and inevitable force. This is the kind of covert idealism Schneider rightly objects to. So despite Lepore's great sensitivity to the political consequences of performance remains, there is something finally too disciplinarily complacent about her version of historical narration. Beyond the sacralizing originalism she objects to and the secular progressivism she would commit us to, I would argue that there are is another direction in which we could go, one that moves us in closer proximity to the perlocutionary affects and dispossessive force of radical black profanation.

Performing the Fourteenth Amendment

Advocates of a living Constitution can point to the historical process of amendment which, while it does nothing to refute originalism per se, takes some of the rhetorical wind out of originalist sails, insofar as it would seem to imply that the original intentions of the amenders would need to be studied and revered at least as much as those of the framers. Sacred texts cannot typically be amended (although they can be translated and interpreted). For this reason, one extreme right-wing variant of originalism has held that certain amendments are either invalid, or have created a second-tier class of citizenship. According to this white supremacist ideology, the Constitution and Bill of Rights confirmed whites as "sovereign citizens," whereas the Civil War had succeeded only in establishing "fourteenth-amendment citizens." The Constitution is the original, and the Fourteenth Amendment its monstrous double. Sovereign citizens, Stephen Atkins explains, believe they "have no obligations to follow any laws of the federal government. Only the Fourteenth Amendment citizens must follow federal laws. This distinction according to antigovernment theorists mean that 'natural' citizens can regain sovereign status by renouncing all contracts with the U.S. government and renouncing their U.S. citizenship."[45] Rightly considered a fringe movement, sovereign citizens nevertheless give explicit voice to the racial contract that Charles Mills argues implicitly underlies consensual liberalism.[46] For Mills, a social contract such as the U.S. Constitution is deemed egalitarian because the racial inequality of the society out of which the contracting parties emerge has been hidden from view. Sovereign citizens hysterically give this structure away when they contrast the revocable, contractual version of citizenship they enjoy, based on their natural racial sovereignty, from the irrevocable, biopolitical citizenship of African Americans and other racial minorities, based only on the positive law of the amendments. This is one reason why their racism is so annoying to liberalism: it threatens to give the game away. One might even say of liberalism what Adorno said of psychoanalysis: that "nothing is true except the exaggerations."[47] Analytically speaking the excessive and fanatic interpretation of originalism provided by the sovereign citizens is more revealing than the respectable legalisms of influential conservative jurists, than even the moderate historical perspectivalism of progressives like Lepore, who seek to establish a firewall between history and antihistory in order to safeguard the present from the Constitution's perlocutionary affects. Sovereign citizens (and more mainstream variants such as the growing numbers who believe that while the Fourteenth Amendment granted blacks equal citizenship, it excludes from citizenship those born on U.S. soil of foreign parentage) by contrast push the masquerade fairly close to the limits, although the carnival of time they prepare for might look more like a bloodbath than anything else.

This extremist backdrop is helpful in reading the tensions within the mainstream originalism of the House Republicans, who dissociate themselves from sovereign citizens and other extremists such as the loud "birther" protestor who disrupted the reading of the Constitution during the clause restricting eligibility to serve as U.S. president to a "natural-born citizen."[48] Yelling "except Obama!" repeatedly until she was removed from the gallery, this activist's disruption served as a kind of obscene supplement to the official performance, repeating back its logic with unsettling fervor. Such scenes of perlocutionary affect were precisely what the dramatic reading strove to both elicit and control. In devising the performance, Representative Goodlatte took on the role of impromptu dramaturg, deciding exactly which parts of the Constitution-as-script would be read. Faced not simply with a basic law but a text for oral interpretation, he confronted the issue of repealed sections, which are no longer "good law." He chose to omit such sections, deciding to consider them, as one fellow member of the Republican Congress objected, "deletions" rather than "amendments."[49] Here was a quandary for originalist stagecraft. Should the reading of the Constitution, which has changed over time, be read aloud in such a way as to foreground the accretion and exfoliation of its meanings? Is that part of its illocutionary force, or not? Reading the complete text might confuse or offend auditors, especially that majority of auditors who would hear the reading only in snippets, perhaps while visiting Congress, perhaps while watching C-SPAN or YouTube, or perhaps in a political attack ad exploiting decontextualized clips from C-SPAN's online archive. Not only would a reading of the Constitution to the letter make evident apparent contradictions, it would impose a secular or at least a sequential temporality on the performance, against originalist intentions.

For reasons of such dangers, the performed corollary of the jurisprudential doctrine of originalism turned out to be an industrious revisionism. A document had to be expurgated in order to preserve its aura as integral. The *New York Times* found the results a pleasingly ironic enactment of the "living" Constitution hypothesis: "For roughly 90 minutes, sentence by sentence, the words of the Constitution fluttered through the chamber, in accents reflecting myriad districts that did not even exist when the document came into being, and in the voices of women and African-Americans whose full rights were not recognized at the hour of its drafting."[50] Here, the newspaper of record joined progressive social historians like Lepore in striving to show the very archive the right appeals to a source of singular, crypto-racial identity, is itself a fount of diversity. America is a remedy for America, as the "hour" of national creation is reaudited through the "voices" of twenty-first-century women and men of multiple races and regions.[51] But this placid reading, intended to rebut the fiercely partisan motivations of the House Republicans, itself belied another story of antagonism the reading suppressed: the countermemories of many of the minority subjects participating in the reading.

Publicly objecting to the reading of an expurgated Constitution, Representative Jesse Jackson, Jr., of Illinois told the house that "[t]his is very emotional for me given the struggle of African Americans. . . . Many of us don't [want] that to be lost on the reading of our sacred document."[52] Between the concept of the Constitution as inerrant, and the placid affirmation of its status as "living," Jackson evoked another sense in which the law seemed rather to accumulate, one in which even a dead letter, *especially* a dead letter, might be crucial to read and consider for its perlocutionary affects. While seemingly genuflecting to both the originalist belief in the "sacred" status of the basic law and to progressive idea of a living Constitution, Jackson's objection actually reasserted a sense of accumulative time that belonged to neither, and invoked the struggle of African Americans as a struggle against both. A statement released from his office put the matter this way:

> Our expectation was that the new Republican majority would read the Constitution as written and its subsequent amendments. There is a broad body of law and interpretation that has developed from 1787 until the adoption of the last Amendment in 1992 that has turned our Constitution into a living document, paid for by the blood, sweat and tears of millions of Americans from the Revolutionary War, through the Civil War to even our current conflicts. The . . . redacted Constitutional

reading gives little deference to the long history of improving the Constitution and only seeks an interpretation of our Constitution based on the now, not the historic, broad body of law and struggle that it has taken to get there.[53]

While seemingly siding with the "living document" school of constitutional interpretation, Jackson's statement also points to an aspect of African American collective memory regarding the Constitution, one that undermines the sacred/secular divide and even, as the philosopher Giorgio Agamben might have put it, *profanes* it. For his particular bone of contention was clearly not the missed opportunity to present a constitutional law seminar within the House of Representatives, but what consequence the the redaction had for the reading of the notorious "three-fifths clause" in Article 1, Section 2, Paragraph 3 of the Constitution.

The three-fifths clause—popularly misconstrued as the belief that the framers considered blacks to be three-fifths a human being—is a touchstone of radical black collective memory, deployed in an antithetical register to resist both the sacralization of the founding fathers and the progressive story of secular evolution. It is a particular dense and potent textual site of countermemory, insofar as it has been interpreted as both pro- and (however incongruously at first approach) antislavery. At the root of this difference were antebellum debates among abolitionists over whether the Constitution was, or could be construed to be, antislavery. Where Garrisonians indicted the Constitution as "an agreement with hell," others like Douglass (after his break with Garrison) construed a Constitutional authority and even obligation to abolish inequality.[54] Douglass, in an 1860 pamphlet defending an antislavery Constitution, pointed out that the "three-fifths" clause gave a free man of color "two-fifths" greater political standing than his enslaved counterpart, empowering the free states while weakening the slave states, and thus demonstrating an antislavery impulse within the language of even this notorious compromise.[55] The political stakes of this argument are clear when set in context of the then-prevailing law of the land, which reflected the conclusion of Supreme Court Justice Taney in *Dred Scott v. Sanford* (1856), that the Constitution excluded the possibility of black citizenship. Douglass's antislavery Constitution was thus in an important sense a *virtual* Constitution, one that was not enforced by the government that was nevertheless created by it, but which still existed as a set of possibilities immanent to the political field. While couched in a legal analysis, the idea of an antislavery Constitution is more perlocutionary than illocutionary, more invested that is "in the field of human interaction which is not governed by the conventions or conditions or rituals" of the performative, but by the "complementary field [of] improvisation and passion and aggression" in its perimeter.[56]

Wishing to include the three-fifths clause in a public recitation of the Constitution is thus much more than a taking of sides in the sacred/secular divide; it is closer to a *profanation* of that very divide. In his essay "In Praise of Profanation," Agamben writes: "If consecration was the term that denoted the leaving of the sphere of human law, profanation signified the return to the free usage [*ad libero uso*] of mankind. To profane does not simply mean to abolish or cancel separations, but to learn to make new uses of them."[57] The perlocutionary force of the law seems a prime site for such a learning of new uses. What would it mean, what would it take, to profane the Constitution, a secular document that has become sacralized? What we might see as Jackson's wish to profane the reading of the consecrated Constitution—by including text that is already in it—calls attention to a blind spot in our contemporary sacred/secular binarism. It points us toward what we should not have needed Agamben to have taught us to call *naked life*.

Agamben has argued that sovereignty asserts its power neither by including nor by excluding, per se, but by asserting authority over the decision.[58] Sovereign citizens are mistaken when they see a contrast between a direct, originary white sovereignty and vicarious, derivative black and brown citizenship emerging later. Biopower resides not on either side of the charmed circle of citizenship, but in the act of separation itself. The apparatus of sovereignty "realizes a pure activity of governance" that must always "imply a process of subjectification, that is to say, they must produce their subject."[59] As a process, governmentality is necessarily time bound. This time is not however a natural phenomenon like gravity, but a naturalized phenomenon that produces the subject that would seek to comprehend and perhaps even disrupt it. Profanation sets a different time to work within and against the time of governmentality.[60] Subjectification is dissimulated by performances of white racial innocence, which veil it in a myth of historical identity. Black countermemory, such as that evoked by Jackson, thus works as a "counterapparatus" to such strategic forgetting.[61] The Constitution asserts a biopolitical decision at several places, but no more curious and contested at our present time than in its specification that the president be a "natural-born citizen." This clause has become relevant in the past two years because of the insistence of a lunatic fringe that the sitting president has failed to produce proof he is such a natural-born citizen. But what is a "natural-born citizen" if not a zone of exception, a point where life and law meet at a point of arbitrary decision and exclusion? Birth, as feminist theory has shown, is hardly a natural phenomenon upon which social and cultural arrangements are founded, but a deeply gendered event that naturalizes culture and cultures nature. The performatives that assign sex and gender begin well before birth; the battle over women's autonomy in reproduction long precedes conception.[62] "Natural birth" is an effect of language, history, technology, and power, as well as of human reproduction. But the resonances of the birther objection to Obama's presidency do not stop here. Most legal discussions of the birther controversy have focused on the first half of the phrase—the meaning of "natural born"—but in so doing left mostly uncontested its biopolitical link to the latter half: the meaning of "citizen." Yet the citizen/alien binarism operates as one of the most vicious and ugly modes of justifying the brutal treatment of humans in our time. Here Obama's race links the clause specifying that the president be a "natural-born citizen"—at least associatively—to the Fourteenth Amendment provisions clarifying that all persons, regardless of race, born in the United States are citizens. This amendment bears directly upon the fierce struggle over who counts as naturally born American, with a vocal right wing asserting those born of foreign parentage do not qualify, and a liberal wing defending birthright citizenship. Both views, however, reproduce the sovereign decision over citizenship, casting the person whose citizenship cannot be definitely decided for or against (such as the American brought into the U.S. as an infant or child) into a zone of exception. Progressive appeals for "pathways to citizenship" or even "rights for the undocumented" are certainly worth supporting, but neither untangle the subjectifying power of sovereignty as a governmental apparatus. Alongside these political and legal performatives, we need to restore a domain of periperformative and perlocutionary speech and action, not to cancel the legal efficacy of citizenship, but to learn to make new uses of it.

In this respect, Jacobus tenBroek's classic account of the abolitionist roots of the Fourteenth Amendment can be usefully contrasted with black abolitionist David Walker's celebrated 1829 *Appeal*. TenBroek's chronological, progressive, impeccably sourced legal and political history attributes to white male abolitionist lawyers and politicians the development of a concept of paramount national citizenship that triumphed over the state and sectional identities that prevailed before the U.S. Civil War. Intriguingly, he points to early legal and rhetorical ambiguities in abolitionist uses of the word "citizen":

> The conception of national citizenship and of certain privileges and immunities attaching to it, though vague, rudimentary, and ill defined, was yet basically present in abolitionist constitutional theory as early as 1834–35. Appearing as a part of the undifferentiated mass of the total religious, ethical, natural rights argument, the expression "American citizen"—sometimes "citizens of the United States"—was roughly interchanged with "human beings" or "persons having inalienable rights."[63]

Such a loose concept of citizenship was wielded by the Supreme Court in the *Dred Scott* decision, when Dred Scott was found to lack citizenship because he lacked rights, and to lack rights because he lacked citizenship. But this very zone of indetermination and ambiguity could be used, as Douglass used the three-fifths clause, in a double-edged fashion. Whereas the antebellum rhetorical deployment of "citizen" as including within the category of "American citizen" all persons naturally born on U.S. soil, black abolitionists like Walker and Douglass pointed to the inverse implication: the notion that being a naturally born person included within itself a concept of "citizenship" that could not be bound by any particular nation.[64]

This black conception of a world citizenship is visible in the full title of David Walker's *Appeal, in Four Articles; Together with a Preamble, to the Coloured Citizens of the World, but in Particular, and Very Expressly, to Those of the United States of America, Written in Boston, State of Massachusetts, September 28, 1829*. Walker's preamble opens with a greeting to "my dearly beloved Brethren and Fellow Citizens," and the ensuing document repeatedly returns to variations of these appeals to brothers, citizens, and fellow men. His language is deeply gendered, and for the most part directed at the present situation in "these United States." So he is an unlikely champion, perhaps, for a feminist cosmopolitanism. And yet Walker's insistence that his appeal be heard—or overheard—by the "coloured citizens of the world" at least potentially expands beyond the frame of national manhood, insofar as it strikes at the biopolitical root of the concept of the "natural-born citizen." In addition to those it hails particularly and expressly, it also invites an indeterminate broader group, spatially and, I would also suggest, temporally distanced. This again is the realm of the perlocutionary, and Walker is a wonderfully insightful guide to its affective potentiality.

Much as Jackson urged contemporary Americans to reread the Constitution for its blemishes and imperfections, to reactivate its dead letters in unexpected and subversive acts of antiphonal citizenship, Walker guided his readers through the biopolitical thicket of revolution-era racial thought (such as Thomas Jefferson's *Notes on the State of Virginia*). Delving into this racial and national archive, Walker produces neither a progressive account of gradual triumph over a benighted past, nor an idealized national point of origin. History for Walker is not a natural force; it is a naturalized one that needs to be denaturalized, a set of racial and national habits that must be dehabituated. His *Appeal* is itself a scriptive thing for undoing white racial innocence, an archival remain that persists long after its author's premature disappearance, long after the political conditions he responded to have passed, its rhetorical fire undiminished in its fierce opposition to complacent identity.[65] In contrast to Douglass's later defense of antislavery constitutionalism, Walker repeatedly highlights the dehumanizing acts and attitudes of American slaveholders, cruelties he asserts can be found in no prior "page of history, either sacred or profane."[66] Walker's *Appeal* may well belong to the tradition of a specifically American jeremiad, but it also contributes to a negative cosmopolitanism that sets up black collective memory as a counterapparatus to sovereign subjectification. As an archival performative, it reminds us the power of the past to give not so much pleasure or pain as a kind of pure passion, one that reckons fearlessly with the masks and ruses of history.

NOTES

1. Danny Yadron, "House Reads Constitution, Gets Civics Lesson," *Washington Wire* (blog), *Wall Street Journal*, January 6, 2011, http://blogs.wsj.com/washwire/2011/01/06/house-reads-constitution-gets-civics-lesson/.

2. J. L. Austin, *How to Do Things with Words*, 2nd. ed. (Cambridge, MA: Harvard University Press, 1975), 22.

3. Ibid., 94–108.

4. Eve Kosofsky Sedgwick, *Epistemology of the Closet* (Berkeley and Los Angeles: University of California Press, 2008), 149.

5. Eve Kosofsky Sedgwick, *Touching Feeling: Affect, Pedagogy, Performativity* (Durham, NC: Duke University Press, 2003), 74–75.

6. Ibid., 75.

7. I further discuss the direct/vicarious binarism as Sedgwick excavates it in *Epistemology of the Closet*, below.

8. Michel Foucault, *The History of Sexuality*, vol. 1, An Introduction (New York: Vintage, 1990). On queer temporality, see Elizabeth Freeman, *Time Binds: Queer Temporalities, Queer Histories* (Durham, NC: Duke University Press, 2010); Heather Love, *Feeling Backward: Loss and the Politics of Queer History* (Cambridge, MA: Harvard University Press, 2007); Judith Halberstam, *In a Queer Time and Place: Transgender Bodies, Subcultural Lives* (New York: New York University Press, 2005). On performance and political surrogation, see Joseph Roach, *Cities of the Dead: Circum-Atlantic Performance* (New York: Columbia University Press, 1996).

   As I hope to detail in what follows, queer theory and performance studies have similarly come to valorize a subjective and open-ended relation to time and temporality, which is often aligned against a normative, chronological time associated with heterosexuality, capitalism, and the state. In some ways this valorization bears comparison to Foucault's proposal to displace psychoanalytic accounts of desire— with their Oedipal teleologies—with more experimental, subjective and collectivist uses of pleasure. While I am clearly writing from within this theoretical horizon, I am querying our relative inattention to the politically ambidextrous uses of pleasure, surrogation, and free-wheeling time. This ambidexterity is more than an unfortunate empirical observation; it seems to me to require a robust accounting of what we feel entitled to hope for on behalf of the pleasurable uses of time.

9. Rebecca Schneider, *Performing Remains: Art and War in Times of Theatrical Reenactment* (New York: Routledge, 2011); Jill Lepore, *The Whites of Their Eyes: The Tea Party's Revolution and the Battle over American History* (Princeton, NJ: Princeton University Press, 2010).

10. Ian Baucom, *Specters of the Atlantic: Finance Capital, Slavery, and the Philosophy of History* (Durham, NC: Duke University Press, 2005), 24.

11. Alice Moore Dunbar-Nelson, *Masterpieces of Negro Eloquence* (New York: Bookery Publishing, 1914), 43.

12. On the national Thing, see Rinaldo Walcott, "Beyond the 'Nation Thing': Black Studies, Cultural Studies, and Diaspora Discourse (or the Post-Black Studies Moment)," in *Decolonizing the Academy: African Diaspora Studies*, ed. Carole Boyce Davies et al. (New York: African World Press, 2003), 107–24. On the dispossessive force of blackness, see Fred Moten, *In the Break: The Aesthetics of the Black Radical Tradition* (Minneapolis: University of Minnesota Press, 2003).

13. Saxton follows Pierre van den Berghe in this usage. See Alexander Saxton, *The Rise and Fall of the White Republic: Class Politics and Mass Culture in Nineteenth-century America* (London: Verso, 1990), 16.

14. This argument of course extends into the late nineteenth century and twentieth century as well, as right-wing activists fiercely object to a series of purportedly unconstitutional extensions of labor rights, welfare rights, occupational health and safety regulations, the minimum wage, and so on. "It has evolved to the point," a progressive critic of the Tea Party has been quoted in the *New York Times*, "where it seems many in the Tea Party believe the entire 20th century is unconstitutional." Kate Zernike, "Constitution Has Its Day Amid a Struggle for Its Spirit," *New York Times*, September 16, 2011, http://www.nytimes.com/2011/09/17/us/constitution-has-its-day-amid-a-struggle-for-its-spirit.html.

15. Right-wing opposition to Progressive-era legislation and constitutional amendments—in particular the Sixteenth Amendment (ratified 1913) granting Congress the right to collect an income tax—in some ways repeats these acts of reverse-historiography. Insofar as women's suffrage (Nineteenth Amendment, ratified 1920) is among the accomplishments of this era, hostility to Progressivism is at least an oblique hostility to, if not the present-day reality of women's full citizenship, then to the set of historical forces that made that citizenship actual (above all, the self-organization and activism of American women).

16. I have reversed the order in the quoted text, but his larger point stands. Michel Foucault, *Power/Knowledge: Selected Interviews & Other Writings 1972–1977*, ed. Colin Gordon (New York: Pantheon, 1980), 194.

17. On the ongoing salience of the political culture of abolitionism for a contemporary politics of human rights, see chapter 2 of *Paul Gilroy, Darker Than Blue: On the Moral Economies of Black Atlantic Culture* (Cambridge, MA: Harvard University Press, 2010).

18. Stanley Cavell, Foreword to Shoshana Felman, *The Scandal of the Speaking Body* (Stanford, CA: Stanford University Press, 2002), xx.

19. Schneider makes much of one quote a reenactor provides her: "Of course we know that *our pain is relative*—none of us really die, and no one is badly hurt, one third of us do not have dystentery, most of us are much older than the average soldier's age, etc., etc., etc." With textbook disavowal, this reenactor immediately proffers all the reasons why, logically, his experience cannot be felt as real while nonetheless asserting a community of those in the know for whom their pain, however relative, is for all that still real. Schneider, *Performing Remains*, 53.

20. Keith Jenkins, *Rethinking History*, 3rd ed. (New York: Routledge, 2003).

21. Schneider, *Performing Remains*, 30.

22. Freeman, *Time Binds*, 3; Sedgwick, *Epistemology of the Closet*.

23. Walter Benjamin, *Walter Benjamin: Selected Writings, 1938–1940*, ed. Howard Eiland and Michael William Jennings, vol. 4 (Cambridge, MA: Harvard University Press, 2003), 395. The quotation in which this well-worn phrase appears is worth citing in full: "The concept of mankind's historical progress cannot be sundered from the concept of its progression through a homogenous, empty time. A critique of the concept of such a progression must underlie any criticism of the concept of progress itself" (394–95).

24. See especially Michael Foucault, "Nietzsche, Genealogy, History," in *The Foucault Reader* (New York: Pantheon, 1984), 76–100.

25. Ibid., 93–94.

26. I thank Dana Luciano for pointing out this connection between historicist pleasures taken and the ancillary pains often produced in others in the process.

27. Robin Bernstein, *Racial Innocence: Performing American Childhood and Race from Slavery to Civil Rights* (New York: New York University Press, 2011).

28. On the performativity of the nonhuman world, see Karen Barad, "Posthumanist Performativity: Toward and Understanding of How Matter Comes to Matter," *Signs* 28, no. 3 (2003): 801–31.

29. Foucault, *The Foucault Reader*, 83.

30. And it is not simply the gullible historical enthusiast who gets trapped in this dualistic tangle. At seemingly another level of sophistication entirely, performance artists establishing a reportorial canon of masterpieces avow their connection to almost any art form other than theater, for fear of relinquishing the direct appearance, within their exhibitions, of a body denuded of artifice or impersonation.

31. Schneider, *Performing Remains*, 54.

32. Bernstein, *Racial Innocence*, 80–81.

33. Schneider, *Performing Remains*, 32.

34. Through the psychoanalytic category of disavowal, we can extend the insights Bernstein restricts to the culture of childhood to broader patterns of white supremacist culture, as indeed she suggests when she points to the broad legal and cultural impact of "doll tests" in the era of desegregation.

35. Jay Fliegelman, *Declaring Independence: Jefferson, Natural Language and the Culture of Performance* (Stanford, CA: Stanford University Press, 1993).

36. Steven Calabresi, *Originalism: A Quarter-Century of Debate* (Washington, DC: Regnery, 2007).

37. See chapter 2 of Bernstein, *Racial Innocence*.

38. I am indebted to conversations with Karen Shimakawa for my understanding of how legal scholarship operates to identify and cite "good law."

39. Lepore, *The Whites of Their Eyes*, 15.

40. Ibid., 8.

41. They did not follow through on this idea, although, as Lepore notes, a variety of political groups and causes have thrown items into the harbor over the decades, in the spirit of '73. Ibid., 84.

42. David Strauss, *The Living Constitution* (Oxford: Oxford University Press, 2010).

43. Scott Malcomson, *One Drop of Blood: The American Misadventure of Race* (New York: Farrar Straus and Giroux, 2000).

44. Bernstein, *Racial Innocence*, 19.

45. Stephen E. Atkins, *Encyclopedia of Right-Wing Extremism in Modern American History* (Santa Barbara, CA: ABC-CLIO, 2011), 179.

46. Charles Mills, *The Racial Contract* (Ithaca, NY: Cornell University Press, 1997).

47. Theodor Adorno, *Minima Moralia: Reflections from Damaged Life*, trans. E. F. N. Jephcott (London and New York: Verso, 2006), 49.

48. "'Birther' Interrupts Reading of Constitution in Congress," Associated Press, January 6, 2011, http://www.thegrio.com/politics/birther-interrupts-congress-constitution-reading.php.

49. Yadron, "House Reads Constitution, Gets Civics Lesson."

50. Jennifer Steinhauer, "Congress Members Read Constitution Aloud," *New York Times*, January 6, 2011, http://www.nytimes.com/2011/01/07/us/politics/07constitution.html.

51. Even the legacy of the U.S.-Mexican War is obliquely registered in reference to those "accented" representatives whose districts did not exist in 1787, as if the process by which those districts were established had been motivated by a multicultural impulse to diversify political representation beyond the white male propertied framers.

52. Yadron, "House Reads Constitution, Gets Civics Lesson."

53. Chris Good, "Should Congress Have Read the Whole Constitution? Jesse Jackson, Jr. Makes the Case," *Atlantic*, January 6, 2011, http://www.theatlantic.com/politics/archive/2011/01/should-congress-have-read-the-whole-constitution-jesse-jackson-jr-makes-the-case/68983/.

54. See John Stauffer, *The Black Hearts of Men: Radical Abolitionists and the Transformation of Race* (Cambridge, MA: Harvard University Press, 2004), 23 and passim.

55. James A. Colaiaco, *Frederick Douglass and the Fourth of July* (New York: Palgrave Macmillan, 2006), 175; William S. McFeely, *Frederick Douglass* (New York: W. W. Norton, 1995), 205–7.

56. Cavell, Foreword to Felman, *The Scandal of the Speaking Body*, xx.

57. Giorgio Agamben, *Profanations* (New York: Zone Books, 2007).

58. Giorgio Agamben, *Homo Sacer: Sovereign Power and Bare Life* (Stanford, CA: Stanford University Press, 1998).

59. Giorgio Agamben, *What Is an Apparatus? and Other Essays*, trans. David Kishik and Stefan Pedatella (Stanford, CA: Stanford University Press, 2009), 11.

60. Antonio Negri, *Time for Revolution* (New York and London: Continuum, 2003).

61. On profanation as counterapparatus, see Agamben, *What Is an Apparatus?*, 19.

62. Judith Butler, *Gender Trouble: Feminism and the Subversion of Identity* (New York: Routledge, 1990).

63. Jacobus tenBroek, *The Antislavery Origins of the Fourteenth Amendment.* (Berkeley: University of California Press, 1951), 72–73.

64. Here would be another difference with Garrisonians who, in rejecting a constitutional route to abolition, placed little importance in the rights of the citizen, as opposed to the rights of the human.

65. The very typography of his *Appeal* reflects its status as a performative, scriptive thing. See Marcy J. Dinius, "'Look!! Look!!! at This!!!!': The Radical Typography of David Walker's Appeal," *PMLA* 126, no. 1 (January 2011): 55–72.

66. Davis Walker, "Walker's Appeal, in Four Articles; Together with a Preamble, to the Coloured Citizens of the World, but in Particular, and Very Expressly, to Those of the United States of America, Written in Boston, State of Massachusetts, September 28, 1829": 12, *Documenting the American South*, http://docsouth.unc.edu/nc/walker/menu.html.

4

Doing Justice to the Archive

Beyond Literature

SHELLEY STREEBY

In 1913, Lucy Parsons, whose career as a radical writer, speaker, editor, and publisher spanned the labor wars of the long-19th-century and early-20th-century world wars and revolutions, was arrested on the streets of Los Angeles and charged with selling literature without a license. The literature in question was *The Famous Speeches of the Eight Chicago Anarchists in Court*, according to William C. Owen, the editor of the English page of *Regeneración*, a bilingual newspaper published by Mexican revolutionaries living in exile in Los Angeles. Parsons, a black, Indian, and Mexican woman who was probably born a slave in Texas, became a leader of the Chicago anarchist movement in the 1880s along with her husband, Albert Parsons, a former Confederate solder turned Radical Republican who was threatened with lynching after the Civil War when he tried to register black voters in Texas, where he met Lucy. In 1887 Albert was infamously executed, along with four others, for the murder of a police officer, who was killed by the blast of a bomb of unknown origin in Chicago's Haymarket Square. In the years that followed, Lucy Parsons compiled and self-published several editions of a slim volume of the Haymarket anarchists' speeches in court. On the 20th anniversary of the event, however, as she issued a new memorial edition, she worried in the preface that the anarchists' words "remained in the archives of history, almost forgotten."

Was this slim volume of speeches literature? According to the LAPD and the law, it was, though it was punitively demarcated as a kind of outlaw literature. In this context and according to these definitions, the *Famous Speeches* are what Jacques Derrida calls literature as "public writing": that which is published.[1] If, in its broader significance literature is, for Derrida, following Hélène Cixous, "Omnipotence-Other," the "undecidable writing for which as yet no complete formalization exists" (15), then *Famous Speeches* also counts as literature within this frame. But Derrida also wonders about the problem of drawing the line between "literature and the others," between literature and "non-literature, between the material and the form, private and public, secret and not-secret, the decipherable and the undecipherable, decidable and undecidable" (24). It is precisely the investment in drawing the line of literary value that distinguishes these more expansive definitions of literature from the narrower ones demarcated by the literary apparatus of the time and our time—by the institutions, periodicals, syllabi, publishing houses, marketing categories, prizes, and so forth that shape and alter the meanings of literature at particular moments. In the 1910s, *Famous Speeches* was not valued by the literary institutions of the day and would not have been taught as literature in schools, which raises questions about how the category of the literary is constructed in relation to state power and ideas about policing more broadly. It might have been considered "propaganda," though that word did not have the negative connotations it has now during the early-20th-century period of its emergence.[2] Today, the *Famous Speeches* would still be an unusual choice in an English or literature class, though a more capacious definition of the literary might include it within the category of notable speeches or crime literature. More likely, however, it would be viewed as belonging, like history, with those "others" of literature—those texts that the literary apparatus cannot or decides not to value within the category of literature.

But we might also ask: what is history and what is an archive? When Lucy Parsons worried that the *Famous Speeches* remained in the archives of history, almost forgotten, what kind of archives and history did she mean? Was she referring to the archives of the state, which classified the Haymarket anarchists as murderous criminals? Was her labor as a publisher part of an effort to push the men's words from the state's juridical and punitive archive into another kind of archive where what happened might be remembered differently and where the past might cross back over into the present and the future rather than remaining safely encased in its containers? Should we call this archive "literature," even though the gate-keeping guardians of the aesthetic, whose predictable jeremiads intermittently warn that only they are capable of analyzing form, have rarely included it within that category? What forms might these archives take other than literature? Are they part of history, that strange space where Parsons imagines memories are stored away and "almost forgotten"?

For Parsons, the space of history is both danger and consolation, for if the radical past is almost forgotten there in the archives, it is also retained for a future when another movement might reanimate its meanings for the present. Perhaps this dialectical view of the archives of history was shaped by her own losses over the years when police and detectives raided the offices of newspapers she wrote for and groups she organized, often disappearing or destroying what they seized. In a final blow to the archives of radical memory, after Parsons died in 1942 in a Chicago house fire, police seized her papers as well as the library of more than 1,500 books and newspapers that she had collected over her long lifetime; because of earlier raids, it was already only a remnant of a once much larger whole. The role of state and corporate power in all this archival destruction and preservation, as well as their investments in defining history, should not go unnoticed. While with Ann Laura Stoler we may wish to avoid fetishizing the "finite boundaries of the official state archives" in order to explore "their surplus production, what defines their interior ridges and porous seams, what closures are transgressed by unanticipated exposition and writerly forms," we must also acknowledge the limits and regulatory frames that official archives impose upon the subjects of history.[3]

But what is history, anyway? Like literature, it has multiple meanings. Within literary studies, history is sometimes viewed as the bad other, a realm of facticity that literature transcends, or a discipline that privileges other kinds of evidence, thereby marginalizing literature or deeming it suspect and insufficient. And yet, if we consider history as an apparatus, it is also, like literature, a heterogeneous ensemble of institutions, texts, syllabi, and so forth, many versions of which now both draw on literary and cultural texts and question the linear, progressive historicisms famously critiqued by Walter Benjamin and the subaltern studies historiographers, among others. Indeed, the disciplines of English/literature and history have shared this tendency to regulate and exclude and to establish privileged canons of value that shore up progressive, linear, national, and nationalist histories.

This is one of the historical limits of disciplinary thinking, and one of many reasons it is important, especially at this moment of danger when formations with closer relationships to social movements, such as ethnic studies and women's/gender studies, are under attack in the neoliberal university, to foster robustly interdisciplinary methods and formations. While the incorporation of the demands of social movements into universities has been a complex and contradictory process, the last decade of shock-doctrine downsizing of higher education has altered the terrain of struggle and we are now in a different moment than the late 1990s/early 2000s, when the incorporation of difference appeared to be the main problem confronting scholars and teachers committed to social justice. Although traditional humanities disciplines are also under attack, interdisciplinary formations, especially those that challenge the neoliberal university's ways of doing academic business, are now often most vulnerable to cuts and elimination. Thus, despite the limits of the repressive hypothesis, there is indeed some repression going on as neoliberal cuts, downsizing, and the violent police response to student movements throughout the University of California, for example, have clarified in the last few years. While as Rod Ferguson suggests it is imperative to attend to and bring to crisis the "networks of power that align minority difference with institutional dominance," a "reinvigorated interdisciplinary life" is also necessary to "disrupt dominant forms of institutionality" and interrupt the detachment and withdrawal of higher education from movements pressing for change.[4]

For disciplinary ways of seeing and institutional hierarchies of knowledge production and management of difference may encircle objects of memory in ways that isolate them from social conflicts, movements, and struggles and thereby both diminish our understanding of them and radically shrink the boundaries of the "we" who participate in defining and shaping the contradictory project of higher education.

How does the scholar in the archive decide where literature begins and ends? What effects does the encircling of the literary in the archive have, if the scholar desires to encircle it and if it even can be encircled? How are its boundaries drawn and what gets cut off and detached in the process? And how might different kinds of archives challenge the boundaries of the apparatuses of English/literature and history?

Each of the excellent essays in the "Archives Unbound" section begins with a problem in the present that is connected to the racial past and future of the United States, thereby refusing the static historicisms and linear, progressive temporality that organize many discipline-bound literary and empiricist histories. Each also raises questions about what counts as history, as literature, and as an archive. Lloyd Pratt analyzes a recent novel, Edward P. Jones's *The Known World*, in order to explore the solutions African American writers have imagined to the problem of representing historical traumas such as the Middle Passage and slavery. Instead of "[subordinating] the spread of detail inherent to the archive into a coherent linear narrative of cause, effect, and transformation," Pratt writes, African American writers often turned to other representational modes, such as the historical romance, to "write a history of totality in a world of partial vision." Rodrigo Lazo, on the other hand, focuses on scholars of "Hispanic/Latino literature" who hope to document the "often-overlooked participation of Hispanics in U.S. historical events," but end up finding "unexpected discoveries" and "uncomfortable histories" in the "capacious and messy Hispanic archive," such as evidence of Hispanic "Confederates in the Attic." Although Latina/o scholars may wish to "posit continuity from people in the past to the present," Lazo warns that such linear continuities are "likely to clash against some of the material that is ultimately gathered within the archive," and disturb the formation of Latina/o studies as a field that "has gained momentum in the last thirty years from the work of scholars who sought to challenge exclusion and white supremacy in U.S. society." Finally, Tavia Nyong'o speculates on the 2011 reading aloud of the U.S. Constitution on the floor of the House of Representatives in hopes that performance studies' "attunement to the present and subjective encounter with the past" may foreground "what history takes pride in delegating to other disciplines." Swerving around in time, Nyong'o reads David Walker's 1829 *Appeal* in relation to debates over the expurgation of the three-fifths clause and readings of the 13th and 14th amendments in order to expose an "abolitionist legacy" of the "profanation" of citizenship as a critique of constitutionalism. All three essays take issue with the writing of history as a linear narrative of national progress and all three turn to other kinds of archives, representational modes, and temporalities to reimagine the relations among past, present, and future.

In thinking critically about history making as a cultural activity of the present, however, Nyong'o suggests that simply mixing up different times is not enough, since lingering in the past can align with conservative historicism rather than historical materialism. In the case of many reenactors of the Civil War and the Tea Party, such time bending may rather serve as a "bastion of white male identity politics," promoting the idealization of a historical period prior to black citizenship and foreclosing "a reckoning with the black radical strivings that are immanent to but never fully contained by the nation's story." Calling for a 19th-century studies interested "less in the question of how time passes, and more in the question of how time accumulates—in and as forms of (racial and national) property," Nyong'o appeals to the "dispossessive force" of a radical black countermemory that he finds in Walker's *Appeal* and the performance of the Constitution. Pratt also explores how what he calls the "black intellectual and expressive traditions" of "African diasporic culture" challenge the ordering of time in dominant history-writing, especially in an emergent liberal historiography. But rather than giving up on the ideal of imagining historical totality, Pratt argues, African American writers were on the contrary more adept at "producing an anti-reifying and totalizing historicization such as Lukács describes in *History and Class Consciousness.*" Asking questions about how time accumulates and imagining a historical totality, then, remain relevant and urgent for Nyong'o and Pratt as they were for the writers and cultural producers they discuss in their essays.

If for Nyong'o and Pratt other archives of the black diaspora and other modes of representation such as Walker's *Appeal*, the performance of the Constitution, and African American history writing and historical romances enable a fuller, more critical reckoning with U.S. history and the accumulation of time as racialized national property, however, Lazo emphasizes how archives may resist the stories the scholar wants to tell. When Latina/o studies scholars are confronted in the archive with discoveries they did not expect to make, for instance, such as the existence of Hispanic Confederates, their findings may call into crisis, Lazo suggests, the "hopeful recuperation" of an elided Hispanic past that is the "hallmark of Latino studies" and that "drives research agendas." Lazo understands the "archive" both as "a repository of documents" and as "an analogy for the collection of information that sustains an academic field" and an "identity." He defines the "mega-Hispanic archive" as the domain where "popular representation and media circulation meet academic research: an accumulation of information, discourses, and texts that motivate a problem of subjectivity." He also isolates a second meaning of "Hispanic archive": "the accumulation of knowledge as a result of fields of study that emerge from the ethnic labels Hispanic/Latino, in other words the scholarly collection of texts that make up the historical record," including the Recovering the U.S. Hispanic Literary Heritage Project as well as "various scholarly and critical projects that contribute to the Hispanic archive.'" Ultimately Lazo urges scholars to attend to the "contradictions that emerge" when archives clash with their frames of study and archival concepts (e.g., the nation), which are animated by the intricate nexus of desire and investment that draws the scholar to the archive in the first place.

Here Lazo joins other scholars such as Kirsten Silva Gruesz in confronting what she calls the "vexed question at the heart of the endeavor of Latino studies: what are the outer limits of Latino identity?"[5] Lazo privileges the terms "Hispanic" and "Latino" even as he notes that they are sometimes used "interchangeably" (thereby generating "contradictions") and distinguishes "Latino" as "a contemporary term linked to university-based programs and post–Civil Rights social movements" from "Hispanic" as "an ethnic label for people of Spanish and Latin American descent." Calling the field that has emerged in the last 30 years Hispanic/Latino studies, however, elides some of the other names that have contributed to this project, such as Chicana/o studies, Puerto Rican and Nuyorican studies, Cuban American studies, and Dominican American studies:[6] in other words, the study of the "Latino subgroups," which map onto different spaces and nations of origin and which was the dominant way what today often goes by the name of Latina/o studies began to be institutionalized in the "later years of the Civil Rights movement" in response "to minoritarian political pressures," as Gruesz helpfully reminds us. During this period of war, decolonization, and racial unrest, educational activists and social movements pressed for changes in school curricula, which often happened at the local or state level in response to specific struggles, such as California State University, Los Angeles's founding of the first Chicano studies department in 1968 in the wake of the L.A. Blowouts, when students walked out of L.A. high schools to express their dissatisfaction with the education system.[7] It is also worth noting that the formations aligning with what we now call Latina/o studies were interdisciplinary in their origins; the titles of early journals, such as *El Grito: A Journal of Contemporary Mexican American Thought* (UC Berkeley) and *Aztlan: A Chicano Journal of the Social Sciences and the Arts* (UCLA), are revealing in this regard.

In the late 1980s and 1990s, traditional disciplines such as English and history were slowly affected by these changes, as Latina/o texts sometimes appeared on syllabi in the wake of the archival and revisionary work of a generation of scholars, including Rosaura Sánchez and Beatrice Pita, who "recovered" the novels and letters of María Amparo Ruiz de Burton that Lazo discusses at length in his essay. During the same years, partly in response to demographic shifts, marketing appeals, and official categories, "Latino" began to organize fields of study, a shift marked by the proliferation of projects in the late 1990s under that name. Many scholars who now, like Lazo and Gruesz, prefer the umbrella term "Latino," despite what she calls its "suspect legacy as a term of governmental power," seek "the still invisible linkages among different populations" and points of intersection and comparison rather than emphasizing the distinct particularity of "the different remnants" of Spain's empire (118). Many also criticize the limits of the ethnic nationalisms of the 1960s and 1970s as articulated by the Chicano Movement and other movements out of which the push to institutionalize what is now Latina/o studies initially emerged. They emphasize a multiplicity of experiences instead of looking for what some characterize as a reductive counter-narrative of resistance that they argue has dominated past scholarly discussions. More and more, these scholars work in history, English, and literature departments as well as in Spanish departments and interdisciplinary formations such as Latina/o studies, Chicana/o studies, ethnic studies, American studies, and so forth.

Even as "Latino studies" moves into traditional disciplines, however, what we might call the Latina/o literary archive pressures narrow definitions of literature, as Lazo recognizes when he observes that some of the evidence in the Latina/o literary archive, such as Ambrosio Gonzales's pamphlet *Manifesto on Cuban Affairs* (1853), "would not be classified as Literature by aesthetic archivists." This problem is a familiar one for many Latina/o studies scholars, who have grown accustomed to doing the hard work of archival retrieval and then also having to educate colleagues with narrow understandings of aesthetics about the particular significance of form, genre, and language in the Latina/o archive. At the same time, many remain committed, like the earlier generation, to doing such archival work: Gruesz argues that this labor is necessary to counter the "foreshortening of the Latino past" (130) and "the denial of coevalness in past time" (132), which assume "all Latinos are 'recent arrivals' in the United States" and thereby deny them "the common occupation of past time with other U.S. Americans" (121). This helps to explain why what Lazo calls a "critical archive" quickly formed around the work of Ruiz de Burton when her novels were republished in the 1990s. As Lazo remembers, scholars "in the field of Latino studies as well as those more generally interested in American literature published a variety of articles, and she became a keystone in the Recovering the U.S. Hispanic Literary Heritage Project."

Even though Ruiz de Burton wrote novels in English that have been reissued in readily available modern editions, however, her status in relation to the 19th-century U.S. literary field remains relatively tenuous compared to Nathaniel Hawthorne or Henry James, which is why Lazo calls her, along with José Martí, "the only other Hispanic writer who has approached canonical status in nineteenth-century U.S. literary studies." Lazo's refusal to situate Ruiz de Burton squarely within the realm of the canonical registers ongoing struggles over the boundaries of the canon and the significance of diverse aesthetics for U.S. literary history.

Nonetheless, these novels helped make a place for Latina/o studies in 19th-century American literary studies and many scholars of Latina/o literature have written about them. Many of this generation of Latina/o literary scholars, like José Aranda, cited by both Lazo and Gruesz, focus on how Ruiz de Burton embodies the contradictions in what Lazo calls "the Hispanic archive." Pita and Sánchez initially claimed Ruiz de Burton "as part of a Hispanic past," according to Lazo, by emphasizing her dispossession as a "Latina," "a Catholic," a "Spanish speaker," and an "outsider in Yankee territory." But the "contours of Ruiz de Burton's life soon raised complications" and Lazo suggests critics such as Aranda "called our attention to the problems of heritage by questioning the critical investment in framing an upper-class light-skinned woman as a writer of resistance to white hegemony." In this scholarly genealogy, the new generation corrects the mistakes of the past: this logic suggests that while Pita and Sánchez did not probe these "problems of heritage" and framed Ruiz de Burton, despite her upper-class status and light skin, as a "writer of resistance to white hegemony," 21st-century Latina/o literary scholars can now read the novels more critically, as examples of how "Hispanic literary history's claim to a counter-narrative can stumble across its own troublesome past."

I wonder, though, whether this rather linear genealogy of "Hispanic literary history" depends upon authorizing Latina/o literary studies as a distinctive endeavor and encircling the literary in ways that detach the novels from other fields, texts, and contexts that give them meaning. Even back in 1995, three years before Aranda's *American Literature* essay appeared, in their preface to *Who Would Have Thought It?*, Pita and Sánchez were already calling our attention to how Ruiz de Burton imagined "a construction of upper-class Latinos/as as white, a perhaps defensive—though not defensible—move . . . in view of the fact that Congressional records of the period refer to Mexicans in the southwest as a 'mongrel race.'"[8] Their interest in complexities of class and race becomes even more apparent when we move from the novel prefaces to their wider body of writing and scholarship, especially Sánchez's *Telling Identities: The Californio Testimonios* (1995), where she situates Ruiz de Burton in relation to the elite class of Mexican-origin settlers of California who lost most of their land and power in the wake of the U.S.-Mexico War of 1846–1848. Sánchez devotes big chunks of the book

to analyzing the complexities of class and racial formations and constructions of ethnicity as well as the hierarchies and power relations of
settler colonialism, specifically the dispossession of Indians through
force and liberal land laws and their exploitation in the missions, even
as she argues that the Californios themselves were rendered subaltern
in relation to the Anglo invaders after 1848. Sánchez situates Ruiz de
Burton in relation to historically changing, complex vectors of class,
race, and colonialism as she explains how the Californios appealed to
the "construct of *criollismo*" in "an attempt to appear on the same racial
plane with the Yankee invaders, as if national origin and race could be
wielded as a strategic discourse to combat racist representations of the
conquered Californios as half-civilized Indians" (59). *Telling Identities* is not as widely read in literary circles as the prefaces to Ruiz de
Burton's novels, perhaps because its main focus is on the *testimonio*, a
genre in which, as Sánchez puts it, "literary and nonliterary, popular
and elite, historical and fictional discourses overlap and intersect" in
ways that require an "interdisciplinary methodology" (xi) to understand. If we rally around the literary and privilege the novel as a form,
we risk detaching Ruiz de Burton's writing from these other fields, contexts, forms, and histories. Broadening the purview of Latina/o studies beyond the literary narrowly conceived, as many Latina/o studies
scholars have taken the lead in doing, on the other hand, illuminates
diverse genealogies for the field that disrupt linear histories of scholarly
progress and enlightenment and make visible the heterogeneous, often
interdisciplinary work of earlier generations and its affiliations with the
present.

A wide range of cultural forms that push disciplinary boundaries are
also central to what Pratt calls "the black intellectual and expressive traditions" of "African diasporic culture" and what Nyong'o names "black
collective memory." Although Pratt focuses on the writing of history
and especially the historical romance as it "descended from Sir Walter
Scott," he recognizes that literature is only of the forms through which
African Americans have imagined alternative approaches to historical representation. In response to what is missing in the archive, to the
"exclusion of African Americans from the documentary trail of evidence, except as entries in chattel bookkeeping or the emerging scriptive
technologies of the American judicial system," as well as the problem of

representing historical traumas such as slavery and the Middle Passage that resisted representation, what Ernest Hall refers to as "oral, vernacular, and commemorative culture and historical memory" emerged as important forms through which African Americans reenvisioned their past. Pratt emphasizes that African American literature, a significant "archive of past experience rearticulated in the present moment," is also essential to any such list of cultural forms that respond to history. To do so, he critically engages Madhu Dubey's claim that writers of African American speculative fiction "turn away from history" to "more fully" address "the truth of the past" by "way of an antirealist literary imagination that can fluidly cross temporal boundaries and affectively immerse readers into the world of slavery." While Pratt concludes that Dubey ultimately implies that such speculative fictions propose that "the inequities of the past have rendered the past a useless resource," however, I wonder whether instead she suggests that speculative fiction turns away from the past only as it has been reductively imagined in more conventional forms of history writing and thereby rejects not a confrontation with time and history as such but rather the limits of linear, progressive narratives of liberal historiography.

But although Pratt focuses on how Jones's *The Known World* embraces the idea of a "totalizing history" in contrast to what he sees as black speculative fiction's turning away from the past and history, he also emphasizes how Jones's novel acknowledges and values connections between different forms of expressive culture through its focus on "Alice's creations," which are central to the novel's representation of the world. Alice's multimedia maps are a mode of historical representation that the novel incorporates by registering the impossibility of ever fully doing so, in a scene of "ekphrasis" or "the verbal description of visual art forms," as Pratt explains. The novel's insistence on this impossibility suggests not only that the "history writer might in the end find herself required to work in a variety of different representational modes if she is to achieve the goal of a total history," but that the historical romance and canonical literature are, by themselves, inadequate ways of responding to the problems of representing the history of the African diaspora and that other expressive and speculative forms, sometimes with lower and less respectable genealogies, are also necessary.

If Pratt encircles the historical romance in his analysis even as he remarks on the broad range of expressive forms through which African Americans have responded to gaps in the archives and the trauma of history, Nyong'o foregrounds his interdisciplinary method in reading the U.S. Constitution as political theater in relation to what we now call an important work of early African American literature, Walker's *Appeal*. Walker is a late addition to U.S. literary anthologies partly because African American literature has only relatively recently been accorded value by the literary apparatus. And although the pamphlet and the appeal, like the Constitution, count as literature within early republican definitions of the literary, these texts have more often been consigned to history by a discipline that privileges novels, short stories, and poetry. Nyong'o's interdisciplinary method, on the other hand, is sparked by insights from feminist social and cultural history, political theory, social movement scholarship, and especially performance studies. In speculating on how the black radical tradition has imagined alternate modes of historical representation, Nyong'o also uses tools from U.S. literary studies, analyzing Walker's *Appeal* as a jeremiad with a difference, whose meaning is determined not only by that classic American literary form, but also by other texts and contexts beyond its boundaries, which together articulate "a negative cosmopolitanism that sets up black collective memory as a counter-apparatus to sovereign subjectification." That is, if the jeremiad form always brings U.S. Americans back to the sovereignty of sacred nation-time and the citizen/alien binarism after a ritualized recognition of a problem or declension in the present,[9] Walker's *Appeal* opens up onto a broader and more heterogeneous black radical tradition that both draws on and transmits an abolitionist legacy of profaning citizenship as it voices "strivings that are immanent to but never fully contained by the nation's story."

Although Nyong'o warns that we cannot simply privilege the repertoire and embodied forms of knowing over texts and the archive, he concludes that a "performance genealogy" is necessary to restore the full ambiguity of this evocation of the black world as a counter-apparatus to the sovereign subjectification of sacred nation-time. These evocations come in many different forms, including literature, although we may miss their manifold ambiguities, associations, connections, meanings, and larger significance if we discipline the archive by encircling the literary. For it takes an interdisciplinary methodology to begin to do justice to what Nyong'o calls the "dispossessive force" of a radical black countermemory, and perhaps, also, to 19th-century American literature, whatever that may be.

NOTES

1. Jacques Derrida, *Geneses, Genealogies, Genres, and Genius: The Secrets of the Archive*, trans. Beverley Bie Brahic (New York: Columbia University Press, 2003), 23. Hereafter cited in text. In "The Future of the Profession," Derrida also connects literature to public space and "the right to say everything publicly, or to keep it secret, if only in the form of fiction." Quoted in McQuillan, "Foreword: 'What is Called Literature,'" *Geneses*, vii.

2. For more on how literature was imagined in relation to transnational anarchist cultures and state power during this period, see Streeby, *Radical Sensations: World Movements, Violence, and Visual Culture* (Durham: Duke University Press, 2013). Chapter 2 situates Parsons in relation to Mexican anarchists who were imprisoned in the U.S. after they were judged guilty of obscenity for the content of their newspaper, *Regeneración*.

3. Ann Laura Stoler, *Along the Archival Grain: Epistemic Anxieties and Colonial Common Sense* (Princeton: Princeton University Press, 2009), 14.

4. Roderick A. Ferguson, *The Reorder of Things: The University and its Pedagogies of Minority Difference* (Minneapolis: University of Minnesota Press, 2012), 231, 230.

5. Kirsten Silva Gruesz, "The Once and Future Latino: Notes Toward a Literary History Todavía Para Llegar," *Contemporary U.S. Latino/a Literary Criticism*, ed. Lyn Sandin and Richard Perez (New York: Palgrave Macmillan, 2007), 116. Hereafter cited in text.

6. The term "Latina/o Studies" can also elide the related yet distinct trajectories of an emergent Central American studies, and the complicated significance of blackness and indigeneity that cuts across such fields.

7. See Melissa Hidalgo, "Schooling La Raza: A Chicana/o Cultural History of Education, 1968-2008," Ph.D. dissertation, University of California, San Diego, 2011.

8. Beatrice Pita and Rosaura Sánchez, "Introduction" to María Amparo Ruiz de Burton, *Who Would Have Thought It?* (Houston: Arte Publico Press, 1995), xx.

9. Sacvan Bercovitch, *The American Jeremiad* (Madison: University of Wisconsin Press, 1978).

PART II

States of Exception

5

Unsettled Life

Early Liberia's Epistolary Equivocations

DAVID KAZANJIAN

Your letter bears to us the very information we have for years longed to recieve, telling us in detail the history and fate of most all White and Collored that was dear to us, and that we had left behind us, the story is a Melloncholy one. and after all leaves us the victory who chose Africa & became seekers of Liberty, so far as the Collored people are Concerned. Sinthia died 1836. Gilbert in 1839. Mother died of dropsey in 1845. George Crawford died suddenly in 1846. I was at that time away off in the interier of Africa preaching to the natives, on the Goulab and Pessa lines. We have suffered in Africa, and suffered greatley. It was so long before we Could find Africa out, how to live in it, and what to do to live, that it all most cost us death seeking life.
Rev. Alfred Russell to Robert Wickliffe, 1855[1]

Nineteenth-century Liberia was an unsettled state on many levels. Between 1821 and 1847, it was a colony over which no state formally exercised sovereignty, having been founded and ruled by a private philanthropic organization from the U.S. called the American Colonization Society (ACS). In 1847, Liberian independence was declared by black American settler-colonists, many of whom had been freed from slavery so that the ACS could deport and settle them on lands that had been appropriated by coercive "fee simple" treaties with, and expropriated at gunpoint from, West Africans. The newly independent black settler-colonists, in turn, promptly disenfranchised those very West

Africans. During its colonial years of forced settlement and conquest, then, Liberia was never formally settled by or as a state; in turn, after its independence Liberia disenfranchised the region's native inhabitants, generating antagonistic ethnic and class distinctions that have echoed throughout the country's twentieth- and twenty-first-century civil conflicts.

Yet those black settlers who came to live in colonial Liberia also lived unsettled *states of being* or *life* that cannot be reduced to the formal, political, and governmental history I just sketched and upon which they reflected in letters written to their former masters, family, and friends in the United States. These unsettled lives can be glimpsed in questions raised by my epigraph, which comes from a letter written in 1855 by a settler-colonist named Rev. Alfred Russell to Robert Wickliffe, the second husband of Russell's former owner, Mary Owen Todd Russell. What kind of "life"—so close to "death" and yet with "Liberty" in its sights—did these emancipated slaves "seek" in "cho[osing] Africa"? What life did Russell and his fellow black American settler-colonists "find out" that was at once a "victory" and a sufferance? How was that life lived, geographically and temporally, both as a "longing" for "information" from the U.S. and as "so long" a time in "the interior of Africa," both as a "Melloncholy story" about what was "left behind" and as a series of deaths of those who left the U.S. for Africa? And what do the lives Russell and his kin came to live tell us about the freedom they sought?

Unfortunately, much contemporary scholarship has foreclosed such questions about Liberia's unsettled lives because it has been organized around two conflicting interpretations of the black settler-colonists: a return-to-Africa interpretation, in which those settler-colonists are represented as freedom-seeking ex-slaves returning to their ancestral homeland; and an anti-imperial interpretation, in which the settler-colonists and their white sponsors are represented as unjustly imposing their will upon innocent West African natives. As opposed as these two interpretations seem, they both displace reflection on Liberia's unsettled lives with histories of settlement by taking for granted the willful autonomy of the settlers and the meaning of the freedom they sought. In the case of the return-to-Africa interpretation, black American settlers are assumed to have settled their own freedom by leaving chattel slavery in the U.S. for national-citizenship in the putative land of their forbearers; in the case of the anti-imperial interpretation, black American colonists and/or their white sponsors are assumed to have settled their own imperial rule by rapaciously wresting land and freedom from West Africans.[2]

In this essay, I would like to complicate these two interpretations by reading the settlers' epistolary archive for reflections on early-to-mid-nineteenth-century Liberia's unsettled lives, and ultimately to offer some answers to the questions Russell's letter raises. In this archive one rarely finds the settler-colonists simply or straightforwardly imagining Africa as their original homeland, or disdaining native West Africans as savages to be killed or converted, or writing of freedom as something to be calculated, owned, accumulated, authorized by a state, developed from capitalist relations of production, earned by the conversion of non-Christians, appropriated for individuals, or expropriated from others. Or perhaps I should say that one does find all of those plans for Liberian freedom in the letters, yet those plans are never simple or straightforward because they are persistently set in apposition to more equivocal and capacious accounts of the effort to live a free life in Liberia with, among, and against native West Africans and in the wake of slavery's ongoing legacies. Consequently, we should read the letters counterpunctually, attending to the ways those familiar plans—which seem to lend themselves either to the return-to-Africa interpretation or to the anti-imperialist interpretation—are continually undone.

To limn this undoing, in what follows I first trace a genealogy of the two predominant interpretations of African colonization to the late-eighteenth-century writings of two influential black diasporans: Phillis Wheatley and Olaudah Equiano. Their respective involvements with the British colony of Sierra Leone proved foundational for the ACS's colonization of Liberia, and at first glance they seem to fall neatly into—and thus to inaugurate—the anti-imperial interpretation (Wheatley) and the return-to-Africa interpretation (Equiano). By looking closely at Wheatley's and Equiano's texts, however, I argue that African colonization was, at its black diasporan foundations, a site of more nuanced and equivocal thought about how to live a free life in the Atlantic world than either interpretation grants. I then turn to the epistolary archive of early

Liberia in order to show how the settlers' reflections on "return" and "the natives" generate a speculative body of thought about living unsettled states of being or life. From this thought we learn that living free in Liberia did not just mean returning to a putative African homeland or conquering and converting native West Africans—although those meanings do circulate in the archive. Alongside those meanings, counterpunctually, freedom in Liberia could also mean ongoing, improvised encounters with the legacies of chattel slavery; fragile and volatile interactions between settler and native; a life on the brink of death, as well as a death haunting life itself; and a future sought skeptically and critically. Consequently, instead of simply documenting the settlers' quest for a settled state of freedom—embodied, for instance, by formal emancipation from slavery, national citizenship, evangelical Christianity, an autonomous will, hard work, violent conquest, or the accumulation of material wealth—this archive also shows how intimately many settlers came to know an unsettled life characterized by a temporality more recursive and open-ended than progressive or teleological, and a territoriality for which "home" remained strange and unbounded.

Toward a Genealogy of African Colonization

On October 30, 1774, the enslaved African American poet Phillis Wheatley critiqued the African colonization movement in a letter to English merchant and philanthropist John Thornton. Thornton had asked her to serve with two black missionaries, Bristol Yamma and John Quamine, in Annamaboe, a slave-trading post in what is now Ghana. Writes Wheatley,

> You propose my returning to Africa with Bristol Yamma and John Quamine; if either of them upon strict enquiry is such, as I dare give my heart and hand to, I believe they are either of them good enough if not too good for me, or they would not be fit for Missionaries; but why do you hon'd sir, wish those poor men so much trouble as to carry me so long a voyage? Upon my arrival, how like a Barbarian shou'd I look to the Natives; I can promise that my tongue shall be quiet for a strong reason indeed being an utter stranger to the language of Anamaboe. Now to be serious, this undertaking appears too hazardous, and not sufficiently

Eligible, to go—and leave my British & American Friends—I am also
unacquainted with those Missionaries in Person.[3]

In this passage, as I have argued in *The Colonizing Trick*, Wheatley
turns the tables on Thornton's imperial presuppositions about Africans: "how like a Barbarian shou'd I look to the Natives."[4] She then
lays claim to Anglo-America—"my British & American Friends"—
while wryly reminding Thornton that she does not happen to know
all black diasporans: "I am also unacquainted with those Missionaries
in Person." Wheatley thus rejects the presumption of racial affiliation
that undergirded much eighteenth-century colonizationist thinking, at
once exposing the imperial aspirations of the Sierra Leone project and
asserting her role in the struggle for freedom in Britain and America.

By apparent contrast, consider the final chapter of *The Interesting Narrative of the Life of Olaudah Equiano*, first published in 1789. Equiano, who
like Wheatley was enslaved as a child, describes his extensive involvement
during the 1780s in the very colonization ventures that Wheatley abjures
in her letter to Thornton. Indeed, Equiano seems much more sanguine
about the entire effort. Claiming the racial and national affiliation with
West Africans that Wheatley questioned, he explains that he agreed to be
"sent out as a missionary to Africa" by the British Sierra Leone Company
"in hope of doing good, if possible, amongst my countrymen."[5] Equiano
then describes his willingness to lobby the British government to support the colonization of Sierra Leone with emancipated slaves: "These are
designs . . . connected with views of empire and dominion, [and] suited
to the benevolence and solid merit of the legislature. . . . As the inhuman
traffic of slavery is now taken into the consideration of the British legislature, I doubt not, if a system of commerce was established in Africa,
the demand for manufactures would most rapidly augment, as the native
inhabitants would insensibly adopt the British fashions, manners, customs, &c. In proportion to the civilization, so will be the consumption of
British manufactures" (233). Equiano's praise for "empire and dominion"
over "insensible" natives makes him seem like an imperial agent of capital penetration and Christian conversion who justifies his intervention by
representing himself both as British and as African.

However, upon closer consideration Wheatley and Equiano do not
fit so neatly into these interpretations. Consider a letter Wheatley wrote

to the white colonizationist Samuel Hopkins on May 6, 1774, shortly before her letter to Thornton:

> I am very sorry to hear, that Philip Quaque has very little or no apparent Success in his mission. Yet, I wish that what you hear respecting him may be only a misrepresentation. Let us not be discouraged, but still hope, that God will bring about his great work, tho' Philip may not be the instrument in the Divine Hand, to perform this work of wonder, turning the African "from darkness to light." Possibly, if Philip would introduce himself properly to them, (I don't know the reverse) he might be more Successful, and in setting a good example which is more powerfully winning than Instruction.[6]

As in her letter to Thornton, Wheatley casts doubt on the African colonizationists' presumption of racial affiliation between black diasporans and Africans by foregrounding the difficulty of communication. Unlike her letter to Thornton, however, here Wheatley also holds out the possibility of a certain communication between West Africans and African diasporans, a communication across the Atlantic divide. This possible communication is asymmetrical, to be sure, but not unidirectional, and thus not simply imperial. Quaque is called upon to "introduce himself properly" and "set . . . a good example," but by distinguishing courteous exemplarity, couched in the conditional with the modal verbs "would" and "might," from the pedantic noun "instruction," Wheatley leaves open the possibility of unscripted encounters. In turn, "the African" is silent not because he or she has nothing to say, but rather because Wheatley recognizes that she does not know what "the African" might say: "I don't know the reverse." African colonization here seems less the straightforward imposition of a Euro-American will upon innocent natives, and more an equivocal scene of encounter and communication, a scene whose unfolding is as important as it is fragile and fraught with risk.

In turn, if we read the last chapter of Equiano's narrative more closely, we can raise doubts about his apparently enthusiastic endorsement of colonization. Indeed, he explains that he was wary when he first was asked by the white British governor of Senegambia to become a colonial agent in Sierra Leone: "I at first refused going, and told him how I had been served on a like occasion by some white people the last voyage I went to Jamaica, when I attempted, (if it were the will of God) to be the means of converting the Indian prince. . . . He told me not to fear, for he would apply to the Bishop of London to get me ordained. On these terms I consented to the Governor's proposal to go to Africa" (221). Equiano is referring to his attempt to convert a Miskito Indian prince named George when they were shipmates bound from England through Jamaica to the Miskito coast of Central America; according to Equiano's *Narrative*, the prince had originally been taken to England "by some English traders for some selfish ends" (202). This analogy between converting a Miskito prince on the way to Central America and converting Africans in Sierra Leone undercuts the presumptive racial affiliation between black diasporans like himself and native Africans, an affiliation Equiano had seemed to embrace by calling Africans "my countrymen." With this analogy, West Africans are more akin to Native Americans as non-Christians than they are to black diasporans as black or African. As Equiano explains, his effort to convert "the Indian prince" initially seemed to be succeeding, but then some white sailors on the ship began mocking the spectacle of an African talking about Christianity with an Indian. This eventually caused Prince George to spurn both Christianity and Equiano all together. Equiano is thus wary of what he calls the "mock Christianity" of his presumptive white patrons, and is finally persuaded to go to Sierra Leone not so much because of his desire to follow his patrons' plans to convert Africans in Africa, as because of his tactical interest in garnering some institutional recognition for himself in Britain: "He told me not to fear, for he would apply to the Bishop of London to get me ordained."

Equiano's wariness turned out to be well warranted. In this last chapter of his narrative, he also refers obliquely to the complicated conditions under which he was driven out of the colonization movement. As he tells it, he was falsely and publicly accused of corruption by some well-placed white colonial officials, which forced him to resign his position. Upon closer consideration, however, we learn that Equiano might not have gone to Africa simply to convert natives and spread capitalism, or even to get ordained, and that he might have been accused of something other than corruption. One of the white officials who accused Equiano, Thomas Boulden Thompson, wrote a letter to the British Navy

Board on March 21, 1787, claiming that Equiano had been an instiga-
tor of sedition: Thompson is appalled at "the conduct of [Equiano] . . . ,
which has been since he held the situation of Commissary, turbulent and
discontented, taking every means to actuate the minds of the Blacks to
discord; and I am convinced that unless some means are taken to quell
his spirit of sedition, it will be fatal to the peace of the settlement and
dangerous to those intrusted with guiding it" (299). If we read Thompson's account against the grain of his overt intentions, we could say that
Equiano was willing to agitate with others in Sierra Leone to challenge
white visions of colonization. What that challenge consisted in remains
unclear; we are left to wonder exactly what Equiano's "means to actuate
the minds of the Blacks to discord" might have been, and how a less
biased observer than Thompson might have described those "means"
and that "discord."

Although Equiano himself does not elaborate upon these details of
his West African venture in the last chapter of his narrative, we can still
read that chapter, counterintuitively, as a certain critique of African
colonization. One of the literary devices he deploys most often in *The
Interesting Narrative* is that of representing his initial naïveté in the face
of white people followed by his subsequent shock at their "ill-usage" of
him. Thus, Equiano's representation of his imperial desire to help spread
British culture, religion, and economics at the beginning of the chapter
could be read as the critical staging of an initial, naïve trust in white
intentions; in turn, his subsequent disillusionment at being defamed for
his efforts, toward the end of the chapter, could be read as a perfor-
matively cautionary tale to black diasporans who might be tempted to
believe white promises about African colonization.

For Wheatley and Equiano, then, African colonization is caught in
a complex temporality and geography captured neither by a foundationalist assertion of origins (the return-to-Africa perspective) nor by a
strict binary between colonizer and colonized (the anti-imperialist perspective). These two black diasporans writing at the beginning of the
African colonization movement teach us that both interpretations in
fact impoverish the history they try to capture. Specifically, if we marshal the most foundationalist notion of diaspora and argue that black
settler-colonists really were returning to their origins in Africa, we participate in the imperial gesture that Wheatley questions so directly and

that Equiano at once advocates and undermines. Furthermore, a foundationalist celebration of "return" erases the real violence done by black
settlers and their white sponsors to West Africans. However, if we argue
that black diasporans are not returning because there is no connection
between the diaspora and Africa, we ignore the potential lines of communication across the Atlantic divide that Wheatley mentions in her
letter to Hopkins and that Equiano seems to have participated in on the
ground in Sierra Leone. Additionally, a strict critique of return, which
would position black settlers as simple agents of Western interests and
West Africans as mere victims of Western imperialism, by itself is also
not adequate because it represents the formerly enslaved settlers either
as children who did not know what they were doing or as unabashedly
rapacious and unreflective plunderers—representations that the epistolary archive of Liberia makes untenable, as we will see. This stark anti-
imperialist perspective also participates in the nativist fantasy of West
Africans as pure and untouched victims unprepared for their encounter with the capitalist world-system brought by imperial diasporan settlers. In fact, we know that by the turn of the nineteenth-century West
Africans had already been through centuries of volatile contact with the
capitalist world-system, and had become savvy, if not always successful, manipulators of that system, including vigorous participants in the
slave trade itself.[7]

This question of how to interpret a diasporan return to Africa was
of course a venerable one throughout the twentieth century, extending
from W. E. B. Du Bois's work on Pan Africanism, through the "Africa
interest" period, to St. Clair Drake's critical account of "Africa interest" in the 1950s, to Adalaide Cromwell and Martin Kilson's under-
appreciated reformulation of "return" in their *Apropos of Africa*, to
Carter Woodson's and George Shepperson's elaborations of diaspora,
to name just a few of the most important touchstones.[8] One drawback
of the flowering of such thought about "return," however, has been a
tendency in even more recent scholarship to represent this twentieth-
century intellectual history as infinitely more subtle and complex than
the supposed back-to-Africa obsessions of the nineteenth century. For
instance, in both "The Uses of Diaspora" and his *The Practice of Diaspora*, Brent Hayes Edwards has shown us the richness of George Shepperson's work on return. But Edwards follows Shepperson in tending

to celebrate twentieth-century thought at the expense of the putatively more simplistic and foundationalist thought of the nineteenth century.[9] In "The Uses of Diaspora," Edwards writes disapprovingly that "at times the 'Africa interest' [discourse] was inflected toward a return to the African continent itself, as in the nineteenth-century colonization and missionary movements, for instance."[10] Edwards's presumption that "nineteenth-century colonization and missionary movements" were too caught up in a literal understanding of "return," and that the most problematic of twentieth-century "Africa interest" discourse mimics these movements, appears to be a result of thinking about the nineteenth century in the terms of just a few, well known, late-nineteenth-century black intellectuals (he cites Martin Delany and Edward Wilmont Blyden). After the Liberian state declares independence in 1847, we certainly do see the rise of a discourse of what Edwards calls "a return to the African continent itself" both in Liberia and in various segments of the African diaspora. However, as I hope to show below by way of contrast with Edwards, a rich challenge to both foundationalist celebrations of return as well as blunt dismissals of return can come to us from the early to mid-nineteenth century itself—from the other side, if you will, of the "Africa interest" period of the twentieth century as well as the return-to-Africa period of Delany's and Blyden's later nineteenth century.

Wheatley's and Equiano's texts actually orient us toward this challenge. Just as the black settler-colonist and missionary Philip Quaque was Wheatley's figure for the fraught and fragile possibility of linkages across the black Atlantic, so too does he make an appearance in the last chapter of Equiano's narrative: Quaque is Equiano's contact in Sierra Leone, the man to whom the white British governor of Senegambia sends Equiano. To the extent that we can read Wheatley's and Equiano's texts as converging on a subtle and equivocal attempt to grapple with what a free life under African colonization might have meant to black diasporans and West Africans alike, then the settlers themselves— figured in both Wheatley's and Equiano's texts by Philip Quaque— embody that convergence.[11] The most extensive textual trace of these settlers in Liberia can be found in the archive of letters they wrote to their former masters, family, and friends in the United States. During Liberia's colonial and early national periods in particular, these letters offer remarkably fecund if unsystematic accounts of the effort to live a free life through African colonization.

The Epistolary Archive: "Return"

When one reads these letters one is immediately struck by the relative lack of discourse about a "return to Africa," indeed the rarity even of the very word "return." When this word is used, it is usually by way of discussing a return to the U.S. by the many settlers who find themselves or others around them overwhelmed by Liberia's difficult conditions and stricken by the separation from friends and family left behind in slavery. Even when settlers do represent Liberia as a homeland of sorts, that representation is undone by remembrances of their former lives, and at times by accounts of their own aspirations, or of the aspirations of others, to travel back to the United States. If Liberia is not, according to this archive, an African homeland to which African American settler-colonists imagined themselves simply "returning," then what are the temporalities and geographies of the free life they sought there?

The desire to return to the U.S.—either literally or in spirit, via salutations, remembrances, and even dreams—regularly punctuates this archive. For instance, Wesley J. Horland, writing from Bassa Cove to James Moore in Kentucky on January 18, 1846, declares both that "I am hapay to say this is a very good countray, and any man may make a living in this countray if he will," and that "I expect to come to the U. States before long, if you think it advisabel."[12] In a second letter written one day later to Moore, Horland continues: "if the Lord is willing, I intend to see yore face once more. I do hope you will advise me what to do in this respect. I would like to come thare verry well; but I do not know the law that you have among you as yet. I would be glad if you would wright me all the newse. Write to my pepel for me."[13] Peyton Skipwith, who arrived in Liberia in 1833, writes: "I wonce had a notion of coming home and still have a notion but I want to go up to Sirrilione. . . . If not will return back to America and give my respects to your family also to the people let my Mother know that you have received a letter from me. I don't want you to say any thing to about my being blind but let her know that I will return. Dianah send her love to Miss Sally and all of the family and is very desirous of returning back again."[14] Peyton's daughter Diana Skipwith also imagines such a return: "I should like to come Back thire a gain and the we expect of coming back again gave my love to ant Lizy and to ant Cissiah and to uncle Ned gave my love to awl encureing friends."[15] Indeed, as Diana explains in another letter to Sally Cocke dated May 7, 1838, this expectation had a deep hold on her unconscious: "I wish that I could See your faice for I cannot take rest of nights Dreaming A bout you Some times I think I am thire I am thire and when I awoke I am hear in Liberia & how that dos greave me but I cannot healp my Self I am verry fraid I shal never see your faice a gain."[16] On July 11, 1858, Peter Ross wrote to Ralph R. Gurley, an ACS agent, pleading for help in securing funds from the estate of his master, Captain Isaac Ross of Mississippi: "my Dear Sir, i would be glad to Com and see you. if you is willing and Can get money anogh to Com."[17] Ross and his kin in Liberia apparently thought carefully through this desire "to Com," for he writes to Gurley on July 19: "i beg you all to see to it that we would Get sum of our money for we stan in kneed of it. our object is to buil a ship to sail Cross the atlantic osion there for we beg you all to help us. africa is a Good place. but we want to be much better."[18]

By using the verb "to come" more often even than the verb "to return," letters like these place the emphasis not so much on a turning back to what was before, as they do on approaching anew: both a new approach and an approach to something that, while familiar, might have become different. That the verb "to come" can be used predictively, as a dative infinitive in the sense of an action whose completion lies in the future, further amplifies the sense in which "the U. States" to which many of these settlers imagine coming could be as much an unrealized ideal as a familiar place from their past.[19] Also, the relationship between the verb "to return" and its subject is more secure and active than the relationship between the dative infinitive "to come" and its subject, since "to come" also carries the sense of an action befalling or falling to someone. Diana Skipwith's "we expect of coming back again" bears a trace of this ambivalent subject-verb relationship, one that is not quite a passive construction but also one that falls short of a fully active subject performing an action willfully.

Consequently, the temporality of the desires expressed by these letters cannot simply be described as a nostalgic preference for the prior familiarity of slavery over the present and future unfamiliarity of freedom. Rather, these settlers continually stage and restage imaginative returns to the U.S. that swerve between what life in Liberia might become after living in the U.S. and what life in the U.S. might come to be in the wake of living in Liberia. The letters veer between slavery and freedom in a context where neither state of being is as clear-cut as it might seem, and where daily life—in and through the letters' very sentences—shifts between incomplete experiences of each. These letters' "returns," then, are less about choosing slavery over freedom, or the U.S. over Liberia, than they are about the turns or swerves that coming to be free entails. For instance, they turn toward seeing familiar "faces" from a new angle, in a new context, after an estranging experience. Such sight befalls these settler-colonists, taking them out of the life they had known and turning them toward the familiar as if it were other. We could thus read these swerves between Liberia and the U.S. as ongoing expressions of an inchoate, unpredictable, and unauthorizable desire "to be much better," as Peter Ross writes.

Even among settler-colonists who explicitly embrace Liberia as a homeland in their letters, a certain dissonant backbeat usually sounds through. H. W. Ellis was born enslaved in Virginia, lived in Tennessee and Alabama, and became a Presbyterian minister of such renown that the Synod of Alabama purchased, emancipated, and sent him, with his wife and daughter, to be a missionary in Liberia. Shortly after arriving in Liberia in 1847, Ellis began to correspond with Rev. William McLain, treasurer of the ACS, with the initial goal of securing ACS funding for a college. "As I cautiously take the liberty of writing, I humbly solicit the condescension of your honor and reverence to accept a communication from a transmarine stranger," Ellis writes in his first letter to McLain on November 20, 1849.[20] Since "stranger" meant both an unknown person and a foreigner, Ellis here effectively declares himself at once personally unknown to McLain and no longer quite American; as a *transmarine stranger*," Ellis also declares himself to be perpetually in motion across the Atlantic, poised between being *in* Africa and *from* the U.S.

This estranged state echoes throughout Ellis's letters. On the one hand, writing again to McLain on April 15, 1850—as well as to his kin *through* McLain—Ellis sounds convinced that "Africa" is his proper home: "I have a word of advice, and, I think, of consolation too, to my colored friends in Alabama. I am a pure and undefiled African, in every honorable sense of the word; I hope to live, labor and die in Africa."[21] On the other hand, continuing to address his "colored friends in Alabama," Ellis also insists that Alabama is a certain homeland too: "I do not think it to be the will of our Heavenly Father that you should leave home and go to any place except Africa. If your superiors say, Go to Liberia, come right along. But, excepting Liberia, go to no place, from Alabama, under Heaven."[22] This split allegiance is also reflected in Ellis's November 20, 1849, letter to McLain:

> That portion of our people who are intelligent and good, who love themselves as they should, love Liberia their country; they are worthy and useful citizens, and these are they who love America! Now there is this remarkable fact about it, that those of the above named quality love America from proper motives, and for proper reasons, but would not go back there upon any terms whatever; but you know that we, of course, have some trifling, indolent persons here, as well as every other place, who never were, nor ever will be any important use to themselves or country; these always are murmuring and grumbling, even in America; they grumble here—yea, every place![23]

The category of "trifling, indolent persons" seems to emerge here as a way of differentiating two kinds of love for America: those who love Liberia also love America "from proper motives," while those who "are murmuring and grumbling" about Liberia and, presumably, considering returning to America, love America for all the wrong reasons. Ellis's effort to police a boundary between good and bad love of country, and his judgmental dismissal of Liberia's black settler critics, betray his own unease about life in Liberia. Thus, though he describes himself as "a pure and undefiled African," Ellis's letters depict a Liberian life that oscillates between Georgia and Africa, a life that murmurs and grumbles with antagonism and impurity. This is not exactly what Peter Linebaugh and Marcus Rediker have called a "revolutionary Atlantic," for Ellis does not enlist in the kind of self-conscious radicalism they so carefully trace in *The Many-Headed Hydra*.[24] And Ellis certainly does not proffer what Kwame Anthony Appiah has called "cosmopolitanism," or "ethics in a world of strangers."[25] For the diverse unity Ellis at times celebrates in Liberia—"Here we have excellent neighbours, both Americans and natives. . . . Come and be happy!"[26]—is neither nationally all-inclusive nor transatlantically extensive, as it excludes those "trifling, indolent persons" in American and in Liberia who "always are murmuring and grumbling," and it both limits and compartmentalizes its reach: "excepting Liberia, go to no place, from Alabama." Rather, Ellis names a state of being that remains critically estranged from—even when it seems to pursue—heroic collectivities and global networks.

James W. Wilson also reveals murmurings and grumblings about Liberia in the very act of presenting it as the proper land for black freedom. In an August 5, 1858, letter to ACS treasurer McLain, Wilson attempts to counter the public charges of two other settlers—James and William Watson—against the ACS: "I Larn thire is a Report floting in the Unided States that the agent of the Colinizathion Socety had Pur saled them to Pucherd som Chep Calico & Brest Julls and on thir arivel thay Ware disopinted and thair by defroded out of thir money."[27] The case of "the Watson men," as Wilson describes them, was that same year exposed on the propagandistic pages of the ACS's official organ, the *African Repository and Colonial Journal*, by A. M. Cowan, a white agent of the Kentucky Colonization Society. As Cowan put it, the Watson brothers "returned to slavery, believing that freedom to the negro in Africa is the greatest curse that could possibly befall him; and that had the Liberians the means of getting away, seven-eighths of them would gladly return to the United States and serve the hardest masters to be found in the South, feeling that the condition of the slave here is far preferable to that of the most favored of the inhabitants of Liberia."[28] Wilson similarly seeks to portray "the Watson men's" criticisms of Liberia, and their return to the U.S., as an embrace of slavery:

> I am all so despose to think he that Would not Work for his benifite will not Work for others unlest he is forst With the Whipe but if it is thir path to have som one to make thim work for a Liven Let it be so for as thir path is So shal it be un to you Sayes the Criptures as for my Part I do not know What William & James Watson Return for unlest it Was for the Whipe. . . . I can not See What a man of Coller Want to go Back to the united States to Live for un Lest he has no Sol in him for Whare thire is

a sine of a Sole With in a man it Panc for fredom in this Life & the Life to Com.[29]

In the process of insisting that "a man of Coller" can have freedom only in Liberia, Wilson reveals the unfreedom "the Watson men" encountered. It is as if their return to the U.S. threatens the very meaning of Liberia as freedom's homeland for African Americans, such that both Wilson and Cowan have to charge the Watsons with a love of slavery and, in Wilson's hyperbolic terms, with soullessness. Nonetheless, "the Watson men's" challenge to stark depictions of Liberian life continues, as a textual trace in the archive, to backbeat Wilson and Cowan's polemics. This trace of "murmuring and grumbling" about Liberia reminds us that the free life for which one "Panc," or pants—"it Panc for fredom in this Life & the Life to Com"—is at once at hand and out of reach, resisting governmental or geographic settlement.

In other letters, the notion of Liberia as the homeland of black freedom breaks down less spectacularly, over a number of years and across the written experiences of interconnected settler-colonists. Consider, for instance, the large, extended family that had been enslaved to the family of John Hartwell Cocke of Jamestown, Virginia.[30] Cocke had inherited a large plantation and over one hundred slaves from his wealthy father, but his education at William and Mary College and his religious views led him to become an ardent colonizationist as early as 1817. Cocke and his second wife, Louisa Maxwell Holmes, went to great lengths to "train" the slaves they hoped to emancipate and deport in skills that would supposedly help them in Africa. Cocke eventually sent eight former slaves to Liberia in 1833: Peyton and Lydia Skipwith, and their six children, Diana, Matilda, Felicia, Martha, Nash, and Napoleon.[31] The Skipwiths' subsequent struggles across the Atlantic led Cocke to establish a colonization school of sorts on two plantations he purchased in Alabama. During the 1840s and 1850s, Cocke sent scores of his slaves to these sites, called Hopewell and New Hope, although he would eventually deem only a fraction of them sufficiently "trained" to send to Liberia. Among those whom Cocke emancipated and deported from the Alabama "school" as well as directly from Virginia during these decades were Leander Sterdivant and his children Diana, Rose, and William; brothers Richard Cannon, James Nicholas, and Peter

Jones; Julia Nicholas; and Peyton Skipwith's brother Erasmus Nicholas, who had been owned by Cocke's son, Philip St. George Cocke.

Like H. W. Ellis, Erasmus Nicholas's early letters convey an unsteady conviction that Liberia is his proper home. As he wrote to his mother from Monrovia on March 5, 1843: "on my first sight of this part of the world [manuscript torn] so Differrent to the part where I was born that it appeared to me as though I was in a new world, but since I have gotten nearly over the african fever I like the place better & Better for I find it is the only Place for the man of Colour."[32] However, as we learn in letters from his niece, Matilda Skipwith, and her father, Peyton Skipwith, by 1846 Erasmus had found Liberia to be too new of a "new world" and had returned to the U.S.: Matilda writes on October 23, 1844, to Sally Cocke that "Erasmus has Left us and gone to Philadelphia," and Peyton writes to his mother on June 27, 1846, that "Erasmus has not returned since he left here for the states & it appears as if I cannot receive any intelligence from him. I would like much to hear something of him if he is in the States. You will be please to write me by Mr. Williams and let me know whether you have heard any thing of him or no."[33] On July 4, 1848, Matilda suggests—at the end of a letter with different sections addressed to Sally Cocke and to her grandmother Lucy Nicholas Skipwith—that Erasmus did return to Liberia, only to leave again: "NB. Uncle Erasmus has been out to Liberia since you request that we should give you some account of him—he is now on his way to the States & will leave for Africa, again by the return of the 'Liberia Packet.'"[34]

Erasmus's comings and goings figure the ambivalence his extended family expresses about life in what he tried to understand as "the only Place for the man of Colour." Elsewhere in his June 27, 1846, letter to his mother, Peyton Skipwith gives full vent to this ambivalence: "In your last to me you expressed an anxiety for me to come over, but I am afraid that I shall never be enabled to cross the atlantice again though I would like much to see you once more in the flesh. . . . Dear Mother I find that the people are afraid to come to this country." Drawn by and toward his mother, his fear that he will never see her in the U.S. resonates with the fear he admits others black Americans have about Liberia itself. In this context, Peyton's next sentence—"I can assure you that any person can live here if they has a little money"—reads like a tepid endorsement.[35] In a letter written to his former master Cocke on June 25, 1846, Peyton also reveals that James Nicholas "left this place for *Jamaca* & I have not been enable to hear from him since."[36] As James Nicholas's brother Richard Cannon elaborates in a September 29, 1844, letter to Cocke: "Brother James Could not Contente himself here & lift Some months, ago for Kingston, Jamaca & I has never been enable to heare from him Since theire he has been."[37] On August 13, 1857, Leander Sterdivant starkly puts James's fate in the context of the fate of the rest of his kin in a letter also written to Cocke: "my self and 3 children are well diana and Rose are married the Rest that came out with me are all dead but James he went back."[38]

However, Matilda's letters do the most to undo her uncle Erasmus's initial enthusiasm. After the deaths and departures of many of her relatives, on May 19, 1852, she also writes to Cocke: "I have seen a great Deal of trouble since the Death of my People and all my hold hart is on the Lord this is avery hard Country for a poor widow to get along."[39] A year later, on September 26, 1853, Matilda tells Cocke: "Please to give my Best Respects to all the family and now I will try Indevr to tell them the state of my mind now I am left a lone in this Lonsum Cuntry now one to look up to . . . and sometimes I live in hopes to see you all again and then again it seemes that the way looks so gloomy and if I ar not see you now more in this world, I expect to meet you in hevin."[40] For these settler-colonists, then, Liberia was as much "Lonsum Cuntry" as homeland, as much "trouble" and "Death" as promised land. For some it was, paradoxically, as much a place to leave for the U.S. in search of freedom as it was a place to which freedom comes. Freedom here fails to be a state toward which one moves directly, a threshold one crosses definitively, or a subjectivity one achieves masterfully. Rather, freedom takes the form of Matilda's "again and then again," a return that is a repeated turning, paradoxically recursive and open-ended.

Even those rare settlers who do write of Liberia in the most foundationalist of terms cannot be taken to represent a straightforward, "return to Africa" perspective. Consider the letters of James Cephas Minor, who was apprenticed in a printing house in Fredericksburg, Virginia, by his master with an eye to sending Minor to Liberia with a trade. Soon after arriving in Monrovia, Minor writes to his former master on February 11, 1833, that "[w]e hope many months will not pass away before we shall see our harbour glittering with ropes that have been the bearers of the people destined to return to the land of their forefathers." Repeating this sentiment later in the same letter and perfectly summarizing the period's predominant argument for African colonization, Minor writes: "Africa is a land of freedom; where else can the man of color enjoy temporal freedom but in Africa? They may flee to Hayti or to Canada, but it will not do; they must fulfil the sayings of Thomas Jefferson, 'Let an ocean divide the white man from the man of color.' Seeking refuge in other parts of the world has been tried, it is useless. We own that this is the land of our forefathers, destined to be the home of their decendants."[41] But thirteen years later, Minor writes to his former mistress of his own nostalgia for Virginia, which he calls "home," and admits that many former slaves want to return to the U.S.: "George and James Marshall . . . myself, and Abram gets together, and sits down, and cherishes the recollection of home, and the remembrance of old acquaintances. The Marshalls talk of returning home, they had expected to have gone back in the vessel tha brings this letter; but they have foregone their intentions for the present. George, however, was much inclined on returning, but James was not. I have advised them to be content, and turn their attention to some sort of occupation."[42] At the same time, on September 23, 1851, James Minor's mother, Mary, writes to the Maryland Colonization Society agent who was responsible for transporting her to Liberia that "I have been at Africa A Long time & I wish to come home if I can possibel. You will please Send me an answer."[43] James himself, some years later, imaginatively returns to the U.S. in a letter to his former mistress: "Very often, by reflection, I can take a view of Fredericksburg—Toppen Castle, Edgewood, and many other places, over which, I have walked, in your beloved country in the days of early youthhood."[44]

Read in this light, the letters of Mary Ann Clay and her niece Lucy Clay to the family of their former master Sidney B. Clay pose a problem about nativity: are African Americans native to Africa or the U.S., and is the nativity of native Africans to be expunged or identified with? Enslaved in Bourbon County, Kentucky until the death of their master, Mary Ann and Lucy were then emancipated and deported on the ship *Alida*, which sailed from New Orleans for Monrovia on February 13, 1851. Although they both lost their children on the voyage or during their first months in Liberia, on September 27, 1853, Mary Ann nonetheless writes that "I can asshure you that I am very much please with Liberia Since I have had the feaver, and I can asshure you that I am more thankful for you for Sending us to the Land of our Four Fathers and where we can enjoy our freedom. It is true that I have been a great deal of afflicted Since I left America But I hope that I will Soon be well again."[45] On September 28, 1853, Lucy echoes Mary Ann's hopes in the face of personal suffering, but complicates her aunt's presumption that Liberia is "the Land of our Four Fathers": "Myself and Aunt has been much afflicted since we have been here, but notwithstanding I feel quite satisfied with the place, and like it very well. I have not as yet regretted that I left my native home, though I have often been unwelcomly circunstanced. One of the children died with the smal pox on the voyage out, and two with the fever after their arrival here."[46] Opening up an equivocal gap between "the Land of our Four Fathers" and "my native home," Mary Ann's and Lucy Clay's letters show how tenuously early black settler-colonists embraced the discourse of a return to Africa. Underscoring this tenuousness, according to letters in the Clay Family Papers, two other people enslaved by Sidney B. Clay refused deportation to Liberia, claiming to prefer drowning to such a fate, and thus were sold into further bondage in Texas rather than accompany Mary Ann and Lucy Clay on the *Alida*.[47]

For the settler-colonists who went to Liberia during its early years, then, the idea of Africa as a place to which African Americans could "return" was either absent or backbeat by its own undoing. On their epistolary stage, we read numerous speculative reflections from which a free life emerges less as a formal state of manumission or citizenship in a settled nation-state, and more as an unsettled, ongoing state of improvised being that is continually intimate with slavery and a diasporic Atlantic. The discourse of return in this archive is inflected less by the inevitably tragic, foundationalist dream of which Saidiya Hartman is so carefully critical in *Lose Your Mother: A Journey along the Atlantic Slave Route*: "return is what you hold on to after you have been taken from your country, or when you realize that there is no future in the New World, or that death is the only future."[48] Rather, in their imaginary and literal returns to the U.S., these settler-colonists in Liberia hesitate on liberty's threshold, such that the servitude they left continues to be a reckoning and the freedom they seek is to be found in returns to the U.S. staged from Liberia. Writes Hartman, "return and remaking, or restoration and transformation, can't be separated into tidy opposing categories. Sometimes *going back to* and *moving toward* coincide."[49] In early- to mid-nineteenth-century Liberia, the epistolary scenes of that coincidence emerge as recursive and open-ended encounters with—to borrow again from H. W. Ellis's letters—temporally and geographically strange, transmarine states of inchoate slavery and freedom.

The Epistolary Archive: "The Natives"

Just as the letters frustrate the tendency to read African colonization from a straightforward, "return to Africa" perspective, so too do they frustrate the tendency to read the settler-colonists as unabashed imperialists devoted solely to wiping out or converting and assimilating passive and innocent West Africans. For though we read extensively of settlers assuming their imperial righteousness and exercising their colonial power, we also read both of powerful West African efforts to counter colonization and of settler efforts to disrupt West African participation in the slave trade. Perhaps more strikingly, however, we read in these letters candid expressions of the settlers' inability to make sense of native lives. At times, we even read of the subtle and equivocally acknowledged ways in which the settler-colonists' assumptions about "the natives" are undone, and of moments in which the settlers themselves are moved and remade by the very "natives" they work so hard to move and remake.

Black settler Alexander Hance can introduce us to this complex and uneven scene. Writing to ACS president J. H. B. Latrobe in 1838, Hance depicts a settler community rife with division and conflict. Having recently returned to Cape Palmas from a short trip to the U.S. to recruit more settlers, Hance explains:

> you will be informed of the present situation of the colony which at this time is far different to what it was when I left here for america. On my return it had altered so much that it really astonished me to see it in that time how the colony had fallen from its former prospects. And it now is in quite abad sutuation both in regard to provisions & Government. . . . The colonist generally are very much disatisfied especially the new emigrants. They are all extremely so. I regret my trop to America, for the new emigrants connected with some of the old colonist would

deprive me of my existance were it in their power. They have raised a great many false reports about me & have attempted to excommunicated me from the church.[50]

In this context of settler infighting and disaffection, West African resistance to colonization was unsurprisingly strong: "One fact is this: the natives do not like to be governed by a colored Man and they do just as they please almost."[51]

Such tensions made settler-colonists rethink their ideas about their own ties to Africa. Peyton Skipwith—who as we saw above arrived in Liberia with his family in 1833—writes on April 22, 1840, to his former master John H. Cocke that "it is something strange to thank that those people of africa are calld our ancestors in my present thinking if we have any ancestors they could not have been like these hostile tribes in this part of africa for you may try and distill that principle and belief in them and do all you can for them and they still will be your enemy." Skipwith apparently questioned this "return to Africa" narrative because of the violence with which West Africans met the settlers' own, often brutal attempts to appropriate West African land and transform West African cultures:

I must say that the greaset war that ever was fought by man was fought at Headengton, a Missionary establishment about five miles form Millsburg it was said that a savage host of this man that we took occasion to against sent about four Hundred men to attack this place about day Break . . . it has been said that a great number died but how many I do not no with the lost of one Native man Mortally wounded they then persued them and found the Generals body slightly intomed about twenty miles from the field of Battle his head was taken from his body and now made an ornament in the Hands of the Governor Buchanan the Battle lasted about one Hour fifteen minutes how this was done they had an over quanty of musket loded and had nothing to do but take them up and poor the Bullets in thire flesh and they would fall takeeng fingers and tearing the flesh assunder.[52]

Massacres like this grew not only out of the settlers' efforts to seize land and convert "natives," but also out of native resistance to settler disruption of West African trade, including native participation in the slave trade. As Skipwith explained to Cocke less then a year earlier, on November 11, 1839:

> A Slave dealer for somitime had a slave factory at Little Bassa and Gov. Buchanan after he came out orderd him away and said to him that he had no right to deal in Slaves in that teritory and that he must remove in so many days . . . he would not believe but still remaind and we went down and broke up the factory and brought away all the effects say in goods and destroyd about fifty puncheons Rum which was turn loose on the ground say the effect in goods &c to the amt of ten thousand Dollars after we had taken the goods or a part we had to contend with the natives which fought us two days very hard but we got the victory and form a treaty before we left with one of the chiefs but not with the other and only got four Slaves so we cannot say that we concluded a final peace without the other partys consent.[53]

By linking the conflict with the slave dealer to the sudden need "to contend with the natives," Skipwith seems to understand the participation of West Africans in the Euro-American slave trade. Perhaps this participation contributes to his deep disillusionment about the fact that "these people of Africa are calld our ancestors." Skipwith is not moved enough by this encounter, however, to question his own collaboration with white officials of the ACS, like Buchanan, both to police West African trade and to appropriate West African land. Indeed, the very articulation of a certain antislavery activism with land appropriation through militarism and political double dealing makes "the victory" a dubious one, which Skipwith perhaps acknowledges by admitting that "we cannot say that we concluded a final peace without the other partys consent."

Like Peyton Skipwith, Sion Harris—a manumitted carpenter and farmer who arrived in Liberia on the ship *Liberia* in 1830 when he was just nineteen—writes on January 5, 1848, of "Africa" as "the Land of our fore Fathers" and exclaims on May 20, 1849, that he would never be content to live in the U.S. again: "I can say that I thank God that I am at home in Africa. I found my family well. I never expect to contend with the collard man in America no more, if they come I will, if not well with me. I expect to die in Africa where the free air blows for here are Liberty. . . . I have no more business in America."[54] But Sion Harris's letters are most striking because of his apparent glee in writing extensive accounts of violent conflict with "the Enemy." Like Skipwith, he is untroubled by the linkages among antislavery activism, land appropriation, and colonial violence: "have broak up the great slaver factory and liberated a great manny slaves there was none of our men lost none crippled they burnt up a great many towns."[55] In fact, he seems content to secure his own settler-colonial "rights" at the expense of any consideration of native West African rights: "we have been appressed long enough we mean to stand our ground & contend for our rights until we die, O if my cullard friends would only believe and feel the love of liberty they would not Stay in the United Stats."[56]

As Harris explains in an April 16, 1840, letter to Samuel Wilkeson of the Maryland Colonization Society, he participated in the very massacre Peyton Skipwith describes above, claiming for himself the honor of having secured the head of the general to which Skipwith referred: "Many wished the head, but I reserved it for the Governor, with Greegrees, a great quantity which I delivered to the Governor."[57] In details that were excised by the ACS when they published this letter in the *African Repository*, Harris writes of one of the indigenous leaders: "Goterah returned, back to the kitchen, which he siesed and shook with one hand, and brandished a Dreadful knife with the other about 6 inches broad. and about a hundred and 50 men came up to the fence, to whom he said letus go in. I took deliberate aim at him (he was half bent-shaking) and brought him to the ground cut off his knee shot him in the lungs and cut of his privets."[58] Harris seems untroubled by his own brutality, declaring that "I examined myself and saw all was right," and admitting that he only prayed so that God would make the conditions more favorable for the battle.[59] However, he does add a "P.S." to this letter in which he undercuts his own professed connection to Africa and rejection of America:

I desire to go to America to see my frinds who are in East Tenasee Knox County and I would like your advice about it whether it would be safe or right. I have no Family but My self and wife and means to come. If you think it difficult to go to tenesee I would like to visit a Merica any how some where or other. . . . I would be very glad to have a frind to exchange Curiosities with or give Curiosities for other little things because I have in my power to collect many One reason for my wishing to go see my frinds is I write and I write without answers.[60]

Harris's loneliness is striking here, and though in subsequent letters he continues to criticize America and extol Liberia, the exuberance with which he colonizes West Africa fails to make up for his own sense of being out of place. In fact, this troubled articulation of loneliness with imperial violence is echoed in a brief paragraph he writes to his sister on November 29, 1849, at the end of a letter to ACS treasurer McLain: "I dream of seeing you often & would like to see you, But I could not concent to come to America. My love to you & all the children. how large is John? I love him. I wish I could see him, when he grows up, he must send me a present."[61] Oscillating between violent imperial enthusiasm and intimate, personal longing across many years, Sion Harris's letters simultaneously assert settler-colonial rights and unsettle that very assertion.

Even as they seek to draw sharp distinctions between "natives" and themselves, the settler-colonists betray the fragility of the divide between colonizer and colonized, a fragility that the settlers cannot always instrumentalize for conquest—as do Skipwith and Harris—or conversion and assimilation. For instance, James Minor—whom I mentioned in the previous section—writes to his former mistress Mary B. Blackford in 1852 that "[t]he religion, habits, manners, customs, and dress of the unattended to portions of the aboriginees, among us, are so vague and insignificant, that the children are imbibing some of the lowest principles. We hope for better, if worse Come."[62] Though he is critical of "the aboriginees" here, Minor also reveals that subsequent generations are already rejecting settler separatism by allowing themselves to be transformed by the very people they have displaced and disenfranchised. Diana Skipwith, Peyton's daughter whom I also discussed above, explains in a similar vein to Louisa Cocke on May 20, 1839, that "there is not a Native that i have see that i think that i could make my self hapy with ware you to see them you would think that i am write in my oppinion all though they ar verry ingenious people they make some Beautiful Bags which i inted sending you all some."[63] At once eager to proclaim her lack of attraction to the "Native" and struck by how "ingenious" they are, Diana Skipwith perhaps offers an example of the attitudes of "the children" whom Minor criticizes: her "write . . . oppinions" are subtly, grudgingly undone by her own quotidian encounters.

Diana Skipwith further reveals how the fragility of the settler-colonists' power was exposed by the very "natives" the settlers sought to control. As she writes to her former mistress Sally Cocke on March 6, 1843:

> I wrote you a long catalogue about the Natives customs which I am inhopes that you have found very amusing in conversing with one of them I ask him how was it that the could not read & write like white man (they call us all white man) & had not as much sence as the white man & he said that it was thire own foult that god give them the choice either to learn book proper as thy says or make Rice & thy told god they had rather make rice I labored with him & told him that it was a misstaken Idear altogether I farther told him that god had bless them with as many Sences as the white man and if thy ware to only put them in exersise that he would be the same as white man after talking with him some time he said in answer you tell true too much.[64]

It is difficult to tell whether Diana understands how this man is likely challenging her assumptions and making fun of her claims. She does acknowledge that "the Natives" have countered the racial formations settlers brought with them from the U.S. when she explains parenthetically that "they call us all white man." Indeed, she seems to have accepted this appellation "white man" by including herself among those who can "read & write" and whom "the Natives" should emulate. The man's response reads like a ruse, however, because at the very time when many settlers are on the brink of starvation, he wryly explains that God made his people choose between "rice" and "book proper" and that "it was thire own fault" they chose not to starve. That Diana's response is to urge the man to "be the same as the white man" by choosing both "rice" and "book proper" may well have deepened the man's sense of irony, as he observed how this former slave's people both emulate "the white man" and go hungry. Perhaps his "answer" to Diana—that "you tell true too much"—was more of a challenge than Diana could fathom.

In a letter written on July 3, 1855, from Liberia's Clay-Ashland settlement to Robert Wickliffe of Lexington, Kentucky—a letter from
which the epigraph of this essay comes—Rev. Alfred F. Russell speculates at length about the very meaning of "nativity" in early Liberia,
at once elaborating and complicating the accounts I have considered
in this section. Russell and his mother, Milly, had been emancipated
and deported from Kentucky to Liberia in 1833 by their owner, Wickliffe's wife Mary, who had inherited them from her own mother. Russell
writes in reply to a letter he had just received from his former master,
and although we do not have Wickliffe's letter, it is not surprising that
Russell describes it as "so unexpected."[65] Wickliffe was a well-known
and powerful proslavery politician; in fact, by 1830 he was Kentucky's
wealthiest man and largest slaveholder. So it is not clear what would
have motivated him to contact his former slave, apparently for the first
time, more than twenty years after Russell had been emancipated and
deported by Wickliffe's wife. As Russell explains in the letter's opening
lines, "we had ever held the impression that you were not well pleased
with our Coming to Africa, and some how thought you opposed to
both Collonisation & abolition." Wickliffe's letter was apparently solici-
tous, however, since Russell follows up with an apology—"Pardon us
for this misjudgment of you"—and then leaves aside the odd nature of
the correspondence, adopting a candid and familiar tone.[66] Russell proceeds to offer a quite detailed evaluation of Liberia just eight years after
it declared independence.

Toward the end of the letter, Russell reflects upon the status of the
most recent black American settlers in Africa, in the context of debates
over how to define citizenship in Liberia:

He that comes from Your shores to this Offspring of American benevolence, is no stranger or alien, aney more than I was. Their birth, tongue,
education, religion, and Country is the same. The very Object and end
of their Coming is the same with my own. The same Philanthropy that
sent me, places them hear, on the very same footing, Condition & for
the same Cause. I hold Liberia has no right now, to meat the American Emigrant more freighted with intelligence & industry than formerly,
with unjust & unconstitutional naturalization laws. (We are all foreigners) because a party will hold office. The American emigrant bears no

comparison with the Irish, Germans, Polls, with strange tongue & strange Religion. Pouring into your Country, bought by the Revolution- ary blood of her Natural born sons, But who are our Natural inhabitants but our natives? for whom Liberia has eve made naturalisation rules. But time will work all right. We have a splendid country, rich in soil, metals, & resources of maney kinds & large enough for all the blacks in America. They would not trouble me by coming Ten thousand a month.

What starts as a gesture of inclusion for all new immigrants from the U.S. to Liberia leads to a recognition that "we are all foreigners." Russell then draws a curious distinction between two different kinds of "for- eigners": those new black American immigrants to Liberia and Euro- pean immigrants to the United States. His recognition that motley and multilingual European immigrants were driven into migrancy because of their "Natural born" militancy somehow then leads Russell from that natural European migrant militancy to "our Natural inhabitants . . . our natives," which in turn leads him to question Liberia's ironic effort to restrict the citizenship status of native West Africans. Finally escaping from this jumble of descriptive and proscriptive claims about nativity with the optimistic phrase "But time will work all right," Russell con- cludes by throwing the shores of Liberia wide open to all who may come from the U.S.

This passage interests me not as a statement of policy to clarify, but rather in its very resistance to clarity. That is, Russell is unable to control the figures of coming and going, of immigrant and emi- grant, of American and Liberian, of native and foreign. They circulate recklessly, and it is as if that very recklessness gives him his hope. Of course, such recklessness would not last long in the increasingly set- tled nation-state of Liberia. Yet the trace of it in Russell's letter ought to remind us of the unsettled states of being or life that survived during Liberia's volatile and potent early years. That Russell himself would become a representative of Montserrado County in the Libe- rian Senate during the 1850s, and in the 1880s both vice president and president of Liberia before his death in 1884, deepens the import of his epistolary equivocations. As one who would become a representa- tive of the Liberian state, he fails to state definitively his own under- standing of Liberian freedom, and through that failure itself he leaves

a trace of freedom's ongoing, unsettled elaboration in Liberia's epistolary archive.

Certainly, the settler-colonists' accounts of "the natives" expose their
participation in brutal imperial land appropriation, political exclusion,
economic disruption, and cultural repression. Yet these letters also
reveal the fragility of settler-colonization in Liberia, to the point where
the settlers' very lives are occasionally unmade by "the natives" they
seek to remake. When settlers fail to resist such fragility—when their
often vigorous and violent efforts to settle their own lives by unsettling
the lives of others falter—we glimpse the unsettlement of living free in
colonial Liberia.

"It all most cost us death seeking life"

The rest of Rev. Russell's letter to Robert Wickliffe reflects extensively
on the very meaning of such an unsettled life, a reflection with which
I would like to conclude this essay. As Russell explains: "I live in Clay
Ashland, a district bought by the Kentuckey Collonisation Society."
Clay-Ashland was named after Kentucky Congressman Henry Clay,
whose plantation outside Lexington was called Ashland. Clay was an
ardent supporter of African colonization because, as he put it on the
floor of the U.S. House of Representatives in 1816, it would clear "our
country of a useless and pernicious, if not a dangerous portion of its
population," namely free blacks and rebellious slaves.[67] When Russell
says the land was "bought" by the Kentucky Colonization Society, he
references the "fee simple" treaties, often coerced at gunpoint, by which
Colonization Society agents seized West African land from its native
inhabitants, who did not even recognize the concept of property the
Americans thought they were securing.[68]

Russell does not explicitly discuss this Liberian memorialization
of Clay's racist Whig nationalism or Liberia's history of colonial land
appropriation. However, he does insist that his fellow settlers have made
Clay-Ashland so successful that it has become "an object of jealousey
& hatred from maney who should encourage foster & protect, & not
try to break it down." He continues, "the people in [Clay-Ashland] are
not inclined to bow to Old Chairs Tables or Combinations, they feel
that they left masters & lords behind. and venture to contend for their

equal & Constitutional rights." In this passage, Russell describes Liberian freedom as a "feeling" for and a "venture to contend" with chattel slavery's past, as much as a practical struggle with the difficult material conditions of Liberia's present. By invoking the "Old Chairs," "Tables," "Combinations," "masters & lords" to which his fellow settlers are "not inclined to bow," Russell effectively summons the very servitude memorialized by the name of the town in which the settlers are venturing to contend for a new life. Though that past is summoned in order to be refused and transformed into something else, which Russell here names "equal and Constitutional rights," such a refusal still contains within itself a certain recognition of the past's continuing power. That is, he must acknowledge that past in some form in order to perform the refusal to bow to it. Indeed, for this refusal to remain what Russell calls an "inclination," the past itself must be kept alive and in sight, for that past is both dead (as an old "Chair" or "Table" is) and deadly (as a "master," "lord," or "Combination" might dispense disenfranchisement to the extent even of death). Paradoxically, then, the refusal to bow not only allows one to seek life, but also commits one to keeping death itself alive, particularly the threat of one's own death. To call this refusal an "inclination," as Russell does, is at once to express confidence in the refusal, as if it were a likely choice, and to be reminded of its tenuousness, as if it could just as easily be inclined otherwise, at the risk of the very life being sought. Perhaps this deep imbrication of life and death is figured by the shift from "seeking Liberty," as Russell describes the aim of his fellow settlers in my epigraph, to this passage's more attenuated formulation "venture to contend," a phrase that describes not so much a direct contention as it does a potentiality: the effort it takes to begin such a contention, or the venture that is a condition of possibility for contending.

In the next section of the letter, Rev. Russell delves even more deeply into the settlers' feeling for the past as well as the paradoxical relationship between life and death. In the process, he makes a case for understanding freedom as a tenuous, unrealized potentiality that has thus far exceeded any attempt to institutionalize or authorize it. As he continues,

Coming to Liberia 22 years ago as I did, and becoming we all once thought a crippled youth. With no rich brothers, no resources. Seeing all around me, large families, influential and united & reunited by marriage, holding all the offices in the Country & the avanues to every immolument, working every thing aparently from hand to hand and into & for each other, and looking upon all else as a third rate thing. Made aney sky dark. This kissing the "big toe" and this very "big negro" business. Has to me been the greatest "night mair" that ever crippled the energies of Liberia, and to this day the roots and limbs of those combined and self seeking influences, sway a heavy sceptre, and to a Country in which all around, every chief is King, & to emigrants from where every master is Sovreign, men taught to bow before powers seen & influences felt, Espeshialy when the love of power & office is Concidered & well weiged—and then the possession of office from the foundation of both the Collony & the Republic in the same Channels—until what was once a favor, seemes to be now aright. Though the popular vote is heard of, the ignorant thoughtless & promised hord may be both voters, & jurymen. things are not as liberal as they might be Still the true heart of Liberia feels that if our independance is declared the battle of Liberty is still to be won.

Due to a leg disease he contracted as a child shortly after arriving in Liberia, Russell walked with crutches for much of his Liberian life. But here he insists that an increasingly codified system of class and political privilege among black settlers presents a much more "crippling" obstacle to seeking freedom in Liberia than personal, physical ailments like his own. Remarkably, he figures that system in the language of servitude. The servile bowing he earlier said ex-slaves were *not* inclined to perform because they venture to contend for their rights is here precisely what "right" has come to mean to many of those very ex-slaves: "men taught to bow before powers seen & influences felt . . . until what was once a favor, seemes to be now aright." That is, some settlers have inclined toward the power of mastery and have even deftly articulated it with democracy and civil rights. Consequently, their efforts to restage life end up reiterating, even revivifying all too familiar norms of power. And yet it is this very reiteration that provokes Russell to begin to theorize a kind of liberty that is neither achieved by nor reducible to the conventional procedures of democracy or the formal freedom of rights and national citizenship. At this point in the letter, liberty is no longer an individual matter at all. Whereas earlier Russell personified the feeling of freedom in individual settlers, here it is the idealized figure of "the true heart of Liberia" that feels an as-yet-unrealized liberty. This liberty is a kind of potential: what he calls "the energies of Liberia," where "Liberia" is not so much a nation-state as it is a universal that exceeds institutional settlement, a freedom that remains open to articulation with ever-changing particulars, an articulation that in turn restages the universal itself.[69]

Rev. Russell's letter can thus be read as a critical, speculative account of the equivocal volatility of an unsettled life in colonial Liberia, a life that seeks liberty. This does not mean that Russell is unrealistic, that he loses touch with the material reality of life in Liberia, or that he abandons the empirical analysis of practical problems for idealist abstractions: nineteenth-century Liberian history is replete with countless ACS agents and bureaucrats who embodied just such an approach to its struggles. Rather, Russell turns to the critical and the speculative at precisely the moment when his account of Liberian life reveals how Liberian freedom has become *too* abstract, formal, conventional, and procedural. The letter suggests that when freedom assumes the abstract, settled forms of the national citizen and the nation-state, it begins to exhibit traces of the very mode of servitude it was supposedly excluding and overcoming.[70]

In this context, we can finally return to the passage from Russell's letter that stands as my epigraph. After expressing a mix of nostalgia and sadness for the life he left behind in the U.S.—"Your letter bears to us the very information we have for years longed to recieve, telling us in detail the history and fate of most all White and Collored that was dear to us, and that we had left behind us, the story is a Melloncholy one"—Russell makes a bold declaration: "and after all leaves us the victory who chose Africa & became seekers of Liberty, so far as the Collored people are Concerned." Whatever "information" Wickliffe communicated in his letter, Russell suggests it was so "Melloncholy" that it vindicated the choice his family made to leave for Liberia in 1833, a choice he represents as becoming "seekers of Liberty." Yet this sense of vindication is immediately and paradoxically followed by a chronicle of family deaths that began just three years after their arrival in Monrovia, a chronicle that itself tells a melancholy story: "Sinthia died 1836.

Gilbert in 1839. Mother died of dropsey in 1845. George Crawford died suddenly in 1846." Russell's missionary work "preaching to the natives, on the Goulab and Pessa lines" is then presented not as redemptive good works, but rather as melancholy in its own right: as that which prevented him from being with his kin when they died. It would seem that "the victory" these "seekers of Liberty" won to some extent restages the melancholy story Wickliffe told of life back in the U.S., as the letter's next sentence underscores: "We have suffered in Africa, and suffered greatly." In what sense, then, were the settler-colonists victorious? What "Liberty" did these "collored people" find?

Russell's next sentence can be read as a kind of answer to these questions: "It was so long before we Could find Africa out, how to live in it, and what to do to live, that it all most cost us death seeking life." To have "chose Africa" and become a "seeker of Liberty" as settler-colonists, then, became seeking life in the midst of death, coming to the brink— "all most"—of paying for life with death. Coming to the brink of death is represented as an action that continually befalls one rather than an action that one either masterfully controls and manipulates or tragically suffers. From Rev. Russell's letter, we thus learn that seeking liberty means remaining skeptical about its institutionalization and speculative about its renewed performance, opting for the actively equivocal over the formally settled. The temporality of this speculative thought, as we have seen throughout the epistolary archive of early Liberia, is recursive in that it continually returns—"again and then again," as Matilda Skipwith wrote—to ongoing legacies of U.S. slavery. But that temporality is also open-ended, in that those returns are poised on the cusp of inchoate futures called "freedom" or "liberty." In turn, the geography of that thought resists a bounded sense of home, be it what James Cephas Minor called a "land of our forefathers" or what Rev. Russell called "a Country . . . where every master is Sovreign." It becomes a geography of the "transmarine stranger," as H. W. Ellis put it, whose settlements refuse to settle.

* * *

I would like to thank Ivy Wilson and Dana Luciano for their encouragement and extremely helpful suggestions about early drafts of this essay. For their assistance with manuscript sources, I am most grateful to Matthew A. Harris, research and reference coordinator, Special Collections, University of Kentucky; Matthew Turi, manuscripts research librarian, Special Collections, University of North Carolina, Chapell Hill; and Margaret Hrabe, reference coordinator, Special Collections, University of Virginia.

NOTE ON SOURCES

I have consulted the following manuscript collections: Wickliffe-Preston Family Papers, University of Kentucky Special Collections; American Colonization Society Papers, Library of Congress, Washington, D.C.; Blackford Family Papers, Southern Historical Collection, Wilson Library, University of North Carolina, Chapel Hill; Clay Family Papers, University of Kentucky, Lexington; Cocke Family Papers, University of Virginia Special Collections.

When manuscript sources were unavailable, I have relied on letters published in nineteenth-century periodicals. It should be noted, however, that procolonization periodicals such as the *African Repository and Colonial Journal* routinely excised critical comments about Liberia from the letters they published, so their transcriptions are not entirely reliable. When nineteenth-century periodical sources were also unavailable, I have used letters transcribed and published in Bell I. Wiley's *Slaves No More: Letters from Liberia, 1833–1869* (Lexington: University Press of Kentucky, 1980). It should be noted that Wiley's transcriptions are also unreliable, in that he at times silently "corrects" grammar, syntax, and punctuation, and so manuscript sources should be consulted whenever possible, as I have done. When I have used Wiley's text, I have deleted the bracketed interpolations he adds to the letters in an apparent attempt to clarify meaning, because I have found them either unnecessary, inaccurate, or obfuscating.

NOTES

1. Reverend Alfred F. Russell to Robert Wickliffe, Wickliffe-Preston Family Papers, Box 8. A transcription of Russell's letter is available at http://legacy.bluegrass.kctcs.edu/LCC/HIS/scraps/liberia2.html.
2. For scholarship on these questions, and on the history of Liberia more generally, I refer the reader to footnotes 7 and 8 of my "The Speculative Freedom of Colonial Liberia," *American Quarterly* 63.4 (2011): 890–91.
3. Phillis Wheatley, *The Collected Works of Phillis Wheatley*, ed. John C. Shields (New York: Oxford University Press, 1988), 184.
4. See David Kazanjian, *The Colonizing Trick: National Culture and Imperial Citizenship in Early America* (Minneapolis: University of Minnesota Press, 2003): 93, 124–26.
5. Olaudah Equiano, *The Interesting Narrative and Other Writings*, ed. Vincent Carretta (New York: Penguin Books, 1995 [1789]), 221. Subsequent citations will be given parenthetically.

6. Wheatley, *Collected Works*, 181–82.

7. See L. B. Breitborde, "City, Countryside, and Kru Ethnicity," *Africa: Journal of the International African Institute* 6.2 (1991): 186–201; Vernon R. Dorjahn and Barry L. Isaac, eds., *Essays on the Economic Anthropology of Liberia and Sierra Leone* (Philadelphia: Institute for Liberian Studies, 1979); Svend E. Holsoe, "A Study of Relations between Settlers and Indigenous Peoples in Western Liberia, 1821–1847," *African Historical Studies* 4.2 (1971): 357–62; Frederick D. McEvoy, "Understanding Ethnic Realities among the Grebo and Kru Peoples of West Africa," *Africa: Journal of the International African Institute* 47.1 (1977): 62–80; W. W. Schmokel, "Settlers and Tribes: The Origins of the Liberian Dilemma," *Western Arican History, Boston University Papers on Africa, volume IV*, ed. Daniel F. McCall, Norman R. Bennett, and Jeffrey Butler (New York: Frederick A. Praeger, Publishers, 1969), 153–81.

8. A crucial account of "return" that stands apart from this tradition in significant ways is Saidiya Hartman's *Lose Your Mother: A Journey along the Atlantic Slave Route* (New York: Farrar, Straus and Giroux, 2007); I touch on her text briefly later in this essay. For touchstones on the discourse of return, see Adelaide Cromwell and Martin Kilson, *Apropos of Africa: Sentiments of Negro American Leaders on Africa from the 1800s to the 1950s* (London: Frank Cass, 1969); St. Clair Drake, "Negro Americans and the Africa Interest," in *The American Negro Reference Book*, ed. John P. Davis (Englewood Cliffs, N.J.: Prentice Hall, 1966), 662–705; Drake, "Diaspora Studies and Pan-Africanism," in *Global Dimensions of the African Diaspora*, ed. Joseph Harris (Washington, D.C.: Howard University Press, 1982), 359–66; W. E. B. Du Bois, "Pan-Africa and the New Racial Philosophy," *Crisis* 40 (November 1933); Du Bois, *The World and Africa: An Inquiry into the Part which Africa has Played in World History* (New York: International Publishers, 1946); George Shepperson, "Notes on Negro American Influences on the Emergence of African Nationalism," *Journal of African History* 1.2 (1960): 299–312; Shepperson, "The Afro-American Contribution to African Studies," *Journal of American Studies* 8 (December 1974): 281–301; Carter G. Woodson, *The Education of the Negro Prior to 1861* (Washington, D.C.: Associated Publisher Inc., 1968); Woodson, *The Mis-Education of the Negro* (Trenton, N.J.: Associated Publishers, 1933); Woodson, *The African Background Outlined or Handbook for the Study of the Negro* (Washington, D.C.: Association for the Study of African American Life and History, 1936). See also Harold R. Isaacs, "The American Negro and Africa: Some Notes," *Phylon* 20 (1959): 219–33; E. U. Essien-Udom, "The Relationship of Afro-Americans to African Nationalism," *Freedomways* 2 (1962): 391–407; Richard B. Moore, "Africa Conscious Harlem," *Freedomways* 3 (1963): 315–34; Essien-Udom, "Black Identity in the International Context," in *Key Issues in the Afro-American Experience, vol. 2: Since 1865*, ed. Nathan Huggins, Martin Kilson, and Daniel Fox (New York: Harcourt Brace Jovanovich, 1971), 233–58; Sterling Stuckey, "Black Americans and African Consciousness: Du Bois, Woodson, and the Spell of Africa," in *Going through the Storm: The*

Influence of African American Art in History (New York: Oxford University Press, 1994), 120–37.

9. Brent Edwards, "The Uses of Diaspora," *Social Text* 66.3 (2001): 45–73; Edwards, *The Practice of Diaspora: Literature, Translation, and the Rise of Black Internationalism* (Cambridge, Mass.: Harvard University Press, 2003).

10. Edwards, "The Uses of Diaspora," 47.

11. To pursue this convergence in Sierra Leone, see *The Life and Letters of Philip Quaque: The First African Anglican Missionary*, ed. Vincent Carretta and Ty M. Reese (Athens: University of Georgia Press, 2010).

12. Wesley J. Horland to James Moore, 18 January 1846, *African Repository and Colonial Journal* 23.9 (September 1847): 280.

13. Wesley J. Horland to James Moore, 19 January 1846, *African Repository and Colonial Journal* 23.9 (September 1847): 281.

14. Peyton Skipwith to John H. Cocke, 6 March 1835, Cocke Family Papers, Special Collections Library, University of Virginia, Accession No. 640, Box 81.

15. Diana Skipwith to Sally Cocke, 24 August 1837, Cocke Family Papers, Special Collections Library, University of Virginia, Accession No. 9513, Box 9.

16. Diana Skipwith to Sally Cocke, 7 May 1838, Cocke Family Papers, Cocke and Brent Family Correspondence, Special Collections Library, University of Virginia, Accession No. 9513-C, Box 1.

17. Peter Ross to Ralph R. Gurley, 11 July 1858, American Colonization Society Papers, Box I: B8, pt. 1. Isaac Ross had died in 1837 and left a will that gave his slaves the choice of being sold to another slave master in the U.S. or being freed and deported to Liberia. Although the will also stipulated that some proceeds from the sale of the estate should aid any of the enslaved who chose Liberia, Ross's heirs challenged the provision. In turn, the ASC sued the heirs to enforce Ross's colonizationist wishes. Although the ACS won the suit, money never made it to the 176 who left for Liberia. See Wiley, *Slaves No More*, 155–57.

18. Peter Ross to Ralph R. Gurley, 19 July 1858, American Colonization Society Papers, Box I: B8 pt. 2.

19. As the OED notes, this dative infinitive use of the verb "to come" is akin to the French *à venir*. Jacques Derrida has elaborated this verb extensively; see, for instance, Jacques Derrida, "Force of Law: The Mystical Foundation of Authority," *Deconstruction and the Possibility of Justice*, ed. Drucilla Cornell et al. (New York: Routledge, 1992), 3–66, as well as one of Derrida's last written works, "Enlightenment Past and to Come," in *Le Monde diplomatique*, English edition, November 2004 (http://mondediplo.com/2004/11/06derrida).

20. H. W. Ellis to Rev. William McLain, 20 November 1849, *African Repository and Colonial Journal* 26.4 (April 1850): 118.

21. H. W. Ellis to Rev. William McLain, 15 April 1850, *African Repository and Colonial Journal* 27.1 (January 1851): 4.

22. Ibid.

23. Ellis to McLain, 20 November 1849: 118.

24. Peter Linebaugh and Marcus Rediker, *The Many-Headed Hydra: Sailors, Slaves, Commoners, and the Hidden History of the Revolutionary Atlantic* (Boston: Beacon Press, 2000).

25. Kwame Anthony Appiah, *Cosmopolitanism: Ethics in a World of Strangers* (New York: W. W. Norton, 2006).

26. Ellis to McLain, 20 November 1849: 118–19.

27. James W. Wilson to Rev. William McLain, 5 August 1858, American Colonization Society Papers, Box I: B8, pt. 2.

28. A. M. Cowan, *African Repository and Colonial Journal* 34.7 (July 1858): 199.

29. Wilson to McLain, 5 August 1858: B8, pt. 2.

30. Wiley, *Slaves No More*, 33–35.

31. For a contemporary novel that echoes this collection of letters, see Caryl Phillips, *Crossing the River* (New York: Vintage, 1995).

32. Erasmus Nicholas to Lucy Nicholas, 5 March 1843, Cocke Family Papers, Special Collections Library, University of Virginia, Accession No. 9513-f, Box 8.

33. Matilda Skipwith to Sally Cocke, 23 October 1844, in Wiley, *Slaves No More*, 62; Peyton Skipwith to Lucy Nicholas Skipwith, 27 June 1846, Cocke Family Papers, Special Collections Library, University of Virginia, Accession No. 640, Box 117.

34. Matilda Skipwith Lomax to Sally Cocke and Lucy Nicholas Skipwith, 4 July 1848, Cocke Family Papers, Special Collections Library, University of Virginia, Accession No. 640, Box 125.

35. Peyton Skipwith to Lucy Nicholas Skipwith, 27 June 1846, Cocke Family Papers, Special Collections Library, University of Virginia, Accession No. 640, Box 117.

36. Peyton Skipwith to John H. Cocke, 25 June 1846, Cocke Family Papers, Special Collections Library, University of Virginia, Accession No. 640, Box 117.

37. Richard Cannon to John H. Cocke, 29 September 1844, Cocke Family Papers, Special Collections Library, University of Virginia, Accession No. 640, Box 112.

38. Leander Sterdivant to John H. Cocke, 13 August 1857, Cocke Family Papers, Special Collections Library, University of Virginia, Accession No. 640, Box 153.

39. Matilda Skipwith Lomax to John H. Cocke, 19 May 1852, Cocke Family Papers, Special Collections Library, University of Virginia, Accession No. 640, Box 140.

40. Matilda Skipwith Lomax to John H. Cocke, 26 September 1853, Cocke Family Papers, Special Collections Library, University of Virginia, Accession No. 640, Box 144.

41. James C. Minor to John Minor, 11 February 1833, *African Repository and Colonial Journal* 9.4 (June 1833): 126.

42. James C. Minor to Mary B. Blackford, 12 February 1846, *African Repository and Colonial Journal* 22.8 (August 1846): 261.

43. Wiley, *Slaves No More*, 26.

44. James C. Minor to Mary B. Blackford, n.d. 1852, Blackford Family Papers, Southern Historical Collection, Wilson Library, University of North Carolina at Chapel Hill.

45. Wiley, *Slaves No More*, 265.

46. Ibid., 266.

47. See letters by A. M. Cowan to Brutus J. Clay, 10 January 1851, and C. T. Field to Brutus J. Clay, March 22, 1856, in Clay Family Papers. Also mentioned by Wiley, *Slaves No More*, 335–36.

48. Hartman, *Lose Your Mother*, 99.

49. Ibid., 96.

50. Wiley, *Slaves No More*, 118.

51. Ibid.

52. Peyton Skipwith to John H. Cocke, 22 April 1840, Cocke Family Papers, Special Collections Library, University of Virginia, Accession No. 640, Box 98.

53. Peyton Skipwith to John H. Cocke, 11 November 1839, Cocke Family Papers, Special Collections Library, University of Virginia, Accession No. 640, Box 96.

54. Sion Harris to William McLain, 5 January 1848, American Colonization Society Papers, Box I: B3, pt. 1; Sion Harris to William McLain, 20 May 1849, American Colonization Society Papers, Box I: B3, pt. 2. On Sion Harris, see *Sanctified Trial: The Diary of Eliza Rhea Anderson Fain*, ed. John Fain (Knoxville: University of Tennessee Press, 2004), xxxiii; Tom W. Shick, *Emigrants to Liberia, 1820–1843: An Alphabetical Listing* (Newark, Del.: Liberian Studies Association of America, 1971), 43; Wiley, *Slaves No More*, 331.

55. Sion Harris to William McLain, 20 May 1849, American Colonization Society Papers, Box I: B3, pt. 2.

56. Ibid.

57. Sion Harris to Samuel Wilkeson, 16 April 1840, American Colonization Society Papers, Box I: B2.

58. Ibid. For the censored, published version of this letter, see *African Repository and Colonial Journal* 16.13 (July 1, 1840): 195–97. Wiley also mentions this censorship (*Slaves No More*, 332).

59. Ibid.

60. Ibid.

61. Sion Harris to William McLain, November 29, 1849, American Colonization Society Papers, Box I: B3, pt. 2.

62. James C. Minor to Mary B. Blackford, n.d. 1852, Blackford Family Papers, Southern Historical Collection, Wilson Library, University of North Carolina at Chapel Hill.

63. Diana Skipwith to Louisa Cocke, 20 May 1839, Cocke Family Papers, Special Collections Library, University of Virginia, Accession No. 640, Box 95.

64. Diana Skipwith to Sally Cocke, 6 March 1843, Cocke Family Papers, Special Collections Library, University of Virginia, Accession No. 9513-f, Box 8.

65. Reverend Alfred F. Russell to Robert Wickliffe, Wickliffe-Preston Family Papers, Box 8. A transcription of Russell's letter is available at http://legacy.bluegrass.kctcs.edu/LCC/HIS/scraps/liberia2.html.

66. Wickliffe, who was also a lawyer, might well have been trying to determine the fate of Russell and his family, or even to angle for some kind of supporting

testimony from them, given that Wickliffe was being sued by his wife's heirs over her inheritance. See http://legacy.bluegrass.kctcs.edu/LCC/HIS/scraps/liberia2.html.

67. Clegg, *The Price of Liberty*, 30.

68. Ibid., 37–38.

69. Judith Butler, "Restaging the Universal," in Butler, Ernesto Laclau, and Slavoj Žižek, *Contingency, Hegemony, Universality: Contemporary Dialogues on the Left* (New York: Verso, 2000), 41.

70. For an extended account of the speculative texture of the Liberia letters, see my "Hegel, Liberia," *Diacritics* 40.1 (2012): 6–39, as well as my "The Speculative Freedom of Colonial Liberia."

6

The News at the Ends of the Earth

Polar Periodicals

HESTER BLUM

> A newspaper . . . always represents an association, the members of which are its regular readers. That association can be more or less well-defined, more or less restricted, and more or less numerous, but the seed of it, at least, must exist in people's minds, as evidenced by nothing more than the fact that the newspaper does not die.
>
> Alexis de Tocqueville, *Democracy in America*, Vol. 2, Part II, Chapter 6

The mutually constitutive relationship between an association and its newspaper, as Tocqueville describes it in *Democracy in America*,[1] takes many forms throughout the eighteenth and nineteenth centuries, perhaps most influentially in the imagined community of the nation theorized by Benedict Anderson. Tocqueville's claims are derived from the smaller, voluntary associations he observed in the U.S. in the 1830s, what Anthony Ashley Cooper, third Earl of Shaftesbury, identified in the previous century as forms of "private society,"[2] an oxymoron whose axes of meaning have subsequently converged. The elements Anderson stipulates as essential to the literary genre of the national newspaper are also found in smaller collectives on a local or private scale—for instance, the assembly of seemingly unrelated parts into a fictive whole conjoined only by their "calendrical coincidence," their temporal or spatial proximity.[3] For Anderson the newspaper and the book are necessarily "mass-produced industrial commodit[ies]" that can reach a large and dispersed population seemingly simultaneously; he finds "community in anonymity."[4] Shaftesbury's coteries, on the other hand, along with Tocqueville's voluntary associations, are characterized instead by their intimacy, their ephemerality, rather than by their vast scale or their facelessness.[5] To what extent, then, can the national and the anonymous attributes of the newspaper themselves be imagined, even when the circulation of the newspaper is restricted? I am interested, in other words, in how the genre of the newspaper is itself imagined by communities.

This essay emerges from a place of paradox within these discourses of newspaper, print culture, community, and nation by studying tiny bodies of shared interest that in and of themselves constitute the mass totality of a culture. I take as my subject polar periodicals: the perhaps surprising fact of the existence of newspaper production and circulation in the Arctic by Anglo-American polar expedition members, who collectively wrote, published, read, and critically reacted to a series of gazettes and newspapers produced in extremity and directed at a restricted readership of fellow crew members. But rather than the coteries or associations mentioned above, which were contained within a broader world of sociability and print, the polar literary communities were completely isolated from any possibility of communication with other polities or individuals—even as their missions represented a nation's interest. The newspapers that Arctic expeditions produced, then, were at once mass-market commodities and privately circulated bits of ephemera. Rather than focusing on the attributes of the genre alone, I am interested in exploring a literary collective that occupies the medium itself, that takes a form of print culture associated with the nation, and locates it in a different world.

In what follows, I delineate a literary exchange whose circuits are both familiar and outlandish: the transmission of literary periodicals written and, perhaps surprisingly, *published* (largely on table-top presses) within a few degrees of the poles by expedition members for their private consumption. The newspapers were part of a full literary and artistic life aboard polar ships during the sunless winter months, in which ice-immobilized ships formed the stage for plays, literary readings, "pops" (light classical music), and lecture series. But while the journals and other voyage narratives written by expedition members were published upon their return home—and, in the case of British ventures, only after the Admiralty had approved their contents—shipboard newspapers were printed and circulated for intended consumption by the polar community aboard individual ships alone. This bifurcated model of literary exchange, at once the most quotidian in the world and the most eccentric, emerges from the dynamic of limit-excess that has been brought to bear on the polar regions, in the sense that their blank-ness and barrenness both exceed the kinds of traffic we think of as part of global or intranational exchange, and also stand as its limit.[6]

More particularly, as I detail in the second half of this essay, the existence and function of polar newspapers raises questions about the nature of collectivity in closed, isolated, literary communities repre-senting national interests—however remote from the polity. In the first North American Arctic newspaper, the *North Georgia Gazette, and Winter Chronicle* (1819–20) of William Edward Parry's first Arctic expe-dition, the question of community was quite explicitly debated within the paper itself, as contributors arranged themselves rhetorically against the "N.C.s" or "non-contributors" to the paper.[7] But as we will see, the register in which the expedition's officers (who constituted the paper's stringers) understood their playful attacks on journalistic non-contri-bution had no resonance when replayed within national borders. Arti-cles that suggested that the mission's collectivity was fragile or threat-ened, however humorous, were suppressed upon the voyage's return to Britain. The economies of literary circulation—of the barely public sphere of the polar mission—constitute this essay's focus. Aboard the *Hecla* and the *Griper*, Parry's ships, this literary economy was defined by the officer corps, by and for whom the paper was created. And yet the terms of their literary output did not compute among the "men" or non-officers of the mission (who outnumbered officers by four to one). Nor, as I will discuss below, were those terms trusted to signify in the non-polar Anglo-American literary world.

The geophysical and imaginative remoteness of the North and South Poles has drawn interest in the regions from the perspective of science, exploration, and poetic and artistic imagination. The poles have cap-tivated popular attention in Europe and the U.S. ever since the earli-est attempts to find a Northwest Passage, and the voyages south that followed in the wake of James Cook's circumnavigation of Antarctica. Science has been a primary organizing force for polar exploration dur-ing the past 250 years, even as scientific expeditions were organized by states who took a nationalist interest in the results. Unfolding on an oceanic surface of different states of matter, from liquid to solid, polar missions were staffed by scientists and a somewhat more elite class of sailors than the usual maritime crews, given the international visibility and promotion of the expeditions. After sailing as far north or south as possible during the brief polar summers, expeditions would plan to "winter over" in a harbor with relatively stable ice, ships encased by the frozen ocean and yet still jostled by shifting bergs. The men lived aboard ship during the dark winter months and prepared for overland/ ice sledging operations (either dog-, pony-, or man-hauled) in early spring, for the purposes of hydrography, scientific experimentation, or a sprint to the poles. Most expeditions launched with great fanfare, and the published voyage narratives they later generated in turn enjoyed wide circulation among a general readership, and continue to fuel public interest in bestselling popular histories today.[8]

Yet while the familiar narratives of adventurous voyage (and their fictional counterparts[9]) have been the most visible forms of literary production generated by Arctic and Antarctic exploration, the existence of printing and other forms of publishing in the polar regions themselves has been largely unremarked upon.[10] After 1850 many expeditions brought a nonstandard piece of nautical equipment aboard ship: a printing press. With such presses, polar-voyaging sailors wrote and printed newspapers, broadsides, plays, and other reading matter beyond the Arctic and Antarctic Circles. These publications were produced almost exclusively for a reading audience comprised of the mission's crew members. Their status as private, coterie literature has remained fixed in literary history; in the popular histories of Arctic and Antarctic exploration the existence of polar printing and expedition newspapers warrants barely a line or two of recognition. And yet shipboard newspapers, written and circulated among expedition members, provide an alternative account of the experiential conditions of polar exploration. Furthermore, as I argue, they also constitute an important economy in themselves: they became an alternative medium through which expedition members established terms of shared value, community, and association. While polar print culture shares many characteristics with other coterie publishing circles, whether in the eighteenth century or those identified with the elite private presses and salons of the modern era, I am interested in the collective, confined literary culture of late-nineteenth-century working men at the scene of their labor. And not just their labor: they are in a totalizing environment, one in which polar conditions determine work and leisure, interior and exterior, alike. Like all sailors, polar crew members were always on their job site; their leisure time was neither spatially separate nor guaranteed.[11] This economy of shipboard literary production is consistent with other economies—at once fiscal, manufactural, and cultural. And also like other economies, as we will see in what follows, not every partner in the exchange contributed equally. The Arctic and Antarctic regions have long presented imaginative and strategic impediments to stable possession, given the geophysical challenges of sustaining human life. But when faced with the natural antagonism of the extremity of polar conditions, nineteenth-century expedition members did not draw blanks; they printed gazettes.

Extreme Printing

The existence of shipboard literary culture was not in and of itself unusual over the course of the nineteenth century. Many long-voyaging ships were provided with libraries; sailors read histories, novels, and periodicals, intensively reading (and sharing among themselves) the small stock of reading material at hand. And polar voyages, which could plan on enforced periods of relative inactivity during the winter, had larger libraries than most ships; Sir John Franklin's *Erebus* and *Terror* ships had 3,000 volumes between them (a copy of *The Vicar of Wakefield* was found among the few artifacts recovered from the lost ships). Some sailors kept personal journals, while officers contributed to shipboard textual production in the form of logbooks, ship accounts, progress diaries, or—on more official, grander expeditions—narratives of their voyages and discoveries, which often became strong sellers. This was enabled in part by the unusual rates of literacy among seamen, estimated at 75–90% by the mid-nineteenth century.[12] As a laboring class their literacy was encouraged by onboard schools (focused on mathematics and navigation as well as letters, all necessary for nautical advancement) and a maritime culture in which leisure time was often spent in storytelling or in theatricals, a particular mainstay of British naval practice adopted at times aboard U.S. ships.

Newspapers, however, were much rarer among the literary circles of mariners. While Jason Rudy's work on the shipboard poetical practices of Victorian passengers aboard ships bound for Australia and South Africa has revealed a practice of periodical production by which men and women entertained themselves on long passages, relatively few newspapers were produced by sailors, for sailors, on open-water journeys.[13] On polar expeditions, however, shipboard newspapers became a frequent activity—even an expectation—during the several months of polar darkness in which expeditions wintered over, their ships bound by ice and their crews relatively stilled (and looking for ways to mark the time, as David and Deirdre Stam have argued[14]). In proportion to non-polar nautical missions, the percentage of newspapers aboard polar-voyaging expeditions in the nineteenth and early twentieth centuries was exceptionally high. The first polar newspaper, which will be the subject of much of this essay's discussion, was the *North* [originally *New*] *Georgia Gazette, and Winter Chronicle* (1819–20), a manuscript newspaper produced by the officers of William Edward Parry's British Northwest Passage Expedition.

Beginning in 1850, however, most polar newspapers were actually printed on presses whose initial presence on the ships' catalogue of supplies was not intended for literary recreational use. The first printing presses in the Arctic had been brought to assist in the broad dispersal of messages via balloons as an ultimately futile tool in the search for the missing Northwest Passage explorer Sir John Franklin. The red-silk-printed balloon messages were printed by the thousand and distributed across the ice in eight-foot fire balloons, in vain (fig. 1). But once table-top printing presses found their way aboard ship, expedition members found ways to adapt the press to their literary and theatrical ends. When winter storms made fire-balloon messaging impractical, the presses were recruited into more creative outfits, however ephemeral. In addition to newspapers such presses printed broadsides and playbills for shipboard theatricals (fig. 2), menus for holiday dinners, captains' orders, and songs and occasional poems composed by mission members. Sailors even carved their own large-font type in some instances. In all cases these imprints have been treated as ephemera both by expedition sponsors and members, and by print cultural history. They constitute a small and dispersed archive (Elaine Hoag estimates the number of imprints produced in the Arctic at around one hundred; she doesn't treat Antarctica),[15] found in the miscellaneous folders, perhaps, of those expedition members whose papers have been collected, those who kept samples of polar printing as souvenirs.

The literary periodicals generated near the poles include the *Illustrated Arctic News* (fig. 3) and the *Aurora Borealis*, newspapers printed in the Arctic by two sister ships engaged in the search for the lost Franklin expedition (1850–51); the *Port Foulke Weekly News* (fig. 4), written aboard Isaac Israel Hayes's Arctic voyage in the *United States*;[16] the *Arctic Moon*, a newspaper written by members of the Lady Franklin Bay Expedition (1881–82); the *Midnight Sun*, a single issue produced by the Baldwin-Ziegler Polar Expedition (1901); the *Arctic Eagle*, a gazette printed by the men on the Ziegler Polar Expedition (1903–5); the *South Polar Times*, a lavish, extensive magazine published by Scott's National Antarctic Expedition (1902–3) (that same mission had an offshoot, comic newspaper, *The Blizzard*, for pieces deemed unsuitable for *South Polar Times* inclusion); and the first book published in Antarctica, *Aurora Australis* (fig. 5). This last consists of 120 pages of mixed-genre material written by members of Shackleton's 1907–9 British Expedition, who bound copies with whatever materials were at hand, from orange crates to horse halters to boxes that once contained stewed kidneys. Newspapers were not confined to Anglo-American ventures; Norwegian Fridtjof Nansen's *Fram* expedition (1893–96) produced the manuscript newspaper *Framsjaa*, and the German Arctic Expedition led by Carl Koldewey aboard the *Hansa* (1869–70) published the *Ostgrönlandische zeitung*. Polar gazettes were generally comical, focused primarily on interpersonal affairs and cool wit rather than on the sober proceedings of the expedition proper.

Of all the ways that a polar expedition might find to pass the tedium of long, dark winters trapped in or on ice, why would crew members feel an imperative not just to write stories, poems, or travelogues, but to publish or print them? And in doing so, in what manner did they inhabit and reflect upon the genre of their literary production? I am interested in what this drive toward what we might call "extreme printing" tells us about the state of print culture and coterie publication in the nineteenth-century Anglo-American world.[17] The nearly simultaneous and necessarily limited production and consumption of these texts by polar voyagers represent an unusual print circuit—intensified but not exceptional—that emerges from the intersection of the scientific and nationalist aims of expeditions, the manual labor performed by polar voyagers, and the developing technologies of print and literary culture.

The travel accounts that were written for an interested domestic readership—that is, those in the genre of the book-length narrative of voyages and travels—had a very different orientation than the ephemera produced by the expedition members for their private consumption. Indeed, when several of the polar periodicals were later reprinted for select non-expedition members, they expurgated materials from the originals. We might think of polar periodicals as farcical locked-room mysteries, whose narrative of a given expedition is perfectly contained, yet inaccessible to the wider world. And like locked-room mysteries, polar periodicals are rigged—the key is linked to the broader readerly economy of the ship, in its situational jokes, its cant, and its circuit of referentiality. While polar expeditions might have had nationalist aims, the gazettes produced on such missions kept their focus on the local and intimate, unlike the newspapers that Benedict Anderson has argued are coextensive with nationalist projects.[18] Yet like the periodicals of Anderson's focus, polar gazettes sought to realize their function in creating community (not always successfully, as we will see).[19] The difference lies in scale and spatiotemporality: Anderson presumes the simultaneity of newspaper reading among far-flung individuals,[20] although Trish Loughran has recently made a persuasive argument that in the early U.S. such presumptions are not historically accurate. Rather than a networked national print culture, Loughran describes localized, fragmented communities of print that are more akin to what we see aboard polar ships; as she writes, "if the newspaper denies, in its casual columnar form, the scatteredness of the spaces from which it collects its information, it nevertheless bears . . . the telltale traces of that scatteredness."[21] That is, if for Anderson newspapers allowed a broadly dispersed population a sense of belonging to the imagined community of the nation, then the polar newspapers, in an alternative move, enabled a close-knit local community—one flung far from the geophysical place of the nation—to establish an imagined community apart from it. Contrary to the "silent privacy" of newspaper reading "in the lair of the skull" that Anderson describes, polar newspapers were read aloud and in common to the collective.[22] The polar community both constitutes and is constituted by the newspaper's production.

Polar voyages were confined within both the ship and the ice that made transit impossible for much of a given year. As such, we can observe a tension between the global ambitions of such voyages and the remarkably circumscribed conditions of their practice. At a terrific remove from the usual spheres of literary circulation, communities of expedition members produced new works for exchange, debate, and provocation. Polar printing emerged from the intersection of the scientific and nationalist aims of expeditions, their need to sustain morale, the manual labor performed by polar voyagers, and the developing technologies of print and literary culture. The remarkable fact of these printed works reveals, for one, the sustaining power of collective reading practices to generate forms of communal sociability, understanding, and sustenance. The employment of polar publishing, furthermore, highlights in suggestive ways the classes of people who—apart from those credited as professional authors—were writing creatively and forming coteries through the medium of the newspaper.

Expedition members, I maintain, were quite aware of these questions in crafting their papers. We see this, for example, in the *Aurora Borealis*, an Arctic newspaper from 1851[23] (the rival to the *Illustrated Arctic News*, both of Horatio Austin's Franklin search mission). In an article entitled "The Rise and Progress of Printing in the Arctic Searching Expeditions"—itself, I will note, only the second instance of printing in the Arctic, so quickly does it rise and progress—the *Aurora's* editor writes that in the Arctic "we find, in a manner little to have been expecting, printing forwarding, even here, the great cause of humanity."[24] The invocation of the "great cause of humanity" is mock-grandiose, certainly, but elsewhere in writing about the *Aurora* an officer of the expedition cites controversies and suppressions of the press that had been taking place on the European continent as part of the mid-nineteenth-century revolutions. In an argument that directly anticipates Benedict Anderson, the *Aurora Borealis* contributor writes, "A great paper like the 'Times' no longer addresses itself to one empire or to a single people. The telegraph and the railroad have destroyed space, and a truth now uttered in London in a few minutes later vibrates through the heart of France, or is heard on the shores of the Adriatic."[25] The point of this officer is not, however, to claim a relationship to this scattered empire, but to establish the paper's bona fides in worldmaking on its own terms. He continues: "The 'Aurora Borealis' was the public organ of the little world on board Captain Austin's squadron in the Arctic Seas, and its pages are a reflection of the harmony and good-fellowship, the order and the Christian union, which prevailed in the Expedition."[26] This is the sense of humanity meant in the paper's account of the rise of Arctic printing: creating little worlds through shared experience of literary circles.

The News in the *United States*

The *Aurora* officer quoted above observes the annihilation of "space" in the print culture of the newspaper. Lloyd Pratt has similarly challenged the belief that a national print culture in the early U.S. would serve the function of "homogenizing time," as "national literature, national newspapers, and other nation-based print media would function as the nation's temporal infrastructure."[27] The periodicity of polar newspapers, indeed, was wildly irregular, as David and Deirdre Stam have shown, due to "lack of paper and ink or other supplies, the inability of men to work together, novelty worn thin, and hurt feelings from jokes gone bad," in addition to "growing lassitude."[28] Intended in part to mark time through the obscurity of the polar winter, the newspapers registered the futility in doing so at the same time that they established the terms for what constituted news at the ends of the earth. In polar papers the coexistence of the everyday and the exceptional in the very existence of polar newspapers is quite consciously framed. Here I turn to the manuscript newspaper produced in the winter quarters of Isaac Israel Hayes's privately-funded North Pole mission aboard the ship *United States* (1860–1). Hayes had been the surgeon aboard fellow Philadelphian Elisha Kent Kane's closely followed Second Grinnell Expedition (1853–5), which was searching for the fate of the Franklin expedition (and which produced its own newspaper, the *Ice-Blink*). In addition to their ambitions for the North Pole or Franklinia recovery, both Kane and Hayes sought the imagined Open Polar Sea beyond the ice.[29] In the aftermath of that mission's new record for a "Farthest North"—even though it failed to produce new information about the Franklin catastrophe—Hayes ventured anew, and again participated in the publication of a polar newspaper.[30] Like many mid-century U.S. polar missions, Hayes's expedition was not federally sponsored, but supported by private patrons and the revenue from lecture tours.

In launching the newspaper, the *Port Foulke Weekly News* (fig. 4), Hayes declared, "The free press follows the flag all over the world, and the North Pole rejoices in 'The Port Foulke Weekly News.'"[31] The crew had issued handbills and posters to advertise the periodical—this, for an expedition totaling only fourteen men. The expedition members had intended to print the paper (there was in fact a press aboard) but as the editors explain in the opening number: "we hurried our paper through the press, without using our new font of type, and as it came through so well, we will probably reserve the type to make either balls of, for the purposes of sending dispatches to, and dispatching any troublesome neighbors."[32] The gesture to "troublesome neighbors" likely refers to polar bears, often shot at by venturers to the Arctic; the comic tone is consistent with most polar newspapers' imagination of the extra-expedition communities of animal life. This lighthearted balance of the voyagers' material demands and speculative fancies can also be seen in the establishment of the paper itself. As Hayes reports in his narrative, *The Open Polar Sea*, "All the details of its getting-up have been conducted with a most farcical adherence to the customs prevailing at home. There is a regular corps of editors and reporters, and office for 'general news,' and 'editorial department,' and a 'telegraph station,' where information is supposed to be received from all quarters of the world, and the relations existing between the sun, moon, and stars are duly reported by 'reliable correspondents,' and pictorial representations of extraordinary occurrences are also received from 'our artist on the spot.'"[33] The *Port Foulke Weekly News* was not alone in its "farcical" inhabitation of the expected beats for a newspaper; Hayes's description of its contents can stand for a general one: "There is a fair sprinkling of 'enigmas,' 'original jokes,' 'items of domestic and foreign intelligence,' 'personals,' 'advertisements,' &c., &c., among a larger allowance of more pretentious effusions."[34] In the "private society" described by Shaftesbury, shared wit was the basis of community building.

But even as this newspaper was intended for "the private family circle" of the expedition—as all polar periodicals were, explicitly—it had a clear idea of how its very existence reoriented the expedition's perspective on the world.[35] We see this in the following excerpt from the speech made by the paper's editor, George Knorr, upon its inauguration: "we have, at the cost of much time, labor, and means, supplied a want which has been too long been felt by the people of Port Foulke. We are, fellow-citizens, no longer without that inalienable birthright of every American citizen,—a Free Press and an Exponent of Public Opinion." After reiterating how very remote their location is from their nonetheless "wide-spread country," Knorr takes a larger view:

> Have we not left that vague border of the national domain far behind us? Yes, fellow-citizens! and it now devolves upon us to bring the vexed question of national boundaries, which has been opened by our enterprise, to a point—to a point, sir! We must carry it to the very Pole itself!—and there, sir, we will nail the Stars and Stripes, and our flag-staff will become the spindle of the world, and the Universal Yankee Nation will go whirling round it like a top. Fellow-citizens and friends:—In conclusion, allow me to propose a sentiment befitting the occasion,—A Free Press and the Universal Yankee Nation: May the former continue in times to come, as in times gone by, the handmaiden of Liberty and the emblem of Progress; and may the latter absorb all Creation and become the grand Celestial Whirligig.[36]

Knorr's reference to the "vexed question" of the "vague border" of the nation functions in several ways. Most immediately, he gestures to mid-century expansionist policies as well as to the sectional conflicts in the U.S. that would erupt into war while the ship *United States* was far above the Arctic Circle, surprising the crew upon its return. Furthermore, the invocation of nationalist terms in which to cast "Liberty" and the "Free Press" was common to the period, in which many newspapers (especially British and European) were still subject to stamp taxes and governmental censorship. But Knorr's lack of clarity about the limits of the "national domain" also serves to raise the question of what relationship polar missions had to colonialist voyages. Although expeditions to the Arctic regions were not generally designed for territorial claiming (other than the imperialist imposition of place names), this passage records a cheeky awareness that behind the interests of science and hydrographic discovery lies a grander imperial ambition. This is especially seen in the use of the phrase "Universal Yankee Nation," which originated in the 1820s as a counterpoint to the South's "Virginia race." By mid-century, though, the Universal Yankee Nation was used more sardonically to describe a certain kind of New England ingenuity and proprietary expansiveness. Knorr's toast, then, becomes an acknowledgment of the forces of acquisitional control operating behind polar expeditions, while claiming a space for parodic worldmaking within the "vague" territory of the newspaper.

I see more than the tired metaphors of colonialism here, however playfully or parodically offered. Knorr invites us to reorient our critical perception, taking a proprioceptive stance—by which I mean one mindful of the place and conditions from which it originates—that looks to planetary spaces not from a position rooted in an already-established national space, but from a new *point*, a new perspectival pole, a reorientation of our map of the world (fig. 6). Polar periodical coteries, I am arguing, are aware of the nationalizing and generalizing aspects of the genre of the newspaper, too; the *Port Foulke Weekly News* recognizes such moves as part of the demands of a newspaper. The notion of planetary spaces (as opposed to global ones), in the terms offered by Gayatri Chakravorty Spivak and Wai Chee Dimock, allow us to imagine a world organized not by relations between globalized nation-states, but a world comprised of extranational resources on a planetary scale. This point, like the "grand Celestial Whirligig" imagined by the *Port Foulke Weekly News*, sets us a-spin, and allows us to imagine Anglo-American literary studies at the ends of the earth.

Discontent in the *Winter Chronicle*

For the balance of this essay I turn to the news at the ends of the earth by way of the first newspaper written in the polar regions: the *North Georgia Gazette, and Winter Chronicle* (1819–1820) (fig. 7).[37] The *Winter Chronicle*, as it was called within its own pages, was a manuscript expedition newspaper written in the Arctic by the officers of William Edward Parry's British Northwest Passage Expedition, which consisted of just over one hundred men, about twenty of whom were officers. The widely praised expedition achieved records of latitude, which earned them a parliamentary prize. Parry also pioneered the tactic of deliberately spending the winter on the ice: whereas previous Arctic missions had foundered when unable to return to open water before the cold season set in, Parry embraced the prospect of a long, frozen sojourn above the Arctic Circle. He arranged for shipboard theatricals (a mainstay of British naval recreational practice) and, "In order still further to promote good-humour among ourselves, as well as to furnish amusing occupation, during the hours of constant darkness," Parry determined that the ship would "set on foot a weekly newspaper." He named Captain Edward Sabine (who helmed the expedition's sister ship) as editor, and hoped the gazette would serve the purpose of "diverting the mind from the gloomy prospect which would sometimes obtrude itself on the stoutest heart."[38]

As we shall see, however, the newspaper's charge to bring recreation and pleasure to its intimate sphere of circulation found a more electric transference than Parry had anticipated. The newspaper's sense of fun and play began to rest over the course of its issues on a staged feud between the contributors and the non-contributors (or "N.C.s") to the paper—all of whom were officers. But when the expedition's success and popularity resulted in London republication of the *North Georgia Gazette, and Winter Chronicle,* Parry suppressed many of the most barbed articles on the N.C.s. The wit that had circulated among their coterie was prevented from circulation in the literary sphere outside of the ship's own economy. In other words, the expedition's officers' presumptions of private, intimate, collaborative mutuality were compromised in and altered by publication, thus calling into question the very premises of joint endeavor and mutuality undergirding the expedition itself. Tracing the breakdown in the *Chronicle* gives us an opportunity to rethink the kinds of community associations formed outside of the imagined communities we have thought of as constituting both the nation and national print culture.

The initial number of the *Chronicle* proposed to circulate the paper "amongst the Officers of the Expedition," whom were presumably to provide the content, too, as editor Sabine claimed that he was "wholly dependent on the Gentleman of the Expedition" for the success of the paper.[39] A letter of approbation from "Philo Comus" (a pseudonym of Parry's, indicating a love of revels and play) was published in the first number, expressing hope that the *Chronicle* would "serve to relieve the *tedium* of our one hundred days of darkness"—the three-month-plus portion of the polar winter in which the sun would never appear (I:1, emphases in original unless otherwise noted). The contributions were delivered anonymously and published pseudonymously (a manuscript copy of the *New Georgia Gazette, and Winter Chronicle* held at the Scott Polar Research Institute identifies the contributors to the newspaper).[40] The tone of the contributions to the *Chronicle* responds to this desire to keep the expedition members pleasantly occupied: the articles are largely witty and playful, and include reviews of shipboard theatricals in addition to the lyrics of expedition-themed songs written and performed at the ship's winter quarters. Other genres featured in the paper are riddles and enigmas, mock advertisements and notices, and analyses of the social habits of the expedition's dogs. One "Nauticus" tried to submit a mathematical problem, but it was rejected for its simplicity—it failed to "exercise the ingenuity" of the crew (I:15). These categories were not necessarily trifling. The genre of the riddle, as David Shields has written, presumes an audience "something more than witless"; as such, riddles "could be considered the citizenship exam for membership in the republic of letters."[41]

Even though the paper's editor, Captain Sabine, later wrote that "at the time [the issues] were composed, not the remotest idea was entertained of their fulfilling any other purpose than that of relieving the tedium of an Arctic Winter, and perhaps of afterwards affording amusement to a few private friends at home," the *Chronicle* was in fact printed in London a year after the expedition's return, in response to "the interest which the Public took in all that had passed during the voyage." The interest was so high, in fact, that sources were leaking information to the press in advance of the British Admiralty's approval of the publication of Parry's official voyage narratives. As a review of the reprint of the *Chronicle* explains, "By the rules of the Admiralty, every person employed in public Expeditions, is bound, on returning home, to give up his Journals and other memoranda at a certain latitude, and not to publish or cause them to be made known until Government has sanctioned their publication" ("A Journal of a Voyage"). In the prefatory note to the printed edition of the paper, Sabine trusts that the contributors "may be allowed to claim from the general reader the same indulgence, which they would have received, had the perusal of the Chronicle been confined to the partial circle to which they originally intended it should have been limited" (*North Georgia Gazette* v).[42] The implied reader of the *Winter Chronicle*, ideally, remains Arctic-bound, even as Sabine's language evokes the conventions of first-person narrative writing: an apology for deficiencies of circumstance, which we are told have been uncorrected upon publication.

Yet despite Sabine's promise that "no alteration has been attempted in the respective papers, in preparing them for the press," the printed edition nevertheless excises a good number of articles and letters from the manuscript version. The decision about what pieces to cut seems to have been made by expedition leader Parry himself, judging from a manuscript edition of the newspaper that he had given to his sister, which is preserved at the Scott Polar Research Institute. Parry's copy was written in ink, but has been corrected with penciled annotations. Although there are a number of grammatical or minor stylistic emendations, the most visible editorial marks indicate the excision of a good number of letters, articles, and other pieces for the newspaper. In some examples individual paragraphs are crossed out; in most, the penciled hand—almost certainly Parry's—strikes through whole contributions. In several instances the word "omit" has been written at the head of an entry. In all cases but one (mentioned below), the omissions proposed in the manuscript paper were indeed left out of the printed version.

One might expect that the excisions made for the sake of public circulation of the gazette would be of material that was racy, crude, or nonsensical. This is not, however, the case: Parry's censorship focuses largely on articles that concern a supposed feud among the officers over the question of whom is adequately contributing to the expedition's mission. Strikingly, the majority of the excised pieces consist of an ongoing series of editorials, letters, and fictional stories proposing outlandishly violent reprisals against what the gazette calls the "N.C.s," or the "non-contributors," to the *Winter Chronicle* (the N.C.s are singled out for not contributing specifically to the paper, I will stress; there is no indication otherwise that their contributions to the broader polar mission are deficient). This is not to say that concerns about the non-contributors did not make it into the print version—in fact, the contents of the late issues in the twenty-one-number run of the *Chronicle* were increasingly dominated by articles on the N.C.s. At their most mild, the articles wonder whether the non-contributors lack the wit to contribute; at their most heated, the contributors threaten to multiply behead the "many-headed monster, the *Encea Borealis*, vulgarly called N.C."; or to brand their counterparts "with a red-hotte ironne, fashioned after the letters N.C." The latter, in fact, is drawn from the one piece Parry identified for omission that for an unknown reason made its way into the paper: an example of the genre of fiction in which a narrator finds a superannuated manuscript account, which he in turn presents to the reader. In this instance the manuscript describes an expedition to the Arctic in which certain members refuse to participate in "merrie-making"; the Captain withholds their rations in punishment, for "those which do not benefitte the Communitie, the Communitie is not bounded to benefittee *them*."[43] I make the assumption that these tensions were largely rhetorical not just because of the amusing extremity of its language, but because Parry's identification of the pseudonymous contributors shows that the fight was pitched between and among the top-ranking officers writing variously as N.C.s and as contributors.

But even though the tone of both the printed and excised articles is satirical, the rhetorical playfulness of the attacks on the non-contributors cannot disguise a very serious concern: that not all expedition members are fairly sharing in the mission's labors and in its rewards. The suppressed pieces, in particular, reveal an escalating distress and mock anger over the differences between the contributing and non-contributing members of the expedition. Sabine's notion of a "partial circle" of readers is key, I am arguing. And as a reflexive gesture to the severely limited circulation of the paper, it is also disingenuous, like all such gestures within such genres of coterie writing. The articles in the *North Georgia Gazette, and Winter Chronicle*—and indeed, that of other polar newspapers as well—are finely tuned to their intimate sphere of circulation, given all the inside jokes and event- and place-specific references. In the *Winter Chronicle* this attention is most keenly felt in terms of the paper's role in fostering and reflecting collaborative labor. The paper's existence was wholly reliant on full participation in its production, the editorial statements said repeatedly. In just the second issue of the paper, Sabine was sounding the alarm to those who had not yet contributed: "I would also remind those who are yet silent," he wrote, "that *now* is the time when support is most needed; when, if every person will put his shoulder to the wheel in earnest, (and each individual may command his own exertions,) there can be no doubt that your Paper will go on with spirit" (II:15). Sabine's metaphor of self-directed manual labor aside, this call for writerly work was issued to a coterie within a coterie: the twenty-odd officers sharing exceptionally tight quarters with nearly eighty "men," the seamen not holding officer status. On polar expeditions, it should be noted, extreme conditions and small crews necessarily required that officers would to do a far more balanced share of the mission's manual work than on open-water ventures; there was far less difference in onboard functions between officer and "man" than on other naval or merchant ships.

We see this worry about the failure of collectivity in a poem directed to the N.C.s by one of the expedition's lieutenants, writing as "Timothy Tickle'em." In the poem—which was one of the ones Parry struck from appearance in print—we learn of the contributors' plan "To tear their characters to bits" upon the expedition's return home:

> The Churls, I vow, who *cannot* write
> Aught to be hang'd, or shot outright,
> As useless Vermin who destroy
> The food we should alone enjoy
> But wherefore spend our words in vain,
> When all our hints inflict no pain?
> We'll roar it out to all the world,
> When once again our sails are furl'd: . . .
> Thus, my dear friends, we'll serve each knave,
> Who does not chuse to send his stave,
> And if we can't excite their shame,
> At home, at last, we'll brand their name.[44]

This poem excited "considerable foment" among the N.C.s, we learn from a suppressed letter to the editor, written by Parry himself. The vow, when back in England, to "shame" or "brand" the name of those who did not contribute is seen in other contributions, such as the punishment mentioned above of branding the letters *N.C.* on an offender's cheeks. This, we are told, is done so that "our friends in old Englande might aske and know theyre historie" (MS *Chronicle* No. 9). What is notable is that these threats to expose the non-contributors to the broader social and professional world—however humorously intended in the manuscript or coterie newspaper—are nevertheless censored from the public record of the printed newspaper. Parry wished to keep the rhetorical exercise of non-contribution within the world of the expedition only.

Even though threats of beating or hanging non-contributors are not meant to be taken literally, one presumes, a response from a supposed N.C.-sympathizer (identified as Lieutenant Hoppner, a very frequent contributor) in the form of a letter to the editor (likewise censored from the print version) seems to take the larger social and professional threat more seriously. The poem by Timothy Tickle'em, the correspondent writes, "seemed to express a degree of malice that I imagined never would have been permitted to creep into [the *Chronicle*'s] columns, which I always fancied, were originally intended to afford amusement to *our own little circle*." The writer's stress here on the *"little circle"* of this coterie newspaper's audience is significant; the frequency of the attacks on those not writing for the paper means the non-contributors had legitimate reasons to fear losing face in the social and professional spheres back home. What is more, the N.C.s' concerns seem to have been ongoing, as the letter continues: "The spiteful pleasure which your Correspondent anticipates in pointing out the Non-Contributors to those who have no concern in the affair will, I fear, give just grounds for strengthening the apprehensions that many entertained before, of similar intentions" (MS *Chronicle* No. 15). The fear on behalf of the N.C.s of the possibility of a "stain on their characters" seems to hit a nerve; as the letter from the defender of the non-contributors concludes, "although the N.C.'s may be wrong, still they do not deserve . . . that stain upon their Characters which this, and some other Articles are likely to impress on the minds of readers who are unacquainted with circumstances" (MS *Chronicle* No. 15). This remark, made by a pseudonymous contributor, shows a presumption of an audience outside the orbit of their polar sphere. The social tension staged is palpable here, and the paper's editor, Captain Sabine, appended a judicious note to the letter of protest, which said that Sabine would have questioned the letter writer had he known who he were. The "lines in question did not strike us as written with any such ill-design," Sabine explains, but allows that although "we may . . . have been mistaken, but we really do not perceive what occasion any individual among amongst us can have for a 'malicious feeling' toward the persons who have not written for the Winter Chronicle" (MS *Chronicle* No. 15). This measured justifica-tion stands in contrast to the bombastic affectation of the newspaper's previously published threats against the bodies and reputations of the non-contributors.

A follow-up letter from the author of the threatening poem, Timo-thy Tickle'em (again, one omitted from the London publication of the paper) asks facetiously what the N.C.s fear—that the "Admiralty will seek out the names of those two or three individuals out of 20, who have never written for the Winter Chronicle?" No, the contributor argues; "the N.C.'s must know, that the knowledge even of the *existence* of a paper among us must necessarily be confined to a very limited cir-cle; & that whatever stigma is brought upon them on this account, is one of their own seeking." The presumption of intimacy, of a private society outside of state relations, is key to this contributor's position, as he continues: "If the contributions to the Winter Chronicle were to be regulated by law, like the Income-tax, according to each man's *ability* to contribute, it is evident how woefully the N.C.'s would be in arrears!" (MS *Chronicle* No. 16). This letter relocates the social threat of non-con-tribution to the immediate coterie of the expedition itself, rather than the broader English professional world.

As it turns out, Parry's manuscript edition of the *Chronicle* reveals that the proportion of contributors was far less than the 85%-plus from the letter quoted above (that is, the claim that only "two or three indi-viduals out of 20" were N.C.s). Parry's copy identifies virtually all the authors of the pseudonymous contributions, and we find there were a total of ten contributors. Three of the ten, however, contributed only one or two pieces to the paper. The seven frequent contributors include Parry, Captain Sabine, several other lieutenants, and the ship's clerk and purser. The three who made only a few contributions, however, were all midshipmen, the lowest class of officers. And among these midshipmen we find John Bushnan, whom Parry identifies as the author of the let-ters from "N.C."—his only contribution to the *Chronicle*. Midshipmen, who had just begun their professional naval careers, would have the most to fear from threats to their reputation. This would be especially true in the case of the *Chronicle*, in which the spats and disputes are all staged among high-ranking officers writing pseudonymously.

But officers, of course, were not the only members of the expedition. None of the "men" aboard ship—the able seamen, boatswain's and carpenter's mates, eighty-odd all told—seem to have contributed to the paper. Nor is it clear that they necessarily read it, although the men serving at the officers' mess table would have the occasion to overhear the reading aloud of the *Chronicle* over a meal, and perhaps spread its contents among the common seamen.[45] Perhaps a seaman might have been passed one of the manuscript copies of the paper, but it would likely have been something acquired under the table. This sense is reinforced by another unprinted letter to the editor. This short note is signed by "Timothy Hint," and expresses pointedly the stresses of keeping labor expectations in balance. Here is the note, in full: "It is a well-known fact in the Natural History of Bees, that a certain part of the year, the working Bees confederate to turn the *Drones* out of the Hive; perhaps some one of your Correspondents may know at what part of the year this circumstance usually takes place, and whether it differs in different climates" (MS *Chronicle*, 14). The worker bees do virtually all of the labor in the beehive, including catering to the drones, whose only function is to be available to impregnate the queen bee—at which point the drone dies. (Also relevant, given the Arctic setting, is the fact that the turning out of the drones from the hive usually happens in early winter, when the *Winter Chronicle* was launched.) The letter, written by second-in-command (and *Chronicle* editor) Sabine, could indicate a coded fear, however wry, that the workers (that is, the common seamen of the voyage) might feel collectively mutinous against the drones (the officers).

The potential for insurrection would be no laughing matter at sea, of course, where mutinous sailors potentially faced death. Less than two months before the *North Georgia Gazette, and Winter Chronicle* shut down production, a letter from a correspondent named "Peter Plainway"— Parry himself—asserted a resurgence of collective work and good will. Notably, this letter appears in the fourteenth volume of the London version—where it was printed in place of the provocative Timothy Tickle'em poem, which had opened that particular issue in the manuscript version of the *Chronicle*. Parry claims that it "is evident, that the number of [the paper's] Correspondents is weekly increasing. . . . The N.C.s!—but alas the very name is now almost extinct" (XIV: 53). "Extinct" in the printed *North Georgia Gazette,* perhaps—but alive and kicking in the manuscript version, and therefore among the officers during the expedition.

Parry had intended for the newspaper to "emplo[y] the mind" and "divert the leisure hours"; he had anticipated no "unpleasant conse-quences" of giving his men a literary outlet for their opinions.[46] Yet the expedition's surgeon, Alexander Fisher, reveals in his own narrative of the voyage that there was reason to worry about the consequences of giving the men license to free expression. Fisher's narrative is taken from the journal he kept during the voyage; the following concerns about the *Winter Chronicle* were presumably recorded before its first numbers appeared:

> I have no doubt but it will answer its end, that is, of diverting the men; but . . . I am not quite so certain of its answering its purpose so well, for I have seen one or two instances, and have heard of many more, where newspapers on board of ship, instead of affording general amusement, and promoting friendship and a good understanding amongst officers, tended in a short time to destroy both: . . . until at length the paper, instead of being the source of amusement and instruction, becomes the vehicle of sarcasms and bitter reflections. (Fisher, *Journal of a Voyage* 152)

I need hardly add that Fisher was himself a non-contributor. Provoca-tively, even though Fisher is not recorded as a contributor to the news-paper, he did hustle his *Journal* through the press so quickly that the Admiralty investigated to see if he had kept a private copy of his let-ters, which would have been in violation of the Admiralty's early-nine-teenth-century practice of collecting all written material from an expe-dition. As a review of his journal put it, he was "unjustly suspected of having kept a duplicate of his Journal, in order to forestall Capt. Parry's promised work" ("A Journal of a Voyage of Discovery").[47]

Yet a contemporary review of the *Chronicle* (not familiar with the unexpurgated version of the gazette) points out that injunctions against wounding the feelings of members of the group serve only to weaken the junto's literary output: forbidding hurt feelings is "a law as destruc-tive to mirth and quizzery, as that of political libel would be to free opinion. . . . It seems absolutely to have assisted the climate to freeze up the spirit of *fun* altogether."[48] Another review noted what seemed to be Parry's proprietary—or censorious—practices. In introducing its review of the *Chronicle*, the *Literary Gazette* explains, at length:

> soon after the expedition returned, we had a file of these Gazettes lent to us, with permission to extract such articles as we thought would afford pleasure to the readers of the Literary Gazette. In a fit of extra politeness, we thought it would be a compliment to Captain Parry to mention our purpose to him, and to obtain his sanction. To this we received the annexed letter,* and as we had committed ourselves by the request, we could not, as gentlemen, proceed any further. We accordingly cancelled what was printed for our forthcoming Number; and the readers of the polar newspaper must consequently exhibit their half-guinea for what in our pages would not have cost them half-a-crown.

> * Captain Parry presents his compliments to the Editor of the Literary Gazette, and begs to acquaint him, in reply to his letter of yesterday, that the officers who contributed to the paper in question, have some time ago consented to have the *whole* to be printed in one volume, to be at the disposal of the publisher, after a certain number of copies have been given to each of the contributors, and that they are now in the press. Captain P., therefore, cannot but express a hope, in his own name, and that of the officers, that no extracts from it may be published in any other shape. ("North Georgia Gazette, and Winter Chronicle" 325)

We see here Parry's desire to control, above and beyond even the Admiralty's own regulation, how the Anglo-American literary world encountered the productions of the Arctic literary sphere. Even though Parry commanded several further hugely successful Arctic expeditions, his crews never again produced a newspaper. What is more, future polar papers on other missions did not confine their contributor list to the officer corps.

Joking about non-contribution by high-ranking officers was all very well when it was an internal matter, a private manuscript newspaper. But as the more incendiary pieces in the *Chronicle*—actually written by major officers—were withheld from the printed version for the public, the actual attribution of the suppressed articles says something all the more powerful about how they imagined the non-transmissability of their experience to the broader world, how they imagined their literary collectivity as something apart from their professional collectivity. While these can seem like the kind of debates that take place in a boarding school newspaper, or in the amateur journalism produced by American teenagers in the late nineteenth century, it is important to keep in mind the totality of their lives that sailors devoted to the oceanic world. As one officer wrote in a private letter about the *Chronicle*, "when it is considered at what an early period the officers of the navy are sent to sea generally at eleven or twelve years of age and that the education which they receive on board can scarcely be supposed to be on the best or most enlarged plan it will we think be admitted that many of the papers in the North Georgia Gazette are far superior to what might reasonably be expected and such as would not discredit the more regular scholar and practised writer."[49]

In the sharp-witted and somewhat poisonous debates about the non-contributors in the *Chronicle*, we see a concern about how hierarchies were maintained in an environment demanding collective labor. The contributors' periodical assaults on the non-contributors reveal, I argue, that in brutal conditions in which none had comfort or leisure, the force of distinction came down to the literary. Given the generic self-reflexivity of polar periodicals, a change in the circumference of a paper's sphere of reception alters fundamentally the nature of the genre itself. The reason that non-contribution was so very threatening, ultimately, has to do with the very nature of polar periodicals as cultural and social markers. If an Arctic newspaper exists functionally and materially on board in its textual circulation, but not imaginatively in the space it occupies in service to the ship's "humanity," then non-contribution breaks the fantasy that the polar expedition is still connected to the world. Not necessarily the settled world, or what we might think of it as the "inside" world to the polar regions' "outside"—but the expedition's own world, constituted by the ship, the crew, its materials, and the literary imagination that populates it. The news at the ends of the earth, then, circulates both at the poles and in the fictive elsewhere that functions, for expedition members, as the world itself. If this mode of exchange is not globalist in the sense of current rhetorics of transnational criticism, it is nonetheless planetary in its imagination of literature produced in extremity as both remarkable and as inevitable as the daily paper.

Figure 1. National
Maritime Museum
AAA3970.

Figure 2. Personal collection belonging to
Edward N Harrison, clerk in charge HMS
ASSISTANCE, National Maritime Museum
MSS/75/061.

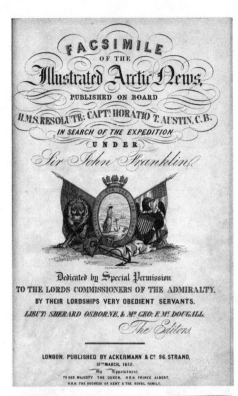

Figure 3. Facsimile of the *Illustrated Arctic News,* printed aboard HMS *Resolute*, 1850–51. Stefansson Collection, Dartmouth College.

Figure 4. *Port Foulke Weekly News,* MS newspaper aboard *United States,* Isaac Israel Hayes's Arctic Expedition, 1860–61. New-York Historical Society.

Figure 5. Title page of
Aurora Australis, printed at
the Sign of "the Penguins"
by Joyce and Wild, 1908–9.
Image courtesy State Library
of South Australia.

Figure 6.
*The Arctic
Region,
Showing
Explo-
ration
toward the
North Pole.*
Library
Company
of Phila-
delphia.

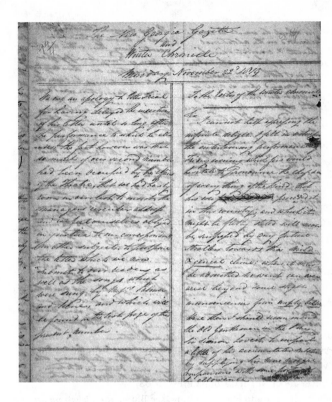

Figure 7. Copy of *New Georgia Gazette* given to Sir John Franklin. Pasted in to *Sir John Franklin, The Discoverer of the North West Passage, Original Letters Written During his Arctic Expeditions*, National Maritime Museum FRN/1.

NOTES

1. Alexis de Tocqueville, *Democracy in America*, trans. Arthur Goldhammer (New York: Library of America, 2004).

2. Anthony Ashely Cooper, Third Earl of Shaftesbury, *Sensus Communis: An Essay on the Freedom of Wit and Humour. . . .* (London: 1709), 1.

3. Benedict Anderson, *Imagined Communities: Reflections on the Origin and Spread of Nationalism* (London: Verso, 1991), 33.

4. Anderson, *Imagined Communities*, 34, 36.

5. Scholars of print culture—I am thinking particularly of Trish Loughran and Meredith McGill—have described how paying closer attention to the operations of transnational and local spheres of circulation dismantles some elements of Anderson's model and shores up others.

6. For a discussion of presumed nonproductiveness of polar spaces, see Hester Blum, "John Cleves Symmes and the Planetary Reach of Polar Exploration," *American Literature* 84: 2 (2012): 243–71.

7. *North Georgia Gazette and Winter Chronicle*, in William Edward Parry, *Journal of a Voyage for the Discovery of a North-West Passage from the Atlantic to the Pacific:*

Performed in the Years, 1819–20, in His Majesty's Ships Hecla and Griper under the Orders of William Edward Parry (Philadelphia: Abraham Small, 1821).

8. On the early-nineteenth-century publications emerging from Arctic missions, see the work of Janice Cavell in *Tracing the Connected Narrative: Artic Exploration in British Print Culture, 1818–1860* (Toronto: University of Toronto Press, 2008) and Adriana Craciun in "Writing the Disaster: Franklin and Frankenstein," *Nineteenth-Century Literature* 65:4 (2011): 433–80. See also Russell Potter's *Arctic Spectacles: The Frozen North in Visual Culture, 1818–1875* (Seattle: University of Washington Press, 2007) and Michael Robinson's *The Coldest Crucible: Artic Exploration and American Culture* (Chicago: University of Chicago Press, 2006).

9. On Arctic-inspired nineteenth-century fiction, Jen Hill is particularly sharp; see her *White Horizon: The Arctic in the Nineteenth-Century British Imagination* (Albany: SUNY Press, 2009).

10. The exception has been the excellent bibliographic work done by David and Deidre Stam and by Elaine Hoag, cited below in notes 14 and 15.

11. As Cesare Casarino notes, maritime labor in the nineteenth century was "altogether resistant to the increasingly parcelized and mechanic rhythms of an industrial environment such as the factory" (*Modernity at Sea: Melville, Marx, Conrad in Crisis* [Minneapolis: University of Minnesota Press, 2002], 54). For more on sailors' labor and leisure conditions, see also Hester Blum, *View from the Masthead: Maritime Imagination and Antebellum American Sea Narratives* (Chapel Hill: University of North Carolina Press, 2008).

12. For more on sailors' literacy and literary culture, see Blum, *The View from the Masthead.*

13. See Jason R. Rudy, "Floating Worlds: Émigré Poetry and British Culture," *ELH* 81: 1 (2014): 325–50. In my research I have seen a handful of manuscript newspapers aboard British ships in the India trades; six of these are located at the National Maritime Museum archives in Greenwich, England. Even fewer American seamen's journals mention the presence of a shipboard newspaper. The Kemble Maritime Collection at the Huntington Library, which largely covers cruise ships from the late nineteenth through the late twentieth century, holds ship newspapers for under thirty vessels out of nine hundred collected; but most of those thirty-odd newspapers were aggregations of wire reports from the electronic ages of communication, rather than content produced aboard ship.

14. David H. Stam and Deirdre C. Stam, "Bending Time: The Function of Periodicals in Nineteenth-Century Polar Naval Expeditions," *Victorian Periodicals Review* 41, no. 4 (Winter 2008).

15. Elaine Hoag, "Caxtons of the North," *Book History* 4 (2001): 81–114.

16. *Port Foulke Weekly News.* MS in New-York Historical Society. 1860–61.

17. In coining this phrase I register the echo of Anderson's description of the newspaper as "an 'extreme form' of the book, a book sold on a colossal scale, but of

ephemeral popularity," mindful of "the obsolescence of the newspaper on the morrow of its printing" (*Imagined Communities*, 34–35).

18. Anderson, *Imagined Communities*.

19. Ibid.

20. Ibid.

21. Trish Loughran, *The Republic in Print: Print Culture in the Age of U.S. Nation Building, 1770–1870* (New York: Columbia University Press, 2007), 11.

22. Anderson, *Imagined Communities*, 35.

23. *Arctic Miscellanies: A Souvenir of the Late Polar Search*. [Horatio Austin.] (London: Colburn and Co., 1852).

24. Ibid., 246.

25. Ibid., xxiii.

26. Ibid., xxiv.

27. Lloyd Pratt, *Archives of American Time: Literature and Modernity in the Nineteenth-Century* (Philadelphia: University of Pennsylvania Press, 2010), 4.

28. Stam and Stam, "Bending Time."

29. Isaac Israel Hayes, *The Open Polar Sea: A Narrative of a Voyage of Discovery Towards the North Pole, in the Schooner "United States"* (New York: Hurd and Houghton, 1867).

30. Hayes would continue to support newspapers in unexpected places. As the surgeon in charge of Satterlee Hospital in Philadelphia during the Civil War, Hayes promoted the formation of a hospital newspaper, the *West Philadelphia Hospital Register* (1863). Hayes wrote in the *Register*: "For the information of those who may feel an interest in the success of our 'little sheet,' we would say that it is printed and published, within the walls of the Hospital.—The type is set up, and the press-work performed by Soldiers, whose names are given below.—convalescent patients, partially disabled by service in the field" (I:ii:7).

31. Hayes, *The Open Polar Sea*, 176.

32. *Port Foulke Weekly News*, 11 Nov. 1860, 1:1.

33. Hayes, *The Open Polar Sea*, 177.

34. Ibid., 181.

35. *Port Foulke Weekly News*, 11 Nov. 1860, 1:1

36. Hayes, *The Open Polar Sea*, 179–80.

37. The original manuscript version was entitled *New Georgia Gazette and Winter Chronicle*, after the land that Parry named "New Georgia." Upon the expedition's return, however, Parry discovered that there already was a New Georgia, so the name of the land and of the gazette was changed in future iterations to "North Georgia." Henceforth all references to the paper were to the *North Georgia Gazette, and Winter Chronicle*.

    A note on sources: the *North Georgia Gazette* was printed as an appendix to Parry's journal of the voyage. When I quote from the printed version, I will refer to the pagination in Parry's journal as well as the periodical's number.

Elsewhere in this essay I cite the manuscript version of the *New Georgia Gazette*, which contains material that is not printed in the North Georgia version in Parry's journal; when I refer to the manuscript version, I will cite the newspaper's number, as there is no pagination in the manuscript version.

38. *Journal*, 99.

39. *North Georgia Gazette*, vi.

40. *New Georgia Gazette, and Winter Chronicle*, Scott Polar Research Institute, MS 438/12.

41. David S. Shields, *Civil Tongues and Polite Letters in British America* (Chapel Hill: University of North Carolina Press, 1997), 162.

42. The few reviewers who commented upon the *North Georgia Gazette* accepted this cue, noting that standard critical energies would be inappropriate. As one review put it, "though the volume before us has a claim beyond that of most, if not of all others, that we have every perused, to be excepted from the severities, and even the justice of criticism; we may be permitted equally to admire and eulogize those compositions, which sprang into existence amidst the regions of eternal frost" (*European Magazine*, 541). The only complaint of most reviewers was the high half-guinea price for the volume.

43. *North Georgia Gazette*, MS No. 9.

44. Ibid., MS No. 14.

45. This degree of rank-based exclusivity would be significantly smaller in the polar publications in the decades to come.

46. "A Journal of a Voyage of Discovery to the Arctic Regions, in his Majesty's Ship Hecla and Griper, in the years 1819 and 1820," *Gentleman's Magazine* (May 1821): 99.

47. "Journal of a Voyage," 442–43.

48. *Examiner*, 3 June 1821: 348.

49. *Letters Written During the Late Voyage of Discovery in the Western Arctic Sea, by an Officer of the Expedition* (London: Printed for Sir Richard Phillips, 1821), 59.

7

Feeling Like a State

Writing the 1863 New York City Draft Riots

GLENN HENDLER

Passed by Congress on March 3, 1863, the "Act for enrolling and calling out the national Forces, and for other Purposes" proclaimed that "all able-bodied male citizens of the United States, and persons of foreign birth who shall have declared on oath their intention to become citizens under and in pursuance of the laws thereof, between the ages of twenty and forty-five years . . . are hereby declared to constitute the national forces." These citizens and proto-citizens were to be transformed into "national forces" through a census-like survey of homes by government agents, a division of each state into "enrolment districts" with numerical quotas for draftees, and then a set of lotteries to determine who would be called up for military service.[1] In short, the first military draft ever imposed in the United States entailed an unprecedented quantification and instrumentalization of the nation's white male population in order to make it available for use by the state.[2]

Conscription had been deemed necessary because of the mixed military record of Union troops up to that point in the war—which had already lasted far longer than many northerners had expected—and especially because of the increasingly serious problem of retention; desertion and other illegal acts had reduced Union forces by more than a hundred thousand.[3] Even so, the act provoked resistance even before it passed Congress. Democrats immediately put the legislation in the context of what they saw as the Republicans' unwarranted extension of U.S. state power and bureaucracy, noting that it authorized a new apparatus of enforcement headed by a provost marshal general, whose agents were to arrest "deserters, spies, traitors, and other people deemed disloyal to the northern war effort."[4] Critics also complained about the bill's complexity, its intrusiveness, and the arbitrariness of its lottery system. But the most controversial component of the law stipulated that those who could afford to hire a substitute or present three hundred dollars were exempt from conscription. Class antagonisms accentuated by this provision were conjoined in the public mind with the politics of race and slavery, a conflation best exemplified in the oft-repeated complaint that the price of a substitute was lower than the price of a slave; by that logic poor whites had been reduced to a status lower than chattel slavery.[5] Thus, not only were white male citizens being systematically quantified; the opposition had at hand a similarly quantitative way of describing this process as comparable to enslavement.

The U.S. state began this expansion of governmentality just as it had all but lost two features traditionally seen as constitutive of state sovereignty: control over its own territory and its monopoly on violence. Within the area it still ruled after the secession of eleven of thirty-four states, the federal state's legitimacy was nowhere more in question than in New York City. As early as January 1861, Mayor Fernando Wood had called for the formation of a neutral and independent city-state to be called Tri-Insula, which was to consist of Manhattan, Staten Island, and Long Island, and would prosper by trading with both the Union and the nascent Confederacy. While Wood's proposal garnered little support, the city remained a stronghold of Copperhead and antiwar sentiment. Some opposition was rooted in explicit proslavery and pro-Confederacy opinion, though the most prominent factor was probably the city's economic dependence on the trade in cotton. Then, just days after the Union army barely turned back a massive military incursion into northern territory at the battle of Gettysburg, the beleaguered nation's largest city erupted into violent, open rebellion in response to the federal government's assertion that it had the power to conscript its white male citizens' bodies into that army. Viewed in this light, the New York City draft riots represented one of the greatest threats to the authority of the U.S. state in that or any other era.[6]

Violence broke out on July 13, 1863, just as the machinery for conducting the lottery and the bureaucracy for implementing the draft were being put into place. At first the rioters directed their rage at such state apparatuses, starting with the office of the provost marshal. These purposeful acts of sabotage quickly expanded, however, into a full-scale revolt that lasted for several days and was astonishingly brutal and destructive. Mob violence was directed at any symbol of authority, at the homes of the wealthy, at newspapers perceived to be prowar or abolitionist, and at any person or building seen as representing the federal government. As was common during the dozens of riots that convulsed northern cities throughout the antebellum years, however, bearing the brunt of the rioters' rage were free African Americans, several of whom were tortured, lynched, and burned alive, and many more of whose homes and public institutions were destroyed. The most widely publicized act of the mob was the looting and burning of the Colored Orphan's Asylum, which was targeted, it seems, as a symbol of both black public visibility and elite white philanthropy. The riots were quashed only when troops, including some that had just the previous week fought at Gettysburg, were pulled from the battlefront to retake the city, in the course of which they may have killed more people than had the rioters. Similar events were occurring on a smaller scale in other cities from Boston to Detroit; it is no wonder many observers thought a pro-Confederate revolution was under way across the North.[7]

In the draft riots a class fraction expressed its resistance to its own quantification by attacking every institution of the public sphere it saw as complicit in the process of making it visible and vulnerable. The riots thus made starkly visible an emerging conflict between the modernizing U.S. state and a substantial portion of its population.[8] This polarization of state and society was simultaneously a division *within* the social, since in theory a democratic state is not exterior to the society it rules. In this essay I explore this division of state and society in three 1860s texts about riots: *Anticipations of the Future*, an epistolary novel by the

Virginia slave owner and secessionist Edmund Ruffin that includes a chapter depicting the destruction of New York City by a mob; *What Answer?*, a sentimental interracial romance by the young abolitionist orator Anna Elizabeth Dickinson that culminates in the deaths of its main characters in the draft riots; and a poem by Herman Melville titled "The House-Top: A Night-Piece," in which the riots are observed from a distance. While the texts' genres and styles differ as widely as their authors' express political sympathies, what they have in common is the depiction of antistate violence as an outburst of public sentiment, as if a riot were an enactment of a social emotion.

Each of these texts registers the social meaning of a riot not just at the manifest thematic level, but also by formal means. Representation of the riots—and of the state as both their cause and the agent of their suppression—occasions some very peculiar formal anomalies in each of these texts, which push at the generic limits of the novel and the lyric poem. I argue that these formal experiments (however anachronistic that phrase may seem within a nineteenth-century literary context) are aimed at understanding and registering at the affective level the social fractures that were both revealed and exacerbated by the draft riots. In theorizing relationships between affect and social causality, each resorts to a rhetoric and narrative stance that can best be described as *impersonal*, and thus seems in tension with the insistently *personalizing* affective structures usually seen as characteristic of the novel and the lyric poem as well as the narrative and characterological conventions of nineteenth-century sentimentality. If the novel is designed to express individualized, privatized, bourgeois interiority, and if the lyric is commonly conceived as "eternal, placeless, overheard speech" that disavows the mediation of an audience or public (and of the lyric form itself),[9] when writers use these genres to represent a collective, public, primarily proletarian, externalized social experience such as a riot, the boundaries of each genre are stretched almost to their breaking points.

Ruffin, Dickinson, and Melville write the draft riots not just through different generic forms, but also through divergent social and political lenses. As we will see, though his text is at least as formally and generically peculiar as the other two, Ruffin's avid Confederate nationalism makes him very much the odd man out in this trio, in that he cheers on the riots even as he scorns the rioters themselves as the inevitable consequences of a barbaric northern free labor system and a radical abolitionist movement. The political differences between Dickinson (a Garrisonian abolitionist who had only very recently reconciled herself to supporting the Republican Party and the Union) and Melville (whose evolving political affiliations during and after the Civil War have been notoriously difficult to categorize) are less stark.[10] But while they share with Ruffin an almost visceral disdain for the perpetrators of riotous violence, for the two northerners this disidentification puts them in the uncomfortable position of contemplating an affective identification with the state itself, in the form of the police and military forces that were brought in to suppress the violence and restore order.[11] I read their texts as efforts to diagnose (and to some degree, to repair) the ruptures in the structure of feeling that—within their understanding of a democratic social space—both constitute the social and at the same time suture society to the state. Their responses have in common a deep anxiety about what it meant that, at this moment of multiple legitimation crises, their authors found themselves in a position where nationalist feeling seemed to require an identification not with a national symbolic, but with the concrete and even repressive institutions of the state itself. In other words, *What Answer?* and "The House-Top" pose the question of what it means to feel with—and feel like—a state.[12]

The formal anomalies in these two texts, I will argue, are traces of Melville's and Dickinson's efforts to imagine the state both as an active agent—an effort just as challenging to the conventions of the novel and the lyric as is representing the agency of a mob—and as a point of identification. Americanist literary and cultural scholarship possesses few tools for analyzing such an affective relation to the state.[13] As my invocation of Lauren Berlant's concept of a "national symbolic" implies, there is an extensive research conversation about how nineteenth-century cultural forms—most notably sentimentalism in its various genres and modes—provide the affective glue for either the *nation* or a broadly conceived *public sphere*. Numerous scholarly works (including some of my own) have explored the role of affect in the production, reproduction, and dissemination of U.S. nationality and nationalism. But the theorization of the nation-form that has been most influential on this scholarship—Benedict Anderson's *Imagined Communities*—for all its immense value, has often been deployed in American literary studies in a way that brackets out the state.[14] Too often, we have written as if the nation existed primarily as a structure of feeling and not as a set of institutions, as Foucauldian governmentality but not as a concrete set of government agencies and powers, as ideological state apparatuses without repressive state apparatuses.[15] Seldom has this scholarship considered an affective relation to the state itself. As such, analyzing texts in which the state plays a role as an agent—and even, as we will see, as an object of both identification and longing—requires both an extension and a complication of the frameworks within which we have come to understand the operation of nineteenth-century structures of feeling.

* * *

Looking at a formally unconventional and resolutely unsentimental text such as the Virginia slaveholder Edmund Ruffin's first and only novel, *Anticipations of the Future, To Serve as Lessons for the Present Time* takes us far from such familiar frameworks.[16] Branching out from his early career as an agronomist, over the course of the 1850s Ruffin became a leader of the Southern nationalists known as "Fire-Eaters," identifying himself fully with the Confederate cause.[17]

Ruffin serialized *Anticipations* in South Carolina's *Charleston Mercury*; it was shortly thereafter issued in book form by the Richmond publisher J. W. Randolph. The New York City riots take place in the fifty-second of the book's sixty-three chapters, titled "Outbreaks of disorder and violence in the northern cities. Sack of New York." The chapter starts, as its title implies, by describing uprisings in cities across the north in response to the imposition of a military draft. Like many of the events narrated in this section of the novel, this one corresponds to the facts; resistance to the draft was widespread and often violent from the time Congress passed the conscription law. Throughout the passages on the riots, Ruffin is concerned with the question of their causes, and why they were not effectively and immediately suppressed. So he places the events in a military-historical context, noting that many federal troops were away at the front fighting the South, that local militias "sympathised [sic] too much with either the previous sufferings or the present excesses of the rioters, to heartily oppose them in arms," and that "not a few joined the plunderers" (288). These details, too, are all quite close to contemporaneous historical accounts, and confirmed by more recent scholarship on the riots.

That much of Ruffin's narrative matches the historical record would be unremarkable had the novel not been written in 1860, three years *before* the New York City draft riots took place. *Anticipations* is a futuristic fantasy of Confederate nationalism triumphant and the destruction of the North, not, like Melville's and Dickinson's postbellum texts, a rumination on recent history. However prescient Ruffin may seem in this one chapter, the book is full of plot developments that have turned out to be wildly counterfactual. Early on, Lincoln is revealed as a stalking horse for the radical abolitionist presidency of William Seward, but even so, the timidity of Southern moderates keeps a Civil War from breaking out till 1868. Once the conflict does begin, it goes swimmingly for the South, in part due to that region's agricultural self-sufficiency.[18] The Confederacy quickly captures Washington, D.C., making it the capital of its new nation. Riots and uprisings destroy the North's industrial base and most of its cities, and gradually the Northwestern states join the confederacy as well, so all that remains is a rump Union of the abolitionist and increasingly impoverished New England states.

Though it depicts entirely imaginary events, Ruffin's *Anticipations of the Future* aspires to verisimilitude in its social analysis. So it draws on discourses such as the nascent disciplines of sociology and crowd psychology that had informed depictions of real riots in the period.[19] We can see one example of a social discourse not initially designed to explain riotous violence being deployed for that purpose when Ruffin's narrator describes what happens after the mob pillages the city's liquor stores: "When thus tempted, and stimulated, thousands of the lower classes who had designed merely to be inactive spectators, became, in their subsequent drunken excitement, active rioters, plunderers, and, in many cases, murderers" (286–87). Here the rhetoric of "stimulation" and "excitement," as well as the narrative trajectory from "inactive spectators" to "active rioters" both draws on and contributes to the construction of the social imaginary emerging out of the antebellum temperance movement and other body reform discourses.[20]

In keeping with his interest in social causality, Ruffin's narrator spends a good deal of time explaining how a few thousand rioters are able to terrorize an entire city, claiming that "[t]he few who at first had

attempted resistance, were promptly stabbed, and their bleeding bodies thrown into the streets," producing such fear that "the hundreds of
thousands of peaceable inhabitants [were made] submissive to every
command, and silent under every outrage of a few thousand despera-
does" (287). His explicit analogy is with the French Revolution; he
compares the terror the rioters deployed with the fear provoked by
those he calls the "Septembrisers," the "less than one thousand assas-
sins" who subdued Paris in 1793. Here Ruffin draws on a revolutionary political precedent, to be sure, but also on an understanding, common in sensational fiction of the period, of the affective structures by
which the "lower million" could be manipulated and controlled by a
small faction or conspiracy. Similarly, one eyewitness to the draft riots
who had served as a "Volunteer Special" recruited to suppress the riots
titled his account *The Volcano Under the City*; invoking in his title and
text imagery of the "slumbering volcano" found in narratives about
slave revolt, sensationalistic invocations of an underworld, "Mysteries
of the City" novels by Ned Buntline and George Lippard, and the figure of the "many-headed hydra" of working-class rebellion.[21] In short, a
wide range of genres and traditions informed the understanding of the
causes of violence in both literary and journalistic depictions of such
riots, and their rhetorics made their way into Ruffin's text.

What is most unsettling about *Anticipations of the Future* is that,
while he includes all these literary and paraliterary elements, he does
almost nothing to integrate them into a recognizably novelistic framework. *Anticipations* is, it is true, epistolary; as the book's title page
asserts, its narrative unfolds "[i]*n the form of Extracts of Letters from an
English Resident in the United States, to the London Times, from 1864 to
1870*." And Ruffin asserts in his preface that he has chosen "to present
his general propositions and argument in a novel, and therefore a more
impressive form" (vi). Though Ruffin here draws on the commonplace
view that the novel was the genre best calculated to "impress" its arguments on the reader's emotions, in both form and content *Anticipations of the Future* seems more journalistic than novelistic. Unlike most
epistolary novels, which typically present an exchange of letters among
several characters whose relationships and individual interiority unfold
through their correspondence, the letters in *Anticipations* all come from
a single person. The novel describes no other characters, nor are there

plot developments other than the political and military events signaled in each chapter's flat, descriptive title, such as "Army. Land Grants" or "Political movements of border states." It is as if Ruffin chose to reduce the novel form to pure "news," abjuring any tendency toward the individuated, interior psychology usually seen as definitional of the genre.

As such, *Anticipations* barely registers to a reader *as* a novel; rather, it reads as a narrative with all elements of the personal, the psychological, and the individual rigorously removed. This impersonality—which is a matter not just of tone, but also of narrative form—corresponds to the theory of social causality the text articulates. While social affects do play their roles in motivating the riots, the primary causal forces throughout the text are never individualistic or personal. This is clear from the way the novel's transitions are dominated by economically and politically deterministic rhetoric; for instance, one chapter begins, "The economical and commercial results, to this time, in both the northern and southern confederacies, are such as might have been anticipated from the operations of the previous and existing causes" (331). In this impersonal mode, Ruffin found an "impressive" form that fit not just his "general propositions and argument," but also his social and historical theory.

An Excursus on Sympathy and Impersonality

Such rigorous impersonality engendered by the novel's very form, especially in the chapter about the riots, would seem to place *Anticipations of the Future* entirely outside the sentimental literary tradition. To be clear, it is not the mere depiction of violence that makes it un- or antisentimental. After all, both the philosophy of moral sentiment and its literary manifestations arose as ways of addressing the problem of representation posed by human suffering, positing a personalized, psychological concept of sympathy as the morally and emotionally proper response to violence, terror, and similar acts and affects. For instance, a central parable in Smith's *Theory of Moral Sentiment* considers the ability of a viewer to share the emotions of another man being tortured "on the rack" and concludes that the viewer's capacity for sympathy is not only a moral virtue, but also the glue that holds society together.[22] Rather, it is Ruffin's decision to nearly evacuate the sympathetic and the psychological from his account of violence that appears perverse and anomalous from a sentimental perspective; he has replaced the affective theory of social cohesion—the theory articulated by Smith and developed in the sentimental literary tradition—with a political-economic theory that reads as reductive at best.

But not all accounts of sentimental affective exchange have placed the impersonal and the affective in stark opposition to one another.[23] One literary-historical analysis of the sentimental politics of affect in American fiction, Philip Fisher's *Hard Facts: Setting and Form in the American Novel*, turns not to Smith's man on the rack but to a parable related in Rousseau's "Discourse on the Origin and Foundations of Inequality Among Men." To support and illustrate his claim that nature has provided humans with a spontaneous and disinterested "pity" that complements their "reason," Rousseau cites an image from Mandeville's *Fable of the Bees*. Rousseau's paraphrase presents us with "the pathetic picture of a man locked up, who outside sees a ferocious Beast tearing a Child from his Mother's breast, breaking his weak limbs with its murderous fangs, and tearing the Child's throbbing entrails with its claws."[24] Fisher uses this image to illuminate the structural dynamics of sentimentalism. He emphasizes that while there are four figures in this scenario—an imprisoned man, a mother, a child, and a beast who kills the child as the imprisoned man watches— "only three of [these figures] are given psychological reality. The oppressor is merely a wild beast, no further attention is given to his reasons or to his experience. Instead, the experience is given only for the three who suffer in different ways the violence of the beast." And that experience is crucially differentiated, individuated. The mother experiences what Fisher calls "separation and mental anguish," which is a doubled form of loss: the loss of her child but also the loss of her family, of her *relation* to her child.[25] And it is especially apt that Fisher uses this scene to set up a reading of *Uncle Tom's Cabin*, since Stowe famously overlays that sentimental convention onto the family separations that for her are the essence of slavery as a system. As he puts it, "Slavery is, in effect, redescribed so that the reader sees it, not as a form of labor, but as an ordeal of separations."[26] And Stowe, still more problematically, asserts that all family separations are affectively identical; indeed, that all pain is ultimately the same.

For Rousseau, however, this scene is not about the mother *or* the child; his own affective cathexis extends less to those figures than to the imprisoned man, who suffers "dreadful agitation" and "anguish" due to being unable to "give any help to the fainted mother or to the dying child!"[27] The imprisoned man thus becomes a stand-in for the reader, who is structurally positioned as a passive but sympathetic spectator to what is happening in the text. What makes the *prisoner* human, and thus distinguishes him from the "ferocious Beast," is that he experiences such affects in response to someone else's pain. As in Adam Smith, the capacity to sympathize—or, in more modern terms, to empathize—is definitional of the human. Less often noted is Rousseau's insistence that the imprisoned man "takes no personal interest whatsoever" in the child's distress. This disinterested impersonality—which I will argue here is a crucial element not just in Ruffin's theory of social causality, but also in Dickinson's and Melville's representation of the draft riots— places the man in a structural position more like that of the perpetrator of the violence than it is like that of the victims. For the beast as well is portrayed as being no "personal" relation to what is being destroyed in the parable. In other words, neither the beast *nor* the spectator has an "interested" relation to the bond between mother and child, though this fact leads to opposite affective consequences.

While Fisher says that in this tale there are three figures granted "psychological reality," in fact there are only two. Unlike the prisoner and the mother, the child in the scene is portrayed as merely a suffering body. Fisher ably analyzes the way the structure of sentimental experience renders the humanity of the victim, and even enlists his reader's imagination in that rendering, but somewhat unwittingly he finds himself *participating* in that process in his own analysis by imagining that to feel sympathy for the mother's loss is tantamount to granting "psychological reality" to the infant thereby understanding its suffering. My point here is not to "correct" Fisher, especially because I think his chapter on Stowe is still an invaluable theorization of the politics of sympathy. Rather, I am interested in further unpacking the role played by the *impersonal* in the sentimental structure of feeling.

The impersonal is not antithetical to the attribution of interiorized subjectivity—of the "personal"—but an inextricable part of it. Both in Rousseau's scene and in Fisher's analysis, impersonality functions to prevent the extension of "psychological reality" to the perpetrator (and, perhaps more surprisingly, to the victim); but at the same time it is essential to the way the attribution of such psychological interiority is performed. This dynamic will turn out to be crucial for understanding Melville's and Dickinson's representations of collective public violence, which deploy what I am calling "impersonality" in different but equally complex ways.[28]

* * *

Unlike Ruffin's novel, Anna E. Dickinson's *What Answer?* sets itself up squarely within a sentimental tradition, and most of the narrative is driven by affective forces similar to those that drive the plots of other sentimental novels.[29] Dickinson—a precocious white Philadelphia native who published her first antislavery essay in the *Liberator* at age fourteen, quickly became one of the most celebrated orators of the century, at twenty-two gave a speech in the House of Representatives attended by Senators, Congressmen, cabinet members, and Abraham Lincoln himself, and was likely a model for the character of Verena Tarrant in Henry James's *The Bostonians*—published *What Answer?* in 1868.[30] The book—her first effort at fiction—centers on a romance between Willie Surrey, a wealthy young white New Yorker, and a light-skinned free black woman named Francesca Ercildoune. When he first sees Francesca performing a controversial antislavery reading, Willie falls instantly in love, at first unaware of her racial identity but evincing no prejudice once he learns her father is black.[31] Many tragic misunderstandings ensue, including Francesca's rejection of Willie because she wrongly presumes that he is as racist as his parents are. Willie joins the Union army, loses an arm in battle, and returns to woo, win, and wed Francesca, planning afterward to recruit a black brigade for the cause.

Through its first seventeen chapters, *What Answer?* reads as a somewhat quirky interracial romance, with the evident overlay of a mostly Garrisonian abolitionist polemic tempered by Unionist rhetoric. But the boundaries of sentimental convention are stretched beyond their limits when Dickinson introduces a riot scene. As Willie pauses to aid an ill black friend in New York, abruptly the friend's wounded, bleeding mother bursts into the room shouting "'O Lord! O Lord Jesus! . . . The day of wrath has come!'" (258). Willie's heroic antiracist intentions and Francesca's newfound happiness are being thwarted by the outbreak of the draft riots.

In the following chapter depicting the riots, the novel changes tone, style, and form in nearly every way, abandoning novelistic conventions almost as completely as does Ruffin's *Anticipations of the Future*. First, the romance plot comes to a halt, and all the characters that have populated the novel thus far disappear from view. Dickinson's narrator announces the shift in the chapter's opening paragraph with an uncharacteristically self-referential statement: "Here it will be necessary to consider some facts which, while they are rather in the domain of the grave recorder of historical events, than in that of the narrator of personal experiences, are yet essential to the comprehension of the scenes in which Surrey and Francesca took such tragic parts" (259). It is as if Dickinson decided that the only way to describe the massive brutality of the riots was to resort to Ruffin's impersonal, deterministic historical perspective, that for this event the voice of the novelist—"a narrator of personal experiences"—had to give way to that of "the grave recorder of historical events." The thematic and formal break marks the other events in the novel—including not just the romance, but also abolitionist meetings and Civil War battles—as "personal," and marks the riot as a fundamentally different kind of event: public, social, "historical."

Accordingly, in this chapter even the grammar and syntax shift. Up to this point, the narration has been, as Dickinson here implies, novelistic in a characteristically sentimental way: epistemologically omniscient, but especially attentive to the emotions of the characters with whom readers are meant to sympathize, sometimes deploying free indirect discourse to enter such characters' minds to grant them "psychological reality," and occasionally resorting to a polemical direct address to the reader. Stylistically, *What Answer?* would feel quite familiar to anyone who has read *Uncle Tom's Cabin*, for instance. But in the chapter about the riots, the vast majority of sentences are in the passive voice, as if Dickinson had trouble attributing a subject, an agent, to these events. When her narrator does use the active voice, the subjects of the sentences are collective, for instance: "A body of these, five or six hundred strong, gathered about one of the enrolling-offices" (261). As the riot progresses, the forms of collectivity get more complex: "it was no longer one vast crowd collected in a single section, but great numbers of gatherings, scattered over the whole length and breadth of the city . . . with no definite atrocity to perpetrate, but ready for any iniquity that might offer" (266). All the particular points of identification necessary to produce sentimental sympathy are evacuated from the text, leaving amorphous, nonspecific subjects of uncertain agency in their place.

The most marked effect of the narrative shift in this chapter is to raise for Dickinson's readers the question of how to think—and perhaps more importantly, how to *feel*—about the events being depicted. This is not to say that the posture of the "grave recorder of historical events" is morally neutral but it is, in contrast with much of the rest of the novel, analytical, as if the narrator's task required a kind of impersonal distance from the violent events of this chapter. In this analytic mode, Dickinson does not emphasize the sort of emotional cause of the riots that could be attributed to an individual psyche. Rather, she seeks to identify a *social* source for the violence. And she explicitly locates the source of this non-state public violence in the relation between the people and the state—which perhaps explains why she did not feel the need to create a similar narratorial, characterological, and stylistic shift in her description of the state-sanctioned violence of war in the earlier chapter in which she effectively narrates a bloody battle from the perspectives of her novel's main characters.

Thus Dickinson's description of the riots begins—with her typical attention to historical accuracy—by describing an attack on one of the offices where the draft lottery was to be held.[32] The violence is at first highly organized and directed at the instruments of state administration: "Lists, records, books, the drafting-wheel, every article of furniture or work in the room was rent in pieces, and strewn about the floor or flung into the street" (261). Then the rioters shift their attention from the objects being used to instrumentalize them to the persons who embody state power. A man tries to keep the mob from setting fire to the building because "helpless women and little children were in the house"; but the mob, "by his dress recognizing in him a government official," rejects his appeal to their sympathies.

Alice Rutkowski is mostly right, in her discussion of the novel, when she writes that Dickinson's "portrait of the mob is basically one-dimensional: according to her telling, it was made up of wholly ignorant, foreign-born hooligans." Using Fisher's argument that sentimentalism depersonalizes the perpetrator of violence in order to avoid arousing "interest in the motives or psychology of the oppressor," Rutkowski goes on to assert that "[s]takes are simply too high for Dickinson to imagine what the rioters might have felt, why they might have rioted. The victim and villain must be distinctive in order to enable both sympathy and, ideally, action on the part of the reader."[33] It is true that in this chapter there is not exactly an analysis of what the rioters "felt," since—like the beast in the Rousseau scenario Fisher analyzes—they are granted no psychological interiority or emotional nuance. However, Dickinson does provide a salient analysis of the causes of their actions by emphasizing that early in the riots all the targets of violence have a close relation to the state. "Police-stations, enrolling-offices, rooms or buildings used in any way by government authority, or obnoxious as representing the dignity of law, were gutted, destroyed, then left to the mercy of the flames" (265). The only non-state buildings mentioned here are the offices of newspapers "that had been faithful to loyalty and law," and are thus closely associated with state policy.

As "myriads of wretched, drunken women" join the crowd, it moves on to another state institution, "an armory where were manufactured and stored carbines and guns for the government" (263). Here Dickinson makes her first effort to produce the state as a site of identification, emphasizing the "gallant defense" attempted by the officers guarding the armory, contrasting them with the rioters' leader, "a big, brutal, Irish ruffian," and noting in particular that "terrible yells and cries, filled the air in every accent of the English tongue save that spoken by a native American. Such were there mingled with the sea of sound, but they were so few and weak as to be unnoticeable in the roar of voices" (264). The rioters' antipathy to the state thus has two sources: their rage at the injustice of the draft, certainly, but also their marginality to the nation, symbolized here by the inarticulacy of their voices as well as by their accents.

Then the mob shifts from attacking the state to attacking every "inoffensive negro, who crossed the line of their vision." The crucial turn comes later in the afternoon of July 13, when "a crowd which could have numbered not less than ten thousand, the majority of whom were ragged, frowsy, drunken women" targets "the Orphan Asylum for Colored

Children,—a large and beautiful building, and one of the most admirable and noble charities of the city" (266). Dickinson does not emphasize the fact that the orphanage was a private charity, but from this point in the chapter she shifts from analyzing the riots as a violent response to state power to seeing them as pure "terror," an unlocalizable affect that pervades the public sphere, without specific agency, source, or object.

Dickinson invokes sentimental rhetoric in her description of the attack on the Orphan Asylum, but in a way that demonstrates sentimentalism's limits as a way of explaining the events she depicts. First she makes clear that it is the rioters' inability to sympathize that allows them to commit their atrocities. As the crowd is about to set fire to the building, "an appeal was made in [the children's] behalf . . . to every sentiment of humanity which these beings might possess,—a vain appeal! Whatever human feeling had ever, if ever, filled these souls was utterly drowned and washed away in the tide of rapine and blood in which they had been steeping themselves" (266). Dickinson depicts the rioters as savage, though the interjected "if ever" makes it ambiguous whether they have always been so, or if it is the riots themselves that have made them such "beings." In other words, once the rioters no longer target the state as their antagonist, Dickinson can account, in a sentimental idiom, for the reproduction of their savage (lack of) feeling. However, she is hesitant to provide an explanation for the production of violence, to suggest an originating cause for the "tide of rapine and blood" less circular than the claim that it is caused by the excess or lack of feeling that is itself a result of participating in violence.[34]

The appeal to the crowd's sympathies "was answered on all sides by yells and execrations, and frenzied shrieks of 'Down with the nagurs!' coupled with every oath and every curse that malignant hate of the blacks could devise, and drunken, Irish tongues could speak" (267–68). It is specifically the mob's conflation of antistate violence with antiblack racism that pushes Dickinson's sentimental explanatory logic past its limits. The most she can do is identify a pattern, an internal logic, to the violence; the rioters attack "every stray police officer, or solitary soldier, or inoffensive negro, who crossed the line of their vision; these three objects—the badge of a defender of the law,—the uniform of the Union army,—the skin of a helpless and outraged race—acted upon these madmen as water acts upon a rabid dog" (266). The mob's rage is spurred metonymically by elements *external* to the person: the badge, the uniform, the skin. The first two are obviously figures for state authority itself, while the third represents the race that, in the minds of the rioters, has become the cause of the state's intervention in the social sphere. At the same time, each of these three substitutes, in a sentimental logic, for the imagined *interiority* that might have provoked a more humane response—again, the sympathy that the rioters either have never been capable of, or that have been blocked or foreclosed by their participation in the violence of the day.

The problem of racism pushes Dickinson to search for political, social, and structural explanations. As she insists, the targeting of blacks is not caused by spontaneous human feelings, but rather by "the prejudice fostered by public opinion, incorporated in our statute-books, sanctioned by our laws, which here and thus found legitimate outgrowth and action. . . . The horrors . . . were but the bloody harvest of fields sown by society, by cultured men and women, by speech, and book, and press, by professions and politics, nay, by the pulpit itself" (273). One can undoubtedly hear in this rhythmic, cataloguing language something of Dickinson's oratorical style, but it is also a serious effort to locate the causes for these events in, as she says, "*society*," conceived of not in amorphous terms, but as a structure organized by both the institutions of the public sphere ("speech, and book, and press") and the ideological state apparatuses of "professions and politics" as well as "the pulpit itself." Here she is working toward language that will help her describe how these social institutions have produced a violent break within society between the white working class and the state.

The narrative break that marks this chapter is, I am suggesting, an effort to represent such a social-structural break at the level of literary form. As the first day of the riots ends, Dickinson makes two rhetorical moves that underscore this point. The first is a paragraph in which the chapter's peculiarly objective and impersonal narrator pulls back, almost cinematically, to survey the events of the day, and expresses an unnervingly impersonal emotion that verges on pleasure, even as it simultaneously invokes the Romantic sublime: "Standing on some elevated point, looking over the great city which presented, as usual, at night, a solemn and impressive show, the spectator was thrilled with a fearful admiration by the sights and sounds which gave to it a mysterious and awful interest. A thousand fires streamed up against the sky, making darkness visible; and from all sides came a combination of noises such as might be heard from an asylum in which were gathered the madmen of the world" (268–69).

We will return to this high, distant vantage point shortly, when we turn to Melville's "House-Top." In *What Answer?* it gives the reader a strange, brief respite before her narrator plunges us into the second day of the riots. At this point Dickinson turns to more familiar figures for the events, referring to them as a "reign of terror," but she also accelerates her use of the passive voice. To list only half the passive verbs on a single page: "Outbreaks were made, crowds gathered, houses burned, streets barricaded, fights enacted . . . stores were closed, the business portion of the city deserted . . . every telegraph wire was cut, the posts torn up, the operators driven from their offices" (269). Dickinson also makes reference to the passivity or even complicity of local and state government officials, briefly praising Republican Mayor George Opdyke for correctly assessing that federal troops would be needed, and condemning Democratic Governor Horatio Seymour—who had vocally opposed the draft and publicly promised to prevent it from being enforced—for appearing at City Hall on the morning of the second day to deliver a speech that quickly became infamous, in which he repeatedly addressed the rioters as "My friends."

Even when she invokes a standard Unionist explanation for the riots—attributing them to the failure of subhuman Irish immigrants to integrate into the nation[35]—she insists on characterizing the riots as an attack on the state itself. They are "an effort on the part of Northern rebels to help Southern ones, at the most critical moment of the war," and she calls Copperhead editors and supporters of Governor Seymour "traitors to the Government and the flag of their country,—renegade Americans." Dickinson goes on to say that "the tribes of savages—the hordes of ruffians—found ready to do their loathsome bidding, were not of native growth, nor American born" but "that the masses, the rank and file, the almost entire body of rioters, were the worst classes of Irish emigrants, infuriated by artful appeals, and maddened by the atrocious whiskey of thousands of grog-shops," and joined by "the most degraded of the German population (272).[36] Here ethnic identities, read as disaffiliation from national identity, map all too neatly onto antipathies both to the state and to civilization itself.

This nativist rhetoric implies a fairly simplistic analysis of the causes of the riots, and there is no necessary conflict between such civilizationist discourse and sentimentalism's theory of social causality. Thus, we can read much of the chapter as consistent with the sentimental aversion to ascribing agency to the perpetrators of violence, which she accomplishes by using the passive voice and by narrating from a distance that does not allow the rioters any interiority. But by the end of the chapter, as the riots reach their climax, agency and causality become increasingly hard to pin down. First the riot itself seems to develop a kind of agency. Dickinson writes that "the riot, begun ostensibly to oppose a single law, developed itself into a burning and pillaging assault upon the homes and property of peaceful citizens" (273). After this resort to a peculiarly recursive causal structure by making "developed" into a reflexive verb, Dickinson decides to bring into the narration a recognizably human witness to these atrocities. However, this figure is remarkably abstract and hypothetical, thus retaining a high degree of impersonality: "it was only necessary to walk the streets, if that were possible, through those days of riot and conflagration, observe the materials gathered into the vast, moving multitudes, and scrutinize the faces" of the rioters (273). This hypothetical person's nearly ethnographic gaze provides the reader with access to the affective responses of the citizenry affected by the riots, white and black. But these affects do not personalize or specify these citizens; Dickinson resists turning them into *characters*. "The knowledge of these people [the rioters] and their deeds," she continues, "was sufficient to create a paralysis of fear, even where they were not seen. Indeed, there was terror everywhere" (274). These free-floating affects ("fear," "terror") are then, in the chapter's final paragraph, attached not to specific, individuated characters, but to abstract and plural "women" and "men" who are terrified by the experience. None of them get names; none appear in the rest of the novel; until the chapter's final two sentences, none of them even get singular pronouns.

In these concluding sentences, two singular persons emerge from this amorphous social mass, though they too are presented as impersonal types. The first of these gets no markers of his identity attached to his person, though his "surroundings" are indicative of his upper-class status and probably his whiteness: "Here one surveyed all his costly store of rare and exquisite surroundings, and shook his head as he gazed, ominous and foreboding" (274). The final adjectives reference affective states, but leave ambiguous their location; are the words "ominous and foreboding" attached to the person's gaze or to the violent acts at which he gazes? Dickinson then uses indexical shifters to mark a contrast between this figure "here" and the other, who is introduced by the words: "There, another of darker hue," a phrase that serves as the subject of a grammatically unwieldy and notably longer sentence of over 130 words. This second figure is, like the previous hypothetical figure walking through the riots, an impersonal mediator. In contrast with the wealthier and presumably white man who seems to be in his own home, this "darker" figure's abstract nature is emphasized by the ambiguity of his location, signaled by the repetition of the word *or* in the account of his location: he "peered out from garret casement, *or* cellar light, *or* broken window pane." And what he sees has a nonspecificity emphasized by a similar reiteration of the word *some*: he sees "some woman stoned and beaten till she died; some child shot down, while thousands of heavy, brutal feet trod over it till the hard stones were red with its blood, and the little prostrate form, yet warm, lost every likeness of humanity, and lay there, a sickening mass of mangled flesh and bones" (274). These anonymous women and children are granted physical materiality but not personality, like the child in Rousseau's scenario. Their brutal dehumanization has its formal and stylistic correlative in the fact that their deaths are witnessed only by a viewer and narrator who occupies no specific point of view. Dickinson seems to be experimenting here with the possibility of representing and provoking sympathy in a context of almost complete impersonality.

Another Excursus on Sympathy and Impersonality

At the end of *What Answer*'s chapter about the draft riots, the impersonal man she has just introduced—again, the only specific details Dickinson has provided about him are his "darker hue" and a gendered pronoun—watches a brutal lynching. The chapter's long last sentence ends with a phrase that briefly opens up the possibility of this abstract figure's affective humanization: "and watching this, and cowering as he watched, held his breath, and waited his own turn, not knowing when it might come" (274). Like Rousseau's and Mandeville's prisoner in the tower, this man is simultaneously capable of sympathetic identification and unable to act to help the victim of the violence. Within the logic of sympathy limned in Fisher's analysis of Rousseau, the combination of emotional cathexis with enforced immobility marks this otherwise impersonal figure as fully human.

Dickinson's language here resonates with a scene of violence and sentimental response that is more familiar to Americanists than is Rousseau's parable: Frederick Douglass's account in his 1845 *Narrative* of hiding in the closet, watching his Aunt Hester's whipping. Douglass's scene is in many ways parallel to the one in Rousseau, though with the narrative functions distributed slightly differently. The role of the beast is clearly taken up by the master, Captain Anthony, who whips Hester mercilessly while the young Frederick watches, powerless to intervene, from the "closet" in which he is hidden. Douglass situates himself in relation to the scene by saying that he "was doomed to be a witness and a participant" in "a long series of such outrages." He then, famously, figures this event as "the blood-stained gate, the entrance to the hell of slavery, through which I was about to pass." Douglass concludes this framing with a reference to the limits of language and his own expressive capacities, writing that "[i]t was a most terrible spectacle. I wish I could commit to paper the feelings with which I beheld it" (6).

Like both Rousseau and Dickinson, Douglass aligns the reader with a spectator who is structurally unable to act and is *therefore* sympathetic; from that viewer's perspective he can graphically describe the visual and auditory signs of Aunt Hester's pain. Essential to each scene is the fact that the viewer witnesses violence from a small but critical distance. Unlike the other writers, however, Douglass focuses in very careful and particular ways on the affect of the perpetrator of the violence as well as the victim's agony. Put another way, Douglass here follows sentimental convention (which is also abolitionist convention) in displaying, verbally, the signs of pain for his readers to examine and verify the horrors of slavery, invoking the readers' affective responses to make them witnesses and perhaps even to think of themselves as "participants."[37] But in contrast with Rousseau's scenario, where the "beast" is granted no human agency or interiority, here it is Captain Anthony's feelings and actions, *not* Aunt Hester's responses, which take up the most narrative space. Douglass makes clear that Captain Anthony's violence is an expression of the white man's own jealousy and rage, because he lusts after Hester and assumes, correctly, that she has been sneaking out to be with her chosen lover. Thematically at least, the impersonality that figures in Rousseau's scenario plays no part in Douglass's characterization of Captain Anthony, whose motives are purely personal, of Aunt Hester, who is granted—in condensed form—a thwarted romantic narrative; nor of his own young self, who has every personal reason to sympathize with the pain of his own relative.

In an analysis of this scene, Saidiya Hartman poses two probing questions: "Does the pain of the other merely provide us with the opportunity for self-reflection?" she asks, following with: "how does one give expression to these outrages without exacerbating the indifference to suffering that is the consequence of the benumbing spectacle or contend with the narcissistic identification that obliterates the other or the prurience that too often is the response to such displays?" (4). Ultimately, she implies, to make us see this scene of violence—or at least to make us see it repeatedly—is not primarily, as Douglass or Stowe would have it, to make us feel the victim's pain; it is, rather, to distance us from it. In this, Hartman's take on sentimental sympathy is in the tradition of James Baldwin, who famously characterized such sympathy as "the inability to feel" and argued that "it is always, therefore, the signal of secret and violent inhumanity, the mask of cruelty."[38]

This distancing, Hartman argues, does not contradict the idea that viewing a depiction of an act of violence can bring us closer to the victim's experience; rather, it is a result of that fantasy itself.[39] Douglass, by focusing in his abolitionist autobiography on the pain of Hester and connecting it to the painful identifications experienced by his young self, evinces a faith in the same abolitionist allegory of sentimental reading about which Hartman is dubious, and in an idea, general in sentimental culture, that the production of sympathy for the victim is a more effective use of representations of unjust violence than an examination of the causes and motivations of the perpetrator's violence would be. The concern, for critics like Hartman who are skeptical about the political efficacy of sentimentalism, is the dialectic of distance and proximity constructed in relation to the victims of violence. Sympathy, especially when narrativized or presented as an image, *is* a relation of distance, even though it entails a fantasy of proximity produced by and through the production of affect.

The *Narrative* presents in meticulous detail the positioning of Aunt Hester's body for the torture, the way Captain Anthony instrumentalizes her as the object of his own affective outburst. The most vivid signs of affect in the scene of violence itself, however, interrupt the very syntax of the narration, appearing in a parenthesis placed between the subject and predicate of a sentence about a purely physical response to the violence: "the warm, red blood (amid heart rending shrieks from her, and horrid oaths from him) came dripping to the floor." In the parenthesis, the affective expression of the perpetrator and that of the victim are made parallel (which is of course not the same thing as making them morally equivalent). And Douglass's own response follows immediately thereafter—"I was so terrified and horror-stricken at the sight, that I hid myself in a closet." That response leads directly to an act of identification: "I expected it would be my turn next" (7–8).

It is this identificatory phrase that is echoed in the final words of the riot chapter in *What Answer?*, in which the unnamed black man "waited his own turn, not knowing when it might come."[40] Like the young Douglass, this man is an object for the reader's identification precisely because he is powerless to prevent the act of violence he is witnessing. And like Douglass, he models sympathetic identification for the reader by imaginatively projecting himself, from a slightly safe distance, into the position of the victim. But there is a stark difference between the two at the level of narrative form. In Douglass's *Narrative*, the speaker of these words is the author, narrator, and main *character*, the central point of sympathetic identification in the narrative, while in Dickinson's novel the terrorized black man makes only this single brief appearance; he has virtually no specific *characteristics*, not even a specific location at a specific time. Instead, Dickinson presents him with a degree of abstraction and impersonality that would perhaps be comprehensible in a political speech, where an orator might invoke a pure type, such as "the man on the street." But in a novel, such impersonality seems anomalous at best.

I am suggesting that this apparent anomaly signals the moment where Dickinson experimentally pushes the sentimental logic of sympathy beyond its conventional limits. Any sympathy or identification this abstract figure evokes is purely structural, produced by nothing more than the novel's assertion that he is capable of sympathizing with the man he sees being lynched. What happens, Dickinson seems to ask, if all the personal, individual, interior, psychological particularities are removed from the fictive figures in this chapter of the novel, and yet the reader is asked to respond sympathetically? And in the final passage, the experiment is still more focused: What happens if the only particularities the reader is given to work with are race and gender? Can sentimental sympathy be produced in a condition of almost complete impersonality?

We will never know how either Dickinson or her readers responded to these questions, or the results of her experiment, which does not extend beyond this single chapter of the novel. At the beginning of the following chapter Dickinson returns us to the novel's plot and characters. This comes as no relief from the violence, as Willie's black friend is lynched, Willie himself is brutally beaten to death, and Francesca is killed by a stray bullet as she runs to his mangled body. But these events, however brutal they may be, are represented in the same style and form as the rest of the novel. Though sentimentalism—as affective structure, as narrative style—served her purposes in the rest of her novel, Dickinson's social, structural analysis of the draft riots required her to interpolate this peculiar chapter into her tale, to narrate the development of these events from an emotional and even a spatial distance –"some elevated point" and to resort to a distant, impersonal narrator and narrative form.

* * *

Herman Melville's poem about the draft riots also observes events from an "elevated point," setting up a dynamic of distance and proximity that bears comparison with the stylistic and formal experiments in *What Answer?* Like Dickinson, Melville views the riots through an affective lens, and at the same time invokes a rhetoric of impersonality that exists in tension with the individualized, personal voice of a lyric poem.

"The House-Top" appeared in 1866 in Melville's first published book of poetry, *Battle-Pieces and Aspects of the War.*[41] As Melville puts it in his brief preface, "[w]ith few exceptions, the Pieces in this volume originated in an impulse imparted by the fall of Richmond." In other words, they were nearly all written after April 1865, once the defeat of the Confederacy had become inevitable. Melville continues: "They were composed without reference to collective arrangement, but being brought together in review, naturally fall into the order assumed" (45). That order—what unifies the book's approximately seventy poems—is not style, form, or voice; indeed, the volume is astonishingly eclectic, ranging from very short lyrics to quite complex near-epics, and the

poetic voices include soldiers and officers from both sides, noncomba-
tants affected by the war, impersonal or omniscient narrators, and others. Rather, what organizes the main section of *Battle-Pieces* is, simply,
chronology. The first, "The Portent (1859)," is a short lyric about the execution of John Brown, and most of the following fifty-two poems refer
to specific events and include parenthetical dates under their titles.
After several pages of endnotes to the poems, the book concludes with
a prose "Supplement" that argues for sectional reconciliation.

Battle-Pieces then, is an effort to represent epic historical events in
lyric form, an experiment in genre that puzzled reviewers at the time,
and has made this collection of poems challenging to read since.[42] What
makes the lyric form not entirely inappropriate is that, at least according to the preface, the subject matter of the poems is not so much political or military history as it is the impressions made by that history. In
Melville's words: "The events and incidents of the conflict – making up
a whole, in varied amplitude, corresponding with the geographical area
covered by the war – from these but a few themes have been taken, such
as for any cause chanced to imprint themselves upon the mind" (45).
Having invoked geography and history—space and time—Melville goes
on to use affective terms—"feelings" and "moods"—to describe what
the poems are really meant to represent, words that correspond inter-
estingly to the qualifying terms "pieces" and "aspects" in the books'
title: "The aspects which the strife as a memory assumes are as manifold as
are the moods of involuntary meditation – moods variable, and at times
widely at variance. Yielding instinctively, one after another, to feelings
not inspired from any one source exclusively, and unmindful, without
purposing to be, of consistency, I seem, in most of these verses, to have
but placed a harp in a window, and noted the contrasted airs which
wayward winds have played upon the strings" (45). Like the music produced without human agency by an Aeolian harp, then, the volume sets
out to display "moods" and "feelings" that are similarly "involuntary."[43]
And like the notes played on such a harp, the source of the free-floating
"feelings" to which the lyric speaker "yield[s] instinctively" is external
to the subject, much as the "fear" and "terror" late in the draft riot chapter of *What Answer?* exist in an impersonal and abstract social space.

The opening of "The House-Top" is perfectly consistent with this
account of the book's project, thematizing "feelings" and "moods"

that are detached from any specific person. Here is the complete poem, except for the endnote Melville signals with the superscripted letter at the end of the sixteenth line; I will quote and discuss that note below.

THE HOUSE-TOP.

A Night Piece.
(July, 1863)

No sleep. The sultriness pervades the air
And binds the brain – a dense oppression, such
As tawny tigers feel in matted shades,
Vexing their blood and making apt for ravage.
Beneath the stars the roofy desert spreads
Vacant as Libya. All is hushed near by.
Yet fitfully from far breaks a mixed surf
Of muffled sound, the Atheist roar of riot.
Yonder, where parching Sirius set in drought,
Balefully glares red Arson–there-and there.
The Town is taken by its rats – ship-rats.
And rats of the wharves. All civil charms
And priestly spells which late held hearts in awe—
Fear-bound, subjected to a better sway
Than sway of self; these like a dream dissolve,
And man rebounds whole aeons back in nature.[i]
Hail to the low dull rumble, dull and dead,
And ponderous drag that shakes the wall.
Wise Draco comes, deep in the midnight roll
Of black artillery; he comes, though late;
In code corroborating Calvin's creed
And cynic tyrannies of honest kings;
    He comes, nor parlies; and the Town, redeemed,
Give thanks devout; nor, being thankful, heeds
The grimy slur on the Republic's faith implied,
Which holds that Man is naturally good,
And – more – is Nature's Roman, never to be scourged.

The title of the poem provides the reader with both a spatial location (a "roofy" one, to cite the most whimsical word in the poem) and a temporal one (a month, a year). We are especially clearly situated chronologically because immediately preceding "The House-Top" is Melville's poem about the battle of Gettysburg, also dated July 1863; any reader in 1866 attentive to the chronological structuring of *Battle-Pieces* would likely have recalled that the draft riots followed hard on the heels of that battle. However, the poem—which is written, unusually for Melville, in blank verse[44]—quickly undoes this spatial and temporal specificity by emphasizing the speaker's affective states. The startlingly emphatic first two words, "No sleep," obviously, lack a subject. Though in the next few lines we get some fragments indicating the presence of this initially absent or at least ambiguous subject, that implication of asubjectivity persists, and makes the various affective and bodily states that pervade the poem all the more ambiguous. The poem's next lines blur the distinction between the internal mental state of the speaker and the external factors that produce it, depicting a "sultriness" that is in both "the air" and "the brain" and invoking "a dense oppression" in which neither oppressor nor oppressed is specified.

The poem then turns, extravagantly, to a metaphorical register that Toni Morrison might call "Africanist." The potentially racial connotations of the word "tawny" are accentuated by the location of the "tiger" in "matted shades" and the reference to Libya that follows shortly thereafter. (For American readers at least, Libya was associated with black Africans; hence Harriet Beecher Stowe's widely read profile of Sojourner Truth was titled "The Libyan Sybil"). It is curious, to say the least, that Africa is invoked in this oblique and metaphorical way and no other, given that the rioters targeted New York's free black population, a fact that Melville surely knew but nowhere mentions. Deak Nabers astutely points out that throughout *Battle-Pieces* "slaves become African, rather than Africans becoming American"; I'd add only that free blacks are Africanized here as well.[45]

The semantic shift toward the "tawny tigers" also sets up the potential for violence, for "ravage." But then Melville pulls us away still further, to look at the stars, situating us in the genre of "night-piece" or nocturne referenced in the poem's subtitle. And thus the scene is set— at least the scene "near by," where "all is hushed." As we will learn in a moment when we move from a near space to a distant one, things are not hushed everywhere. And Melville builds further spatial tension into the poem by characterizing the "near by" with the use of imagery of a quite distant land, the ostensibly "vacant" desert of Libya.

The line, "All is hushed near by" echoes a lyric that appears in *Battle-Pieces* nine poems before this one: "And all is hushed at Shiloh," is the final line of "Shiloh. A Requiem. (April, 1862)." Like many of the poems about Civil War battles in the volume, "Shiloh" views massive public violence from a spatial distance. But that poem's most important distancing is temporal; like the Civil War photos taken by Matthew Brady and his assistants, it represents not the battle itself, but a moment after the fighting has ended and before the dead and dying have been removed or buried.[46] In contrast, in "The House-Top" the riots are occurring at the moment the speaker's words, thoughts, and feelings are, by lyric convention, being uttered. This poem also stands out from others in the volume because the violence it depicts—or rather, the violence whose effects it views from a distance—is not military violence authorized by a state against another state in a time of war (even with all the problems this description poses in the case of the U.S. Civil War). In this first part of the poem at least, the state is painfully absent, and what remains—"civil charms/and priestly spells," the constraints of civil society and religion, specifically the Catholicism of the mostly Irish American mob—have "dissolve[d]" "like a dream." Even though these constraints were rooted in pure affect—"awe" and "fear" of the state and the church—the speaker of the poem mourns their absence, for such power is "a better sway than sway of self." With all such constraints collapsed, in the dark view and semi-Darwinian vocabulary of the poem, "man" regresses or degenerates "whole aeons back in nature."

Each of these conceptual registers works to designate the rioters' violence as worse than merely illegitimate; it is uncivilized, atavistic. This was a common way of portraying the rioters, both in journalistic writings about the events in New York City and in their literary representation. As we have seen, Dickinson also depicts their violence as barbaric, and even Ruffin, the writer most politically sympathetic to the aims of the rioters he depicts, says that "few of them reasoned, or thought of consequences—but sought only present and unlimited enjoyment, in gratifying every appetite, even at the expense of any amount of crime"

(291). Like Melville, Ruffin represents this barbarism as the result of the withdrawal of the affective constraints characteristically produced by the state: "As soon as it was generally known that all military opposition and defence had ceased," Ruffin writes, "the only previous restraint, that of fear, was removed, and numerous and strong parties of the most criminal of the rioters, set out to spread their depredations to other localities, or to enterprises which they had not before dared to attempt." As in Dickinson, the rioters go on to loot government buildings, though in *Anticipations of the Future* they go still further and vandalize churches as well (291).

Curiously, Melville turns to the classical figures of Sirius and Arson to indicate the consequences of such atavism, and represents the violence in other highly displaced forms: the "muffled sound," or the "rats–ship-rats./And rats of the wharves," which must be his characterization of the immigrant rioters. In the body of the poem, Melville quite rigorously avoids specific mention of the draft riots that turn out to be its subject; they are named only in the peculiar endnote that he places in the back of the volume, displaced even further spatially.[47] In the note he uses strikingly evasive language to say that "some proceedings of the draft-rioters" may be describable as "like" what Froissart "dare[d] not write" about a set of "horrible and inconceivable atrocities" committed in a place perhaps not quite as geographically distant as the Libyan desert, but even more historically distant: the Hundred Years War.[48] The note serves the same purpose as Douglass's claim that he cannot "commit to paper" his own feelings about his aunt's whipping; it asserts the unrepresentability of violence while simultaneously moving the viewer closer—epistemologically and emotionally—to the spectator and narrator of the violence.

Thus, while the poem works to establish multiple forms of distance from the rioters' violence, it positions the reader alongside its witness/ narrator, most notably through a set of spatially indexical shifters— "Yonder" and "there-and there"—that produce the effect of being present on the rooftop as the speaker points out events occurring within view. This close alignment makes all the more startling the shift that comes after the footnote. The encomium announced by the word "Hail" is almost as disorienting as the poem's first two words, especially since what the speaker is demanding that we hail is at first left ambiguous:

> Hail to the low dull rumble, dull and dead,
> And ponderous drag that shakes the wall.

Why this set of noises is any more worthy of praise than the riots' "mixed surf/Of muffled sound" remains unclear until the speaker invokes Draco, the lawgiver. Here the language shifts into a martial (and eventually political and theological) register. We have been placed in the position—perhaps ironically, but no less forcefully for that—of hailing the military intervention that did, finally, suppress the riot.[49] Melville leaves us with little choice; he has represented the violence of the rioters as unambiguously irredeemable, and the polity (the Town, the Republic) can wish only to be "redeemed" *from* the mob's violence by a state-sanctioned use of force, one that leaves the Town "thankful."

"The House-Top" thus poses the same question that Michael Warner draws out in his dazzling reading of the poem it evokes, "Shiloh." He argues that that poem—in particular its crucial and oddly parenthetical line, "(What like a bullet can undeceive!)"—"encapsulates the dilemma of Northern liberal intellectuals" over whether emancipation would "redeem the violence in which they had been involved" or would "promise and require a redemption *from* violence" (42–43). In the process, "The House-Top" avoids the explicit depiction of any violence whatsoever. In particular, it brackets out the very state violence that it hails; there are those sounds (the "low dull rumble" and "ponderous drag") and there is the one grammatically and syntactically confusing phrase in which Draco "comes, nor parlies," perhaps hinting at the idea of giving no quarter, but obliquely at best. At the same time—again in contrast with "Shiloh," which performs its redemptive moves by depicting dying soldiers, in the aftermath of battle, as sufferers ("the parched ones stretched in pain"), "The House-Top" avoids any representation whatsoever of the victims of violence. Here—unlike in *What Answer?*—there are no heroic veterans being set upon by a bloodthirsty mob, no black passersby being strung up, no soldiers dying defending the armory, no philanthropists or black children being forced from an orphanage. It is as if Melville set out to depict the riots without any of the elements that would make up a sentimental scenario, while still claiming to document only the "feelings" and "moods" they provoke in a viewer.

Instead of provoking identification with an object of sympathy, Melville turns in the last lines of the poem to a meditation on political theology, asserting that the events depicted demonstrate the falsity of "the Republic's faith" in the natural virtue of "Man." The concluding lines have generally and correctly been taken as Melville's condemnation of the actions of the mob and the need to call in the military to suppress it, which together "corroborat[e] Calvin's creed" of natural iniquity, though it has been less often noted that what is also "corroborat[ed]" is the "cynic tyrannies of honest kings," implying that even a well-intentioned ruler may be pushed into repressive and excessive "tyrannies." Melville's ambivalence persists throughout the poem; while he has produced identification with the repressive state apparatus, even hailing its most forceful actions, he concludes by mourning the loss of the very illusion that he attributes to "the Town," which still does not heed "the grimy slur" on the faith that underpins American democracy.

Each of the traits I have emphasized in "The House-Top"—the use of a lyric voice in the depiction of epic historical events, the (related) emphasis on affective states, the refusal to posit anything resembling a sentimental scenario, and the pessimistic rumination on political theology—can be found throughout *Battle-Pieces*. It is no wonder, then, that in a review of the volume William Dean Howells complained of its "remoteness," arguing that it too often distances us from our "human feelings." One wonders after reading the book, Howells writes, whether "there has really been a great war, with battles fought by men and bewailed by women? Or is it only that Mr. Melville's inner consciousness has been perturbed" by "phantasms" of "tortured humanity shedding not words and blood, but words alone?" He quotes a poem about the guerilla Mosby, and says that "all the other persons in Mr. Melville's poetry seem as widely removed as he from our actual life."[50] This indignant rhetoric of "remoteness" is prompted in particular by the fact that Melville eschews entirely the fantasy of proximity to suffering that is central to any sentimental scenario, consistently accentuating the speaker's *distance* from what he describes (or in this poem, merely points toward). The distance is spatial, to be sure: the noise of the riot comes "fitfully from far," and the speaker is not proximate to either the riot or its repression. But more than that, and more significantly, Melville's poetic voice here works to distance itself emotionally from the violence that is, ostensibly, its subject matter and the object of its ambivalent critique. Temporal and primarily spatial displacements in the language of the poem allow him to use the assertion of the unrepresentability of collective violence—underscored by the footnote's assertion that he "dare not write" about "some proceedings of the draft-rioters"—to produce a voice, and a reader, positioned at a critical distance from the rioters' violence as well as the violence of the state.

This insistence on distance makes locating the politics of the poem extraordinarily difficult. Even if there is in the poem a peculiar and tentative identification of a political emotion, signaled in the relief when order is restored and in the attribution of "wisdom" to draconian measures, there is no place in it from which to identify, no position to be sympathized *with*. The victims of the violence are neither the black citizenry nor the working-class rioters, but an impersonal "Town" that is "taken" and then "redeemed."[51] The town's only vaguely human action is to "give thanks" that are (again, perhaps ironically) described as "devout." And while draconian measures may be "wise" and the military intervention welcomed, an encomium to the repressive state apparatus is not quite an identification; indeed, it presumes a relation that is more vertical than horizontal.

Some of the ambivalence of "The House-Top" has to do with Melville's project in *Battle-Pieces* as a whole, which he articulates in the volume's prose "Supplement." He says there that he wants to write war poems that tend toward reconciliation, and therefore he narrates battle after battle in ways that forestall clear identification with either side, often by viewing the violence either from a spatial or a temporal distance, as in "Shiloh." However tortuously it is argued, the political position Melville takes up in the "Supplement" is much more straightforward than is the politics of any of the poems. There is no doubt, for instance, that he is strongly repudiating the Radical Republican position that any southerners who were—in Melville's tendentious words—"cajoled" or "entrapped" into joining the rebellion had to be permanently excluded from the national polity. The "Supplement" was recognized as such a statement in one of the few positive reviews of the volume, which appeared anonymously in the *New-York Times* on August 27, 1866, and was the first published review of *Battle-Pieces*.[52] The review approvingly cites a passage in the "Supplement" that is startling both because it invokes the very language of sympathetic identification that "The House-Top" so rigorously avoids, and because it extends that sympathy in an unexpected direction. "In imagination," Melville writes, "let us place ourselves in the unprecedented position of the Southern-ers"—by which he clearly means the *white* Southerners—"their position as regards the millions of ignorant manumitted slaves in their midst, for whom some of us now claim the suffrage." What is "unprecedented" in the "position" of the Southern whites is left somewhat unclear, though Melville's reference to the "millions of ignorant manumitted slaves in their midst" comes perilously close to setting the whites up as the suf-fering objects of sentiment in a way that risks evolving into the dis-course of "black domination" that would later legitimate many acts of brutal antiblack violence during and after Reconstruction.[53]

Melville continues still further down this path in the next sentence of the conclusion (also quoted in the *Times* review): "Let us be Christians toward our fellow-whites, as well as philanthropists toward the blacks, our fellow-men" (244). The ironies of the asymmetry in this sentence are multiple, to say the least. The reason for the different imperatives has already been fully racialized earlier in the same paragraph: "The blacks, in their infant pupilage to freedom, appeal to the sympathies of every humane mind," but the "kindliness" exhibited by the "gov-ernment" toward the freedmen and women "should not be allowed to exclude kindliness to communities who stand nearer to us in nature." Melville here verges on fully committing himself to the "community" of whiteness over and against any felt obligation to emancipated blacks, identifying the former with the nation as a whole: "For the future of the freed slaves we may well be concerned; but the future of the whole country, involving the future of the blacks, urges a paramount claim upon our anxiety" (243).

Ultimately Melville's political position emerges as not at all unusual for a Northern white Unionist; national unity takes precedence over racial justice. What is most interesting for the purposes of my argument is how he gets to this position. Here and throughout the "Supplement," Melville couches a set of policy recommendations in affective rhetoric, making arguments about how the state should distribute its "kindliness" (as opposed to, say, rights and economic resources) while the about-to-be enfranchised black citizens make a "claim upon our "anxiety" (as opposed to demanding justice). This is in keeping with his framing of the essay, in which he contrasts the literary, aesthetic, and affective with the impersonality of the political, only in order ultimately to conflate them. At the same time, he identifies the poet's position with that of the state, characterizing himself as "one who desires to be impartially just in the expression of his views," and contrasting this impartiality with a "passionate sympathy" that would lead to "resentments so close as to be almost domestic in their bitterness." This sympathy, he concludes, "would hardly in the present juncture tend to discreet legislation" (246). In other words, he claims that in this volume he has taken an impersonal stance more akin to that of a legislator or officer of the state than to that of a poet. "We have sung of the soldiers and sailors," he writes, "but who shall hymn the politicians?"

At the very end of the "Supplement," Melville expresses a hope that the experience of the war itself can transform the nation's structure of feeling through a kind of affective pedagogy: "Let us pray that the terrible historic tragedy of our time may not have been enacted without instructing our whole beloved country through terror and pity," he writes, "and may fulfillment verify in the end those expectations which kindle the bards of Progress and humanity" (246). The hopeful second half of the sentence clearly contradicts the dark conclusion of the draft riot poem, which questions the power and even the very existence of either bard. But if we read "Progress and humanity" not as signs of Pollyannaish optimism, but instead as more neutrally descriptive indicators of modernity, we can see Melville as anticipating that the national affect can be restructured in line with the needs of the modernizing postwar state, that the "terror and pity" produced by the war can be not just instructive, but also instrumental in the consolidation of national unity and state power.

But does Melville believe that the poetic *representation* of that war can similarly "instruct our whole beloved country?" Is the purpose of *Battle-Pieces* to be instrumental in this way? Is it meant to restructure the national affect in line with the needs of the modernizing postwar state, consolidating national unity and state power? Such an argument would jibe with some other influential interpretations of the poems. Michael Rogin argues that in *Battle-Pieces* "Melville made imaginative rapprochement with weakened family authority, and strengthened it by transferring it to the state" (267), while Timothy Sweet argues even more bluntly that the poems depict "the mode of political subjectivity prescribed by a militaristic state" (165). Most recently, Deak Nabers has pointed out that the book presents itself as "a contribution to the ongoing debate about the 'just' terms for the 're-establishment' of the Southern states," (10) and argued that it thus addresses legal questions about the foundation and extent of U.S. sovereignty after the Civil War.

Despite the differences among these valuable and influential readings of *Battle-Pieces*, they share a tendency to skim past the fact that Melville so often couches these questions in affective terms. As he tells us in the preface, these poems are about "moods" and "feelings" as much as they are about battles and laws. But they are not, as Howells implies in his review, about such "phantasms" in contradistinction to questions of "actual life." Rather, *Battle-Pieces* explores the affective foundations of state sovereignty. For instance, Melville explains his decision to present his thoughts about "Re-establishment" in the "Supplement" by saying that "so far as feeling is concerned, it depends not mainly on the temper in which the South regards the North, but rather conversely." The contribution of a writer such as himself, he says, is that he can write about the matter of feelings about the "Re-establishment" of the national state, but from a "temperate and charitable" perspective, because he "never was a blind adherent" to an ideology (239).

In short, yes, *Battle-Pieces* is concerned with state authority and with the "victory of law." But it is fundamentally about what I have been calling "*feeling* like a state," exploring affective strategies for aligning a subject with state policy. In this project "The House-Top" is exemplary precisely because it takes on the relationship between the state and a population resistant to the state's efforts to enumerate and thus control it. These are of course the same questions Anna Dickinson asks in her chapter on the draft riots in *What Answer?*, questions that are simultaneously formal and political. What are the affects produced when the structures of feeling suturing society to the state break down? And what formal structures—what genre, style of narration, type of characterization—can best document the dislocating experience of such a violent irruption in the national symbolic?

As we have seen, Dickinson and Melville (and for that matter, Ruffin) perform different experiments in their efforts to address these questions. What these very different texts have in common, though, is that they register the social disruption they are trying to represent by means of a rhetoric of "impersonality" that can take several forms, including the evacuation of psychological interiority; the disappearance of individual character; experimentation with narrative and poetic voice; and a complex and contradictory manipulation of temporal, spatial, and emotional dynamics of proximity and distance. That such experiments can be performed in such different generic contexts may point to some affinities between the sentimental narrator and the lyric speaker that will bear further exploration.

These questions about affect, the state, and cultural form also have political and cultural resonance at a moment early in the twenty-first century when American public discourse about the state is deeply confused and ambivalent, when emergent right-wing political formations such as the Tea Party reproduce themselves through visceral antistate affect, when states are implementing austerity policies that entail disinvestment from cultural organizations and initiatives but culture itself is increasingly an instrument of neoliberal state policy.[54] At such a moment it may be instructive to explore the deep ambivalences and contradictions of an earlier moment in the history of U.S. state formation, when white working-class antipathy to a perceived expansion of governmentality could turn on a dime into racist violence, and when reformist and radical intellectuals and writers like Melville and Dickinson unexpectedly found themselves affectively invested in even the most repressive of state apparatuses. Scholars of American literature and culture need to think more about the state, and in particular about the relationship between, on the one hand, the forms of affect we have grown adept at delineating, and on the other, U.S. state formation in the nineteenth century and beyond. If only because leaving the state out of our analysis resonates, however inadvertently, with contemporary neoliberal and neoconservative understandings of the state as both culturally and economically inessential at best, we should be more attentive to cultural forms that, like these texts, bring in the state as a political question, a thematic issue, and a test of generic forms and conventions.

NOTES

1. "An Act for enrolling and calling out the national Forces, and for other Purposes," *Congressional Record.* 37th Cong. 3d. Sess. Ch. 74, 75. 1863. March 3, 1863 (http://www.yale.edu/glc/archive/962.htm; accessed February 23, 2011).

2. It was the first federal draft in the Union, but the Confederacy had instituted a draft lottery earlier in the war, with some of the same structures.

3. Iver Bernstein, *The New York City Draft Riots: Their Significance for American Society and Politics in the Age of the Civil War* (New York: Oxford University Press, 1990), 7.

4. Barnet Schecter, *The Devil's Own Work: The Civil War Draft Riots and the Fight to Reconstruct America* (New York: Walker & Company, 2005), 23.

5. Bernstein, 10.

6. More than other historians treating the draft riots, Adrian Cook emphasizes the antistate tenor of the riots. See *The Armies of the Streets: The New York City Draft Riots of 1863* (Lexington: University of Kentucky Press, 1974).

7. For basic historical facts about the riots I lean heavily on Bernstein, op. cit., which remains the standard work on the events. See also Brother Basil Leo Lee, F.S.C., *Discontent in New York City, 1861–1865,* diss. (Washington, DC: Catholic University of America Press, 1943); James McCague, *The Second Rebellion: The Story of the New York City Draft Riots of 1863* (New York: Dial Press, 1968); Schecter, op. cit.; and Cook, op. cit. A vivid and compelling account of black elite responses to the riots can be found in Carla L. Peterson, *Black Gotham: A Family History of African Americans in Nineteenth-Century New York City* (New Haven, CT: Yale University Press, 2011), 223–60.

   Like all of these scholars, I also draw more directly on nineteenth-century accounts of the riots, including William Osborn Stoddard, *The Volcano Under the City, by a Volunteer Special* (New York: Fords, Howard, and Hulbert, 1887); David M. Barnes, *The Draft Riots in New York. July, 1863. The Metropolitan Police: Their Services During Riot Week. Their Honorable Record* (New York: Baker & Godwin, 1863); George Templeton Strong, *The Diary of George Templeton Strong,* ed. Allan Nevins and Milton Halsey Thomas, 4 vols. (New York: MacMillan, 1952); *Report of the Committee of Merchants for the Relief of Colored People Suffering from the Late Riots in the City of New York* (New York: George A. Whitehorne, 1863); and Joel Tyler Headley's two compendia of riot narratives, *The Great Riots of New York: 1712–1873* (New York: E. B. Treat, 1873; rpt. New York: Thunder's Mouth Press, 2004), and *Pen and Pencil Sketches of the Great Riots* (New York: E. B. Treat, 1877; rpt. Miami: Mnemosyne, 1969) As Peterson notes, the contemporaneous newspaper reporting of the riots provides a limited historical record because of "the degree to which the newspapers tended to reprint one another's reports" (224), but Horace Greeley's *Tribune* and the New York *Times* are essential sources, as is the black and abolitionist press that Peterson herself discusses.

8. Historians and political scientists all seem to agree that the Civil War marked a turning point in U.S. state formation, though there is a wide range of opinion on how weak the state was before the war, what factors led to the strengthening of the state during the war and Reconstruction, the role played by the short-lived Confederate state in these changes, and whether U.S. state formation was as different from other national state-building projects as is usually presumed. See Richard Franklin Bensel, *Yankee Leviathan: The Origins of Central State Authority in America, 1859–1877* (Cambridge, MA: Cambridge University Press, 1990); Stephen Skoronek, *Building a New American State: The Expansion of National Administrative Capacities, 1877–1920* (Cambridge, MA: Cambridge University Press, 1982); William J. Novak, "The Myth of the 'Weak' American State," *American Historical Review* 113 (June 2008): 752–72, and *The People's Welfare: Law and Regulation in Nineteenth-Century America* (Chapel Hill: University of North Carolina Press, 1996); Edward L. Ayers, *What Caused the Civil War?: Reflections on the South and Southern History* (New York: Norton, 2005). Of the historians treating these issues in the nineteenth century, the one most attentive to citizens' emotional attachment to the state is Gregory P. Downs, *Declarations of Dependence: The Long Reconstruction of Popular Politics in the South* (Chapel Hill: University of North Carolina Press, 2011). My thanks to Downs for helping me with these references, as well as for a series of conversations that led me to bring the question of the state into this analysis.

9. The quotation is Michael Warner's paraphrase of the tradition of lyric criticism dominant since John Stuart Mill's assertion that "Eloquence is *heard*; poetry is *overheard*." "What Like a Bullet Can Undeceive," *Public Culture* 15.1: 51. My understanding of the lyric is strongly influenced by Virginia Jackson's in *Dickinson's Misery: A Theory of Lyric Reading* (Princeton, NJ: Princeton University Press, 2005); her argument is extended in "Who Reads Poetry?" which centers on a reading of the opening poem of *Battle-Pieces*, "The Portent." *PMLA* 123.2 (January 2008): 181–87.

10. Debates in Melville scholarship over his politics, while always heated, get all the more muddled when it comes to his position during the Civil War. For illustratively different views, see Michael Paul Rogin, *Subversive Genealogy: The Politics and Art of Herman Melville* (Berkeley: University of California Press, 1979), and Stanton Garner, *The Civil War World of Herman Melville* (Lawrence: University Press of Kansas, 1993.

11. Melville had been in a similar position once before during the Astor Place riots, an experience that likely informed his response to the draft riots. See Dennis Berthold, "Class Acts: The Astor Place Riots and Melville's 'The Two Temples,'" *American Literature* 71.3m (September 1999): 429–61.

Dickinson's Quaker background, as well as her years of active Garrisonian abolitionism, meant she had been even less likely, before the outbreak of the war, to identify with the state itself or any existing government. Even as late as 1864 she was still deeply ambivalent about the Lincoln administration; the acclaimed speech she gave in the House of Representative (in Lincoln's presence) was mostly a critique of his moderation. However, it is worth noting that by 1863 she had begun touring in support of Republican candidates, so she did not long remain a strict Garrisonian in relation to state-based politics. See J. Matthew Gallman, *America's Joan of Arc: The Life of Anna Elizabeth Dickinson* (New York: Oxford University Press, 2006).

12. In this phrasing, as in the title of this essay, I am playing off the title of James C. Scott's *Seeing Like a State: How Certain Schemes to Improve the Human Condition Have Failed* (New Haven, CT: Yale University Press, 1998), and building on an argument about the identificatory dialectic of "feeling with" and "feeling like" that I made in *Public Sentiments: Structures of Feeling in Nineteenth-Century American Literature* (Chapel Hill: University of North Carolina Press, 2001).

13. A notable effort to provide such tools is Christopher Castiglia's in *Interior States: Institutional Consciousness and the Inner Life of Democracy in the Antebellum United States* (Durham: Duke University Press, 2008).

14. For an argument, now twenty-five years old, that American social sciences was systematically marginalizing the role of the state, see *Bringing the State Back In*, ed. Peter B. Evans, Dietrich Rueschemeyer, and Theda Skocpol (Cambridge, MA: Cambridge University Press, 1985).

15. Each of these rephrasings invokes a different theoretical vocabulary, the first associated with Raymond Williams and cultural studies, the second with the work of Michel Foucault (see note above), and the third with the work of Louis Althusser. I certainly do not intend to conflate these quite different theoretical traditions, nor do I with to imply that any of these theorists themselves leave the state out of their reckonings. Rather, I am venturing a generalization about the ways these theorists have been used in American literary and cultural studies. This generalization applies less well to scholarship on the late eighteenth century, where discussions of republican ideology and especially the Constitution are unable to avoid attention to state formation. See, for instance, Eric Slauter's *The State as a Work of Art: The Cultural Origins of the Constitution* (Chicago: University of Chicago Press, 2009)

16. Edmund Ruffin, *Anticipations of the Future, To Serve as Lessons for the Present Time* (Richmond, VA: J. W. Randolph, 1860). All further citations to this text will be parenthetical.

17. Edmund Ruffin, *An essay on calcareous manures* (Richmond, VA: J. W. Randolph, 1852); Betty L. Mitchell, *Edmund Ruffin, a Biography* (Bloomington: Indiana University Press, 1981); Avery Craven, *Edmund Ruffin, Southerner: A Study in Secession* (New York: D. Appleton, 1932; rpt. Baton Rouge: Louisiana State University Press, 1982).

18. Nick Yablon argues that Ruffin's predictions in *Anticipations of the Future*, "while certainly derived from an agrarian theory of value, were not necessarily antiurban or antimodern." *Untimely Ruins: An Archaeology of American Urban Modernity, 1819–1919* (Chicago: University of Chicago Press, 2009), 87. See also

William M. Matthew, *Edmund Ruffin and the Crisis of Slavery in the Old South: The Failure of Agricultural Reform* (Athens: University of Georgia Press, 1988).

19. On crowds and crowd psychology in literature, see John Plotz, *The Crowd: British Literature and Public Politics* (Berkeley: University of California Press, 2000), and especially Mary Esteve, *The Aesthetics and Politics of the Crowd in American Literature* (Cambridge, MA: Cambridge University Press, 2003).

20. On the concept of a social imaginary, see Charles Taylor, *Modern Social Imaginaries* (Durham, NC: Duke University Press, 2004). On the social imaginary of the temperance movement, see Michael Warner, "Whitman Drunk," in *Publics and Counterpublics* (New York: Zone Books, 2002), 269–89; and Christopher Castiglia and Glenn Hendler, "Introduction" to *Franklin Evans, or The Inebriate: A Tale of the Times* (Durham, NC: Duke University Press, 2007).

21. Stoddard, *Volcano*, op. cit. On these genres, see Maggie Montesinos Sale, *The Slumbering Volcano: American Slave Ship Revolts and the Construction of Rebellious Masculinity* (Durham, NC: Duke University Press, 1997); Michael Denning, *Mechanic Accents: Dime Novels and Working-Class Novels in America* (New York: Verso, 1998); and Peter Linebaugh and Marcus Rediker, *The Many-Headed Hydra: Soldiers, Slaves, Commoners, and the Hidden History of the Revolutionary Atlantic* (Boston: Beacon Press, 2000).

22. Adam Smith, *The Theory of Moral Sentiments*, ed. D. D. Raphael and Al Macfie (Oxford: Clarendon Press, 1976). For Americanist uses of Smith as a key to sentimentalism, see Gregg Camfield, *Sentimental Twain: Samuel Clemens in the Maze of Moral Philosophy* (Philadelphia: University of Pennsylvania Press, 1994); Elizabeth Barnes, *States of Sympathy: Seduction and Democracy in the American Novel* (New York: Columbia University Press, 1997); and Lori Merish, *Sentimental Materialism: Gender, Commodity Culture, and Nineteent-Century American Literature* (Durham, NC: Duke University Press, 2000).

23. Recent developments in affect theory define affect (as distinct from emotion) as a phenomenon simultaneously social and embodied. Neither side of this formulation maps neatly onto the category of the personal. See especially Brian Massumi, *Parables for the Virtual: Movement, Affect, Sensation* (Durham, NC: Duke University Press, 2002) (hi Brian!); *The Affective Turn: Theorizing the Social*, edited by Patricia Ticineto Clough with Jean Halley (Durham, NC: Duke University Press, 2007); and Melissa Gregg and Gregory J. Seigworth, eds., *The Affect Theory Reader* (Durham, NC: Duke University Press, 2010).

24. Jean-Jacques Rousseau, *The Discourses and Other Early Political Writings*, Victor Gourevitch, ed. (Cambridge, MA: Cambridge University Press, 1997), 152.

25. Philip Fisher, *Hard Facts: Setting and Form in the American Novel* (New York: Oxford University Press, 1987), 106.

26. Ibid., 107.

27. Rousseau, op. cit., 152.

28. My use of the term "impersonality" resonates in several ways with Sharon Cameron's in her *Impersonality: Seven Essays* (Chicago: University of Chicago

Press, 2007), which culminates in a discussion of Melville's *Billy Budd*. But while Cameron locates impersonality in a set of philosophical and theological traditions that run from Edwards to Eliot, I am interested in its complex and contradictory historical relation to sentimentalism.

29. Anna E. Dickinson, *What Answer?* (Boston: Fields, Osgood, & Co., 1868; rpt. of the 1869 edition, with an introduction by J. Matthew Gallman, Amherst, NY: Humanity Books, 2003). All references to this text will be parenthetical.

30. See J. Matthew Gallman, *America's Joan of Arc: The Life of Anna Elizabeth Dickinson* (New York: Oxford University Press, 2006), as well as an earlier biography, Giraud Chester's *Embattled Maiden: The Life of Anna Dickinson* (New York: G. P. Putnam's Sons, 1951).

31. As Alice Rutkowski points out in the best (of very few) critical analyses of *What Answer?*, Dickinson had been associated in the public mind with the mixing of races since rumors had spread—in 1863, the year of the draft riots—that she was the author of the pamphlet in which the term "miscegenation" was coined: *Miscegenation: The Theory of the Blending of the Races, Applied to the American White Man and Negro*, which claimed that intermarriage was a goal of the Republican Party, was in actuality a hoax produced by Democrats. It was widely distributed in New York in December 1863, including at a speeches given by Dickinson, and the *New York Herald* speculated in print that she was its author. See Alice Rutkowski, "Gender, Genre, Race, and Nation: The 1863 New York City Draft Riots," *Studies in the Literary Imagination* 40:2 (Fall 2007): 126; and Sidney Kaplan, "The Miscegenation Issue in the Election of 1864," *Journal of Negro History* 34 (July 1949): 274–343. See also Lyde Cullen Sizer, "Still Waiting: Intermarriage in White Women's Civil War Novels," in Martha Hodes, ed., *Sex, Love, Race: Crossing Boundaries in North American History* (New York: NYU Press, 1999), 254–66.

32. Sizer, op. cit., notes that Dickinson had done serious research for the war chapters of the novel; the description of the riots indicates that Dickinson—who was not in New York in the summer of 1863 when the riots took place—carefully researched them as well (259).

33. Rutkowski, op. cit., 116–17.

34. Thanks to Dana Luciano for comments that immensely clarified this passage for me. Her suggestions were helpful here and where I return to this passage below.

35. This is, for instance, the response of Union League Founder George Templeton Strong, whose diary entries on the riots are full of visceral disgust for "Paddy, the asylum burner" (*Diary*, vol. 3: 347).

36. Dickinson's assertion—commonplace at the time, and part of a general hardening of anti-Irish sentiment among Unionists enraged by the riots—is mitigated very slightly by her reference to some Irish, "and Catholic Irish too,—industrious, sober, intelligent people,—who indignantly refused participation in these outrages, and mourned over the barbarities which were disgracing their national name" (272).

37. I am drawing here on the argument of Dwight A. McBride in *Impossible Witness: Truth, Abolitionism, and Slave Testimony* (New York: NYU Press, 2001).

38. James Baldwin, "Everybody's Protest Novel" (1949), in *James Baldwin: Collected Essays* (New York: Library of America, 1998), 12.

39. This is a concern of Susan Sontag's work on war photography in *On Photography* (New York: Farrar, Strauss, and Giroux, 1977), in *Regarding the Pain of Others* (New York: Picador, 2003) and, just before her death, in a piece on the Abu Ghraib photographs, "On the Torture of Others," *New York Times Magazine*, May 23, 2004 (http://www.nytimes.com/2004/05/23/magazine/regarding-the-torture-of-others.html; accessed April 1, 2011). Discussion of the ethics of taking, reproducing, and viewing the Abu Ghraib photographs tended to center on such questions of affective orientation and whether such actions produced a sense of distance from, or empathy with, the victims. For two related but ultimately different takes on this question, see the film *Standard Operating Procedure* (dir. Errol Morris, 2008) and the book of the same title, based on the same interviews, written by Philip Gourevitch (New York: Penguin, 2008), retitled in its paperback edition *The Ballad of Abu Ghraib* (New York: Penguin 2009). Thanks are due to Gourevitch for conversations in which my thoughts on these questions were both complicated and clarified.

40. It is possible that this reference is the result of direct influence. Dickinson was surely aware of Douglass's life and writings, and knew him personally. Just a few days before the draft riots, the two of them had appeared on a stage together in Philadelphia at an event promoting black enlistment in the Union army. See *Addresses of the Hon. W. D. Kelley, Miss Anna E. Dickinson, and Mr. Frederick Douglass, at a Mass Meeting, Held at National Hall, Philadelphia, July 6, 1863, for the Promotion of Colored Enlistments* (http://www.archive.org/details/addressesofhonwdookell; accessed March 22, 2011).

41. Herman Melville, *Battle-Pieces and Aspects of the War* (New York: Harper & Brothers, 1866; rpt., Amherst, NY: Prometheus Books, 2001). All further reference to this text will be parenthetical.

42. Many critics have noted the generic instability of *Battle-Pieces*. See Helen Vendler, "Melville and the Lyric of History," *Southern Review* 35.3 (Summer 1999): 579–94; Rosanna Warren, "Dark Knowledge: Melville's Poems of the Civil War," *Raritan* 19.1 (Summer 1999): 100–21; Virginia Jackson, "Who Reads Poetry?" op. cit.

43. Timothy Sweet traces Melville's three uses of the image of the Aeolian harp here, in *Moby-Dick*, and in a poem in *John Marr and Other Sailors* called "The Aeolian Harp." *Traces of War: Poetry, Photography, and the Crisis of the Union* (Baltimore: Johns Hopkins University Press, 1990), 168–69.

44. William H. Shurr, *The Mystery of Iniquity: Melville as Poet, 1857–1891* (Lexington: University Press of Kentucky, 1972), 49.

45. Deak Nabers, *Victory of Law: The Fourteenth Amendment, the Civil War, and American Literature, 1852–1867* (Baltimore: Johns Hopkins University Press, 2006), 48.

46. Michael Warner has read "Shiloh" as something like a refusal, or at least a strong questioning, of the sort of redemptive violence exemplified by Julia Ward Howe's "The Battle Hymn of the Republic." Howe's poem is designed to provoke a violent and transformative interpellation of national subjects by analogizing Christ's sacrifice with that of Union soldiers: "With a glory in his bosom that transfigures you and me;/As He died to make men holy, let us die to make men free;/While God is marching on." For Warner, Melville counters this "remediating" and "redemptive" project, in "Shiloh," with an implicit affirmation of "a distinctive picture of subjective experience and a baseline sanctification of life." The characteristic rhetorical move of this ethical stance, Warner argues, is a redefinition of violence—violence *per se*, not just particular acts of violence—as illegitimate. The contradictory ethical and aesthetic consequences of delegitimating violence in a series of war poems are pushed still further in "The House-Top." See "What Like a Bullet Can Undeceive?" op. cit.

47. This evasiveness and displacement parallels Melville's avoidance, throughout his career, of any mention of the Astor Place riots of 1849. See Berthold, op. cit.

48. The full endnote reads: "'I dare not write the horrible and inconceivable atrocities committed,' says Froissart, in alluding to the remarkable sedition in France during his time. The like may be hinted of some proceedings of the draft-rioters" (229).

49. Positions on Melville's political positions during the Civil War tend to correspond to the degree of irony attributed to his hailing of the use of military force in this poem. For opposing views, see Shurr and Garner, op. cit.

50. William Dean Howells, *Atlantic Monthly* 19 (February 1867): 252–53, rpt. in *Herman Melville: The Contemporary Reviews*, ed. Brian Higgins and Hershel Parker (Cambridge, MA: Cambridge University Press, 1995), 526–28.

51. This is another, still more surprising parallel to Ruffin's novel; in his prediction of the riots, Northern whites and free blacks loot side by side, and there is no antiblack aspect to the riots.

52. Rpt. in Higgins and Parker, op. cit., 509.

53. Charles Chesnutt's 1901 novel *The Marrow of Tradition* brilliantly explores the process by which the production of white "sympathy" under "black domination" culminates in antiblack violence.

54. See, for instance, George Yúdice, "Culture," in Bruce Burgett and Glenn Hendler, eds., *Keywords for American Cultural Studies* (New York: NYU Press, 2007): 71–76, and *The Expediency of Culture: Uses of Culture in the Global Era* (Durham, NC: Duke University Press, 2003).

8

Impersonating the State of Exception

JONATHAN ELMER

What resonance does the phrase "states of exception" have for a likely reader of this volume? While some might make a quick association with the idea of American "exceptionalism," many will, I imagine, think of the significant outpouring of political commentary dedicated to the post-9/11 era, and perhaps explicitly of the 2005 translation of Giorgio Agamben's *State of Exception*. This short book is the second of three works Agamben dedicated to the relation of sovereign power to what he called, borrowing from Roman law, the *homo sacer*, a paradigmatically defenseless figure reduced to "bare life."[1] The suite of works combines analyses of sovereign power drawn from the thought of Carl Schmitt with meditations on life as the target of power derived from Foucault's investigations into "bio-power." *State of Exception* is the most technical of the books. It offers a theoretical investigation of the "state of exception" as "law's threshold or limit concept," the "suspension of the juridical order itself." But it also makes a historical claim that reaches back well before 9/11: "Under the pressure of the paradigm of the state of exception, the entire politico-constitutional life of Western societies began [around World War I] gradually to assume a new form, which has perhaps only today reached its full development" (4, 13). Agamben analyzes various aporias in the relation between law and power, between a realm of norms and the acts that follow from the more or less complete suspension of norms and the rule of law. Unlike the book in your hands, in other words, *State of Exception* does not concern the U.S. in the nineteenth century (though Lincoln is discussed briefly), nor does it address itself overtly to cultural production. My initial question—how well known is Agamben's text, or indeed the theory of the "state of exception" elaborated in his trilogy?—thus suggests a second: even if well known, how relevant is this theory to the reader of this book?

An answer to the first question was suggested by the appearance of an article by Mark Danner in the *New York Review of Books*, titled simply "After September 11: Our State of Exception."[2] Invoking Clinton Rossiter and Agamben, Danner argues that we live now in a "state of exception" that has become normal: "Call it, then, the state of exception: these years during which, in the name of security, some of our accustomed rights and freedoms are set aside, the years during which we live in a different time. . . . It is possible for most to live their lives without taking note of these practices at all except as phrases in the news—until, every once in a while, like a blind man who lives, all unknowingly, in a very large cage, one or another of us stumbles into the bars" (44). A fundamental disorientation has gripped us, Danner suggests, such that we go about our daily lives, reading the papers, going to work, taking vacations—enjoying civil society—all the while unaware that we live in a very large cage. I invoke "civil society" here to signal the classical notion of liberal political theory that there exists a domain outside of the state, a domain in which certain "accustomed rights and freedoms" reside. When the state suspends these—even to the point of rendering the very suspense illegible, as in Danner's example—we have a "state of exception."

Like Agamben, Danner is centrally concerned—and for perfectly good reasons—with juridical issues of rights and their violation by power: the conflict between the state and civil society takes place wholly on the terrain of rights and sovereign powers. The "juridico-political" idiom saturates the analytic field, as it were, and tilts understanding

decisively toward questions of law and right, toward the political rationality emergent from the classic analyses of sovereignty from Bodin
forward. But this approach has its drawbacks. Despite his repeated
recourse to Foucault's analysis of biopower and the notion of "governmentality," Agamben does not, I would argue, take up that inquiry in
the spirit in which it was intended. In the 1970s, Foucault undertook
analyses that resisted the tendency to subsume all political rationality beneath a concept of state sovereignty. He does this not because he
thinks sovereignty, the state, or concepts of rights are not crucial, but
because imagining that they define or cover the political field—as Danner's image above of a very large cage does—is to miss the working of
alternative, and arguably equally influential, political rationalities. In
this regard, it is telling that in a seminar at the Collège de France in
the winter of 1979, a seminar ostensibly focused on "The Birth of Biopolitics," Foucault spends the entire time in what he characterizes as a
kind of preparatory analysis of the political rationality manifest in economic liberalism: "The year's course ended up being devoted entirely
to what should have been only its introduction."[3] "Liberalism acquired
its modern shape," Foucault argues, "precisely with the formulation of
[the] essential incompatibility between the non-totalizable multiplicity
of economic subjects of interest and the totalizing unity of the juridical sovereign" (282). "The subject of interest"—a figure Foucault equates
with liberalism's *homo oeconomicus*—"constantly overflows the subject of right. He is therefore irreducible to the subject of right" (274).
To return to my original question, then: when thinking about what
the notion of "states of exception" might mean in nineteenth-century
America, we do well to keep in view the constant and vigorous jostling
between juridical thought, and all the apparatus of sovereign power
associated with it, and this other domain defined by the logic of economic liberalism, a domain Foucault suggests "overflows" the domain
of rights and their maintenance or suspension. The grip of the state,
its ability to saturate the social field with its fantasy of totalization—
and one wonders whether Danner's image of the very large cage is not
an expression, in protest, of this very fantasy—is quite uneven in the
nineteenth-century U.S. generally, to say nothing of riotous New York
in 1863, polar expeditions, or the scene of Liberian colonization. Making the "state of exception" usable in a nineteenth-century U.S. context

might mean, paradoxically enough, expanding the concept's meaning beyond the juridico-political dimension.

The editors of this volume have effected just this redirection of emphasis. In response to the complexly disoriented worlds presented in the essays by David Kazanjian, Hester Blum, and Glenn Hendler, they propose an idiom of disruption and spacing: the states of exception they have in mind are not defined by the "removal of citizenship by the power of law" as much as the "tenuousness of nationalized modes of belonging" and "(dis)locations in space and time." In place of an Agambenian idiom of application, force, or "suspension," the editors emphasize a shaded analysis of the "distancing, at once willed and compelled, of norms." These questions of spacing, of distantiation, open up, in the essays included here, a new perspective on the limit to state rationality, if not always state power. This limit is not an asymptote or a final term, but something more like a mediated interval or filter blocking access to the elemental figure of the (other) person. "Exception" in these analyses is not the *result* of an act of state sovereignty—like a declared state of emergency—but rather a *condition* that lies "askew" to the nation-state.

Consider David Kazanjian's patient and moving analysis of the correspondence between Liberian colonists and their sponsors and family in the United States. Neither a state, nor a colonial extension of an existing state, Liberia in these early decades was rather a sponsored settlement program rife with contradictions, leaving those involved in the project essentially "askew" to both the U.S. and Liberia. These contradictions, however, as Kazanjian argues persuasively, are not finally peculiar to the case of Liberia; rather, they reveal a general condition of "unsettled" being in the black Atlantic world, a kind of existential precariousness that cannot be grasped either by logics of sovereignty and citizenship or by rationalities of economic liberalism and civil society. Think of Olaudah Equiano gaining his manumission and wishing to go "home" to England; or the sailors during the War of 1812 who chose prison rather than impressment into the British Navy, not because they felt patriotic attachment to the U.S. but rather because prison represented a better chance of survival.[4] So too the Liberian settlers, whose experiences call into question what would seem to be essential binaries of the social symbolic: home/not-home, slave/free, agency/passivity. As terrifying and perilous as this diasporic condition is, Kazanjian does find a version of freedom in it: "a free life emerges less as a formal state of manumission or citizenship in a settled nation-state, and more as an unsettled, ongoing state of improvised being that is continually intimate with slavery and a diasporic Atlantic."

How can we gain access to *this* sort of state of exception, one for which the analytical tools of the theory of sovereignty are not very useful? Kazanjian suggests an answer through his play with the term "unsettled." There is a zone, his analysis suggests, that lies beyond the authorizations of any state, and equally beyond the volitional expressivity of any "author," a zone that is agitated by rhetorical impulsions that are in essence impersonal, or extra-personal. Discussing one of his letter writers, Kazanjian observes: "Russell is unable to control the figures of coming and going, of immigrant and emigrant, of American and Liberian, or native and foreign. They circulate recklessly, and it is as if that very recklessness gives him his hope." Buffeted as he is by danger and contradictory desires, Russell writes a prose that reveals a drifting "potentiality" beyond him—beyond, that is, the equally reifying concepts of self and sovereign gathered under the rubric of "authorization": "freedom [is] a tenuous, unrealized potentiality that has thus far exceeded any attempt to institutionalize or authorize it." It is possible indeed that "liberty is no longer an individual matter at all."

Kazanjian proposes that an attention to semantic flux and affective drift in the language of his correspondents uncovers a political reality otherwise illegible. It's a powerful critical stance, and one seconded in different ways by Hendler and Blum. If one fundamental contribution of this trio of essays is to torque the concept of "state of exception" away from the problems of authority and toward what Kazanjian calls the "unsettled," the other challenge they pose to their contemporaries concerns the status of literary analysis. It's not even clear that "literary" analysis is the right term. Glenn Hendler does ask searching questions about genre and its limitations in his fascinating essay, but neither Blum nor Kazanjian deal with "literary" texts in any standard acceptation. They deal with writing, of course, and with rhetoric; they attend carefully to the material conditions and occasions of expressive production, and to trope, figure, and image. What I would say, then, is that all three critics bring to bear skills of attentiveness and the conviction that a patient unpacking of the textual evidence before them can lead to insights into historical agency and ideological structure otherwise not accessible. What marks them of our moment, perhaps, is that this interpretive work in understood to open onto an *impersonal dimension of communication and expression.*

Hester Blum's analysis of polar printing allows us to extend this inquiry into the impersonal. First of all, who brings a printing press to the North Pole? Well, quite a few people do, it turns out—just as soldiers and sailors have produced their own newspapers far from home, and apparently for their own consumption.[5] While Blum is interested in the convergence between the "everyday and the exceptional," it is not to privilege the latter: the relation between "everyday" printing and the apparently "exceptional" version that she dubs "extreme printing" is governed rather by a logic of intensification, not one of negation or exemption. Still, something a little strange is going on here. Blum invokes Benedict Anderson to explain the motives behind this shipboard printing, but where Anderson argues that print afforded an "imagined community" for people distant from each other in space and time, the "homogeneous empty time" for those aboard an icebound ship during the months-long Arctic night looks less like a solution, we can imagine, than the problem itself. Blum supposes—and the record bears this out—that the papers were intended to bring everyone together—solidifying community; but the result, as she reveals, was not necessarily that. It seems just as likely that what the members of the shipboard wanted was *distance* from each other. If Anderson's notion of "imagined community" emphasizes the latter word, the men aboard Parry's expedition might well have hungered for the minimal distance that would allow them to treat their over-proximate fellows as only *imagined.*

What printing allowed these explorers, I am suggesting, was liberation into a shared, imagined, and *impersonal* community. Here the impersonal is a minimal distance between individuals, a kind of mediating integument that is neither solitude nor fusion, but a zone in which both (collective) belonging and (individual) exemption can be entertained and granted reality, even as neither position is enforced as supreme. In this regard, the satirical quality of the publications Blum analyzes makes sense. Mock "advertisements" suggest, perhaps, the "fantasy that the polar expedition is still connected to the world," but if so, that fantasy is itself part of the appropriation-at-a-distance made possible by print mediation. This is the world inside out, or upside down, and the global aspirations of the "redeemer nation" are both embraced and satirically miniaturized when compared to a child's toy, as is done in the *Port Foulke Weekly News*. "Non-contribution breaks the fantasy that the polar expedition is still connected to the world," writes Blum, referring to those problematic souls who did not play along in the production of these papers. "The news at the ends of the earth, then, circulates both at the poles and in the fictive elsewhere that functions, for expedition members, as the world itself." There are, in truth, several worlds in play here at the poles—and according to Blum's thesis that the apparently exceptional is in fact merely the intensification of the normal, we might propose that there are several worlds in play wherever mediation interposes its "fictive elsewhere" between the worlds—equally real—of the face-to-face and the "imagined" collectivity of, say, a state.

Does what is still named literature have any special relation to the work of mediation made visible by Liberian letters and polar newspapers? I see as yet no clear answer to this question, but Glenn Hendler's analysis of different writerly responses to the draft riots of 1863 in New York suggest just how much is at stake. Everywhere concerned with the "dialectic of distance and proximity" at work in representations of political belonging, Hendler focuses especially on how violently "unsettled" situations, such as those presented by the draft riots, push at the limits of genre to establish the right distance. Political challenges here are overtly addressed to literary-ideological technologies—discourses of sympathy and sentiment, the special resources of poetry or prose, etc. The result of this challenge, in Hendler's analysis, is the breaching of an "impersonal" figure that cannot be contained by received generic modes. Referring to Anna Elizabeth Dickinson's *What Answer?* (1868), Hendler asks: "What happens . . . if all the personal, individual, interior, psychological particularities are removed from the fictive figures . . . and yet the reader is asked to respond sympathetically. . . . Can sentimental sympathy be produced in a condition of almost complete impersonality?" Of all three essayists treated here, Hendler is most direct in his engagement with the problem of "impersonality," invoking the treatment of this idea in Sharon Cameron's work and elsewhere. In the final analysis, "impersonality" marks the exhaustion of sentimental fantasies of sympathy and affective proximity for Hendler. But rather than indexing a mere failure, such "impersonality," he suggests, makes available a new affective posture, what he calls "feeling like a state." For this reason, Hendler suggests we need to "think more about the state." The pull of the "impersonal" is, as it were, back toward the state, the fantasies of sympathetic proximity in civil society having failed.

I wonder, though, if a turn back to the state is where these analyses of rhetoric, mediation, and the "unsettled" state of exception must necessarily lead us. Hendler is correct that in "The House-Top," and arguably throughout *Battle-Pieces*, Melville "eschews entirely the fantasy of proximity to suffering that is central to any sentimental scenario, consistently accentuating the speaker's *distance* from what he describes." This skeptical project regarding sympathy and distance had, in fact, absorbed Melville throughout the 1850s, surfacing most memorably in those fictions that place the reader in a position from which proximity and distance are equally vexing, because equally unstable. The reader of *The Confidence-Man*, surely as much as any of "his" victims, can neither wholly eschew the effort to know another—perhaps to the point of finding "sympathy" for that other—nor achieve any assurance that such knowing has taken place. The same holds true, of course, for Captain Delano's tumultuous hours aboard the *San Dominick*, or the attorney-narrator's months with Bartleby—this last fiction being perhaps the template of them all. Let me suggest in conclusion how the themes and motifs I have isolated from these three excellent essays might play out in the context of that hypercanonical story, "Bartleby, the Scrivener."

Bartleby certainly is exceptional, we might say, but the dilemma at the heart of his story—and this despite the fact that he ends his days in the Tombs—is not law, but desire. The political rationality at stake is not juridical, that is, but economic: this is a tale about the workplace and matters of "preference." In this sense, I would argue, Melville's tale presents us with a version of the state of exception in keeping with the inflection of that concept pursued in these essays. As Foucault might say, a new (liberal, economic) model of governing is at work here: confronted with the reality that the "economic world is naturally opaque and naturally non-totalizable" (282), power no longer *lets live*, and *makes die* (the older model of sovereign right), but attempts to *make live*—the attorney even invites Bartleby to come live in his home—and when that fails, he *lets* Bartleby *die*.[6] Bartleby lives wholly within a world of obscure and idiosyncratic desires that includes the narrator's, those of Nippers and Turkey, even perhaps Ginger Nut. Bartleby's own opaque nonpreferences represent both the apogee and the vanishing point of this obscure *ratio* of desire. Foucault suggests that for classic liberalism, "economics is a discipline that begins to demonstrate not only the pointlessness, but also the impossibility of a sovereign point of view over the totality of the state he has to govern" (282). It is because of this acceptance of the limitation to sovereign knowledge that liberalism can present itself as a "critique of governmental reason" (283). But this critique is itself dependent on a fantasy of rationality, as Foucault knows well. Ventriloquizing a liberal theory he stands at some distance from, Foucault proposes that "[e]conomic rationality is not only surrounded by, but founded on the unknowability of the totality of the process." Rather: "*Homo Oeconomicus* is the one island of rationality possible within an economic process whose uncontrollable nature does not challenge, but instead founds the rationality of the atomistic behavior of *homo oeconomicus*" (282). Is Bartleby an "island of rationality"? That seems to me a strictly unanswerable question. He certainly does not seem *irrational*. While the narrator's mental and physical maneuvers grow ever more erratic over the course of the story, Bartleby trades in statements of self-evidence: "I know where I am," "I know you and want nothing to say to you," "Do you not see the reason yourself?"[7] Bartleby both typifies and ruins a model of the rationality of preferences, and in this regard is a kind of twin, after all, of the state sovereign, he who both embodies and renders constitutively out of reach a rationality proper to the state. He exposes to view the opaque and impersonal desires that lie at the heart of a mode of governmentality based on the person and his or her desires.

The most urgent question for Melville, I would argue, is whether—political rationalities having failed to account for Bartleby—other discourses, specifically the aesthetic, can do any better. Here the questions of distance and proximity, of sympathy and mediation and the "impersonal," come to the fore again. Bartleby is always both too close and too far away. Placed within the narrator's office, within reach of his voice, Bartleby resides behind his green screen as both always there and inaccessible. The narrator's fantasy is that "privacy and society" are "conjoined" (642) by his arrangement with the green screen: perhaps like the men aboard the polar expedition, the green screen here serves to interpose a self-consciously mediating distance by which negotiations between over-proximity and the abstractions of "society" might be played with, and thus rendered livable. But like those spoilsports described by Blum, Bartleby becomes a problematic "non-contributor." The green screen is available for an analysis more elaborate than can be afforded here, but that it represents literature, the role of a specifically literary mediation or interposition of spacing that both acknowledges inaccessibility and wishes it away, seems indisputable: "Throughout, the scrivener remained standing behind the screen, which I directed to be removed the last thing. It was withdrawn; and being folded up like a huge folio, left him the motionless occupant of a naked room" (664). "The motionless occupant of a naked room" represents a different sort of state of exception, one that escapes the rationalities of state sovereignty and economic liberalism alike; and one, too, unsolaced by the enabling illusions provided by the "huge folio" that also fails in its task.

Bartleby is, it seems, a thoroughly disillusioned figure: there is nothing any longer in play (*il-ludere*) for him, no "potentiality" of freedom of the kind discerned by Kazanjian in the flow of letters from Liberia. The tendency of criticism in recent years has been to attack the narrator for his self-serving fantasies. Chief among these fantasies is that attached to the final word of the story: "humanity." It is not uncommon to read analyses which set themselves squarely against that concept and value, and that propose—perhaps not unlike the role of the "impersonal" in the essays included here—that "Bartleby" exposes an inhuman dimension in excess of, and undermining, the consolations of a shared humanity. I believe Melville does, indeed, ask just this question: as Hendler rightly observes, Melville is quite self-conscious about the traps of sympathetic fantasies, and always on the lookout for how proximity and distance are actually at work. But if he asks the question of humanity, and of something like "literature's" ability to address such a question, it is not so clear to me that he has answered it. I suppose the "state of exception" here is existential, and the kind of questions opened for me by the essays by Kazanjian, Blum, and Hendler concern the ongoing viability of a specifically imaginative response to such a state.

Bartleby is there, he is irrefutably human, and he is just as irrefutably opaque: he can neither be ignored nor understood. He must be lived with, even when he is abandoned. "Humanity"—the story's last word—requires acknowledgment on grounds that can never be provided.

NOTES

1. The three texts are Giorgio Agamben, *Homo Sacer: Sovereign Power and Bare Life*, trans. Daniel Heller-Roazen (Stanford: Stanford University Press, 1998); *State of Exception*, trans. Kevin Attell (Chicago: University of Chicago Press, 2005); and *Remnants of Auschwitz: The Witness and the Archive*, trans. Daniel Heller-Roazen (New York: Zone Books, 2002).

2. Mark Danner, "After September 11: Our State of Exception," *New York Review of Books*, vol. LVIII, no. 15 (October 13, 2001): 44–48.

3. Michel Foucault, *The Birth of Biopolitics: Lectures at the Collège de France, 1978–79*, trans. Graham Burchell, ed. Michel Senellart (New York: Palgrave Macmillan, 2008), 282. Hereafter cited parenthetically in the text.

4. For black sailors, see W. Jeffrey Bolster, *Black Jacks: African American Seamen in the Age of Sail* (Cambridge: Harvard University Press, 1998). Bolster argues that the decision to resist impressment is a kind of practical critique of their exclusion from the state by these black sailors. I suggest the more mundane interpretation in *On Lingering and Being Last: Race and Sovereignty in the New World* (New York: Fordham University Press, 2008), 116–17.

5. See Jim Berkey, "Imperial Correspondence: Soldiers, Writing, and the Imperial Quotidian during the Spanish-American and Philippine-American Wars," unpublished dissertation, Indiana University, 2010.

6. This chiastic formulation—take life/let live becoming make live/let die—is Foucault's. See Michel Foucault, *"Society Must Be Defended": Lectures at the Collège de France 1975–76*, trans. David Macey, ed. Mauro Bertani and Alessandro Fontana (New York: Picador, 2003), 240–41.

7. Herman Melville, "Bartleby, the Scrivener: A Story of Wall Street," in *The Piazza Tales*, ed. Harrison Hayford (New York: Library of America, 1984), quotes from 669, 669, 656.

PART III

Speculative Sexualities

9

Eat, Sex, Race

KYLA WAZANA TOMPKINS

Feminist and queer studies of the last three decades have redrawn—undressed, perhaps—the political map of the Western human body, unpacking and reorienting the genealogy of the viscous, somatic, neurologically vital, mucosal matter that is, in the West, called "body." Much attention has been paid to those parts whose political and erotic baggage is clearly overdetermined by their relationship to normative and reproductive—or, coevally, threateningly nonnormative and counterreproductive—erotic behaviors. Leo Bersani, most famously, has taken up anality as a site of fraught sexual politics: for Bersani, anal sex, particularly in the age of AIDS, represented the apotheosis of counteridentification with both the heteronormative and liberal selfhood: "if the rectum is the grave in which the masculine ideal . . . of proud subjectivity is buried, then it should be celebrated for its very potential for death."[1]

But what of the other end of the alimentary canal? This essay argues that not enough attention has been paid to the mouth as a site of both erotic potential and political investment.[2] Specifically, I will look at two short narratives appended to Sylvester Graham's *A Lecture to Young Men on Chastity*[3] to ask: what is the political life and erotic history of the mouth in the nineteenth-century United States? I will focus particularly on the figure of the sexually dissident (and disciplined) child to think through a concept that I call queer alimentarity: the deployment and representation of the mouth—of orality in its many forms, including kissing and eating—as both a trope for genital pleasure, and as a form of erotic pleasure in and of itself.

Spanning six decades of the nineteenth century and written by a major—and closely connected—figure in the antebellum U.S. reform movement, the *Lecture* is heavily invested in that movement's particularly raced pleasures. That is, as a prescriptive text it is as erotically fixated on the consolidation of whiteness as it is both instrumentally directed toward heterosexual futurity and yet always haunted by its violent projections onto—and material consequences for—the bodies of hyper-raced others. In their preoccupation with race these texts allow us to study the mouth as a sensory space that both actualizes and figuratively represents corporeal encounters in difference, a point not disconnected from the mouth's other sensory pleasures.

I understand orality in these texts to reveal the mouth as not simply a passageway through which food and power travel, but rather as a place or even a stage within and upon which various transgressive and normative desires may be acted out and displayed. Eating in these texts is a biopolitical act, one that asserts and shapes racial identification and embodiment as they are organized around politically charged tropes of health and wellbeing. Encoded as desire *and* disgust, these aesthetic and alimentary relationships work to concretize whiteness as a majoritarian racial position organized around disturbingly violent forms of desire that are simultaneously coded as sexually dissident.

Dietetic and alimentary imagery tied to the construction of whiteness across the nineteenth century coheres in what we might think of as the early and uneven biopolitical impulses of the reform movements of the 1830s. While the birth of biopower, in the classic sense, is linked to what Ann Stoler called the "statization of sexuality," in my understanding of biopower in the American context, various reform projects, including temperance and dietetic reform, were linked and often worked hand in hand with sexual hygiene projects such as the anti-masturbation movement. Sylvester Graham's "farinaceous diet" was directed at curbing specific forms of consumption, but it was also, explicitly, a solution to the "epidemic" in youthful masturbation. It is exactly at this intersection that we might also tie eating and racial embodiment to what Bruce Burgett has called the problem of "sex" in the long eighteenth century. Because for dietetic reformers of the early nineteenth century like Graham, eating and "sex," particularly eating and onanism, or masturbation, were closely linked to each other within the rhetoric of vice, morality, pleasure, and dissident eroticisms.

I am borrowing from Bruce Burgett when I put "sex" into scare quotes. I find his call to reconsider "our commonsense understanding of 'sex' as a coherent set of bodily practices . . . and our related assumption that those 'sexual' practices express a sexuality that constitutes the self's deepest . . . interiority" both essential and provocative in trying to understand, on the one hand, the longstanding metonymic, metaphoric, and catachrestic relationships between eating and sex in literature and culture, and on the other hand, what I believe to be their coeval if uneven emergence as dense transfer points of biopower in the early republic.[4] As Burgett points out, food and sex are tied together as part of the Malthusian calculus of population survival: populations will reproduce until food supplies are overburdened, at which point, starvation and other deprivations will cull the population down to orderly forms. If we place Burgett's insights into Malthusian science in conversation with Foucault's account of the rise of biopower, it seems clear that the impregnation of sex with the political life of the nation might similarly be accompanied by a reordered understanding of food as linked to the fleshly survival, and political coding, of the species.

As one of the century's best-known anti-masturbation campaigners, Sylvester Graham has long been thought of, particularly in popular histories of food and medicine in the nineteenth century, as the apotheosis of nineteenth-century quackery.[5] I'd like to argue against the ongoing tendency to treat Graham's work as a punch line for the rhetorical excesses and perversities of the period. Excessive he is indeed, but as scholars have shown, the perversities with which Graham was associated—masturbation and "vicious" consumption among them— have a significant place in literary history.[6] As we will see, the deeply catachrestic, that is, the slippery, sensual, and savory nature of his writing can make Grahamite logic difficult to parse. Inhabiting that difficulty, however, produces a singular portrait of early-nineteenth-century "sexual" economies, whose signs and practices have hitherto evaded the subject-centered (and genitally oriented) methodologies of post-Foucauldian sexuality studies, but whose unveiling might point us toward new readings of the canonical and noncanonical writers that were impacted by Grahamite thought, Herman Melville among them. Graham's writings illuminate the relationship between eating and sexuality by linking the cultural history of wheat and bread to vice, morality, and national formation; in turn, his implicitly racialized and civilizationist construction of an ideal American diet—what I see as the political unconscious of eating culture in the United States—allows for a reconfiguration of Foucault's theory of biopower in the antebellum context.

The Bio(geo)politics of Bread

Sylvester Graham's particular contribution to the anti-onanist movement was to propose that a vegetarian and bread-centered diet would cure what he saw as the era's epidemic of masturbation. Initially trained as an evangelical minister, Graham first entered into public view in 1830, when he accepted a post with the Pennsylvania Temperance Society. Over the next decade he would produce eight books and extensively tour the Northeastern lecture circuit. The extent of his interests included the importance of Sunday school, the spread of cholera, and, of course, the importance of sobriety. By 1835 he had become a known quantity on the reform circuit, especially for his views concerning the relationship between vice and correct diet; by 1837 he managed to articulate a dietetic program whose highly metaphorical qualities reflected the concerns of the reform period and ultimately spawned a number of influential nineteenth-century health reform movements, often referred to as "Grahamite."[7] In her 1839 edition of *Good Housekeeping*, Sarah Hale introduces the recipe for "brown or dyspepsia bread" with an acknowledgment: "This bread is now best known as 'Graham bread,' not that Doctor Graham invented or discovered the manner of its preparation, but that he has been unwearied and successful in recommending it to the public."[8] Indeed, the modern cracker that bears Graham's name does so not because he invented it but because it was originally produced with his health principles in mind.

Graham's writings on diet brought bread into new focus by crystallizing many of the meanings circulating around this everyday food. Bread, for Graham, signified domestic order, civic health, and moral wellbeing; ingesting more bread, he promised, would produce healthy bodies and homes and ensure America's place in the pantheon of civilized nations. A close reading of the dietetic program uncovers a semiotic economy where eating, domesticity, race, and national formation assume sometimes interchangeable places with relation to each other. In this context, bread becomes far more than a staple carbohydrate: it is a symbol of the intimate relationships between eating, technologies of the self, and the intertwined mythologies of body, race, and nation.

As in many popular writings, in the *Treatise on Bread and Bread-making*[9] the biblically derived rhetoric around bread is heavily laden with the ideology of early nationalist racism, which might more precisely be thought of as "civilizationist."[10] Graham's anxious detailing of bread preparation hinges on establishing the causal link between "farinaceous foods" and civic health, from which he derived a number of insights about American consumer habits. Graham opens the *Treatise* with a history of bread, beginning with "primitive inhabitants of the earth, [who] ate their food with very little, if any artificial preparation."[11] He narrates the beginning of grinding nuts, seeds, and grains on stones and continues through to the discovery of fire, constructing the story of bread as the story of the rise of civilization from the primitives through Mosaic times, perhaps culling his evidence from scripture: "Even after the establishment of the Hebrew nation in Palestine . . . at the period of the highest refinement of the Jews, in the arts of civil and domestic life, their fine flour, from which their choicest bread and cakes were made, was, in comparison with modern superfine flour, extremely coarse,— ground mostly by females, in hand-mills constructed and kept for that purpose."[12] What is interesting in this history is the importance that Hawaii—here called the Sandwich Islands—holds for Graham. Not only does he footnote his story about primitive techniques for baking with fire with the comment, "In this same manner the Sandwich Islanders cooked all their food, when they were first discovered," but he concludes the section in which he describes farinaceous foods around the globe—Asia, Africa, Scotland and Ireland—with a discussion of the Pacific Island diet: "the bread of the inhabitants consists of the plantain, bananas, yams, bread-fruit, and other like vegetables, simply roasted, baked, or boiled."[13] As we will see in the discussion of Graham's *Lecture*, the South Pacific has a key role to play in the United States' self-imagining across the period.

That the commodity chosen to solve the problem of gross sensuality had to be wheat was, I am arguing, no coincidence. By the 1830s, wheat production had begun to spread west to the prairies following behind westward emigration; aided by technological and transportation advances wheat production doubled between the late 1830s and the late 1850s. The soil and climate of the plains states proved to be excellent for wheat cultivation, which required a large scale to be truly profitable.

To advocate for bread as a republican food in this period was thus to advocate an economic model that supported U.S. expansion and economic autonomy. The home in which bread was at "the center of the plate" was a self-sufficient homestead, an image of the Republic in miniature. In its commitment to wheat, then, Graham's work supports the United States' imperial and civilizing agenda and ties it to the intimate and quotidian functioning of bodies. When Graham writes, "They who have never eaten bread made of wheat, recently produced by a pure virgin soil, have but a very imperfect notion of the deliciousness of good bread; such as is often to be met with in the comfortable log houses in our western country," he uses the imperial imagery of virgin soil waiting to be fertilized as a sign upon which pleasure (deliciousness) is displaced.[14] In a further fantasy (playing on an enduring American myth), the scene of the eating of this delicious wheat bread is placed in a "comfortable log cabin" such as is found in the West. What sanctifies this pleasure is its civic meaning, for the bread will enter into the very mouths of an audience he invokes as "us, as a nation."[15] In this way, the bodies of the citizenry—from the inner space of their mouths through the coils of their digestive tracts—are implicated in the rapid expansion of American territories into the apparently empty, untouched—virginal—spaces of the West. Eating becomes what Ann Stoler, borrowing from Albert Hurtado's social history of California, referred to as an "intimate frontier": "a social and cultural space where racial classifications were defined and defied."[16] What the logic of Graham's

Treatise on Bread and Breadmaking also suggests is that through the lens of Graham's admittedly eccentric writing, we might begin to think of eating as a sensual and racializing practice that exists on a rhetorical continuum with other dissident and nonnormative forms of sensuality. And indeed, only two years later, in *A Lecture to Young Men on Chastity,* Graham would go further in tying eating to erotic pleasure.

My inquiry here works in conversation with historians and theorists of sexuality who have taken up Graham's writing to make useful insights into male sexuality in the period, as well as scholars in the separate field of food studies, where Graham has been situated as one character in a pantheon of eccentric nineteenth-century food reformers.[17] Few scholars, however, have put these two seemingly separate concerns—food and sex—into productive conversation; some have even dismissed the idea of eating as a dissident form of pleasure. In her groundbreaking article "Rethinking Sex," for instance, Gayle Rubin writes that "the exercise of erotic capacity, intelligence, curiosity, or creativity all require pretexts that are unnecessary for other pleasures, such as the enjoyment of food, fiction, or astronomy."[18] That Rubin pairs food with fiction in much the same way that Sedgwick paired masturbation with fiction is important: all of these activities point to interiorized and imaginative pleasures that seem to defy capture in language.[19]

In Graham's work, technologies of self-care such as sexual hygiene and diet—the two particularly linked in Graham's work—were tied to civic and state wellbeing. What I am characterizing here as a biopolitical turn in nationalist narratives of food and eating was linked to the culture of reform, which encompassed a disparate group of movements including temperance, abolition, and early feminism. These groups characteristically construed politics to be a matter of collective action, but as a political model, reform politics based that collectivity on the individual body, which they interpreted as a site of personal transformation.

The term "biopower" in this essay thus accounts here for very specific and local discursive moves concerning food in the American antebellum culture, what we might think of, if we were to follow Foucault's narrative of the consolidation of biopower, as the joint workings of anatomopolitics and biopolitics, as an early moment in the consolidation of bodily and regulatory disciplines in the service of capital and state power. It may be useful to recall here the link that Foucault posits between the imposition of medical and psychiatric discourses of wellness and the emergence of the nation state, with its need to track its "'population' as an economic and political problem: population as wealth, population as manpower or labor capacity, population balanced between its own growth and the resources it commanded . . . with its specific phenomena and its peculiar variables: birth and death rates, life expectancy, fertility, state of health, frequency of illnesses, patterns of diet and habitation."[20] Foucault, of course, is thinking of postrevolutionary French and British societies, with their fairly centralized governments. In the context of the nineteenth-century United States, with its weaker and dispersed governmental power, its regional differences, "peculiar institution"—namely, slavery—and less homogeneous secularization, Foucault's formulation can't be applied in quite the same way. Michael Warner has linked the temperance movement to a "statistical consciousness, combined with a vast network of non-state associations and an equally vast body of print," but he is also quick to note that temperance "brought a mass public into awareness of itself and its *distinctness* from the national state."[21] Indeed, in the early nineteenth century, there was not much of a state infrastructure dedicated to the "right of the social body to ensure, maintain or develop its life": that would come later, when, in the early twentieth century, progressive-era reformers built upon the work of their reformist antecedents and implemented change at the federal and state level.[22]

Grahamite biopower is thus located in the interspace between the state, from which it was excluded as a radical movement, the public sphere, where it competed with other reform movements to gain the peoples' ears, and the nation, which it figured as an ideal futurity against which the present might be compared and regulated. As the child of both the temperance movement and anti-onanism campaigns, the dietetic movement also styled itself as an attempt to press politically on the most intimate sphere of domestic life. The movement sought to promote its message by tapping into the political energy of republicanism as a discourse of self-improvement and civic belonging.[23]

As it developed during a period of rapid national expansion—a period marked by an explosion in wheat production as the Western borders and reach of the nation expanded, decimating Native cultures, while whaling and merchant ships made trading inroads into the South Pacific—dietetic reform inevitably encountered the epistemological challenges generated by increasingly fraught definitions of race and empire, which it sought to manage by anchoring the nation to ecological and increasingly essentialized ideas of racial embodiment. In Graham's work—and indeed in many domestic manuals—wheat became symbolically overdetermined in this way because of its connection to what Amy Kaplan identifies as the "paradox of . . . imperial domesticity," in which the home "becomes the engine of national expansion."[24] What Kaplan calls "manifest domesticity" operates through antitheses that absorb and define the foreign: the foreign exists both within and beyond the boundaries of the domestic, as the domestic—here, the nation—expands as part of an imperial project. In the context of this close relationship between the home and the nation, middle-class women's work becomes a process of civilizing and colonizing that is invaluable to the building of empire.[25]

Dietetic expressions of the biopolitical were thus linked to what Ann Stoler has called "the education of desire": the intimate schooling of the body and of sentiment that structured European colonial projects and that saw its own particularly nationalist articulations in the United States in the antebellum period. The period between the Louisiana Purchase and the Civil War saw the acceleration of an expansionist project that, in the end, created the continental United States. These projects of national embodiment were linked to the consolidation of whiteness as the dominant racial position in the United States and took place in a broadly comparative landscape, one in which reformers writing in new republics like the United States looked to three sites to shape a micropolitics of daily life: laterally to other colonial spaces, backward to their own European genealogies, and forward toward their often imperial futures. Within these three temporal landscapes, the United States succeeded in performing what John Carlos Rowe called the "rhetorical legerdemain" of both identifying imperial injustices with the former colonizer, Great Britain, and justifying the expansion of U.S. territory in North America as part of national "consolidation" in the name of democracy.[26]

One important subject of the nation's exceptional future was the figure of the child, what Lee Edelman has called "the Child as the emblem of futurity's unquestioned value."[27] Graham likewise saw the child's story as metaphorical for the nation's. Thus the project of empire building was incontestably linked to what Foucault termed, in the *History of Sexuality*, the "pedagogization of the child" within the heterosexual drama of the family.[28] Foucault writes that "the body of the child, under surveillance, surrounded in his cradle, his bed, or his room by an entire watch-crew of parents, nurses, servants, educators, and doctors, all attentive to the least manifestation of his sex . . . [constituted] another 'local center' of power-knowledge."[29] And yet, it is not enough to consider that project of pedagogization purely on the level of the clinical proliferation and institutional disciplining of sexualities; rather we must also consider dietary technologies and projects that organized themselves around an understanding of race as formed out of and therefore defined by the materials that sustained life. With close examination we see that Foucault's vicious little boy is, if not in bed with, then certainly eating from the same plate as, Graham's unruly little girl. Their cure, however, was far from politically neutral: Graham's reformist eating practices assumed a transnational geospatial imaginary, which lay lightly upon the bones of the United States' commercial and imperial ambitions but sought to enter deeply into the bellies of its citizens, mapping marvelous and perverse geographies of desire along the way.

The Lecture to Young Men on Chastity

A Lecture to Young Men on Chastity elaborates Graham's theory of the body, describes the problem of "self-pollution" in youth, and suggests corrective dietary and hygienic measures. In the *Lecture*, as in Graham's earlier *Treatise on Bread and Breadmaking*, food and reproduction constitute "two grand FUNCTIONS [*sic*] of [man's] system [that] are necessary for his existence as an individual and as a species."[30] Graham echoes the anatomical-cum-architectural schema of the body laid out by William Alcott across the dozens of pages in which he enumerates the effects of excessive masturbation (excessive here defined as anything from once to constantly) and sensual indulgence. The descriptive detail is extraordinary: Graham runs his prose across the skin of the body, through the nervous system, between and inside human organs, and offers a range of affective and behavioral indications from blushing in the company of women to languor and morbid sensibility. The end result of venereal indulgence is either an explosive rupturing or the gradual degradation of the body's borders: "It is by abusing his organs and depraving his instinctive appetites, through the devices of his rational powers, that the body of man has become a living volcano of unclean propensities and passions."[31] The volcanic activity here is not simply a matter of emissions: the masturbator drools and dribbles, he is covered with pustulent sores and pimples, he has tooth decay and diarrhea, his eyes become glassy and fall back into their sockets. The erotic object of Graham's palpating narrative ultimately decays and falls apart and thereby becomes less an object of desire than of disgust.

In the *Lecture*, Graham continues to show the same concern with "farinaceous foods" that had taken him down the path of reformed dietary practice in the earlier *Treatise*. There, Graham starts the discourse on bread as an exegesis of the Bible, in which the term "comprehends all farinaceous vegetable substances that enter into the diet of man."[32] For Graham, all "civilizations" consume some kind of farinaceous food; in this way, he seems interested in tracing similarities across nations and periods, in demonstrating the universality of his regime. At the same time, the idea of "civilization" seems to bleed into Graham's republican notions of "civic life" tying "our"—he and his audiences'— local diet to "virtuous" practices that in turn justify a hierarchy of civilizations: "In all civilized nations, and particularly in civic life, bread, as I have already stated, is far the most important article of food which is artificially prepared; and in our country and climate, it is the most important article that enters into the diet of man."[33] The text vacillates between celebrating primitivism—often associated with "cooling" and raw foods—and distancing the "civilized life" it attributes to its readership in the United States from those primitives except as relics of the civilized world's prehistory.

The bifurcation prefigures Lévi-Strauss's separation of the raw and the cooked and his attribution of cooking to civilization, but the semiotic economy here is more attuned to a language of excitement and sensual disorder that Graham will further develop in the *Lecture*: "if man were to subsist wholly on uncooked food, he would never suffer from the improper temperature of his aliment. Hot substances taken into the mouth . . . serve more directly and powerfully to destroy the teeth . . . and hot food and drink received into the stomach, always in some degree debilitate that organ and through it, every other organ and portion of the whole system . . . increasing the susceptibility of the whole body to the action of disturbing causes."[34] Graham continues, "While man obeys the law of constitution and relation which should govern him in regard to his food, he preserves the health and integrity of his alimentary organs, and through them of his whole nature. . . . [I]f he disregards these laws, and by artificial means greatly departs from the natural adaptation of things, he inevitably brings evil on himself and his posterity."[35]

The issue then is at least in part one of sensory overexcitement, which starts with heat in the mouth and builds until it overcomes the rest of the body, expanding outward until it wreaks havoc on the country and its future generations. The language attached to individual wellbeing easily slips into the language of body politic: "and therefore it is of the first consideration, that its character should, in every respect, be as nearly as possible, consistent with the laws of constitution and relation established in our nature; or with the anatomical construction and vital properties and interest of our systems." "If we contemplate the human constitution in its highest and best condition,—in the possession of its most vigorous and unimpaired powers—and ask, what must be the character of our bread in order to preserve that constitution in that condition? The answer most indubitably is . . . the coarse unleavened bread of early times."[36] While the language of civic life slips into civilizational discourse, here the discourse on eating and embodiment borrows from the republican language of constitutionality and power.

What seems to be substitutive or catachrestic language can make it difficult to parse Grahamite logic. However, it is in exactly these rhetorical strategies that I find a key element of queer alimentarity, which I define as a form of nonnormative sensuality that centers on orality and the mouth. That is to say, even before the publication of his specifically anti-onanist writing, the language of eating in Graham also keeps one foot in the language of sexuality as we generally understand it. For instance, what tears down "the laws of constitution and relation" and the "vital properties and interest of our systems" for Graham is "gross and promiscuous feeding": "the people, generally, are contented to gratify

their depraved appetites on whatever comes before them, without paus-
ing to inquire whether their indulgences are adapted to preserve or to
destroy their life and health . . . there will soon reach us, as a nation,
a voice of calamity which we shall not be able to shut our ears against,
albeit we may in the perverseness of our sensualism, incorrigibly persist
in disregarding its admonitions, till the deep chastisements of outraged
nature shall reach the very 'bone and marrow' of the human constitution."[37] This sense of eating as depraved and promiscuous would seem, to
the modern reader schooled in understanding sexuality as genitally oriented, to *borrow* from the realm of sexuality; certainly, as Foucault tells
us in *The Use of Pleasure*, such language echoes the connection between
"alimentary ethics" and "sexual ethics" as prescribed by the classical
Greeks, although Foucault sees that connection as ultimately uncoupled
with the rise of modernity.[38] Such a reading, however, obscures Graham's anatomizing of a perverse and nonnormative geography of desire,
in which eating—and therefore the mouth—is supercharged with an
erotic intensity that easily spreads through the entire body, "outraging"
nature to its "very bone and marrow." My point here is that in talking
about eating as a form of depravity, we are not dealing in displacement.
Rather, alimentarity is in and of itself an erotic act, one with the power
to disrupt social order. Indeed, each of Graham's terms here—depravity,
grossness, perversity, incorrigibility, outrage—implies that social disorder is the inevitable result of indulging in the senses at the expense of
virtuous behaviors oriented toward upholding orderly systems of feeling, being and acting. Eating is, in this symbolic economy, a mode of
"sensualism" that is described with the same language as forms of "venereal" indulgence, and is literally linked as a practice through a highly
racialized language, to the question of the nation's posterity.

In the *Lecture*, farinaceous food is again praised for providing health-
ful fare for those suffering from "irritation and oppression" in the intes-
tines, for it counters the effects of gluttony, highly spiced foods, and
spirits with its wholesomeness and coolness.[39] He recommends farinaceous foods as counterpoisons, which will return the body to a primitive but morally refined state of virility and virtue. In this sense, *farinaceous* expands to include not only wheat, but also any "indigenous"
foods that provide the digestive system with enough roughage to keep it
both cool and fit, preventing overheating and enervation.

While Graham's writings have been repeatedly discussed by scholars in search of texts on male sexuality in the antebellum United States,
two stories contained in the first appendix to the *Lecture* have surely
not received the attention they deserve. There are fifteen notes listed
alphabetically from A to O at the end of the *Lecture*, which serve either
as elaborations and commentary on the text, or offer case studies that
support Graham's theories. In particular the first appendix, which
Graham offers as anthropological evidence for his project, seals the
latent connections holding between diet, sexuality, domesticity, and
empire by constructing an analogous relationship between the masturbating daughter of a wealthy family and the story of the survivors
of the mutiny on the *Bounty* and their mixed-race progeny. This first
note describes a highly respectable family "of considerable distinction
for their wealth, refinement and piety." Graham makes particular note
of the eldest daughter: "Long before this child could speak with sufficient distinctness to be understood by any but the mother, she was
taught to repeat, morning and evening, and on various occasions, little prayers and hymns, adapted to her age. . . . [A]ll that a pious and
devoted mother could do, by way of religious instruction, was done, to
train her up in the nurture and admonition of the lord."[40] Sixteen years
later, Graham visits the family again and finds the children unruly and
ill behaved. Once again he turns his attention to the eldest daughter:
"what surprised me most was her excessive lasciviousness. Wantonness manifested itself in all her conduct, when in the company of males;
and I ascertained that when she was alone with a gentleman, she would
not only freely allow him to take *improper liberties* with her, without
the least restraint, but would even court his *dalliance* by her lascivious
conduct. Being consulted in regard to her health, I found that she was
addicted to the practice of self-pollution and had greatly injured herself
by it."[41]

The central question that Graham poses is how such a child, raised
under the piety and purview of her religious mother and teachers, could
come to this licentious state. The young woman's injuries are tempera-
mental and moral: excessive masturbation has eroded her self-control,
making it impossible for her to distinguish socially appropriate and
inappropriate behavior. The sexual sin—self-pollution, or masturbation—most closely associated with isolation and sterility here resolves

the social problem of onanism (its essentially antisocial and sterile ded-
ication to self-pleasure) by exhibiting signs of itself in public.[42] This is
one of the feared paradoxes of this "private" vice: that it would contami-
nate others. Graham diagnoses the daughter's fault as a domestic fault,
originating with the mother, who had

> wholly disregarded the relations between the bodies and souls of her
> children—between their dietetic habits and their moral character. She
> truly "made the table a snare to them;" and they literally "fared sump-
> tuously every day." Indeed, she prided herself on setting the best table
> in town. Highly seasoned flesh-meat, rich pastry, and every other kind
> of rich and savory food, and condiments in abundance, together with
> strong coffee and tea, and perhaps occasionally a glass of wine, were set
> before these children for their ordinary fare. The result was just what was
> reasonably to be expected; and sorrow and tears were the reward of the
> afflicted mother.[43]

In this anecdote, Graham identifies the root viciousness of the female-
dominated domestic sphere in the mother's departure from the non-
exciting, republican diet to the conspicuous consumption of excitants
and rich and savory food. The tongue, which is accustomed to such
sensual pleasures at the table, leads to the search for other debilitating
bodily pleasures, such as the daughter finds in "courting [gentlemen's]
dalliance by her lascivious conduct." Hence, a habit of indulging in
sumptuary foods leads to "self-polluting" practices, and to moral blind-
ness. Graham lingers, in the sensuous details above, on the spectacu-
lar carnality of the table, making clear the relationship between female
domestic pride and skill, the eroticized diet, the young woman's licen-
tiousness, and the decadence of an era that has overturned the primitive and healthy diet for the modern saturnalia of foods.

But let us also linger for a moment—as indeed the word begs us
to—over the word "dalliance." The large portion of the narrative on the
masturbating daughter narrates the mother's pedagogical work, paying
attention to the daughter's daily religious education: the mother "daily
prayed with her children . . . [the daughter] was taught to repeat, morning and evening, . . . little prayers and hymns." But by the time that Graham returns to visit the family the daughter's rationalized education

has been entirely dismantled. Graham seems peculiarly focused on the mathematics of his ongoing relationship with the family: he has known them for "about eighteen years," the daughter is five, the youngest is three; she is taught to pray daily, and on Sundays; he visits them again "two years since" and remains "several weeks," discovering that "[s]carcely a day passed when she did not get into a violent passion with her mother."

In this fevered numeration of both his relation to the family and the eldest girl's progress toward womanhood (and oddly, crunching the numbers results in the daughter's age coming out to twenty-one, which puts a whole other spinsterish spin on the story) the word that Graham uses to describe the daughter's "wantonness" is striking: while alone in the company of a gentleman, she courts "his dalliance," a term that means "amorous toying or caressing, flirtation" or "often, in bad sense, wanton toying" but that, perhaps more obscurely, also signals etymologically to a "waste of time in trifling, idle delay."[44] The daughter, in other words, pulls the gentleman into what Kathryn Bond Stockton has called the "sideways temporality" of the queer child, into a "toying" playtime that concedes neither to the timetable of quotidian or weekly religious devotion, nor to the heterosexual imperatives of her seemingly inevitable role as mother to the nation. Rather, fueled by an abundance of alimentary pleasure, and her own "self-polluting" ways, the daughter exercises an erotic agency that takes her out of nation-building futurity, where it does indeed seem as though she is treading water as both child and spinster—and into the lateral pleasures of "improper liberty."

While this story organizes itself around the masturbating daughter, the mother's unchaste consumption occupies the other center to this story, and must ultimately be reined in. Vicious eating is invoked by Graham as a sensual and erotic experience connected to the mother's taste for exotic fare and played out in the daughter's masturbatory activities. In a vaginal term suggestive of both lesbian and incestuous desire, the mother's seductive table, that sign of her spending and shopping pleasure, is described as a "snare"; upon that delicious "snare," eating and masturbation are constituted as related behaviors, whose danger is exceeded only by the "lascivious conduct" invited by the daughter, and perhaps too, as the displaced erotics of consumerism that plays out between the two women implies, by the daughter's "violent passion with her mother."[45]

As Jeanne Boydston has pointed out, at the same time that new forms of gendered domesticity were being produced in the early republic and antebellum period, women were taking on domestic shopping duties formerly allotted to men.[46] Graham's domestic parable is located in the cusp of this shift. What the mother has not resisted outside the house, in the public market, is spending the household wealth on sensual foods that are a sort of prologue to her daughter's inability to restrain herself. The social and moral threat posed by female spending in the public sphere finds its expression in the domestic unconscious; the spending female is an invitation to physical and moral degeneracy because she perversely, if unconsciously, elaborates on the metaphor between unwise spending and the illicit "spending" of sperm; and yet also because she allows herself forbidden oral pleasures.

Most of the foods that constitute a threat to the body in this story are marked as "foreign" and "exotic" to the United States (spices, coffee, sugar, tea, and wine), whereas most, if not all, of the cures for the problem of excessive masturbation and the degeneracy of the body lie in local and domestic produce (milk and bread, for instance). The problem is that of misbehaving bodies, of, literally, "spiced" bodies. Graham writes: "I found that this lasciviousness was not confined to the oldest child: all the children were more or less spiced with it, according to their age."[47]

Here, then, is the threat that middle-class women's financial power and taste for foreign luxury pose to the integrity of the middle-class home: a threat of bodily dissolution and infection through the inappropriate eating of foreign imports. For antebellum middle-class white women, leaving the home—going out the front door—to buy supplies for what William Alcott would call the "most important door" in the body required navigating the contradictory symbolic boundaries of the home which, of course, followed them.[48] It opened the home up to the possibility of infection, just as the emigrants coming through the kitchen opened the interior space up to the alien, and the free borders opened up the national body to the possibility of debility, superstition, and disease. The intervention at the household table of the other, embodied in luxury items like wine, tea, and coffee, drained the coffers and energies of the house and the nation, and presented the threat of sexually coded catalytic changes that would overthrow piety, reverence, and modesty in future generations, dislodging their reproductive energies and turning their desires toward more illicit forms of gratification than those allowed for within the frame of normative reproductive legibility.

However, congress with foreign bodies is not always a matter of uncomplicated relations of inequality. Rather, it involves ambivalent forms of identification and rejection, desire and disgust, intimacy and alienation. In this first story, the foreign excitants threaten to become the totality of the consumer, concretizing diet and sexuality as central terms in the imperial metonymies that link body, home, and nation. [49] In this first story, all three bodies, actual and political, can be returned to the regime of worldly asceticism through the total rejection of the foreign and the return to the unprocessed and primitive, which are, fortunately, offered by domestic growers. The second of Graham's stories in the appendix, however, presents an antithetical dynamic.

Set in the South Pacific, the second story recounts the mutiny on the British ship *Bounty*. Contrary to the first story's representation of a sealed domestic sphere, Graham's second narrative reveals another reality of the political economy—the subordination of the American economy to British hegemony, which created a series of lateral identifications between the antebellum United States and other British colonies. It is important to read the seeming contradictions of antebellum food culture through the history of U.S. imperial expansion and the complex, regionally divided relationship of the United States to Britain, its former ruler and greatest customer, as well as its industrial rival; similarly, one might recall the United States' ambiguous position as a postcolonial power in a world in which the European colonial powers were expanding.

In Graham's story from the 1830s, food and sex emerge as central themes in a premonitory fantasy of imperial expansion. Here commodity consumption and the desire for land serve as catalytic desires for interactions across national, regional, and ethnic differences, despite the fact that racial unity would have to be sacrificed in any expansion of American territory. Absorbing these alien others and "Americanizing them" is a constant preoccupation in a nation that is both militarily aggressive and open to successive waves of immigration. In this story, more than any other, the metaphoric qualities of "farinaceous" foods are stretched to include foods not indigenous to North America but that nonetheless evoke the cooling qualities of Grahamite bread.

The story begins with the mutiny on the *Bounty*. Escaping the ship, the mutineers first go to Tahiti, where they take native wives, and then to Pitcairn's Island, along with some native males and their wives. The natives mutiny against the mutineers, and all adult males "of both colors" are killed, except for one: an Englishman, who rather Edenically renames himself "John Adams," perhaps not coincidentally the name of the second president of the United States. Adams oversees the upbringing of the surviving nineteen children and there, with all of the remaining wives, he raises a race of children "in uniform good health": "Infants were generally bathed three times a day in cold water, and were sometimes not weaned for three or four years; and when that did take place, they were fed upon food made of ripe plantains and boiled taro root, rubbed into a paste. . . . [T]hey have no bowel complaints, and are exempt from those contagious diseases which affect children in large communities."[50] The narrative follows the children into adulthood:

> Their beds were mattresses composed of palm leaves, and covered with native cloth, made of the paper mulberry tree. Yams constitute their principal food, boiled, baked, or mixed with cocoa-nut, made into cakes, and eaten with molasses extracted from the tee root. Taro root is no bad substitute for bread; and bananas, plantains and appoi are wholesome and nutritious fruits. They but seldom kill a pig, living mostly on fruit and vegetables . . . they are subject to few diseases. . . . they are certainly a finer and more athletic race than is usually found among the families of mankind.[51]

A number of representations merge into one another here. First, we see that the model of the noble savage so prevalent in Enlightenment discourses emerges in the ideal of the Pacific Islander raised without the taint or temptation of modern life. Second, we see the parallel that Graham has set up between the idea of the noble savage—here specifically these mixed-race children—and the white child. There is an implicit comparison between the young men that Graham is lecturing to and the allegory of the growing nation into which he inscribes the story of Pitcairn's Island. Because Graham is using the example of mixed-race Tahitian children to make a point about American bodies, it becomes clear that we cannot assume that the racial politic at play here is simply the familiar one that hierarchizes dwellings, body types, and races, and that, in the Southern U.S., had the force of law to enslave a large minority of the population. On the one hand, as in the previous story, white American bodies have to remain untainted by contact with the foreign—they need to remain "unspiced"—an image that gestures to the need to shore up the boundaries of the white body. On the other hand, we see that white American bodies can profit by comparison with the foreign, though only when foreigners are appropriately located in their own bioregional spaces.

Once again, these politics of comparison reveal "[colonial] circuits of knowledge production and racialized forms of governance [that] spanned a global field."[52] In this story, United States bodies are *like* Tahitian bodies, a likeness that is underlined by the mixed British-Tahitian heritage of the subjects. These bodies are not, however, of equal standing: Graham ends the story by informing the reader that the Tahitians will one day become an important race—but are not one yet. However, the importance of the comparison lies in the cultural value assigned to these two sets of subjects, both of whose lineages are simultaneously expatriate and, as the argument seems to go, indigenous. Mixed-race Pitcairn subjects can lay claim both to British origins and to the land they live on. What is at stake in Graham's dietetic program is reforming the epicurean American consumer's body so as to enable it to make a similar claim. As though Graham's narrative is haunted by the American Revolution, we see the same large elements: the sailors revolt against British tyranny and establish their own state, literally becoming the founding fathers of a new race when all adult males except John Adams are killed off, eliminating the threat of native insurgency and the cultural or political—or culinary—legacy of the British sailors.

As in the story of the masturbating daughter, the physiological and in particular the sexual health of the children occupies the center of the narrative: "The manners and demeanor of these young people exhibited a degree of modesty and bashfulness that would have done honor to the most virtuous and enlightened people on earth. Adams assured his visitors that not one instance of debauchery or immoral conduct had occurred among these young people, since their settlement on the island; nor did he ever hear or believe that any one instance had occurred of a young woman's having suffered indecent liberties to be taken with her. Their simple habits of living . . . had hitherto preserved these interesting people from every kind of debauchery."[53] Scott Lauria Morgensen has argued that "the terrorizing sexual colonization of Native peoples was a historical root of the biopolitics of modern sexuality in the United States."[54] The violent erasure of nonheteronormative erotic and gendered behavior on the part of First Nations and indigenous peoples is at the heart of what he terms "settler sexuality": "a white national heteronormativity that regulates Indigenous sexuality and gender by supplanting them with the sexual modernity of settler subjects."[55] In this narrative the dietetic strictures of the inhabitants of Pitcairn's Island are foregrounded as both causal of and coeval to their sexual disciplining, while the violence of the colonial encounter is masked by the language of virtue. Such is the amoral logic of colonial violence that the recurrence of the term "liberty," here once again associated with sexual acts perpetrated on women, somehow readjusts the morality of that violence such that blame and responsibility lie on the women themselves.

The narrative of the mutiny on the *Bounty* compulsively reenacts the colonization of the New World, and thus to a certain degree and by analogy, restages the problem of naturalizing the former British colonists' claim to what had formerly been British North America, through the metaphor of indigeneity. In so doing, the metaphor erases the historic presence and agency of the actual indigenous inhabitants of the land by both murdering the men and sexually conquering the women. Within this miscegenative framework, Graham co-opts indigeneity for the project of colonization. The story becomes a case study for the elaboration of his own domestic dietetic argument, even though, again, the analogies at work here need constant repair, and overlook discontinuities in the story (for instance, John Adams is, on one level, a founder of a race, and, on another level, a traitor to his race, inasmuch as his companions were slaughtered by the Pitcairn Islanders). The inhabitants of Pitcairn's Island are both shining examples of the ideal of human health—existing as they do on yams and their Taro root "substitute for bread"—and, as primitive peoples, sign and symbol of the physical possibilities that Americans have abandoned in their commitment to consumer lifestyles that depend on foreign commodities.

Eight years later Melville published the titillating travel memoir *Typee*, also set in the South Pacific, and surely influenced by the fact that, as his most recent biographer, Andrew Delbanco, points out, Graham's *A Lecture to Young Men on Chastity* was one of the few books in the library of the ship on which Melville sailed to Tahiti. [56] As generations of Melville scholars have pointed out, whaling, especially in the Pacific, was a major New England industry. As a result, by the 1830s the United States was already well established in the South Pacific, though it had yet to lay official claim to any lands.[57] Alongside France, Britain, and Russia, by the late eighteenth century the United States was involved in a race to claim Pacific islands as commercial stopping points on the way to China and Japan.[58] The imperialist desire to consume these lands is readily apparent: beyond the identification with indigeneity, the narrative of Pitcairn's Island recuperates South Pacific bodies into a Euro-American schema, domesticating and suppressing racial and sexual difference. Here, as always in Graham's writing, bread or bread substitutes take on an organizing role. Cooling the senses—keeping the skin cool and lowering sexual activity—takes on an exemplary role in this process not simply because, given the logic of segregated spaces in the home, luxury at the table will lead to transgressions unconsciously designed into these spaces, but also because of an overdetermined imperial logic that linked immigrant European bodies to the geopolitical and ecological spaces to which their newly formed national identities laid claim. Within the schema of nineteenth-century science, bodies, in this argument, were best maintained and cured by local produce—a long-standing nationalist formulation that we can trace back through, for instance, the cultural geography of British medical botanists and other scientists of early nation-states.[59] This logic, however, posed a particular problem for settler nations that had visibly imported their fauna and flora with them—a problem that Graham solved with his formulation of a paradoxical Euro-American indigeneity organized around wheat, that symbolically important European grain that the Jamestown settlers had worked so hard, and so vainly, to cultivate.

The term "paradoxical Euro-American indigeneity" here refers to the ways in which the United States, as a settler nation, both co-opted and erased the bodies of native peoples in order to naturalize the European claim to the land. Yet, the immigrant paradox is that they change the very land that, according to the strictures of nineteenth-century science, produces the foods that are healthiest for their bodies. Between the national health and the national produce, there lies a shadow. For Sylvester Graham, the farinaceous rule, which elevated bread to the fulcrum of bodily health and moral character, governed the semantics of food production. Whether from wheat or from taro root, bread—the biblically appointed heart of the European diet—became the cure-all for bodily woes. Fortunately, the virgin soil of the American West, by its very virginity, allowed the immigrant to create the local plant culture—and it is by this means that the American stakes his claim on the ground by planting the grains which can be milled into the staff of life.

However, if Graham is, on the one hand, claiming that we are what we eat, he is also demonstrating that what we are *like* what we eat: always dislocated and relational, reiterated and reconstructed by our quotidian acts. John Adams, the Edenic first and last man of Pitcairn's Island, passes on his generational wisdom to his heirs, having no store to tempt him out of the path of virtue. The pious, elegant, and wealthy lady of the house in Graham's first story, on the other hand, forgets the frugality that instilled moral character into her generation and debauches her children, corrupting their libidos in the rich and savory foods that she brings to the table. In both constructions, correct eating, like correct sexual behavior, is understood as a performative act of national identification. In eating as national subjects, flesh is called into social being through a model that understands race as anchored to some of the most intimate of biological functions.

Eating is not simply intertwined with sexuality as one of the state's "dense transfer points of power" into the body politic in the antebellum period; left undisciplined eating is an act of sensuality in and of itself. Bringing eating into conversation with other forms of venery—linking it through his particular understanding of the human body—Graham's writing reveals eating culture as one cog in the apparatus of disciplinary intervention into the "anatomo-politics of the human body."[60] It was also one that worked to produce a distinctive politics, and erotics, of racial inequity. Graham's fetishization of "farinaceous" foods allows us to see the murderous centrality of fictional Euro-American indigeneity—and the centrality of the denial of the murder and rape of indigenous peoples—in a settler nation that was, from its inception, always and already an imperial (indeed, a genocidal) space.

In Graham's domestic-dietetic proposal, North American indigenous peoples are entirely absent from nationalist discourse; at the same time, only a few years before the consolidation of the official policy of manifest destiny, in Graham's work we find the national gaze already turning westward toward the Pacific. Far more than a simple contrast of bourgeois white cosmopolitanism against an exotic colonial other, in Graham's discussion of the South Pacific we find both negation and identification alongside nascent hints of an argument for annexation. Not a possession of Otaheite, Britain (although ultimately the Pitcairn Islands would become a British protectorate), or the United States, what we find in Graham's narrative of Pitcairn's Island is an ever-deferred futurity: "there may be expected to rise hereafter, in this little colony, a race of people possessing, in a high degree, the physical qualifications of great strength united with symmetry of form and regularity of features."[61] But to whom will these people belong? Certainly the word "colony" implies that they will never belong to themselves.

* * *

As we follow Graham's palpating gaze through the middle-class U.S. home, over the body of a sexually dissident girl dallying with visiting gentlemen and out to the farthest edges of the U.S.'s imperial ambitions to linger over the semidressed bodies of mixed-race Pacific Islanders, it becomes apparent that colonialism's violent and coercive sexual politics subtend the establishment of modern biopolitics. If the vicious daughter of the first narrative had been entirely ensnared by her mother's luxurious and exotic table, that is, corrupted by the disruption of the fantasy of economic autarky at the level of the home and nation, her virtue, Graham avers, might be entirely recuperated via the consumption of domestic produce, albeit produce paradoxically grown within the borders of the United States' gradually expanding agricultural empire. And while the children of Pitcairn's Island are saved by their isolation from the corrupting influence of transnational trade, not only their very existence but their future is defined through the norms of white reproductive futurity, itself laid upon the foundations of a frightening sexual violence.

How then do we bring these narratives together? If what I am calling queer alimentarity is focused in these stories on the figure of the child—and indeed the *Lecture* itself is directed to young men—it is perhaps because Graham's narrative, as a republican text, is so explicitly bound up in early national anxieties. Children thus recur here as tropes for the biological—that is the biopolitical and thus racial—future. But they also haunt Graham's narrative as always-potentially queer subjects. Eating, for Graham, or more particularly, dissident eating, disrupts the flow of national time into an ordered racial future, as the bodies of white children are breached—spiced—with exotic goods, furthering the connection between dissident sexualities and subjects racialized as nonwhite in the settler-colonial and postrevolutionary Americas that has by now been well established in Black and Native queer studies.

Perhaps, however, in orality's queer pleasures, we might also catch a glimpse of something else, a link to the dangerous possibilities of anal penetration. Perhaps in the breaching of the body's borders we might catch glimpses of the liberal individual's ethical vulnerability to the other, of forms of erotic and racial expression that certainly threatened to transcend the limits of one antebellum reformer's anxious dietetic project.

What these texts allow for is a glimpse—a peep, as it were—at the idea of a form of sensual pleasure apparent to Graham, admittedly an extreme character, but perhaps lost to us as a fully realized erotic site today. In some ways I have tried here to theorize the mouth in much the same way that Bersani theorized anality. The mouth's imbrication in the intensification of biopolitics in the American context however, its connection to biological sustenance, allow for it to be a space where "the controlled insertion of bodies into the machinery of production"[62] is met by the body's insertion into the accelerating and deepening culture of capitalist consumption. In this way, the mouth is anality's pastoral other, a site of life-producing (but also life-threatening) pleasure, and a space of intervention into the wellbeing of the nation.[63]

NOTES

1. Leo Bersani, "Is the Rectum a Grave," *October* 43 (Winter 1987): 197–222. As Eve Sedgwick has pointed out, this utopian vision systematically excludes not only female anality, but in fact women altogether. See Eve Kosokfsky Sedgwick, "Anality," in *The Weather in Proust* (Durham, NC: Duke University Press, 2011), 166–82, 171.

2. Since Freud in any case. It is worth noting that in his discussion of orality as a key stage in sexual development Freud refers to the mouth as a "mucous membrane," as though to emphasize the mouth's porosity, its difference from other, dryer sites on the body on the one hand and, on the other, to emphasize its similarity to the anus and vagina, both of which are described in the same terms. In fact, Freud seems to propose that all skin may *evolve* into mucous membrane, in the case of the development of a sexual aberration. He writes, "in scopophilia and exhibitionism the eye corresponds to an erotogenic zone; while in the case of those components of the sexual instinct which involve pain and cruelty the same role is assumed by the skin—the skin, which in particular parts of the body has become differentiated into sense organs or modified into mucous membrane, and is this the erotogenic zone *par excellence*." See Sigmund Freud, *Three Essays on the History of Sexuality* (New York: Basic Books, 1975), 35, italics in the original.

3. Sylvester Graham, *A Lecture to Young Men on Chastity* (Boston: Light & Stearns, 1837).

4. Bruce Burgett, "Between Speculation and Population: The Problem of Sex in Our Long Eighteenth Century," *Early American Literature* 37:1 (2002): 122.

5. For an example of Graham as a trope of nineteenth-century prurience, see Chuck Klosterman, *Sex, Drugs and Cocoa Puffs: A Low Culture Manifesto* (New York: Scribner, 2003) in which he writes, "Any breakfast historian can tell you that Sylvester Graham (1794–1851) so-called 'philosopher and nutrition crusader,' was the kind of forward-thinking wackmobile that . . . " (119).

6. See Michael Warner, "Whitman Drunk," in *Publics and Counterpublics* (New York: Zone Books, 2002), 269–89. See also Eve Kosofsky Sedgwick, "Jane Austen and the Masturbating Girl," in *Solitary Pleasures: The Historical, Literary, and Artistic Discourses of Autoeroticism*, ed. Paula Bennett and Vernon A. Rosario (New York: Routledge, 1995), 133–55.

7. One example is the Battle Creek Sanatorium, founded and run on Grahamite principles by Harvey Kellogg. The modern analogy to the use of the Graham name would be the use of the word "Atkins" to describe any high-protein, low-carbohydrate meal, or the nineteenth-century usage of the word "Banting" to describe dieting, after William Banting's *Letter on Corpulence*. William Banting, *Letter on Corpulence, Addressed to the Public*, 3rd ed. (London: Harrison, 1864).

8. Sarah Josepha Hale, *The Good Housekeeper* (Boston: Weeks, Jordan & Company, 1839), 17.

9. Sylvester Graham, *Treatise on Bread and Breadmaking* (Boston: Light & Stearns, 1837).

10. Hilton Obenzinger, *American Palestine: Melville, Twain and the Holy Land Mania* (Princeton, NJ: Princeton University Press, 1999). See *American Palestine* for a discussion of the representation of the United States as a modern Israel in the nineteenth century.

11. Graham, *Treatise,* 10.

12. Ibid., 15.

13. Ibid., 12, 16.

14. Ibid., 26.

15. Ibid.

16. Ann Laura Stoler, "Tense and Tender Ties: The Politics of Comparison in North American History and (Post) Colonial Studies," in *Haunted by Empire: Geographies of Intimacy in North American History* (Durham, NC: Duke University Press, 2006), 24.

17. See Ben Barker Benfield, "The Spermatic Economy: A Nineteenth-Century View of Sexuality," *Feminist Studies* 1 (Summer 1972): 45–74; Helen Lefkowitz Horowitz, *Rereading Sex: Battles over Sexual Knowledge and Suppression in Nineteenth-Century America* (New York: Alfred A. Knopf, 2002); and Stephen Nissenbaum, *Sex, Diet and Debility in Jacksonian American* (Belmont, CA: Dorsey Press, 1988).

18. Gayle Rubin, "Thinking Sex: Notes for a Radical Theory of the Politics of Sexuality," in *Pleasure and Danger: Exploring Female Sexuality*, ed. Carole S. Vance (London: Pandora, 1992), 267–93. My thanks to Elizabeth Freeman for pointing me back to Rubin's piece.

19. Indeed, Thomas Laqueur links the rise of anti-onanist discourse to the rise of both the novel and pornography as imaginative, and therefore individuating, media. Thomas W. Laqueur, *Solitary Sex: A Cultural History of Masturbation* (New York: Zone Books, 2003). Sedgwick writes, "masturbation can seem to offer—not least as an analogy to writing—a reservoir of potentially utopian metaphors and energies for independence, self-possession, and a rapture that may owe relatively little to political or interpersonal abjection." Sedgwick, *Jane Austen and the Masturbating Girl*, 135.

20. Michel Foucault, *The History of Sexuality, Volume 1: An Introduction* (New York: Vintage Books, 1990), 25.

21. Warner, "Whitman Drunk," 271.

22. Ronald Walters, *American Reformers, 1815–1860* (New York: Hill and Wang, 1997), 222. Walters writes, "the future of reform belonged to institution users—to men and women who regarded bureaus, agencies, and the government in general as instruments of social policy. I have in mind, of course, the stream of liberalism that flows from Progressivism through the New Deal to the 'Great Society' of the 1960s . . . it tried to make the system run better."

23. Ronald Takaki, *Iron Cages: Race and Culture in 19th-Century America* (New York: Oxford University Press, 1980), 8–9. I am working with Ronald Takaki's definition of republicanism here: "In the republic, the people would no longer have

an external authority over them, a father/king to restrain their passions and deny them luxury; they would instead have to control themselves. Whether or not they would be able to exercise self-control effectively depended on their virtue. . . . Republicanism and virtue would reinforce each other: Moral character would enable republican man to govern himself."

24. Amy Kaplan, "Manifest Domesticity," in *No More Separate Spheres: A Next Wave American Studies Reader*, ed. Cathy N. Davidson and Jessamyn Hatcher (Durham, NC: Duke University Press, 2002), 585.

25. In *Mrs. Hale's New Cookbook*, for instance, the matron of the household is advised to be kind but firm with the Irish cook, conjuring up a scene in which a friend instructed the new Irish maid: "The names of the articles of furniture in the kitchen, as well as their uses, were entirely unknown to her, and she had seen so many new things done which she was expected to remember that it must have made her heart sick to reflect how much she had to learn. But there was one thing she thought she understood which was to cook potatoes. These were done and she would show the lady she knew how to prepare them for the table." As it turns out, she even prepares the potatoes wrongly, which would have caused another "lady" of the house to throw the maid out, where she would have wandered "without knowing a place where to lay down her head in this strange country." But, in Hale's scene, all ends well: "My friend did not act in this manner she expressed no surprise at the attitude of the girl only quietly said 'That is not the best way to peel your potatoes.' Julia just lay them on this plate and I will show you how I like to have them done." In this way, in such kitchen scenes, the ladies in this "strange country" civilize its new inhabitants. Sarah Josepha Hale, *The way to live well and to be well while we live: containing directions for choosing and preparing food, in regard to health, economy and taste* (Boston: Weeks, Jordan & Company, 1839), 123.

26. John Carlos Rowe, *Literary Culture and U.S. Imperialism: From the Revolution to World War II* (New York: Oxford University Press, 2000), 5.

27. Lee Edelman, *No Future: Queer Theory and the Death Drive* (Durham, NC: Duke University Press, 2004), 4.

28. Foucault, *History of Sexuality 1*, 104.

29. Ibid., 98.

30. Graham, *Lecture*, 35.

31. Ibid., 39.

32. Graham, *Treatise*, 9.

33. Ibid., 26.

34. Ibid., 18.

35. Ibid., 19.

36. Ibid., 26.

37. Ibid., 35–36.

38. Michel Foucault, *The History of Sexuality, Volume 2: The Use of Pleasure* (New York: Vintage Books, 1990), 51. Foucault writes, "in the reflection of the Greeks

in the classical period, it does seem that the moral problematization of food, drink, and sexual activity was carried out in a rather similar manner. Foods, wines, and relations with women and boys constituted analogous ethical material."

39. Graham, *Lecture,* 146.
40. Ibid., 166–67.
41. Ibid., italics added.
42. For a more extended discussion of the relationship between invisibility, masturbation, and social control, see Neil Hertz's discussion of Freud's analysis of Dora's sexuality in Neil Hertz, *The End of the Line* (New York: Columbia University Press, 1985), chap. 8.
43. Graham, *Lecture,* 169.
44. Oxford English Dictionary, 2nd ed. (online), s.v. "Dalliance," http://www.oed.com, (accessed June 5, 2012).
45. In *Solitary Sex: A Cultural History of Masturbation,* Laqueur argues that masturbation became an issue in the eighteenth century because it symbolized the conjoining of new forms of individuality with discourses of imagination and addiction. Masturbation, he argues, became a lightening rod for medical concern because it drew attention away from other new behaviors that similarly invoked these three discourses, in particular, novel reading and commodity consumption. Graham's conjoining of consumption with masturbatory behavior is right on point with Laqueur's observations about European medical discourse. That said, the addendum I discuss here points to masturbation's relevance to emerging forms of liberal womanhood.
46. Jeanne Boydston, *Home and Work: Housework, Wages, and the Ideology of Labor in the Early Republic* (New York: Oxford University Press, 1994), 102.
47. Graham, *Lecture,* 168.
48. William Alcott, *The House I Live In* (Boston: Light & Stearns, 1837), 35.
49. Maggie Kilgour, *From Communion to Cannibalism: An Anatomy of Metaphors of Incorporation* (Princeton, NJ: Princeton University Press, 1990). In her work on cannibalism Maggie Kilgour writes, "one of the most important characteristics of eating is its ambivalence: it is the most material need yet is invested with a great deal of significance, an act that involves both desire and aggression, as it creates a total identity between inside and outside, eater and eaten while insisting on the total control—the literal consumption—of the latter by the former. Like all acts of incorporation, it assumes an absolute distinction between inside and outside, eater and eaten, which, however, breaks down, as the law 'you are what you eat' obscures identity and makes it impossible to say who's who."
50. Graham, *Treatise,* 171.
51. Ibid., 172.
52. Stoler, "Tense and Tender Ties," 52.
53. Graham, *Lecture,* 174.

54. Scott Lauria Morgensen, "Settler Homonationalism: Theorizing Settler Colonialism within Queer Modernities," *GLQ: A Journal of Lesbian and Gay Studies* 16, no. 1 (2010): 105–31.

55. Ibid., "Settler Homonationalism," 106.

56. Andrew Delbanco, *Melville: His World and Work* (New York: Knopf, 2005).

57. The first official U.S. expedition to the South Pacific occurred in 1791.

58. See John Carlos Rowe, "Melville's Typee: U.S. Imperialism at Home and Abroad," chap. 4 in *Literary Culture and U.S. Imperialism: From the Revolution to World War II* (New York: Oxford University Press, 2000).

59. See Rachel Poliquin, "Vegetal Prejudice and Healing Territories in Early Modern England," in *Textual Healing: Essays on Medieval And Early Modern Medicine*, ed. Elizabeth Lane Furdell (Leiden: Brill Press, 2005). I am indebted to Rachel Poliquin's work on this issue.

60. Foucault, *History of Sexuality 1*, 139.

61. Graham, *Lecture*, 176.

62. Foucault, *History of Sexuality 1*, 140.

63. I make this argument at greater length in *Racial Indigestion*, 185.

10

Connecticut Yankings

Mark Twain and the Masturbating Dude

ELIZABETH FREEMAN

If you must gamble with your sexuality, don't play a Lone Hand too much. When you feel a revolutionary uprising in your system, get your Vendôme Column down some other way—don't jerk it down.
Mark Twain, "Some Thoughts on the Science of Onanism"

The *four untimely essays* are altogether warlike. They demonstrate that I was no Jack 'o' Dreams, that I derive pleasure from drawing the sword—also, perhaps, that I have a dangerously supple wrist.
Nietzsche, *Ecce Homo*

On November 28, 1884, the *New York World* reported that the sales prospectus for Mark Twain's completed novel *The Adventures of Huckleberry Finn* had been defaced with an obscene illustration, apparently inserted by a disgruntled engraver during the production of the sales booklet.[1] In the offending image Huck Finn, disguised as Tom Sawyer, stands with his back to the audience looking at a wickedly grinning Aunt Sally and a surprised Uncle Silas. The picture's caption corresponds with Aunt Sally's question to Uncle Silas: "Who do you reckon it is?" In the graffitied version, Uncle Silas appears to have a tiny erection sticking out of his unzipped fly.

This little doodle, however unintentionally, plays on the homoeroticism central to American literature; as Leslie Fiedler argued over six decades ago, classic American novels often feature an interracial bond

IN A DILEMMA.   283

what it would take three days to fix it.   If I'd a called it a bolt-head it would a done just as well.

Now I was feeling pretty comfortable all down one side, and pretty uncomfortable all up the other. Being Tom Sawyer was easy and comfortable ; and it stayed easy and comfortable till by-and-by I hear a steamboat coughing along down the river— then I says to myself, spose Tom Sawyer come down on that boat? —and spose he steps in here, any minute, and sings out my name before I can throw him a wink to keep quiet ? Well, I couldn't *have* it that way—it wouldn't do at all. I must go up the road and waylay him. So I told the folks I reckoned I would go up to the town and fetch down my

"WHO DO YOU RECKON IT IS ?"

baggage.   The old gentleman was for going along with me, but I said no, I could drive the horse myself, and I druther he wouldn't take no trouble about me.

Defaced illustration from sales prospectus for *The Adventures of Huckleberry Finn*. Original held in the Clifton Waller Barrett Library of American Literature, Albert and Shirley Small Special Collections Library, University of Virginia.

between a man and a "boy" or infantilized man—and the relationship between Huck and the runaway slave Jim is paradigmatic.[2] In the prank pulled off by Twain's engraver, however, the alibi of racial harmony falls away, leaving a quite literally naked expression of intraracial, intergenerational, homosexual interest, if not precisely love: with the phrase "Who do you reckon it is?" Uncle Silas now seems to be asking Tom/Huck to name or otherwise identify his rather diminutive penis, and Aunt Sally becomes merely a titillated observer. Moreover, the *New York World* reported that the title of the engraving (which may have been different than the caption) was "In a Dilemma; What Shall I Do?" This line is even more polysemous: is Tom/Huck speaking these words, asking what he is supposed to do with his "uncle's" exposed member?

Or is Uncle Silas speaking them, as if asking Tom/Huck about the remedy for an erection? Given the anti-masturbation campaigns that were still active at the time, there would be only one proper solution: not to "play a Lone Hand," as Twain suggests in his mock treatise on onanism cited in the epigraph above, but to "get [it] down some other way."[3]

According to the *New York World,* Twain's publishers tracked down as many of the defaced illustrations as they possibly could, substituted the original illustration without the defect, and went to press with the prospectus. Two years later, however, Twain began writing a novel, *A Connecticut Yankee in King Arthur's Court* (1889), for which, as it happens, this rogue illustration of sexual exhibitionism between white man and white boy might have served very nicely. In this work, a middle-class factory manager named Hank Morgan is clonked on the head by a burly, disgruntled, crowbar-wielding subordinate in the year 1879, and wakes up to find himself in England in the year 528. There, he immediately sets out to modernize medieval England into nineteenth-century industrial-capitalist America, rallying the masses into a revolution against the aristocracy, sorcery, and the Catholic Church. He christens himself "Sir Boss," converts Camelot to capitalism, and, in echoes of Twain's quippy warning against masturbation, even indulges his own cowboy fantasies, playing the part of a "lone" ranch "hand" with a lasso in a jousting competition. During Hank's manufactured revolution, he also blows up Merlin's tower, another phallic Vendôme Column. But Hank's people rise up against him in the Battle of the Sand-Belt, and he ends up defeated, hidden in a cave, sleeping for 1,300 years under Merlin's spell.

It's easy enough to read *Connecticut Yankee* as a text haunted by the specter of nineteenth-century American labor unrest, especially since Hank shares a last name with the nineteenth-century capitalist J. Pierpont Morgan.[4] In fact, Dan Beard's illustrations for the original publication are tantamount to political cartoons on behalf of economic reform: for example, Beard drew a medieval slave driver with the head of American financier Jay Gould, and other times altogether departed from Twain's plot with drawings that advocated free trade, fair taxation, and so on.[5] The way the novel ends, though, suggests that Twain himself took a dim view of class revolt. The peasants' uprising against the freedom that Hank supposedly offers them is not a rational response to his increasingly autocratic rule, but an outgrowth of their bawdy, infantile worldview, congruent with their civilizationally underdeveloped status. Indeed, Twain draws the peasants with the same lines as nineteenth-century representations of not only medieval folk and free black people, but also the white and multiethnic working class: like Hercules, the brawny factory hand who attacks Hank with a phallic tool, the people of Camelot are sexually excessive, physically strong, and given to childish pursuits.[6]

Yet the novel, I want to suggest, is haunted by a different specter than working-class unrest and the hypersexuality typically attributed to the disenfranchised in the nineteenth-century United States. *A Connecticut Yankee in King Arthur's Court* is also rife with perversions coded as bourgeois in Twain's era: the ostensibly democratic, modern, masculine Hank Morgan is clearly nostalgic for the homosociality inherent in chivalry, overly invested in nudity and little children, uninterested in the ramblings of the medieval wife he takes, and too fond of theatrical "effects" (a word he repeats throughout the novel) to pass as completely hetero-masculine. He may aspire to capitalist manhood, but he continually lapses into the homophilia, voyeurism, pedophilia, and flamboyance that characterized the stereotypical late-nineteenth-century sexual deviant of the white leisure classes. Hank is also deliciously punningly named. The last name "Morgan" may suggest Hank's capitalist agenda, and his full name Henry Morgan (after the famous seventeenth-century Welsh pirate) may imply that this program is another form of robbery, but his nicknames add an erotic fillip or two.

In calling him a "Yankee of the Yankees," Twain ostensibly suggests that Hank was a solid New Englander, as per the most popular etymological explanation for the term "Yankee," a North American Indian approximation of the word "English" (*yengee*).[7] More recently, though, Henry Abelove has also traced the word "yankee" to the slang term "yankum," or masturbatory act, rereading the song "Yankee Doodle Dandy" as a bawdy commentary on masturbation—"doodle" was eighteenth-century slang for "penis," and "dandy" carried its current meaning of a fashionable fop; so, in Abelove's words, "a yankee doodle dandy is a primping penis puller."[8] The figure of a "Yankee of the Yankees," then, conjures up two things: first, it evokes the kind of extreme whiteness associated with both racial purity and the pallor incurred by self-abuse, and second, it figures a yanker yanking other yankers in an endless circle jerk. Indeed, the novel's most literally shocking event is just like the latter image's circuit of bodies electric: during the final battle between medieval peasants and modernization, twenty-five thousand English knights in armor die as they hit a high-voltage fence that Hank has built.[9] In a grotesque parody of democratic fraternity and spiritual magnetic attraction alike, the current is passed, man to man, until Hank and his army of fifty-two men are surrounded by an enclosure of corpses.

Then, too, Hank himself expires in a suspiciously onanistic pose: at the closing of the novel's nineteenth-century frame, he dies in bed, glassy-eyed, pale, and delirious, "mutter[ing] and ejaculat[ing]" endlessly while "pick[ing] busily at the coverlet," the very picture of the solitary vice (258). Even his all-American name is not safe from ribald punning: an obsolete meaning for "hank" is "a propensity; an evil habit," from which it's possible we get the verb "to hanker." But it is also "a . . . curbing hold; a power of check or restraint," the psychological equivalent of reins or a noose.[10] A hank embodies both dissolution and restraint, the very dynamic that organized the meanings of both white middle-class selfhood in U.S. industrial capitalism, and masturbation in transatlantic medical and popular literature.[11] It was not an accident that the American literature against masturbation was directed toward white people, even toward Yankees: as Kyla Tompkins argues in this volume, anti-onanistic discourse was part of a "project of national embodiment . . . linked to the consolidation of whiteness as the dominant racial position in the United States." Hank the yanker is, then, an exemplar of what could go terribly wrong with that project.

But why is Hank the masturbator also a time traveler? As Peter Coviello argues, we might think of sexuality as a way of inhabiting temporality otherwise to capitalism.[12] In *Connecticut Yankee*, onanistic sexuality is in a kind of two-step with market-time, even as Hank's body is tuned to an inarticulate *past* of erotic possibility, a fantasy of what Carolyn Dinshaw has named "Getting Medieval."[13] Moreover, masturbation itself has a temporal quality that made it the perfect foil for eighteenth- and early-nineteenth-century anxieties about a changing economic system; this particular form of sexuality rendered the body, paradoxically, both out of step and in lockstep with modernity's sped-up market time. Thomas Laqueur has written of "[t]he disconnected, imaginative, individualist, resolutely ahistorical qualities of masturbation," claiming that "no form of sexuality is more profligate with time or less linked to family and inheritance."[14] Hank Morgan certainly fits this profile of the disconnected, imaginative individualist: unmoored from his own era, he delights in masquerading and in putting on elaborate dramas to fool the medieval masses, and his contempt for them is in part based upon the fact that "they did not exist as individuals, but merely as homogeneous protoplasm, with alloys of iron and buttons" (249). More important, for the bulk of the novel Hank is also socially disconnected, completely delinked from family and inheritance: he is a self-made man; he arrives in Camelot single and childless; he champions the wage system over patrilineal modes of property transfer. In this sense Hank looks like a masturbator simply because he is a financier, and joins the long history of representation in which sexual deviance and the fluctuations endemic to the market stand in for one another.

Even as masturbation was associated with the market and modernity, though, its temporality also invoked the past, for among the many physical and mental ills with which it was associated by the nineteenth century, a strikingly incongruous one is memory loss.[15] With this symptom, masturbation becomes a figure for not only for the time of capitalism, but for history, or historiography, gone awry. Indeed, Hank suffers from memory troubles at the novel's end, when he babbles about times gone by but does not seem to remember his nineteenth-century self. More generally, both Hank and the novel suffer from a kind of cultural amnesia about the complexities of the medieval era. Hank's most damaging quality is that he is completely ahistorical: a living anachronism, he actually supposes that he can introduce new technologies and modes of production to the Middle Ages, and force a revolution against feudalism 1,261 years ahead of time, before the contradictions of this system have come to a head on their own. Eve Sedgwick has cited masturbation's "affinity with amnesia, repetition or the repetition-compulsion, and ahistorical or history-rupturing rhetorics of sublimity," which is an accurate description of Connecticut Yankee as well: Hank goes back in time to repeat the medieval with a modern difference.[16] The novel resolves its own historical contradictions—predominantly the one that Hank's interference in medieval culture would also have resulted in a very different *nineteenth* century—by blowing everything up in a last blast of the technological sublime.

In other words, *Connecticut Yankee* is less a novel about time travel per se, than about doing history badly. By interlacing the themes of sexual deviance and faulty historicism, *Connecticut Yankee* points to a longer history of the problem of history. From at least Enlightenment debates about precedent and casuistry, through the battle between Romantic historiography and scientific disciplinary methods, through the discrediting of amateur historiography as effeminate, through the Frankfurt school condemnation of pleasurable sensation as always already antithetical to proper historical consciousness, to contemporary Marxist dismissals of queer theory as ludic and ahistorical, doing history badly frequently appears as a kind of perversion.[17] Marx and Engels' famous statement that "[p]hilosophy and the study of the actual world have the same relation to one another as onanism and sexual love" puts the issue succinctly: masturbation is as much a part of the sexuality of history as it is part of the history of sexuality.[18] And while we do not generally read Twain as a theorist of history, in addition to penning quite a bit of scatological and obscene humor he was well read in the popular histories of his time, and had an abiding interest in the question of how history might be written.[19] *Connecticut Yankee,* then, is best read as an inquiry into the erotic logic of nineteenth-century habits of historicizing, and perhaps even our own contemporary ones—and an excursus into possibilities for rethinking these habits.

Yanking Backward

In *Connecticut Yankee,* getting at history in the right manner is in the first instance an *American* project. Both Twain's joke about the Vendôme Column in my epigraph above and his novel draw on his reputed hatred of all things French, especially French sexual mores. Indeed, the year Hank gets brained by his factory hand, 1879, marks the year Twain traveled to France and received a lukewarm welcome from the French people, as well as finding himself "appalled by French sexual standards."[20] Critics have also traced the very worst of Camelot's debauchery in *Connecticut Yankee* to descriptions of the revolutionary masses in Carlyle's *The French Revolution*.[21] It is tempting, then, to read the fictional events of 1879 in *Connecticut Yankee* as Twain's commentary not only on his own travels, but also on the events of 1789 and after, as if Twain slyly reversed some digits and the whole novel makes a mockery of the French Revolution. This makes some sense of Twain's invented device of traveling backward in history, since one of the notable accomplishments of the revolutionaries was a form of time travel—a new calendar instantiated on 5 October 1793 but beginning analeptically on 22 September 1793 (and, it might be noted, picked up again by the Paris Commune of 1871, who knocked down the Vendôme Column). In other words, French revolutionaries seemed to possess the capacity both to deform sex and to turn back time, the latter only the most literal of their many deformations of stadial, developmental history. The sexual standards Twain so despised may well have included their temporal standards.

But Twain is not the first author to correlate the bad timing of the French with sexual deviance. As Marx famously writes in his 1852 *Eighteenth Brumaire of Louis Bonaparte*, citing Hegel, events in world history "occur, as it were, twice. [Hegel] forgot to add: the first time as tragedy, the second time as farce."[22] French history's temporal drag— the insistent, distorting pull of its past failed glories on its revolutionary present—appears, in Marx, as camp performance: he describes the Protestant Revolution as "Luther don[ning] the mask of the Apostle Paul," the Revolution of 1789 "drap[ing] itself alternately as the Roman republic and the Roman empire," the Revolution of 1848 as a parody of 1789, and the coup of 1851 as the resurrection of Napoleon I.[23] For the Marx of the *Eighteenth Brumaire*, there is no turning back to the past that is not rearguard, and looking backward is an act of what Hank Morgan might have called dudery, or dress-up.[24] Even that word "farce" is itself charged with implications of sexual impropriety: from the Latin *farcire* (to stuff), through the Old French words *farcir* (to pad out) and *farce* (an interlude of "impromptu buffoonery" in a religious drama), through its English use as a synonym for "force-meat" or stuffing, "farce" combines theatricality with the image of bodily violation, as in the English word "gag."[25]

In Twain's novel, though, the French appear not in the *habille-ments* of yesteryear, but entirely out of linear history, interpolated into the time of the Anglo-Saxons just as a goose might be stuffed: at first, Hank seemingly returns to the period *before* the Norman Conquest, the era celebrated by commentators from Blackstone onward as prior to feudalism and hence possessed of an originary freedom.[26] Hank's use of parodic Germanic "abracadabras" like "Transvaaltrup-pentropentransporttrampelthiertreibertrauungsthraenentragoedie!" (125) to accompany his feats of technological violence skewers an invented political etiology in which the period of Germanic rule counted as the apex of national sovereignty. Yet the denizens of Camelot bear suspiciously Francophone names like Le Fay, Le Desirous, and Le Poulet. The anachronistic Frenchness of Camelot is doubtless influenced by the nineteenth-century vogue for the Arthurian romances pioneered by Chrétien de Troyes in the twelfth century, but it also allows Twain to poke fun at the aristocracy by way of an effeminacy coded as French. And Twain does so through a gendered drag less immediately weighed down by the past than that condemned by Marx: Hank's medieval side-kick Amyas "Clarence" Le Poulet, for example, appears to him at first sight "an airy slim boy in shrimp-colored tights that make him look like a forked carrot" (15), and illustrator Daniel Beard drew him with the head of the French actress Sarah Bernhardt.

Twain's version of Marx's farcical repetition involves age play rather than just play with historical costume. Part of Hank's failure is that he mistakes historically specific difference for infancy, hewing to a linear model in which earlier times stand for the childhood of the human race even as he force-feeds those "children" with developmentally inappropriate technology. But Hank's relationship with Clarence brings out the erotic aspect of this misapprehension: at a banquet, responding to tall tales of Sir Kay the Seneschal's military prowess, Clarence whispers to Hank, "Oh, call me pet names, dearest, call me a marine!" (20), and then "nestle[s] upon [Hank's] shoulder and pretend[s] to go to sleep" (23). Shortly after, both doubling Clarence and for the first time exposing his own nakedness, Hank finds himself stripped of his supposedly enchanted clothes by the King's men, and thus "naked as a pair of tongs!" (26). Over the years, as Hank conquers the Arthurians with nineteenth-century technology disguised as magic, Clarence becomes

Hank's "head executive [and] right hand . . . a darling" (52). Clarence combines servant, infant, romanticized "right hand," and body double, throwing Hank's homoeroticism, pedophilia, and masturbatory narcissism into stark relief. Clarence's real name, "Amyas le Poulet," is perhaps an anachronistic pun on the Puritan Sir Amyas Poulet but most definitely translatable as "love the chicken."[27] That Twain was aware of the sexual innuendo is confirmed by Hank's later reference to Morgan le Fay as "fresh and young as a Vassar pullet" ready, we might say, for stuffing (99). Twain, then, figured French politics as a kind of eroticized, innocent burlesque, troping the Norman aristocracy of Camelot as both hypersexual and childlike in ways that cast suspicion on the possibly prurient nineteenth-century craze for the Arthurian tales. But neither was he a champion of the nineteenth century's other popular historiographical-national project, the Anglo-Saxonism that revived English and American interest in all things medieval and that animated the work of his nemesis, Sir Walter Scott. Hank Morgan's same-sex infatuations and dubious masculinity are a sign not just of his scrambling Norman and Saxon history, but of his investment in coding medieval times as a restorative tonic for American dissipation, as the prototype for British and U.S. manhood in a way typical of many of the writers who retooled the medieval era in the image of the nineteenth century.[28]

As Twain seems to have recognized and exploited, nostalgia could also be associated with gender trouble. Medicalized in Switzerland in 1688 with a newly coined word, nostalgia was, like masturbation, "born from a disorder of the imagination."[29] It was originally considered a disease of the soldier who missed the loving care of his mother and the oral satisfaction of her home cooking (and here we can see the linkage of food, sexuality, and nationalism that Tompkins addresses in her essay for this volume), though later writers on the subject rushed to defend Swiss youth against the implication that they lacked bravery. American writers, who became concerned with the problem during the Civil War, linked nostalgia with all kinds of disorders, including "spermatorrhoea . . . and a general wasting of all the vital powers," and many promoted battle as the most effective remedy, though "[a]ny influence that will tend to render the patient more manly, will exercise a curative power."[30] Having returned from his own war by *Connecticut Yankee's* end, Hank seems undone by his own nostalgic excess: like the degenerate whose longing for a glorious past has sapped his virility, Hank ends up in bed, glassy-eyed, pale, and delirious. And the novel, rather than affirming Hank's Anglo-Saxon heritage, punctures his sentimental remembrances. The Arthurian era anachronistically puts a bullet into his armor, which is on display at the Warwick Museum in the nineteenth-century frame tale. Denizens of the Middle Ages have refused Hank the restorative effects of encounter with a simpler era: *A Connecticut Yankee* is, as Roger Salomon argues, "a desperate attempt to shatter the nostalgic image" of the Anglo-American past, and Twain uses the correlation between nostalgia and effeminacy to counter the postbellum figuration of Anglo-Saxonism as a form of virility.[31]

The Sexual and Textual Politics of Allegory

What *Connecticut Yankee* has in common with *The Eighteenth Brumaire*, then, is the use of stigmatized sexual activity as a metaphor for a faulty relationship to history: just as costume drama stands in for a failure to apprehend the present in Marx, drag, masturbation, and pedophilia in *Connecticut Yankee* stand in for the failure of particular kinds of pseudo-historicist consciousness (Anglo-Saxonism and the Arthurian vogue, at the very least). Both texts suggest that to lack historical consciousness is to be regressive; to be regressive is to be addicted to costume play and/or a bit of a wanker. Finally, both texts also correlate the perversion of history with suspect narrative modes, both the comedic mode of farce and the serious mode of allegory. In *The Eighteenth Brumaire*, Marx faults French political movements not only for their repetition-compulsion, but also for their tendency to overinvest in the literary genre of tragedy. Marx seems to recognize that the revolution will inevitably be narrativized, but worries that in being so it will inhabit aesthetic forms that forestall action: his description of Luther "don[ning] the mask" of the Apostle Paul resonates with Walter Benjamin's description of the melancholic structure of allegory, which "revives the world in the form of a mask."[32] Allegory, writes Benjamin, "give[s] the concrete a more imposing form by getting it up as a person."[33] If farce is suspiciously overtheatrical, then, the melancholic mode of tragedy risks fixation on the historical wound and thus stasis, the way an allegory, if too fixated upon a prior text, stalls in time and becomes metaphor. Marx's poetry of the future, by contrast, is formally so avant-garde as to be unintelligible in literary-historical terms; he simply gestures toward it. *Connecticut Yankee* has its own such generic foils in the person of Merlin and the hocus-pocus of the Catholic Church, who rely on spectacles of violence to subjugate the masses: their mode, it might be said, is horror. But the novel also understands what the telling of history might look like in the absence of received aesthetic form; that is, *Connecticut Yankee*'s poetry of the future fails precisely insofar as it refuses narrative.

Indeed, the novel is staged as a contest not only between medieval and nineteenth-century worldviews, but also between narrative modes. In the opening nineteenth-century frame tale, the narrator retires to bed to read Malory after a chat with the mysterious stranger of Warwick Castle. When the stranger (whom we later learn is Hank) knocks, the narrator puts aside the book and urges Hank to tell his tale, which he immediately labels "THE STRANGER'S HISTORY." This contrast between Malory and some truer "history" sets up the ongoing battle, within the inner tale, between the chronicle—that enumeration of events unbound by the structuring devices of narrative—and other possible ways of telling. At Hank's first encounter with the Round Table, the Knights and Merlin enumerate their conquests in the long, paratactic sentences typical of the medieval chronicle, putting the entire audience to sleep. Throughout his time in Camelot, Hank complains vociferously about the endless ramblings of the sixth-century English, constantly using the figure of the mill: Clarence introduces him to Merlin's "exaggeration-mill" (21); Hank picks up the metaphor and refers to the knight Sir Kay's "history mill," and his fiancée Sandy's "conversation mill" (70). Sandy is also the audience for his most pointed critique:

> The truth is, Alisande, these archaics are a little TOO simple; the vocabulary is too limited, and so, by consequence, descriptions suffer in the matter of variety; they run too much to level Saharas of fact, and not enough to picturesque detail; this throws about them a certain air of the monotonous; in fact the fights are all alike: a couple of people come together with great random . . . and a spear is brast, and one party brake his shield and the other one goes down, horse and man, over his horse-tail and brake his neck, and then the next candidate comes randoming

in, and brast *his* spear, and the other man brast his shield, and down *he* goes, horse and man, over his horse-tail, and brake *his* neck, and then there's another elected, and another and another and still another, till the material is all used up; and when you come to figure up results, you can't tell one fight from another, nor who whipped; and as a *picture*, of living, raging, roaring battle, sho! why, it's pale and noiseless—just ghosts scuffling in a fog. Dear me, what would this barren vocabulary get out of the mightiest spectacle?—the burning of Rome in Nero's time, for instance? (74–75)

If Marx's ghosts appear in comical togas accessorized with too many citations, Twain's ghosts appear as pure ether, bereft of any representational capacity, "randoming" from event to event because they are denied even interesting verbs. Without "the picturesque," insists Hank, we are left wandering in the desert of fact. Yet Hank's interest in "effects," his own overinvestment in theatricality, ends just as badly, for what is the Battle of the Sand-Belt but a "level Sahara" of meaningless corpses once Hank's interventions on history come to a head?

Despite Twain's reputation as a realist, then, and despite Hank's constant condemnations of Merlin for his hocus-pocus, *Connecticut Yankee* does not hold out for some journalistic, unbiased, straight-to-the-facts version of medieval history. Hank's failures as a historian are as much about his inability to come up with a genre or mode for the events he is part of, about his tendency to move beyond figuration, as they are a result of his over-the-top staging of himself as Sir Boss and his use of pyrotechnics to bedazzle the masses. His acts, put simply, appear to follow Sandy's random and sequential style.[34] We can read the terrible destruction that ends the novel, then, as the failure not so much of the genre-saturated historical account, but of the afigural chronicle.

What *Connecticut Yankee* offers instead of genre is mode. Indeed, the theatricality that Marx condemns in *Brumaire* is of a particular kind: Marx faults the revolutionaries for consistently appearing as other than themselves, as literally allo(other)-philic in the way they depend on prior texts to accrue meaning. This is the very essence of allegory, which always sets a new text in relation to a preexisting one, and thus present in relation to past. While medieval allegory often presented personified abstractions in pitched, Manichean battles outside of earthly time, modern allegory tends to "retell" a previous text. As Deborah Madsen writes, the "allegorical paradox [consists of an] intertextual regression that facilitates the text's progression."[35] In other words, modern allegory is a mode of historiography, and its fundamentally regressive movement—two steps backward for every one step forward—contrasts sharply with Marx's "poetry of the future" shorn of historical citation. Yet *Connecticut Yankee* risks the poetry of the past. Not only is Hank himself made sexually regressive through references to his onanistic tendencies and interest in children, and historically regressive through the figure of time travel, but the double-time of the novel is also, itself, structurally allegorical. *Connecticut Yankee* epitomizes "intertextual regression-as-progression" by telling a story of nineteenth-century America's failures through a return to medieval texts such as *Le Morte d'Arthur*. It literalizes this recursive forward movement in Hank Morgan, the yanking Yankee who is thrust backward in time only to attempt to speed it forward.

Given its allegorical structure, and given that the novel clearly could not serve as a critique of the Middle Ages to denizens of the nineteenth century—who would have understood historical time as inexorably forward moving and past events as thereby impossible to change—the novel thus demands to be read as an allegory for *something* from its outset. In other words, the novel is clearly not just about Hank Morgan's individual failure to reckon with the alterity of the past, but about "America's" failure to contend with some aspect of its own history—its own tendency toward the ahistorical, archetypal version of medieval allegory in which bygone events supposedly signaled timeless truths. *Connecticut Yankee* is less what Michael Colacurcio calls "an allegory within history," than it is an insistence on the historicity within allegory.[36] Thus critics have spewed out historicist interpretations of the novel almost as constantly as Hank's "Man Factory" churns out men ready for nineteenth-century life within the novel. According to the scholarship, *Connecticut Yankee* critiques U.S. imperialism. Or it condemns feudalism in Hawaii. Or it accedes to the logic of nineteenth-century industrialization, in which people are machines. Or it transcodes Twain's experiences with the Paige typesetting machine. Or it is about the crisis of realist representation during the Gilded Age.[37] And so on. In this way, *Connecticut Yankee* is as much about an excess of historical meaning-making, or about historical meaning-making as inherently allegorical, as it is about anything else. By making a mockery of all our attempts to historicize it, by generating a surfeit of historicist readings that all boil down to more allegoresis, *Connecticut Yankee* suggests something that the *Eighteenth Brumaire* refuses: the making of history is a process in which events and texts are invested and reinvested with meaning, prepared for future use in a process that, as I shall argue below, is ultimately libidinal.

On Libidinal Historiography

Connecticut Yankee is cited as the first novel-length work in English whose plot features time travel, a device that would seem to offer the most accurate account of the past in that it ensures perfect correspondence between witness and event. But nobody reads the novel for factual information about the Middle Ages; even in its own moment critics both assumed it was a historical novel and dismissed it for its inaccuracies.[38] Twain himself, though, established *Connecticut Yankee* as conjectural, writing in the preface that "[i]t is not pretended that these laws and customs existed in England in the sixth century; no, it is only pretended that inasmuch as they existed in the English and other civilizations of far later times, it is safe to consider that it is no libel upon the sixth century to suppose them to have been in practice in that day also. One is quite justified in inferring that whatever one of these laws or customs was lacking in that remote time, its place was competently filled by a worse one" (4). The language of "pretending," "considering," "supposing," and "inferring" immediately establishes the novel as a self-consciously imaginary account of the past. Twain's historiography, then, has more in common with contemporary *speculative* fiction oriented toward the future than with the disciplinary history proper to his time, or even with the popular histories aimed at mass audiences in which a gripping plot took precedence over factual accuracy.[39]

And indeed, despite its status as a "historical" novel, *Connecticut Yankee* is speculative in both financial and temporal terms. Despite his admonition not to play a Lone Hand, Twain himself gambled on the future: it is well known that he had invested in the Paige typesetting machine during the time he was writing *Connecticut Yankee,* and that this investment ultimately failed. Hank, though, claims to despise speculation:

> Knight-errantry is a most chuckle-headed trade, and it is tedious hard work, too, but I begin to see that there *is* money in it, after all, if you have luck. Not that I would ever engage in it as a business, for I wouldn't. No sound and legitimate business can be established on a basis of speculation. A successful whirl in the knight-errantry line . . . [i]t's just a corner in pork, that's all, and you can't make anything else of it. . . . And moreover, when you come right down to the bed-rock, knight-errantry is *worse* than pork; for whatever happens, the pork's left, and so somebody's benefited, anyway; but when the market breaks, in a knight-errantry whirl, and every knight in the pool passes in his checks, what have you got for assets? Just a rubbish-pile of battered corpses and a barrel or two of busted hardware. (98)

Hank equates financial investing in what we would now call "futures" with a form of courtship he loathes: heterosexual knight-errantry. The problem, as he sees it, is that knights go lumbering quixotically about fighting imagined demons on behalf of unattainable women, returning only with fantastic stories, the equivalent of kited paper checks. But as Hank implies in his critique of the knights-errant as a pool of gamblers, "speculation" also has a nonheteronormative erotic charge, eschewing as it does the "bed-rock" of reproduction. While Hank equates speculation with ostensibly heterosexual chivalrous romance, it is, in fact, masturbation that has cleaved tightly to the idea of risky financial business. Laqueur has demonstrated how masturbation emerged as a site of cultural anxiety in the eighteenth century precisely at the moment that credit and consumerism emerged; a horror of representational excess and of desire unbounded linked the two domains of finance and sex. The problem with investment, it seems, is precisely its capacity to inflame the imagination, as, indeed, anti-masturbation literature recognized in its correlation of onanism with not only checks and credit, but also reading too much of another kind of paper, fiction. Speculative writing, whether of IOUs or of novels, is inherently libidinal.

Yet despite Hank's protests, Twain's invented history of "what might have been" follows the logic of gambling, in which investments tend

toward a future not yet realized, in which high risk may yield high profits, and in which the virtual supplants the material just the way paper
money supplanted the gold standard. Hank rebuilds Camelot in the
image of nineteenth-century America while acknowledging that his
project must remain incomplete. He averts his own execution in what
he calls a "saving trump" (30) by predicting an eclipse and claiming he
has the power to blot out the sun: "in a business way," he claims, "[the
eclipse] would be the making of me" (31). He names the new currency
of Camelot the "mill," and claims that "[o]ur new money was not only
handsomely circulating, but its language was already glibly in use" (175),
suggesting a collapse between linguistic and financial sign that undermines any pretense to a gold standard; indeed, part of what makes
Hank an unreliable narrator is not only his own rambling narration but
also the way his actions fail to back up his words.

Initially, we might read both allegory and historiography as cures for
what ails the libidinalized marketplace that Hank so vociferously critiques. After all, allegory would seem to fix literary meaning by anchoring one text to a historically prior text (something we can see through
a glass darkly in Twain's seeding of his text with so many allusions),
and historiography purports to settle the meaning of the past. Each
would seem to offer a hermeneutic gold standard. Yet as Frederic Jameson reminds us, allegory can also be read as the preparation of a text
"for further ideological investment," that is, for new ways of figuring the
relationship between an individual and "transpersonal realities such as
the social structure or the collective logic of History."[40] In other words,
allegory is a way of critiquing the present, perhaps even of dreaming
the future, by setting up the past as a transactional site—a site that at
once primes the desire to understand one's position within larger coordinates in the present and presumably, through such understandings,
to change those coordinates. On this model, Hank's faulty historicism,
represented variously as masturbatory vicariousness and prurience, as
the failed narrative drive of his tale, as his attempt to short-circuit the
stadial movement of History-with-a-capital-H from feudalism to capitalism, and even signaled by Twain's incitement of the critical desire to
anchor his tale in events of the nineteenth century, looks like something
queer historians might want to claim. While Twain's contemporaries
prepared the Middle Ages for a rearguard ideological investment in

Anglo-Saxonism, he himself seems to have prepared them for something else.

But for what? Martha Vicinus has argued that nineteenth-century nostalgic literature served as a way to encode same-sex love: the passage of time indexed "a series of negatives, of nonfulfillment that, under certain circumstances, could be more fulfilling than consummation."[41] Here, the impossibility of return opens up an erotics of deferral; an aesthetic of going back to bygone histories and historical fictions serves as one of many literary codes for homosexuality. And this is certainly one way to read Connecticut Yankee: in the novel's frame narrative, the narrator "M.T." meets Hank at Warwick Castle, engaging him in conversation, but Hank "seem[s] to drift away imperceptively out of this world and time, and into some remote era and old forgotten country" (5). Like Sandy, he is overcome by "archaisms" ("Wit ye well" [6], he murmurs to the narrator), and by the time of his death he describes himself as "a creature out of a remote unborn age," moaning for the "abyss of thirteen centuries" that separates him from Sandy (257), and preparing for medieval battle. Yet it seems too simple to claim Hank as a homosexual; his perversions are too various and too complexly temporal.

This brings me, at long last, to the second of the two epigraphs with which this essay begins, Nietzsche's remark that his "untimely" meditations, which include "On the Use and Abuse of History for Life," are military in their temporal imprecision. Counterposing fantasy, or "dreaming," with historiography's "drawing [of] the sword," Nietzsche stakes a claim for the "unhistorical" in the battle against the status quo, echoing his assertion in "On the Use and Abuse of History" that forgetting is necessary to action. But this insistent ahistoricism brings with it a dangerous supplement.[42] Drawing the analytic sword of the untimely is not so distinct from the other manual exercises associated with dreaming: indeed, the creative abuse of history that Nietzsche champions implies, with that supple wrist, a bit of self-abuse. By the turn of the twentieth century, the (a)historical allegory—in which the past will neither retreat nor provide a triumphant origin story for the present as in American nationalist allegory, but hovers as a site of potential critical investment—would become the refuge of those whose erotic interests were "wrongly" invested. Fixating upon a past in which they could not have lived, even fixing their own protagonists within an invented but historically specific past, inverts and others whose sexual practices did not fit into the heterosexual-reproductive matrix could practice a kind of dialectical nostalgia: the past might be embarrassing, but it could also signal the validity of a different life-world, including its norms of gender and eroticism. And, crucially, by featuring an archaic historical period that could not be dissolved into a moment on a personal time-line, or even be situated in a coherent, quasi-nationalist political prog-ress narrative, sexual dissidents could signal the absolute inaccessibility of these alternate life-worlds, these *imperiums in imperio,* to normals.[43] Touch the electric circle, and you die.

This logic might explain the peculiarly regressive moves of explic-itly lesbian and gay literature later on, such as the ending of Radclyffe Hall's 1934 "Miss Ogilvy Finds Herself," in which the main character, a classic version of what Esther Newton has called the mythic man-nish lesbian, slips into a dream sequence and finds herself a caveman courting a cavewoman, never returning to consciousness or the present moment.[44] And it may help explain the queer pseudo-historicist oddi-ties, often classed as Decadent works, that were contemporaneous with *A Connecticut Yankee* and spanned the decades in which sexology rose and fell, from Flaubert's *Salammbô* (1862) through Pauline Hopkins's *Of One Blood* (1902–3) through Virginia Woolf's *Orlando* (1928). For these texts, each in their own way, embrace bad historicism as an erot-ics. They toy with allegory's shuttling movement to prior texts, but no overarching interpretive point guides their time travels. They delight in the sheer alterity of other sex/gender systems, but use these as material for fantasy, courtship, and erotic worldmaking rather than for analytic distance.

Since Benjamin, it has been possible to read allegory not only as a form of historiography—a narrative mode that, by pointing to an ante-rior time, can suggest violence, ruination, and change—but also as a form of drag. On this model, Hank's entire career as Sir Boss, a capitalist in fey aristocratic drag, is certainly allegorical. But what is Twain "getting up" in the personae of Hank, or of medieval culture in general? Coun-tering his historicist critics, I would suggest that Twain is less interested in retelling a particular aspect of nineteenth-century culture through the medieval conceit, than he is in revealing and exploiting the libidinal logic of historiography itself. *Connecticut Yankee* suggests that our habit of historicizing—our hank for it—is fundamentally erotic, perhaps even autoerotic, and that this might not be such a bad thing. Twain's looking backward is neither triumphantly nostalgic nor properly political in the Marxist sense of what it means to do history: it simply marks a refusal, like Hank's final one, to accede to contemporary norms of gendered and sexualized identity. Hank ends his life "pick[ing] at the coverlet," supposedly a trope for impending death. But perhaps he too has other designs with his supple wrist. We might say that Hank, unable to reenter a nineteenth century where his erotic inclinations would be stigmatized, prefers to close his eyes and think of England.

NOTES

This essay has had many readers and interlocutors; I thank especially the editors of this volume, Heather Love, Aranye Fradenburg, H. N. Lukes, Molly McGarry, and colleagues at the UC Davis Faculty Symposium (Hsuan Hsu and John Marx in particular).

1. "Mark Twain in a Dilemma: A Victim of a Joke He Thinks is the Most Unkindest Cut of All," *New York World*, 28 November 1884, p. 8.

2. Leslie Fiedler, "Come Back to the Raft Ag'in, Huck, Honey," *Partisan Review* (June 1948).

3. Thomas Laqueur dates the anti-masturbation crusades from 1712, the appearance of Tissot's *Onania,* to about 1920. See *Solitary Sex: A Cultural History of Masturbation* (Brooklyn, NY: Zone Books, 2004). The epigraph is from Mark Twain, "Some Thoughts on the Science of Onania," a speech delivered to the Supper Club in England in 1879. In *The Mammoth Cod and Address to The Stomach Club,* intro. and ed. G. Legman (Milwaukee, WI: Maledicta, 1976), 23–25, at 25.

4. On *Connecticut Yankee* and capitalist labor relations see Martha Banta, "The Boys and the Bosses: Twain's Double Take on Work, Play, and the Democratic Ideal," *ALH* 3.3 (1991): 487–520; Ann Douglas, "Art and Advertising in A Connecticut Yankee: The 'Robber Baron' Revisited," *Canadian Review of American Studies* VI (Fall 1975): 182–195; Ronald M. Johnson, "Future as Past, Past as Future: Edward Bellamy, Mark Twain, and the Crisis of the 1880s," *American Studies in Scandinavia* 22 (1990): 73–80; and Henry Nash Smith, *Mark Twain's Fable of Progress: Political and Economic ideas in A Connecticut Yankee* (New Brunswick, NJ: Rutgers Univeristy Press, 1964).

5. On Beard's drawings, see Beverly R. David, "The Unexpurgated *A Connecticut Yankee*: Mark Twain and His Illustrator, Daniel Carter Beard," *Prospects: Annual of American Cultural Studies* 1 (1975): 99–117.

6. On representations of the working class as hypersexual, see Christine Stansell, *City of Women: Sex and Class in New York, 1789–1860* (Urbana: University

of Illinois Press, 1987). On representations of medieval bodies, see Carolyn Dinshaw, *Getting Medieval: Sexualities and Communities, Pre- and Postmodern* (Durham, NC: Duke University Press, 1999).

7. "Yankee" (n.), etymology. *Oxford English Dictionary* online, at http://www.oed.com/viewdictionaryentry/Entry/231174.

8. Henry Abelove, "Yankee Doodle Dandy," *Massachusetts Review* 49 (Spring/Summer 2008): 13–21, at 14.

9. Samuel Langhorne Clemens [Mark Twain], *A Connecticut Yankee in King Arthur's Court,* ed. Allison R. Ensor (New York: W. W. Norton, 1982), 257, 258. Subsequent page references are to this edition.

10. "hank" (n.), definitions 7 and 4a respectively (rare or dialect). *Oxford English Dictionary,* at http://www.oed.com/viewdictionaryentry/Entry/83999.

11. On middle-class manhood and sexual self-control, see Russ Castronovo, "Sexual Purity, White Men, and Slavery: Emerson and the Self-Reliant Body," *Prospects: An Annual of American Cultural Studies* 25 (2000): 193–227, at 198.

12. Peter Coviello, *Tomorrow's Parties: Sex and the Untimely Nineteenth-Century America* (New York: New York University Press, 2013).

13. Dinshaw, *Getting Medieval.*

14. Laqueur, *Solitary Sex,* 22.

15. Samuel Tissot's *Onanism* (1758) describes "the impairment of memory and the senses"; memory loss is also mentioned in Benjamin Rush's *Medical Inquiries and Observations, Upon Diseases of the Mind* (Philadelphia: Kimber and Richardson, 1812) and Homer Bostwick's *A Treatise on the Nature and Treatment of Seminal Diseases* (New York: Rogers and Co., 1860).

16. Eve Sedgwick, "Jane Austen and the Masturbating Girl," *Critical Inquiry* 17 (1991): 818–37, at 820.

17. On precedent, casuistry, and Romantic historiography, see Mike Goode, *Sentimental Masculinity and the Rise of History, 1790–1890* (Cambridge: Cambridge University Press, 2009); on amateur historiography, see Bonnie G. Scott, *The Gender of History: Men, Women, and Historical Practice* (Cambridge, MA: Harvard University Press, 1998); on the dangers of pleasure, see, for example Max Horkheimer and Theodore W. Adorno, *Dialectic of Enlightenment,* trans. Edmund Jephcott (Stanford, CA: Stanford University Press, 2007); on queer theory's dangerous ahistoricism, see especially the work of Donald Morton.

18. Karl Marx and Fredrich Engels, *The German Ideology, including Theses on Feuerbach* (Amherst, NY: Prometheus Books, 1998), 253–54. I owe the phrase "the sexuality of history" to Mike Goode.

19. The works Twain read before writing *Connecticut Yankee* include William Edward Hartpole Lecky's *History of European Morals,* Hyppolite Taine's *The Ancient Regime,* Carlyle's *The French Revolution,* George Standring's *People's History of English Aristocracy,* and Charles Ball's *Slavery in the United States.* For a comprehensive bibliography of Twain's historical readings that is probably in

need of updating, see James D. Williams, "The Use of History in Mark Twain's *A Connecticut Yankee*," *PMLA* 80 (1965): 102–10.

20. Wesley Britton, "Carlyle, Clemens, and Dickens: Mark Twain's Francophobia, the French Revolution, and Determinism," *Studies in American Fiction* 20 (1992), 197–204.

21. Ibid.

22. Karl Marx, *The Eighteenth Brumaire of Louis Bonaparte* (1869 ed., rep. New York: International Publishers, 1963), 15.

23. Ibid.

24. On anti-theatricality in the *Eighteenth Brumaire,* see Andrew Parker, "Unthinking Sex: Marx, Engels, and the Scene of Writing," *Social Text* 29 (1991): 28–45.

25. Thanks to Kyla Tompkins for encouraging me to play with the word "farce."

26. Reginald Horsman, *Race and Manifest Destiny: The Origins of American Racial Anglo-Saxonism* (Cambridge, MA: Harvard University Press, 1981), 14.

27. The name "Amyas" is derived from the Latin *amare* (to love).

28. See T. J. Jackson Lears, "The Morning of Belief: Medieval Mentalities in a Modern World," in *No Place of Grace: Antimodernism and the Transformation of American Culture* (Chicago: University of Chicago Press, 1994), 141–81.

29. Jean Starobinsky, "The Idea of Nostalgia," trans. William S. Kemp, *Diogenes* 14 (1966), 81–103.

30. "The Evils of Youthful Enlistments—and Nostalgia," *American Journal of Insanity* 19 (1863): 476–79, at 478; Theodore J. Calhoun, M.D., "Nostalgia, as a Disease of Field Service," *Medical and Surgical Reporter* 11 (1864): 130–32, at 132.

31. Roger B. Salomon, "Mark Twain and Victorian Nostalgia," in Marston LaFrance, ed., *Patterns of Commitment in American Literature* (Toronto: University of Toronto Press, 1967), 73–91, at 85.

32. Walter Benjamin, *The Origin of German Tragic Drama,* trans. John Osborne (New York: Verso, 2009), 133.

33. Ibid., 187.

34. See Anita Obermeier, "Medieval Narrative Conventions and the Putative Antimedievalism of Twain's *Connecticut Yankee*," in William F. Gentrup, ed., *Reinventing the Middle Ages and the Renaissance: Constructions of the Medieval and Early Modern Periods* (Turnhout, Belgium: Brepols, 1998), 223–39.

35. Deborah Madsen, *Allegory in America: From Puritanism to Postmodernism* (New York: Palgrave Macmillan, 1996), 146.

36. Michael Colacurcio, *The Province of Piety: Moral History in Hawthorne's Early Tales* (Durham, NC: Duke University Press, 1995), 425.

37. On imperialism, see John Carlos Rowe, "How the Boss Played the Game: Twain's Critique of Imperialism in *A Connecticut Yankee in King Arthur's Court*," in Forrest G. Robinson, ed., *The Cambridge Companion to Mark Twain* (Cambridge: Cambridge University Press, 1995), 175–92. On Hawaii, see Fred W. Lorch, "Hawaiian Feudalism and Mark Twain's *A Connecticut Yankee in King Arthur's Court*," *American Literature* 30 (1958): 50–66. On industrialization

and mechanization, see Cindy Weinstein, "Twain in the Man-Factory," in *The Literature of Labor and the Labors of Literature* (Cambridge: Cambridge University Press, 1995), 129–72. On the Paige typesetting machine, see Ann Gelder, "Justifying the Page," *Qui Parle* 3 (1989): 168–84.

38. William J. Collins, "Hank Morgan in the Garden of Forking Paths: *A Connecticut Yankee in King Arthur's Court* as Alternative History," *Modern Fiction Studies* 32.1 (Spring 1986): 109–14, at 102. Collins distinguishes between narratives where time travel is explicitly rendered as a hallucination, thought experiment, or dream, and fictions of explicitly physical time travel.

39. See Gregory M. Pfitzer, *Popular History and the Literary Marketplace, 1840–1920* (Amherst: University of Massachusetts Press, 2008).

40. Fredric Jameson, *The Political Unconscious* (Ithaca, NY: Cornell University Press, 1982), 30.

41. Martha Vicinus, "A Legion of Ghosts: Vernon Lee (1856–1935) and the Art of Nostalgia," *GLQ* 10.4 (2004): 599–616, at 601–2.

42. See Derrida, "That Dangerous Supplement," chapter 2 of *Of Grammatology,* trans. Gayatri Chavravorty Spivak (Baltimore: Johns Hopkins University Press, 1998).

43. On turns to the archaic, obsolete, and negative in the literature of same-sex love, see Heather Love, *Feeling Backward: Loss and the Politics of Queer History* (Cambridge, MA: Harvard University Press, 2007). For an elegant theory of queer anachronism, see Valerie Rohy, *Anachronism and Its Others: Sexuality, Race, and Temporality* (Albany: SUNY Press, 2009).

44. Esther Newton, "The Mythic Mannish Lesbian: Radclyffe Hall and the New Woman," *Signs* 9 (1984): 557–75.

11

What Came Before

PETER COVIELLO

There are the calendars that, by now, we know. I have in mind the ones that place the invention of a "modern" sexuality squarely at the end of the nineteenth century—think German sexology, think Wilde, think Sedgwick—and understand that novel modernity in several senses. This new sexuality is said to be modern inasmuch as it marks a suddenly quite comprehensive sort of identity, given definition by gendered object-choice; or by virtue of its emergence as an aspect of being whose putative characterological depth makes it a kind of master key for even the most inarticulable mysteries of selfhood; or because of its cultivation as an immensely useful switch point for the control of populations, the optimization of bodily comportments, the production of subjectivities made legible, via this new sexuality, to a whole host of microcalibrated powers.[1] You can take those calendars or you can leave them—they answer better to some sets of analytic imperatives than to others and, like any other master paradigm, can be as obscuring as they are clarifying. But if for the sake of inquiry you go along with them, you'll find that they broach a whole range of suggestive problems.

Here are just a few: How might the history of sexuality read differently in America, where different trajectories of secularism, different developments of solidified state power, and above all different, and differently violent, racial imperatives must alter, in degrees still to be figured precisely, the European genealogy that the work of Michel Foucault has made so indispensable to criticism? Or again, not unrelatedly: If sexuality comes into its modern and legible form there at the end of the century, then what *was* sex—what were its organizations of bodiliness and carnality, its domains of practice and expression—before it became the sexuality we like to think we know? What happens when, as Bruce Burgett encourages us to do, we dislodge "our commonsense understanding of 'sex' as a coherent set of bodily practices . . . and our related assumption that those 'sexual' practices express a sexuality that constitutes the self's deepest . . . interiority"?[2] How too might we begin the labor of recognizing, *as sex*, those things that might not, under the pressure of later epistemologies, appear as such? How do we comport ourselves critically in the presence of a sex that may not look like sex?

The essays by Kyla Wazana Tompkins and Elizabeth Freeman, in their different and beautifully rendered engagements with these questions, make what I take to be a striking intervention. They do not ask us to consider the shapes sex might take as much as they turn us to the question of what might prove to be sex—of what, that is, we have forgotten how to see as sex, and so can appear to us only as a symptom of displacement, an allegory, a figure. But eating, as Tompkins notes, is not simply a sexual metaphor, is not sex by other means. Hence her insistence that "in talking about eating as a form of depravity, we are not dealing in displacement. Rather, *alimentarity is in and of itself an erotic act*, one with the power to disrupt social order" (my emphasis). And this claim rhymes with Freeman's reminder that doing history—and particularly "doing history badly"—is not only a figure for sex gone awry, but an erotic practice in and of itself. Hence her claim that Twain's *Connecticut Yankee* fits in a tradition that links it to Flaubert's *Salammbô* and Pauline Hopkins's *Of One Blood* and Woolf's *Orlando* inasmuch as "these texts, each in their own way, *embrace bad historicism as an erotics*" (my emphasis). At least part of what's at stake here, I think, is a prying open of our critical orientation toward sex—an expansion, in both essays, of the domain in which we imagine "sex" to be operative, both as a vector of a larger project of biopower, and also, possibly, as the scene of intensities not so easily harnessed by normalizing imperatives. So Tompkins, by tracing out in such detail the racial and imperial stakes of dietary continence in the writing of famed anti-onanist polemicist Sylvester Graham, shows decisively that the mouth—hungry or sated, disciplined by denial or tempted toward savor—is as fully a part of the sexual body as, say, the genitals, and so is just as much an anxious site of negotiated optimization. (Tompkins also does the immensely valuable work of finessing the terms of Foucault's genealogy for Americanists, reminding us that in a country far more decentralized than those of Europe biopower was "located in the interspace between the state . . . the public sphere . . . and the nation.") And for Freeman, who in this piece extends in new directions her path-clearing work on "erotohistoriography," that contested sexual body touches *the self that historicizes*—the self, that is, for whom being in history, and tracking the self's place there, is an ineluctably sensual, *libidinal* undertaking, by turns battering and, as Twain's Connecticut Yankee finds, bewildering, provoking, intoxicating.[3] The mouth that eats, the self in the throes of libidinal historicizing: these are not, as Freeman and Tompkins offer them, displacements of a sexuality whose real locus, whose deep truth, is genital; or of a sexuality that, because it is thus located in genitality, ought finally to be apprehended according to the taxonomizing terms of one or another sexual identity. Graham's perverse eater and Twain's time-traveling Yankee may be queer; as Freeman and Tompkins show, though, that does not mean they are homosexual.

There are a wealth of clarities in these essays—about eating as an erotic practice in which the sexual politics of a specifically American imperialism realize themselves with singular vividness; about Twain, of all people, as a dissident theorizer of sex and historiography—but I want to linger a bit on the return, in both pieces, to the auto-erotic. We might ask: If Tompkins and Freeman are not pointing toward some sort of proto-homosexual identity, are they not invoking just the same that famously premonitory figure of sexual definition and sexual identity, the masturbator? In these terms, we could think of these pieces as tracing a few of the differences made by *earliness*. They ask us to note how differently sex might look in a moment before its full captivation by the taxonomizing logics of singular sexual identities that would come to prominence at the end of the century, which the masturbator seems so much to anticipate.[4] But I hear other possibilities as well in these accounts of an auto-eroticism gone awry, possibilities having more to do with the auto-erotic as signifier of the dangerous derangements of a sex refusing to be bound to the normalizing imperatives of reproduction, familial intimacy, racial propriety, and property management more generally. The potentially racially self-polluting auto-erotic pleasure of eating, the masturbatory habit of historicizing: both of these libidinal practices, and the smoke of scandal that follows their different fires, speak to the anxieties that attend stagings of sex in which it is unmoored not only from patterns of liberal normativity but also, I think, from a certain style of *possessiveness*, such as would suit them for the legibilities of sexual identity. Freeman and Tompkins remind us that one of the very most difficult inheritances of modern taxonomies of sexuality is our tendency to think of sex as, inevitably, a *property* in the self, indeed as one of the liberal self's most cherished and indispensable properties, a thing belonging to each of us. It is not always easy to see past the conception of sex, emerging though not fully calcified in the mid- and late nineteenth century, as something isolable in, and the property of, individual persons, as yours or mine. We could think of this as the liberalization of sexuality, a drive to articulate sex in possessivist terms, as another of the accoutrements of the private self.[5] But the auto-erotic figures Tompkins and Freeman find in Graham and in Twain, and to which they pay so agile and finely grained a quality of attention, put pressure on these understandings. They invite us to think about what it would mean to begin to imagine sex as something not quite yours or mine—not a tool to be turned to use and profited from like any other aspect of being organized by the market logics and imperial racializations of possessive individualism, not a mode of relation to be instrumentalized.

Freeman and Tompkins put me in mind of another mid-century American theorist of diet, chastity, and extravagantly eroticized self-relation: Henry David Thoreau. As wonderful readings by critics like Henry Abelove and Milette Shamir and above all Michael Warner have taught us to see, Thoreau is a writer who vexes the promises of liberal individualism in ways that are consistently tuned to the note of intimate yearning and disappointment, of a richly erotic hunger for what

Dana Luciano, in a resonant phrase, calls "an otherwise that is not necessarily elsewhere."[6] Perry Miller, with dramatized distaste, recognizes
as much when we writes that anyone who spends much time reading
in Thoreau's journals "must be impressed—indeed, appalled—not only
by the obviously insatiable drive that brings Thoreau back, again and
again, to 'friendship,' but by the monotony of his rhetorical devices for
translating friendship into no friendship."[7] Less impatiently, and with
the bilious "Economy" section of *Walden* in mind, we could say that
the yearning that speaks through Thoreau's disappointment is, rather,
the affective afterimage of a desire to articulate sexuality away from its
possessivist moorings. That is, sex comes into meaning for Thoreau
because it marks for him a realm of experience not wholly overcoded
by market imperatives, one that thus offers the beguiling possibility of
a more expansively satisfying bodily self-relation. We can think of this
yearned-for corporeal otherwise as a freedom from capture by market
instrumentalization, gender stricture, and not least from the nationalized whiteness that would do so much to fuse these imperatives into a
nation-making biogenerativity. Thoreau wants a body unhooked from
these simultaneous codings, these "projects of national embodiment"
(in Tompkins's rich phrase), in which racialization, sexualization, and
liberalization all are densely interwoven as mutually amplifying elements of optimized corporeality.[8] To want sex as something other than
a property in the self may be to chafe against this civic, managerial
investment in the flesh.

So how to imagine such a thing? What does a "sexuality" so constituted even look like? Would we know it if we saw it? It's worth recalling
that the most erotically satisfying moments in Thoreau's writing involve
not Alek Therien, the handsome Canadian woodchopper, nor chastity,
nor chastity's auto-erotic counterpart, masturbation. The moments that
tend most toward corporeal delight and sensual luxuriation refer, in
fact, to none of these things. They are rooted, instead, in *sound*. "After a
hard day's work," Thoreau writes in his journal,

> without a thought turning my very brain into a mere tool, only in the
> quiet of evening do I so far recover my senses as to hear the cricket
> which in fact has been chirping all day. In my better hours I am con-
> scious of the influx of a serene & unquestionable wisdom which partly

unfits and if I yielded to it more rememberingly would wholly unfit me for what is called the active business of life—for that furnishes nothing on which the eye of reason can rest. What is that other kind of life to which I am thus continually allured?—which alone I love? Is it a life for this world? . . . Are there duties which necessarily interfere with the serene perception of truth? Are our serene moments mere foretastes of heaven joys gratuitously vouchsafed to us as a consolation—or simply a transient realization of what might be the whole tenor of our lives?

. . . All the world goes by us & is reflected in our deeps. Such clarity! obtained by such pure means! by simple living—by honesty of purpose—we live & rejoice. I awoke into a music which no one about me heard—whom shall I thank for it? The luxury of wisdom! the luxury of virtue! are there any intemperate in these things? I feel my maker blessing me. To the sane man the very world is a musical instrument—The very touch affords an exquisite pleasure.[9]

Almost exactly this motif, with the same underscoring of the body's sensual intuition of an ampler, as yet unformed constellation of itself, appears several months later in the journal, as Thoreau describes the aftereffect of a dream:

And then again the instant that I awoke methought I was a musical instrument—from which I heard a strain die out—a bugle—or a clarionet—or a flute—my body was the organ and channel of melody as a flute is of the music that is breathed through it. My flesh sounded and vibrated still to the strain—& my nerves were the chords of the lyre. I awoke therefore to an infinite regret—to find myself not the thoroughfare of glorious & world-stirring inspirations—but a scuttle full of dirt—such a thoroughfare only as the street & the kennel—where perchance the wind may sometimes draw forth a strain of music from a straw. . . .

I heard that last strain or flourish as I woke played on my body as the instrument. Such I knew had been & might be again—and my regret arose from the consciousness how little like a musical instrument my body was now.[10]

I am tempted to say that this exquisite carnal ravishment by sound is as graphic a scene of sex as we get in Thoreau's writing. For sound in

Thoreau—not hearing, precisely, but the flesh-vibrating modulations of sound—induces a sensual responsiveness to the world without, which works abrupt and sweeping changes in the very organization of the corporeal self. As depicted here, sound belongs properly neither to the world nor to the listener, but is one particularly transforming mode of connection between them: "melody" passes through and inhabits the body, just as it passes through and inhabits the world outside the self. Not unlike Emerson's experience of vision, sound provides for kind of contact that, in its instantaneously shaping movement through the body, is freer from captivation by the world's calcified forms of knowing and perceiving, less overcoded by all those misapprehending structures of connection, of mere "familiarity," with which Thoreau is so impatient. It is a type of phenomenon that confounds exterior and interior, and muddles, in an apparently quite delightful way, the borderlands of the self.

But, conspicuously, sound also projects that self forward, if only momentarily, into future constellations that are as yet only dimly discernible: such episodes of sensual suffusion are for him *"foretastes of heaven,"* reminders of what "might be again." Sound delights Thoreau in a way that makes him believe his body carries within it the possibilities of an ampler, richer, more sensually expansive future, a future not reducible to the doings of "the street and the kennel" but in which the body lives as a "thoroughfare of glorious & world-stirring inspirations." If we are right in calling these sex scenes, then sexuality for Thoreau is not something isolated in persons, not something apprehensible in the self alone, and is neither quite allo-erotic nor auto-erotic. Like the imagining of the mouth as the site where the self could as well be dissipated as disciplined, or that of the historicizing self whose inaccessibility to genre lends it a dispersive illegibility, these scenes in Thoreau return us instead to sex as the name for an unstable in-betweenness, a scene of relation not reducible to the "objects" related, even if, from some angles, both look like "the self." Sex would instead be the name for what inheres between selves and the objects around them, for the current that connects and momentarily confounds them, and in doing so suggests back to the self nothing short of a revised template for being. That this doesn't, from many perspectives, look much like sex is, I think, much of the point.

So Thoreau's story, like those brought into relief by Freeman and Tompkins, usefully reminds us that the late-century arrival of identity-languages of sexuality—such that same-sex desire could, in the famous phrase, begin to speak its own name—was a development not without significant losses, and not just to critical or historiographic clarity. They help us begin to make legible some of the possibilities that may have dropped out from our visions of "the sexual" as such—and in so doing, helps us surrender, at least a bit, the self-flattering tendency to regard the sexual past as, in essence, anticipatory: a version of the present in a moment before its (hermeneutic, ethical, political) fulfillment. The matter is perhaps not that our priggish, or prudish, or deluded brethren in the nineteenth century could not confront what we savvy moderns plainly see were sexual longings they feared even to name. It may be that they envisioned sex in ways we ourselves have not learned, or have forgotten, how to see. One of the things we may have forgotten—which Tompkins and Freeman do so much to restore to view—is the turbulent force of a sex not readily written back into the possessive logics that, then as now, make up so much of the recalcitrant analytic grammar of sexuality itself.

NOTES

1. Exemplary texts here would be Eve Kosofsky Sedgwick's *Between Men: English Literature and Male Homosocial Desire* (New York: Columbia University Press, 1985) and *Epistemology of the Closet* (Berkeley: University of California Press, 1990). We might think too of Ed Cohen's *Talk on the Wilde Side: Towards a Genealogy of a Discourse on Male Homosexuality* (New York: Routledge, 1993), of David Halperin's *How to Do The History of Homosexuality* (Chicago: University of Chicago Press, 2002), and of Ann Laura Stoler's *Race and the Education of Desire: Foucault's* History of Sexuality *and the Colonial Order of Things* (Durham: Duke University Press, 1995). Investing them all, of course, is Michel Foucault's *History of Sexuality, Vol. I: An Introduction*, trans. Robert Hurley (New York: Vintage, 1978).

2. Bruce Burgett, "Sex, Panic, Nation," *American Literary History* 21:1 (Spring 2009): 70.

3. See also Elizabeth Freeman, *Time Binds: Queer Temporalities, Queer Histories* (Durham: Duke University Press, 2010).

4. On onanism as an Enlightenment malady, and particularly a disease of the ungoverned imagination, see Thomas W. Laqueur's *Solitary Sex: A Cultural History of Masturbation* (New York: Zone Books, 2003). See also the essays collected in *Solitary Pleasures: The Historical, Literary, and Artistic Discourses of*

Autoeroticism, ed. Paula Bennett and Vernon Rosario (New York: Routledge, 1995). For an excellent consideration of the masturbator as among the earliest iterations of modern sexual identity as such—"modern" sexual identity as tracked and specified by a theorist like Foucault—see Eve Kosofsky Sedgwick's essay "Jane Austen and the Masturbating Girl," in *Tendencies* (Durham: Duke University Press, 1993), 109–29.

5. "The institutional framework of the lesbian and gay movement," Michael Warner wrote more than a decade ago now, "predicated on identitarian thought, sees all politics as requiring a more consolidated gay identity and a form of life more fully conforming to the institutions of privacy." Warner's acute skepticism with respect to the tuning of national queer politics toward "a new form of post-liberationist privatization" seems to me to have been fortified by his rich engagements with figures from the American eighteenth and nineteenth centuries, who are in many ways ill fitted to such privatization.

6. See Henry Abelove, *Deep Gossip* (Minneapolis: University of Minnesota Press, 2003); Milette Shamir, *Inexpressive Privacy: The Interior Life of Antebellum American Fiction* (Philadelphia: University of Pennsylvania Press, 2008); and Michael Warner "Thoreau's Bottom," *Raritan* 11 (1992): 53–79, and "*Walden*'s Erotic Economy," in *Comparative American Identities*, ed. Hortense J. Spillers (New York: Routledge, 1991), 157–74. Dana Luciano quoted from "Touching, Clinging, Haunting, Worlding: On the Spirit Photograph," lecture given at Bowdoin College, 1 May 2010.

7. Perry Miller, *Consciousness in Concord* (Boston: Houghton Mifflin, 1958), 90.

8. My sense of biopower here comes most directly from Foucault's *History of Sexuality, Vol. 1*, though it is inflected too by Giorgio Agamben's *Homo Sacer: Sovereign Power and Bare Life*, trans. Daniel Heller-Roazen (Stanford: Stanford University Press, 1998).

9. Henry David Thoreau, *Journal, Volume 3: 1848–1851*, ed. Robert Sattelmeyer, Mark R. Patterson, and William Rossie, general ed. John C. Broderick (Princeton: Princeton University Press, 1990), 274–75.

10. Henry David Thoreau, *Journal, Volume 4: 1851–1852*, ed. Robert Sattelmeyer, Leonard N. Neufeldt, and Nancy Craig Simmons (Princeton: Princeton University Press, 1992), 155.

P.S.

A Coda

IVY G. WILSON

On December 6, 1856, the *Provincial Freeman and Weekly Advertiser* published an advertisement from one James Monroe Whitfield. Whitfield, an important figure in the mid-nineteenth century debates about emigrationism but little known now, was calling for a dual-language periodical to be published in English and French. Imagined as a "pre-eminent Literary work, for circulation both at home and abroad," Whitfield intended the *Afric-American Quarterly Repository* to feature both U.S. and Haitian authors as an attempt to conceptualize blackness in transnational if not hemispheric terms.[1]

Like New Madrid in 1811, Haiti in 1856 was a most unsettled political state. In the Introduction, we propose that the New Madrid earthquakes marked a geological as well as historiographic fault line, and that these tectonic openings provide apertures through which to view the dynamic "rethinkings of the politics of time and space in the nineteenth-century United States." In the most literal sense Haiti was also unsettled: one of the perverse ironies of having gained its political independence from France in 1804 through a revolution was that the country was forced to pay the European power for the losses it incurred, and the fledgling nation was thus in debt to France on the order of millions of francs that continued well into the next century. But the price of the ticket was exponentially inflated: there is debate among historians that France forced the small country to not only pay for its loss of the slave colony on the Caribbean island but also remunerate its collateral losses on the American continent, specifically the Louisiana territories, in the guise of interest.[2] Burdened even before it began, Haiti stumbled out of the gates of nationhood as a prototype for the dream of postcolonial statehood and the neocolonial debt economy; indeed, as a birthplace for modernity itself.

From its very inception, and even as a colony, the country that would come to be known as Haiti has lingered in the shadows of the U.S. imagination. Haiti has continually challenged the United States' self-authorized narrative of democratic exceptionalism from the presidency of Thomas Jefferson and Abraham Lincoln to Woodrow Wilson, more recently Bill Clinton, and Barack Obama. In the opening years of the nineteenth century, Jefferson, although he supported the revolutionary spirits that underwrote the American colonists and French Jacobins, could not quite let himself imagine that blacks were capable of self-governance and, in his second term, formally created an embargo against the fledgling country.[3] In the maelstrom of the Civil War, Lincoln considered both Liberia and Haiti as sites for black relocation/deportation before settling upon the Caribbean island as the site for a colony; this history illuminates the intertwined impulses of U.S. nationalism and imperialism even in a moment where the nation itself threatened to be dissolved.[4] While Haiti never developed into a fully materialized colony for the U.S. during the nineteenth century, that haunting desire resurrected again in the aftermath of World War I during Wilson's administration. Under the guise of protecting U.S. commercial interests, the U.S. occupied Haiti for some nineteen years— as part of the so-called Banana Wars, the specter of Haiti emerged as one ghost of many (including Panama, Nicaragua, Honduras, Mexico, and the Dominican Republic) that put into high relief the relationship between U.S. exceptionalism and imperialism and, in a broader sense, the relationship of the U.S. to the Americas writ large.[5] Given its history,

Haiti is often seen not only as an unsettled state but a failed state. And yet for all of its future anteriority, Haiti also served as the model of a freedom yet to be, haunting slaveholders across hemispheres and fueling nineteenth-century African American sentiment toward liberation and inspiring global anticolonial struggles and decolonialization movements throughout the twentieth century.

In the half-century between its independence in 1804 and Whitfield's prospectus in 1856, Haiti had witnessed some nine heads-of-state with titles ranging from governor to president, emperor or king to prime minister, each marking the country's radically shifting and unsettled structures of governance. It had fallen from being the Pearl of the Antilles, the richest colony in the Caribbean, to its poorest (a title that would later extend to the poorest country in the Western hemisphere). But in the mid-nineteenth century, the island enjoyed a relative degree of stability for nearly a twelve-year period under the leadership of Faustin Soulouque, through a calmed, highly centralized teapot of a government, while the violent currents of a geopolitical tempest raged all about. Soulouque, like a few of his predecessors, had encouraged African Americans to repatriate themselves to Haiti. In the wake of the emigration debates within the black public sphere, Haiti became the counterpoint to Liberia. It is in the midst of this context that Whitfield's advertisement appears.

Whitfield was seemingly an unlikely candidate for the proposition. As mentioned before, he was an important figure in the emigration debates but he is not remembered in the same registers of other nineteenth-century black intellectuals such as Frederick Douglass, Martin Delany, or Mary Ann Shadd. He did not have extensive experience in publishing and it is not clear that he commanded French, much less creole. But since the question of *how* Whitfield intended to enable this journal is difficult to handle, we should take refuge instead in the question of why.[6]

In Whitfield's prospectus one finds a shadow archive that acts as a history of transnationalism as much as it does as an expression of longing and desire for a cultural, if not political, sensibility set in motion between two registers; that is, in essence, in traffic. One way to approach Whitfield's prospectus is as something that exceeds the singularity of national identity and as something that yearns for a transnational modality *avant la lettre*. Riffing on the discussions, in this volume, of queer futurities, on the ambient lives of queer subjectivity before they were named as such, we can see in Whitfield's prospectus an epistemology of *becoming* premised on a desire that continually imagines an imminent—but tragically never immanent—future lingering on the precipice of arrival. Inasmuch as the journal's failed birth signals a nonexistent archive, thus foreclosing traditional historical analyses, it also abandons and distills the prospectus to the realm of the speculative, opening up questions of what might have been, or perhaps, what is yet to arrive.

The fate of the journal—it never got off the ground—reveals an analogue to the circulatory networks of the black diaspora, present in the epistolary archive analyzed by David Kazanjian or embodied in periodicals such as *La Revue du Monde Noir*. Long considered the special domain of historians and historical studies, the archives have been the subject of recent critical inquiry by theorists such as Jacques Derrida, Diana Taylor, and Elisabeth Kaplan.[7] Disavowing commonplace images of the archive as an inert repository of obscure or rare artifacts, these critics and others have examined these sites (both physical and conceptual) as a means to expose the social lives of the cultural objects housed in these repositories as well as reveal the particular investments held by custodians in circumscribing an archive along certain ideological routes. Closely read, Whitfield's prospectus allows us to interrogate how the archeological impulses of archival work, especially the dynamic interplay whereby a set of seemingly recessed objects are resurrected from the depths of the historical, radiate onto the living political present. Inasmuch as the prospectus remained unanswered in its own moment, reduced or distilled to a call with no ostensible answer, the document should be thought of as an emanation of the kind of yearning and expectancy at work in Peter Coviello's recent reading of Henry David Thoreau, especially in his suggestion that in Thoreau we can find "the outlines of a future that would not come to be."[8] While the head of the prospectus never found a body to literalize Whitfield's desire, this failed moment of nonconcretization might be thought of as forever articulating a desire and longing for alternative cultural and political formations. It is precisely in this failure—that is, our inability to demarcate the would-be journal as having specific chronological coordinates from this moment to that moment—that the prospectus constitutes a theory of futurity insofar as it can only, and must, remain an anticipatory wish or desired promise of something to come.

Something like the stakes involved in moving away from the mandates of "recovering" a figure like Whitfield has recently been articulated by J. Jack Halberstam as the "queer art of failure."[9] While I make no claims here that Whitfield's prospectus itself constitutes the type of queer objects under analysis in Halberstam's book, it nevertheless amounts to one of the most extreme variations, or alternatively the very embodiment, of the kind of "subjugated knowledges" and possibilities Halberstam laments are too often forgotten, eclipsed, or hushed. In thinking about these alternative political formations in relationship to this volume, we have tried to create a series of dialogues underneath certain signs with the hope that acts of critical interlocution, contamination, and eavesdropping move the ground upon which nineteenth-century American literature takes a stand about its own becoming and unbecoming.

We might recall here the maps that appear in Edward P. Jones's *The Known World*, considered in Lloyd Pratt's essay in this volume, as a reflection on the ways that literature stretches (across) time and space. It is worth underscoring that, in the episode detailing Alice's work in the boarding house, Jones has his character identify the maps under the much more nebulous term "creation." The placement of these "creations"—with one conspicuously on the "Eastern" wall and the other on the opposite (and ostensibly "Western") wall—figures these works in relation to a dialectic of distance and proximity. It is only when the aerial view is set against the hyperlocal that Alice's *mappae mundi* creations function as counter-narratives against, as well as new epistemologies for, imagining black life within the regime of slavery. The case of Whitfield, I am suggesting, operates similarly, because it is not distance (signaled as Haiti) or proximity (signaled as the U.S.) alone that is the sign of his desires, but the sensibilities produced by the figurative shuttling between these two registers and the promise of a new hemispheric American orbit.

If there is a "fault line" on the island of Hispaniola connecting to that of the New Madrid earthquakes, it is the natural watercourse alternately known as Massacre River and Dabajon River that partitions the western third of Hispaniola as Haiti and the eastern two-thirds of the island as

the Dominican Republic. But instead of enabling multiple epistemologies, as we saw with the varying interpretations of the New Madrid
earthquakes, the river that geopolitically divides Haiti from the Dominican Republic also balkanizes much of the scholarship on those two
nations along imperial and linguistic lines. There is, perhaps, no better
sign of this kind of partitioning, as a symbol of the balkanized border-
lines of current critical discourse, than the fact that until recently, sending letters directly between the two countries was impossible, frustrat-
ing any attempts at conversation across the border.

I invoke Haiti here—its shadow relationship to the United States; its
minor and minoritarian archives; its role, as Antonio Benítez-Rojo might
say, as a ligament in the body of hemispheric history—to draw parallels
between the various models of minoritarian criticism at play in *Unsettled
States*.[10] Illustrating these parallels also demands that we draw the links
between the figurative and everyday—that is, the visceral *costs* of moving
ground, most recently signified by the recent Haitian earthquake. As we
seek a reframing of the terrain of political critique, the 2010 earthquake
in Haiti stands as an uncomfortable and tragic reminder of its stakes: not
an excavating of deeper and new meanings, but rather the forceful eruption of them.[11] The writers in this volume seek to move critical discourse
out of its balkanized formations, to cross the river, as it were, and wade
in an ongoing uncertainty that can take no refuge in the calm waters lan-
guidly identified as nineteenth-century American literature.

NOTES

This essay has benefited from conversations with Dorris Garraway, Robert S.
Levine, and, especially, Kyla Tompkins.

1. James M. Whitfield, "Prospectus of the Afric-American Quarterly Repository,"
in the *Provincial Freeman and Weekly Advertiser* (6 December 1856), 1. The criticism on transnational blackness is extensive but some of the most important
recent work on the topic include Michelle Stephens, "Black Transnationalism
and the Politics of National Identity: West Indian Intellectuals in Harlem in
the Age of War and Revolution," *American Quarterly*, vol. 50, no. 3 (September
1998), 592–608, and Michael Hanchard, "Black Transnationalism, Africana
Studies, and the 21st Century," *Journal of Black Studies*, vol. 35, no. 2 (November
2004), 139–53. The essay collection *Hemispheric American Studies*, ed. Caroline F.
Levander and Robert S. Levine (New Brunswick, N.J.: Rutgers University Press,
2008), is an important volume on the subject; on the topic of blackness and the

hemisphere, more specifically, see Ifeoma Kiddoe Nwankwo, *Black Cosmopoli-tanism: Racial Consciousness and Transnational Identity in the Nineteenth-Century Americas* (Philadelphia: University of Pennsylvania Press, 2005).

2. On the early history of the Haitian indemnity, more generally, see Colin (Joan) Dayan, *Haiti, History, and the Gods* (Berkeley: University of California Press, 1995), 13, and Laurent Dubois, *Haiti: The Aftershocks of History* (New York: Metropolitan Books/Henry Holt, 2012), 99, 103, 204. On Haiti and Louisiana, more specifically, see John Craig Hammond, "'They Are Very Much Interested in Obtaining an Unlimited Slavery': Rethinking the Expansion of Slavery in the Louisiana Purchase Territories, 1803–1805," *Journal of the Early Republic*, vol. 23, no. 3 (Autumn 2003), 360.

3. For more on Jefferson and Haiti, see Tim Matthewson, "Jefferson and the Non-recognition of Haiti," *Proceedings of the American Philosophical Society*, vol. 140, no. 48 (March 1996), 22–48.

4. For more on Lincoln's thoughts on colonization and black emigration, see James D. Lockett, "Abraham Lincoln and Colonization: An Episode that Ends in Tragedy at L'Ile à Vache, Haiti, 1863–1864," *Journal of Black Studies*, vol. 21, no. 4 (June 1991), 428–44.

5. On the U.S. occupation of Haiti, see Hans Schmidt, *The United States Occupation of Haiti, 1915–1934* (New Brunswick, N.J.: Rutgers University Press, 1995); on the Banana Wars, see Lester D. Langley, *Banana Wars: Inner History of American Empire, 1900–34* (Lexington: University Press of Kentucky, 1984).

6. I am riffing here on a line from Toni Morrison's novel *The Bluest Eye*: "But since why is so difficult to handle, one must take refuge in how."

7. See Jacques Derrida, *Archive Fever: A Freudian Impression* ([1995]; Chicago: University of Chicago Press, 1998); Diana Taylor, *The Archive and the Repertoire: Performing Cultural Memory in the Americas* (Durham, N.C.: Duke University Press, 2003); and Elisabeth Kaplan, "'Many Paths to Partial Truths': Archives, Anthropology, and the Power of Representation," *Archival Science* (2002), 209–20.

8. Peter Coviello, *Tomorrow's Parties: Sex and the Untimely in Nineteenth-Century America* (New York: New York University Press, 2013).

9. Judith Halberstam, *The Queer Art of Failure* (Durham, N.C.: Duke University Press, 2011).

10. Antonio Benítez-Rojo, *The Repeating Island: The Caribbean and the Postmodern Perspective* ([1989]; Durham, N.C.: Duke University Press, 1992), 4.

11. In addition to studies on the history of the earthquake, including Paul Farmer's *Haiti After the Earthquake* (2011) and *Haiti Rising: Haitian History, Culture and the Earthquake of 2010* (2011), edited by Martin Munro, something of this cata-strophic geological eruption setting into motion a rethinking of political critique has recently been explored by Robert Fatton; see "Haiti in the Aftermath of the Earthquake: The Politics of Catastrophe," *Journal of Black Studies*, vol. 42, no. 2 (March 2011), 158–85.

Hester Blum is Associate Professor of English at the Pennsylvania State University. She is the author of *The View from the Masthead: Maritime Imagination and Antebellum American Sea Narratives* (2008), which received the John Gardner Maritime Research Award, and editor of William Ray's Barbary captivity narrative *Horrors of Slavery* (2008).

Peter Coviello is Professor of English at the University of Illinois, Chicago. He is the author of *Intimacy in America: Dreams of Affiliation in Antebellum Literature* (2005) and *Tomorrow's Parties: Sex and the Untimely in Nineteenth-Century America* (NYU Press, 2013), as well as the editor of Walt Whitman's *Memoranda During the War* (2004).

Jonathan Elmer is Professor of English at Indiana University and author of *Reading at the Social Limit: Affect, Mass Culture, and Edgar Allan Poe* (1995) as well as *On Lingering and Being Last: Race and Sovereignty in the New World* (2008).

Elizabeth Freeman is the author of *The Wedding Complex: Forms of Belonging in Modern American Culture* (2002) and *Time Binds: Queer Temporalities, Queer Histories* (2010). She is Professor of English at the University of California, Davis.

Glenn Hendler is Associate Professor and Chair of the English Department at Fordham University. He is the author of *Public Sentiments: Structures of Feeling in Nineteenth-Century American Literature* (2001) and co-editor of three volumes: *Sentimental Men: Masculinity and the Politics of Affect in American Culture* (1999); *Keywords for American Cultural Studies* (NYU Press, 2007; 2nd ed., 2014); and an edition of Walt Whitman's temperance novel *Franklin Evans; or, The Inebriate* (2007).

David Kazanjian is Associate Professor of English at the University of Pennsylvania. He is the author of *The Brink of Freedom: Improvising Life in the Nineteenth-Century Atlantic World* (forthcoming) and *The Colonizing Trick: National Culture and Imperial Citizenship in Early America* (2003), as well as co-editor of *Loss: The Politics of Mourning* (2002) and *The Aunt Lute Anthology of U.S. Women Writers, Volume One: Seventeenth through Nineteenth Centuries* (2004).

Rodrigo Lazo is the author of *Writing to Cuba: Filibustering and Cuban Exiles in the United States* (2005) and co-editor of the collection *A Window Into Cuba and Cuban Studies* (2010). He is Associate Professor of English at the University of California, Irvine.

Dana Luciano is Associate Professor of English at Georgetown University. She is the author of *Arranging Grief: Sacred Time and the Body in Nineteenth-Century America* (NYU Press, 2007), which won the Modern Language Association's First Book Prize in 2008.

Tavia Nyong'o is Associate Professor of Performance Studies at New York University and author of *The Amalgamation Waltz: Race, Performance and the Ruses of Memory* (2009).

Lloyd Pratt is the author of *Archives of American Time: Literature and Modernity in the Nineteenth Century* (2010) and University Lecturer in American Literature at the University of Oxford.

Shelley Streeby is the author of *American Sensations: Class, Empire, and the Production of Popular Culture* (2002) and *Radical Sensations: World Movements, Violence, and Visual Culture* (2013). She is Professor of Ethnic Studies at the University of California, San Diego.

Kyla Wazana Tompkins is an Associate Professor of English and Gender and Women's Studies at Pomona College and author of *Racial Indigestion: Eating Culture in the Nineteenth Century* (NYU Press, 2012).

Ivy G. Wilson is Associate Professor of English as well as Director of the Program in American Studies at Northwestern University and author of *Specters of Democracy: Blackness and the Aesthetics of Politics in the Antebellum U.S.* (2011).

INDEX

Page numbers in italic indicate illustrations.

Tecumseh, 3, 23n7
temperance movement, 252
temporality: in *A Connecticut Yankee in King Arthur's Court,* 282; in "The House-Top," 215, 216; of masturbation, 279–280; sideways, 260
temporal unsettlement, 11–12. *See also* time
tenBroek, Jacobus, 96
Tenskwatawa, 3
testimonios, 112–113
Therien, Alex, 302
Thompson, Thomas Boulden, 125–126
Thoreau, Henry David: on aftereffects of a dream, 303; and sexual longing, 301–305; on sound, 20–21, 302–303; and Whitfield's failed journal, 310
Thornton, John, 122
three-fifths clause, 93–94, 96
time: as accumulation, 79; chrononormativity, 82; linearity of, 82, 108; and performance studies, 98n8; and queer theory, 98n8
Tissot, Samuel, *Onanism,* 295n15
Tocqueville, Alexis de, on newspapers, 158
totality. *See* historical totality
Truth, Sojourner, 215
Twain, Mark: *A Connecticut Yankee in King Arthur's Court,* 277; on *A Connecticut Yankee in King Arthur's Court,* 289; and the French, 281–282; historical readings of, 295n19; "Some Thoughts on the Science of Onanism," 275, 277. See also *Adventures of Huckleberry Finn*
typography, of Walker's *Appeal,* 102n65

University of California, 106
University of Notre Dame, 27n39
unsettlement: definition of, 10; empathic, 12, 27n36; historical, 11–12; and indigenous studies, 9; and Liberia, 145–147, 235–236; and multicultural education, 8–9; narrative, 10–11; pleasure as ethical, 13; and postcolonial studies, 9; vs. queerness, 25–26n26; as scholarly topic, 26n28; temporal, 11–12
U.S. Census, 41
U.S. Constitution: amendments to, 89–93; Congress's reenactment of, 16, 76–78, 86–87, 91, 115; Fourteenth Amendment, 89–97; Nineteenth Amendment, 99n15; sacralization of, 80; Sixteenth

Amendment, 99n15; and slavery, 93–94; three-fifths clause of, 93–94
U.S.-Mexico War (1846-48), 112

Valdes-Rodriguez, Alisa, 42–43, 45
Vallejo, Mariano Guadalupe, 50–51
Velazquez, Loreta Janeta, 32, 36
Vicinus, Martha, 292
violence, 231n46, 231n53, 265

Walker, David: *Appeal, in Four Articles . . .,* 16, 96–97, 102n65; on blacks as world citizens, 70
Walters, Ronald, 271n22
Warner, Michael, 218, 226n9, 231n46, 252, 301, 306n5
War of 1812, 235
war photography, 230n39
Washington, Madison, 62
Watson, James, 133
Watson, William, 133
Weinstein, Cindy, 13
West Philadelphia Hospital Register, 187n30
whaling, 266
What Answer? (Dickinson): and affective foundations of the state, 223–224; anti-Irish sentiment in, 229n36; distance in, 202; impersonal tone in, 201–206, 208, 238–239; overview of, 200; rioters as depersonalized in, 204; social analysis in, 202; the sublime in, 205–206; witness figure in, 208–209, 211
wheat, 250, 253. *See also* bread
Wheatley, Phillis, 18; and anti-imperial interpretation of Liberian settlement, 121; and communication between diasporans and West Africans, 124, 127; critique of African colonization movement, 122–123; and Quaque, 128
whiteness: aligned with sexual normativity, 19, 246–247; and anti-onanistic discourse, 279; and foreignness, 264; and national expansion, 253; and orality, 246
white racial innocence, 16, 86, 89, 94–95
white supremacy: broad patterns of, 100n34; transmission of, 85
Whitfield, James Monroe, 307, 309–311
Wickliffe, Robert, 119–120, 145, 156–157n66
Wiley, Bell I., 152
Wilkeson, Samuel, 142
Williams, Raymond, 227n15